THE LITTLE, B*ROWN COMPACT HANDBOOK

FOURTH
CANADIAN
EDITION

Jane E. Aaron, *New York University*
Murray McArthur, *University of Waterloo*

Pearson Canada
Toronto

Library and Archives Canada Cataloguing in Publication

Aaron, Jane E.
  The Little Brown Compact Handbook/Jane E. Aaron, Murray McArthur.–4th
Canadian ed.

Includes index.
ISBN 978-0-321-54933-4

  1. English language–Rhetoric–Handbooks, manuals, etc.   2. English language–
Grammar–Handbooks, manuals, etc.   I. McArthur, Murray, 1953–   II. Title.

PE1112.A26 2010   808'.042   C2008-905781-3

ISBN-13: 978-0-321-54933-4
ISBN-10: 0-321-54933-3

Vice President, Editorial Director: Gary Bennett
Editor-in-Chief: Ky Pruesse
Acquisitions Editor: David LeGallais
Marketing Manager: Loula March
Associate Editor: Brian Simons
Production Editor: Kevin Leung
Copy Editor: Ann McInnis
Proofreader: Pearl Saban
MLA Editor: Sharon Kirsch
Production Coordinator: Avinash Chandra
Composition: Integra
Art Director: Julia Hall
Cover Design: Hands Design
Interior Design: Gail Ferreira Ng-A-Kien

The author and publisher are grateful to the many students who allowed their
work to be reprinted here and to the copyright holders who are listed on page 481,
which is hereby made part of this copyright page.

Statistics Canada information is used with the permission of Statistics Canada.
Users are forbidden to copy the data and redisseminate them, in an original or modified form, for commercial purposes, without permission from Statistics Canada.
Information on the availability of the wide range of data from Statistics Canada can
be obtained from Statistics Canada's Regional Offices, its World Wide Web site at
http://www.statcan.ca, and its toll-free access number 1-800-263-1136.

1 2 3 4 5   13 12 11 10 09

Printed and bound in Canada.

Contents

Preface for Students

The Little, Brown Compact Handbook contains the basic information you'll need for writing in and out of school. Here you can find out how to get ideas, use commas, search the Internet, cite sources, craft an argument, and write a résumé—all in a convenient, accessible package.

This book is mainly a reference for you to dip into as needs arise. You probably won't read the book all the way through, nor will you use everything it contains: you already know much of the content anyway, whether consciously or not. The trick is to figure out what you *don't* know—taking cues from your own writing experiences and the comments of others—and then to find the answers to your questions in these pages.

The booklet "Exercises to Accompany *The Little, Brown Compact Handbook*" provides more than 100 applied activities to help reinforce your newly learned skills. Each exercise corresponds to the relevant section and page number in the handbook. MyCanadianCompLab offers additional practice through online quizzing and tutorials as well as valuable resources through downloads and Web links.

The following page details the many ways you can find information in the handbook. Also see pages vi–vii for three helpful tutorials on how to use this handbook effectively. You'll want to be familiar with the symbol illustrated below that highlights special information appearing throughout the book:

ESL   • The ESL symbol, which is integrated throughout the handbook, flags material for students using English as a second language. A guide to all the ESL topics appears on the inside back cover of the book.

Before you begin using this book, you may need to clear your mind of a very common misconception: that writing is only, or even mainly, a matter of correctness. True, any written message will find a more receptive audience if it is correct in word choice, grammar, punctuation, and similar matters. But these concerns should come late in the writing process, after you've allowed yourself to discover what you have to say, freeing yourself to make mistakes along the way. As one writer put it, you need to get the clay on the potter's wheel before you can shape it into a bowl, and you need to shape it into a bowl before you can perfect it. So get your clay on the wheel and work with it until it looks like a bowl. Then worry about correctness.

Finding What You Need

Use a directory.

• "Frequently Asked Questions" (inside the front cover) provides questions in everyday language that are commonly asked about the book's main topics.

- The "Contents" provides an overview of the entire book.
- Detailed outlines on the tabbed dividers direct you to the material covered in each part of the book.

Use the index.

An alphabetical list of all topics, terms, and problem words and expressions appears at the end of the book.

Use the elements of the page.

❶ Running head (header) showing the topic being discussed on this page.

❷ Chapter number and title.

❸ Key term for this discussion.

❹ Examples, always indented. Colour underlining highlights sentence elements and revisions.

❺ Page tab, containing the code of the nearest section heading (**31a**) and the symbol or abbreviation for the topic being discussed (**pn agr**).

❻ ESL pointer for students using English as a second language.

❼ Section heading, a main convention or topic labelled with the section code, **31a:** the chapter number (**31**) and the section letter (**a**).

❽ Box defining secondary terms used on the page. Refer to these white boxes whenever a term is unclear. Otherwise, ignore them.

Use the Glossary of Usage.

An alphabetical list of terms provides notes on meaning, choice (*affect* or *effect?*), and spelling (*civilise* or *civilize?*).

Tutorials

The following tutorials will give you practice in using the book's three systems of discovery: (1) the directories, including the

① Agreement of pronoun and antecedent   211

② 31a **Agreement of Pronoun and Antecedent**

③

The ANTECEDENT of a pronoun is the noun or other pronoun to which the pronoun refers:

④ Homeowners fret over their tax bills.
   antecedent   pronoun

Its constant increases make the tax bill a dreaded document.
pronoun   antecedent

For clarity, a pronoun should agree with its antecedent in person, number, and gender.

Note A computerized grammar and style checker cannot help you with agreement between pronoun and antecedent. You'll need to check for errors on your own.

⑥ ESL The gender of a pronoun should match its antecedent, not a noun that the pronoun may modify: *Sara Young invited her* [not *his*] *son to join the company's staff.* Also, nouns in English have only neuter gender unless they specifically refer to males or females. Thus nouns such as *book, table, sun,* and *earth* take the pronoun *it.*

⑤ pn agr
31a

⑦ (31a) Antecedents joined by *and* usually take plural pronouns.

Mr. Bartos and I cannot settle our dispute.

KEY TERMS

PERSON	SINGULAR	PLURAL
FIRST	*I*	*we*
SECOND	*you*	*you*
THIRD	*he, she, it*	*they*
	indefinite pronouns, singular nouns	plural nouns

GENDER		
MASCULINE	*he,* nouns naming males	
FEMININE	*she,* nouns naming females	
NEUTER	*it,* all other nouns	

⑧

Contents, Frequently Asked Questions, and tabbed page directors; (2) the index; (3) the Glossary of Usage.

Tutorial 1: Using the directories

Each of the following sentences violates the principle it expresses. Using the directories, find the section in *The Little, Brown Compact Handbook* that explains the principle. Correct the violation, and note the section and the editing symbol or abbreviation on the tab identifying the section. Examples:

its

A pronoun should agree in number with their antecedent. (**31 pn agr**)

take

Sentence subjects ending in -*s* takes verbs not ending in -*s*. (**29a vb agr**)

1. The sentence fragment? It should be avoided in all formal writing.
2. Equivalent to a full stop: a colon must be preceded by a complete main clause.
3. A comma splice joins main clauses with only a comma, main clauses should be coordinated with a comma and a conjunction or with a semicolon.
4. Its mandatory to use apostrophes for certain possessive's and contraction's.

Tutorial 2: Using the index

You have written the following sentences and want to know the answer to the question in brackets. Use the index to find the information you require and edit the sentence if necessary.

1. Giancarlo Vecchi, a professor, has written several monographs on the development of Italian agriculture. [The proper nouns and adjectives are capitalized, but should the title "professor" be capitalized?]
2. Every municipality and city in the country sent their representative to the national conference. [Should the pronoun modifying *representative* be plural, as in "their," or singular?]
3. In this economy, the consumer only purchases the necessities and shuns luxury items. [Is the modifier "only" placed correctly?]
4. Three characters remain on stage: Vivienne, the heroine, Tom, her husband, and Bertie, the deceiver of them both. [How should a series of items containing commas be punctuated?]

Tutorial 3: **Using the Glossary of Usage**

Consult the Glossary of Usage at the back of the book, at the last tabbed section, to see if the following italicized words are used correctly. Then either identify each usage as correct or revise the sentence.

1. Ross MacDonald *immigrated* from the United States at a very early age.

2. Readers usually *infer* from his excessive language that the hero feels guilty.

3. The book *which* you want is shelved in the basement of the library.

4. The *principle* character in the novel hails from Vancouver.

Answers to Tutorial 1

1. The sentence fragment should be avoided in all formal writing. (35 frag)

2. Equivalent to a full stop, a colon must be preceded by a complete main clause. (41a :)

3. A comma splice joins main clauses with only a comma, and main clauses should be coordinated with a comma and a conjunction or with a semicolon. (36a cs/fs)

4. It's mandatory to use apostrophes for certain possessives and contractions. (42 v̇)

Answers to Tutorial 2

1. The index entry "capitalization" directs you to the subheading "Capitalize titles preceding persons' names" on page 290, which tells us that titles following a proper noun are usually not capitalized.

2. The index entry for *every* sends the reader to "pronoun-antecedent agreement with" on page 212, which notes that when the compound antecedent follows *each* or *every* the pronoun is singular. So the sentence should be edited to read as follows: Every municipality and city in the country sent *its* representative to the national conference.

3. The index entry for *only* directs you to the rule for the "limiting modifier" on page 229. The limiting modifier should be placed immediately before the word or word group you intend to limit. The edited sentence should read as follows: In this economy, the consumer purchases only the necessities and shuns luxury items.

4. The index entry for "series" directs the reader to the section on the semicolon on page 264, which advises that a semicolon should be used between series items containing commas. The sentence should be punctuated as follows: Three characters remain on stage: Vivienne, the heroine; Tom, her husband; and Bertie, the deceiver of them both.

Answers to Tutorial 3

1. Ross MacDonald *emigrated* from the United States at a very early age.
2. Correct.
3. The book *that* you want is shelved in the basement of the library.
4. The *principal* character in the novel hails from Vancouver.

Student supplements

MyCanadianCompLab (www.mycanadiancomplab.ca). Use the access code packaged with every new copy of the *The Little, Brown Compact Handbook*, Fourth Canadian Edition, to access diverse resources for composition in one easy place:

- Sections on writing, research, and grammar cover all the key topics in the text, providing additional instruction, examples, and practice.

- An eBook version of this textbook allows you to review material easily as you work online.

- An online composing space includes tools such as writing tips and editing FAQs, so you can get the help you need when you need it, without ever leaving the writing environment.

- The protfolio feature allows you to create an ePortfolio of your work that you can easily share with your instructor and peers.

Access to MyCanadianCompLab can also be purchased separately from your bookstore or from Pearson Education Canada.

Preface for Instructors

This text is an adaptation for Canadian students and instructors of Jane E. Aaron's very successful sixth edition of *The Little, Brown Compact Handbook*. Aaron's text combines the breadth and authority of *The Little, Brown Handbook* with the economy and accessibility of the compact format, and this text aims to reproduce that successful combination within a Canadian context. To that end, we have adapted the text to reflect Canadian culture, geography, politics, history, academic practices, weights and measures, customs, and folkways. We have tried to recreate or mirror the complexities of Canadian realities, and these complexities include the reality of North American life. Therefore, we have also retained some of the American references that would be familiar to most Canadians. Above all, we have tried to reflect the complexity of our students' concerns and enthusiasms and to represent those issues in the broadest possible regional and multicultural context.

For six editions now, *The Little, Brown Compact Handbook* has provided writers with an accessible reference, one that helps them find what they need and then use what they find. Combining the authority of its parent, *The Little, Brown Handbook*, with a briefer and more convenient format, the *Compact Handbook* addresses writers of varying experience, in varying fields, answering the questions they ask about the writing process, grammar and style, research writing, and more.

The Fourth Canadian Edition improves on the handbook's strengths as a clear, concise, and accessible reference, but it also takes on two subjects that are central to writing today: thinking critically and using computers efficiently and wisely. In the context of the handbook's many reference functions, the following pages highlight the most significant additions and changes.

A reference for writing in and out of post secondary

Two groups of chapters greatly expand the handbook's range. The first, Part 2, gives students the tools for analyzing and composing in many different writing situations:

- New A chapter on academic writing introduces purpose, audience, language, and other elements.
- New A chapter on study skills provides practical tips for managing time, reading for comprehension, and preparing for exams.
- Two chapters detail techniques of critical reading and argument.
- New Three chapters cover online writing (including e-mail and Web composition), oral presentations (including PowerPoint), and public writing (including writing for business and for community work).

Part 8 then offers a strong introduction to writing in the disciplines:

- New A chapter treats the goals and requirements common to writing in all academic disciplines.
- New Complementing the chapter on writing about literature, a chapter discusses the emphases and methods of writing in other humanities, the social sciences, and the natural and applied sciences.
- Extensive, specially tabbed sections cover documentation and format in MLA, APA, Chicago, CSE, and IEEE styles.

A guide to visual literacy

The handbook helps students process visual information and use it effectively in their writing.

- New An expanded section on using illustrations includes annotated examples.
- New An expanded discussion of viewing images critically uses diverse examples to demonstrate identifying and analyzing visual elements.
- New A section on reading and using visual arguments focuses on images' claims, evidence, assumptions, appeals, and fallacies.
- New Illustrations in most of the handbook's student papers show various ways in which visual information can support written ideas.

A reference for researching with computers

New or expanded discussions of research with computers bring the handbook up to the minute.

- A discussion and screen shot show how to find **bibliographic information for online sources**.
- An expanded discussion of **Web research** includes appropriate cautions and a detailed case study.
- An expanded discussion of **evaluating online sources** includes a detailed checklist.
- A section on **acknowledging online sources** addresses issues of copyright.
- **Electronic documentation models** illustrate all styles: MLA, APA, Chicago, CSE, and IEEE.
- A chapter on **plagiarism** addresses the many issues raised by easy Internet downloading of many different kinds of documents.
- New Lists give specific **Web resources** for the academic disciplines.

A reference for research writing

The handbook already provided strong support for research writers: specific tips for planning, finding sources, working with sources, and writing the paper; detailed guidelines for MLA, APA, Chicago, and CSE documentation; and sample MLA and APA papers. Now, in addition to the material on electronic research, several changes have strengthened these chapters:

- Key concerns of research writers receive added attention: **formulating a research question**; **developing a research strategy**, including tapping into one's own knowledge and balancing print and online sources; **integrating quotations**, including introducing, altering, and interpreting them; and **documenting sources**, a conceptual discussion addressing why disciplines' styles vary.
- The chapter on MLA documentation, and the text as a whole, has been thoroughly updated to reflect the new seventh edition of the *MLA Handbook for Writers of Research Papers*, published in 2009.
- The chapter on **plagiarism** discusses all aspects of the three tasks all writers must carry out to avoid plagiarism.
- The MLA and APA systems of citation for Internet sources are incorporated into the sample.
- The APA styles of citation and documentation for both print and online sources are included and clearly explained.
- New The IEEE styles of citation and documentation for engineering have been included and clearly explained.

A reference for critical thinking and argument

The handbook's concise coverage of argument is more useful and more prominent:

- A chapter, placed early in the book, links argument with critical thinking.
- A discussion of **critical thinking and reading** includes a sample annotated reading and an extended example of analyzing a Web site.
- **Fallacies** and **organization of arguments** receive expanded coverage.

A reference for grammar, usage, and punctuation

The handbook's core reference material continues to feature concise explanations and annotated examples from across the curriculum. The changes here are small but significant:

- Three **tutorials** in the Student Preface give students exercises for finding and using relevant information, rules, and examples.

- Frequent tips spell out the uses and limitations of **grammar/ style and spelling checkers**.
- A foregrounded chapter on **emphasis** focuses on strong subjects and verbs and movement from old to new information.
- **Changes in examples** are now more visible, highlighted with colour underlining instead of italics.

A reference for ESL students

The handbook continues to provide rhetorical and grammatical help for ESL students, all integrated into the rest of the book so that students do not have to distinguish between ESL problems and those they share with native speakers. The symbol ESL signals ESL notes and sections, and an ESL guide on the inside back cover pulls all the coverage together in one place.

A reference for the writing process

In well-focused, practical chapters, the handbook provides tips on invention, the thesis, revision, and more.

- The opening chapter now includes a detailed **checklist for assessing the writing situation** and an expanded discussion of **purpose**.
- A student work-in-progress on Internet communication provides examples at every stage, including first, revised, and final drafts.

An accessible reference

The Little, Brown Compact Handbook is an open book for students. It features not only the convenient format of spiral binding and tabbed dividers but also an unusually accessible organization, "Frequently Asked Questions" on the front endpapers, more than forty-five summary and checklist boxes, a self-teaching text with minimal terminology and cross-references, and unique "Key Terms" boxes for essential definitions.

- A new **two-colour design** is more inviting for students but preserves the clean page format.
- **Coloured tabbed dividers** clearly distinguish the handbook's rhetorical, editing, research, and reference sections.

Supplements to the Fourth Canadian Edition

MyCanadianCompLab (www.mycanadiancomplab.ca). MyCanadianCompLab empowers student writers and facilitates writing instruction by integrating a composing space and ePortfolio with proven resources and tools, such as practice exercises, diagnostics, and multimedia assets. Instructor functions include the following:

- The To Do section enables instructors to create and deliver assignments online and helps keep students on track by listing due dates and assignment details in one place.

- The Gradebook captures both student grades from self-grading aspects of the site and grades given to writing assignments by the instructor, allowing instructors to easily assess student and class progress.

- Instructors can integrate MyCanadianCompLab into their traditional or online courses to whatever degree they'd like: from simply using exercises in the Resource section for homework or extra help to delivering their entire course online. Students can use the new MyCanadianCompLab on their own, benefiting from the composing space and its integrated resources, tools, and services with no involvement from the instructor.

See your local sales representation for further information and access.

Acknowledgments

Acknowledgments from Murray McArthur

Thanks are due to the following people for their valuable comments on the manuscript for this Fourth Canadian Edition:

I would especially like to acknowledge all the colleagues both at Pearson who worked on this and previous editions and at the universities and colleges across the country who have contributed to its continuing success.

Acknowledgments from Jane E. Aaron

The Little, Brown Compact Handbook stays fresh and useful because instructors talk with Longman's sales representatives and editors, answer questionnaires, write detailed reviews, and send me personal notes.

For the sixth edition, I am especially grateful to the many instructors who communicated with me directly or through reviews, drawing on their rich experience to offer insights into the handbook and suggestions for its improvement: Michael Burke, Southern Illinois University, Edwardsville; Daniel Compora, University of Toledo; Stephen Ferruci, Eastern Connecticut State University; Virginia K. Freed, Bay Path College; James Grabill, Clackamas Community College; Robert T. Koch, Jr., Gordon College; Karla Saari Kitalong, University of Central Florida; Patricia Kramer, Rock Valley College; Eleanor Latham, Central Oregon Community College; John P. LoVecchio, Elmira College; Sandra D. Lynn, New Mexico State University, Carlsbad; Amy Martin, Pace University; Rich Miller, Suffolk University; Jennifer P. Nesbitt, Pennsylvania State University, York; David Sharpe, Ohio University; James R. Sodon, St. Louis Community College, Florissant Valley; David J. Sorrells, Lamar State College, Port Arthur; Katherine C. Wood, Texas A&M University; Janet Wright Starner, Wilkes University; Wayne Stein, University of Central Oklahoma; and John Ziebell, Community College of Southern Nevada.

In responding to the ideas of these thoughtful critics, I had the help of many creative people. Carol Hollar-Zwick, development editor and sine qua non, is every author's ideal for can-do attitude, smart thinking, and gentle encouragement. Brooke Hessler, Oklahoma City University, was an invaluable consultant on visual literacy and research writing. Caroline Crouse, University of Minnesota, served as a guide through the labyrinth of the contemporary library. Susan Smith Nash, Excelsior College, helped with disabilities issues and new technologies. And Sylvan Barnet, Tufts University, continued to lend his expertise in the chapter "Reading and Writing About Literature," which is adapted from his *Short Guide to Writing About Literature* and *Introduction to Literature* (with William Burto and William E. Cain).

A superb team helped me make this book. At Longman, Brandon Hight, the book's sponsor, offered perceptive insights into instructors' and students' needs. He and Rebecca Gilpin, editorial assistant, responded enthusiastically to my many needs. Megan Galvin-Fak, marketing manager, provided helpful ideas at key moments in development. Donna DeBenedictis applied a long view and a sharp eye to overseeing production. At Nesbitt Graphics, Jerilyn Bockorick created both the striking new design and the clear page layouts, and Susan McIntyre worked her now-customary miracles of scheduling and management to produce the book. I am grateful to all these collaborators.

(1) The Writing Process

1 The Writing Process

1 The Writing Situation

Like most writers (even very experienced ones), you may find writing sometimes easy but more often difficult, sometimes smooth but more often halting. Writing involves creation, and creation requires freedom, experimentation, and, yes, missteps. Instead of proceeding in a straight line over a clear path, you might start writing without knowing what you have to say, circle back to explore a new idea, or keep going even though you're sure you'll have to rewrite later.

As uncertain as the writing process may be, you can bring some control to it by assessing your writing situation, particularly your subject, audience, and purpose.

1a Assessing the writing situation

Any writing you do for others occurs in a context that both limits and clarifies your choices. You are communicating something about a particular subject to a particular audience of readers for a specific reason. You may need to conduct research. You'll probably be up against a length requirement and a deadline. And you may be expected to present your work in a certain format.

These are the elements of the writing situation, and analyzing them at the very start of a project can tell you much about how to proceed. (For more information about the elements, refer to the page numbers given below.)

Subject (pp. 3–4)

- What does your writing assignment instruct you to write about? If you don't have a specific assignment, what do you want to write about?
- What interests you about the subject? What do you already have ideas about or want to know more about?
- What does the assignment require you to do with the subject?

Audience (pp. 4–5)

- Who will read your writing? What do your readers already know and think about your topic?
- Do your readers have any characteristics—such as educational background, experience in your field, or political views—that could influence their reception of your writing?

1

- What is your relationship to your readers? How formal or informal should your writing be?
- What do you want readers to do or think after they read your writing?

Purpose (p. 6)

- What aim does your assignment specify? For instance, does it ask you to explain something or argue a point?
- Why are you writing? What do you want to accomplish?
- How can you best achieve your purpose?

Research (pp. 299–378)

- What kinds of evidence—such as facts, examples, and the opinions of experts—best suit your topic, audience, and purpose?
- Does your assignment require you to consult sources of information or conduct other research, such as interviews, surveys, or experiments?
- Besides the requirements of the assignment, what additional information do you need to develop your topic? How will you obtain it?
- What style should you use to cite your sources? (See pp. 345–46 on source documentation in the academic disciplines.)

Deadline and length

- When is the assignment due? How will you apportion the work you have to do in the available time?
- How long should your writing be? If no length is assigned, what seems appropriate for your topic, audience, and purpose?

Document design

- What organization and format does the assignment require? (See pp. 30–31 on format in the academic disciplines and pp. 114–122 on format in business.)
- Even if a particular format is not required, how might you use margins, headings, illustrations, and other elements to achieve your purpose? (See pp. 55–63.)

Note The elements of the writing situation listed above pertain to traditional academic and business writing. For some online writing, however, the elements may be different. E-mailing a brief query to a discussion group, for instance, may not involve the particulars of research, deadline, length, and document design. Creating material for the World Wide W   will complicate some elements, especially design. St.   ig will require you to consider the essential elemen   he following pages: subject, audience, and purpose.

1b Finding your subject

A subject for writing has several basic requirements:

- It should be suitable for the assignment.
- It should be neither too general nor too limited for the length of paper and deadline assigned.
- It should be something you care about.

When you receive an assignment, study its wording and its implications for your writing situation to guide your choice of subject:

- *What's wanted from you?* Many writing assignments contain words such as *discuss, describe, analyze, report, interpret, explain, define, argue,* or *evaluate.* These words specify the way you are to approach your subject, what kind of thinking is expected of you, and what your general purpose is. (See p. 6.)
- *For whom are you writing?* Some assignments will specify your readers, but usually you will have to figure out for yourself whether your audience is the general reading public, your classmates, your boss, the college or university community, your instructor, or some other group or individual. (For more on analyzing your audience, see pp. 4–5.)
- *What kind of research is required?* Sometimes an assignment specifies the kinds of sources you are expected to consult, and you can use such information to choose your subject. (If you are unsure whether research is required, check with your instructor.)
- *Does the subject need to be narrowed?* To do the subject justice in the length and time required, you'll often need to limit it. (See below.)

Answering questions about your assignment will help set some boundaries for your choice of subject. Then you can explore your own interests and experiences to narrow the subject so that you can cover it adequately within the space and time assigned. Government aid to college and university students could be the subject of a book; the kinds of aid available or why the government should increase aid would be a more appropriate subject for a four-page paper due in a week. Here are some guidelines for narrowing broad subjects:

- Break your broad subject into as many specific topics as you can think of. Make a list.
- For each topic that interests you and fits the assignment, roughly sketch out the main ideas and consider how many

1c

paragraphs or pages of specific facts, examples, and other details you would need to pin those ideas down. This thinking should give you at least a vague idea of how much work you'd have to do and how long the resulting paper might be.

- If an interesting and appropriate topic is still too broad, break it down further and repeat the previous step.

1c Considering your audience

The readers likely to see your work—your audience—may influence your choice of subject and your definition of purpose. Your audience certainly will influence what you say about your subject and how you say it—for instance, how much background information you give and whether you adopt a serious or a friendly tone. Consider, for instance, these two memos written by a student who worked part-time at a small company and wanted to persuade the company to recycle paper:

Addressed to co-workers

Ever notice how much paper collects in your trash basket every day? Well, most of it can be recycled with little effort, I promise. Basically, all you need to do is set a bag or box near your desk and deposit wastepaper in it. I know, space is cramped in these little cubicles. But what's a little more crowding when the earth's at stake? . . .

Information: how employees could handle recycling; no mention of costs

Role: cheerful, equally harried colleague

Tone: informal, personal (*Ever notice; you; what's; Well; I know, space is cramped*)

Addressed to management

In my four months here, I have observed that all of us throw out baskets of potentially recyclable paper every day. Considering the drain on our forest resources and the pressure on landfills that paper causes, we could make a valuable contribution to the environmental movement by helping to recycle the paper we use. At the company where I worked before, the employees separate clean wastepaper from other trash at their desks. The maintenance staff collects trash in two receptacles, and the trash hauler (the same one we use here) makes separate pickups. I do not know what the hauler charges for handling recyclable material. . . .

Information: specific reasons; view of company as a whole; reference to another company; problem of cost

Role: serious, thoughtful, responsible employee

Tone: formal, serious (*Considering the drain; forest resources; valuable contribution;* no *you* or contractions)

The following box contains questions that can help you analyze and address your audience. Depending on your writing situation, some questions will be more helpful than others. For instance, your readers' knowledge of your topic will be important to consider if you are trying to explain how a particular computer program works, whereas readers' beliefs and values may be important if you are trying to gather support for a change in education policy.

Questions about audience

- Who *are* my readers?
- Why are readers going to read my writing? What will they expect?
- What do I want readers to know or do after reading my work, and how should I make that clear to them?
- How will readers' characteristics, such as those below, influence their attitudes toward my topic?

  Age or sex
  Occupation: students, professional colleagues, etc.
  Social or economic role: adult children, car buyers, potential employers, etc.
  Economic or educational background
  Ethnic background
  Political, religious, or moral beliefs and values
  Hobbies or activities

- What do readers already know and *not* know about my topic? How much do I have to tell them?
- If my topic involves specialized language, how much should I use and define?
- What ideas, arguments, or information might surprise readers? Excite them? Offend them? How should I handle these points?
- What misconceptions might readers have of my topic and/or my approach to the topic? How can I dispel these misconceptions?
- What is my relationship to my readers? How formal or informal will they expect me to be? What role and tone should I assume? What role do I want readers to play?
- What will readers do with my writing? Should I expect them to read every word from the top, to scan for information, or to look for conclusions? Can I help them with a summary, headings, illustrations, or other special features? (See pp. 55–63 on document design.)

ESL If English is not your native language, you may not be accustomed to appealing to your readers when you write. In some cultures, for instance, readers may accept a writer's statements with little or no questioning. In English, however, readers expect the writer to reach out to them by being accurate, fair, interesting, and clear.

1d

(1d) Defining your purpose

Your PURPOSE in writing is your chief reason for communicating something about your subject to a particular audience of readers. Most writing you do will have one of four main purposes. Occasionally, you will *entertain* readers or *express yourself*—your feelings or ideas—to readers. More often you will *explain* something to readers or *persuade* readers to respect and accept, and sometimes even act on, your well-supported opinion. These purposes often overlap in a single essay, but usually one predominates. And the dominant purpose will influence your particular slant on your subject, the details you choose, and even the words you use.

Many writing assignments narrow the purpose by using a signal word, such as the following:

- *Report:* survey, organize, and objectively present the available evidence on the subject.
- *Summarize:* concisely state the main points in a text, argument, theory, or other work.
- *Discuss:* examine the main points, competing views, or implications of the subject.
- *Compare and contrast:* explain the similarities and differences between two subjects. (See also p. 47.)
- *Define:* specify the meaning of a term or a concept—distinctive characteristics, boundaries, and so on. (See also pp. 45–46.)
- *Analyze:* identify the elements of the subject, and discuss how they work together. (See also p. 46.)
- *Interpret:* infer the subject's meaning or implications.
- *Evaluate:* judge the quality or significance of the subject, considering pros and cons. (See also p. 87.)
- *Argue:* take a position on the subject, and support your position with evidence. (See also pp. 88–100.)

You can conceive of your purpose more specifically, too, in a way that incorporates your particular topic and the outcome you intend:

- To explain how Carol Shields's "Sailors Lost at Sea" builds to its climax so that readers appreciate the author's skill.
- To explain the steps in a new office procedure so that staffers will be able to follow it without difficulty.
- To persuade readers to support the university administration's plan for more required courses.
- To argue against additional regulation of health-maintenance organizations so that readers will perceive the disadvantages for themselves.

2 Invention

Writers use a host of techniques to help invent or discover ideas and information about their subjects. *Whichever of the following techniques you use, do your work in writing, not just in your head.* Your ideas will be retrievable, and the very act of writing will lead you to fresh insights.

ESL The discovery process encouraged here rewards rapid writing; you won't need to do a lot of thinking beforehand about what you will write or how. Some ESL writers find it helpful initially to do this exploratory writing in their native language and then to translate the worthwhile material for use in their drafts. However, this practice does require the extra work of translating not only sentences but also thought patterns, and it merely postpones the need to think and create in English.

(2a) Keeping a journal

A JOURNAL is a diary of ideas kept on paper or on a computer. It gives you a place to record your thoughts and can provide ideas for writing. Because you write for yourself, you can work out your ideas without the pressure of an audience "out there" who will evaluate logic or organization or correctness. If you write every day, even just for a few minutes, the routine will loosen your writing muscles and improve your confidence.

You can use a journal for varied purposes: perhaps to confide your feelings, explore your responses to movies and other media, practise certain kinds of writing (such as poems or news stories), think critically about what you read (see p. 78), or pursue ideas from your courses. In both examples following, the students planted the seeds for essays they later wrote. Megan Polanyis pondered something she had learned from her biology textbook:

> *Ecology* and *economics* have the same root—Greek word for house. Economy = management of the house. Ecology = study of the house. In ecology the house is all of nature, ourselves, the other animals, the plants, the earth, the air, the whole environment. Ecology has a lot to do with economy: study the house in order to manage it.

7

2c

Sara Ling responded to an experience:

> Had an exchange today with a man who just joined the snowboard-ing forum—only he turns out to be a woman! She says she's been afraid to write to the forum as a woman because the guys there might shout her down. (When she figured out I was a woman, she decided to fess up to me.) She asked about my experiences. Had to admit I'd had problems of the what-does-a-girl-know sort—advised her to keep her gender a secret to see what happens. Wish I'd thought of it myself. Maybe I'll start over with a new screen name.

(Further examples of Ling's writing appear on pp. 9–10 and in the next three chapters.)

ESL   A journal can be especially helpful if you're writing in English as a second language. You can practise writing to improve your fluency, try out sentence patterns, and experiment with vocab-ulary words. Equally important, you can experiment with applying what you know from experience to what you read and observe.

(2b)   Observing your surroundings

Sometimes you can find a good subject or good ideas by look-ing around you, not in the half-conscious way most of us move from place to place in our daily lives but deliberately, all senses alert. On a bus, for instance, are there certain types of passengers? What seems to be on the driver's mind? To get the most from observation, you should have a pad and pen or pencil handy for notes and sketches. Back at your desk, study your notes and sketches for oddi-ties or patterns that you'd like to explore further.

(2c)   Freewriting

Writing into a subject

Many writers find subjects or discover ideas by FREEWRITING: writing without stopping for a certain amount of time (say, ten minutes) or to a certain length (say, one page). The goal of freewrit-ing is to generate ideas and information from *within* yourself by going around the part of your mind that doesn't want to write or can't think of anything to write. You let words themselves suggest other words. *What* you write is not important; that you *keep* writing is. Don't stop, even if that means repeating the same words until new words come. Don't go back to reread, don't censor ideas that seem dumb or repetitious, and above all don't stop to edit: grammar, punc-tuation, spelling, and the like are irrelevant at this stage.

2c

The physical act of freewriting may give you access to ideas you were unaware of. For example, the following freewriting by a student, Robert Benday, gave him the subject of writing as a disguise:

> Write to write. Seems pretty obvious, also weird. What to gain by writing? Never anything before. Writing seems always—always—getting corrected for trying too hard to please the teacher, getting corrected for not trying hard enuf. Frustration, nail biting, sometimes getting carried away making sentences to tell stories, not even true stories, *esp.* not true stories, that feels like creating something. Writing just pulls the story out of me. The story lets me be someone else, gives me a disguise.

(A later phase of Benday's writing appears on p. 11.)

If you write on a computer, you can ensure that your freewriting keeps moving forward by turning off your computer's monitor or turning its brightness control all the way down so that the screen is dark. The computer will record what you type but keep it from you and thus prevent you from tinkering with your prose. This INVISIBLE WRITING may feel uncomfortable at first, but it can free the mind for very creative results. When you've finished freewriting, simply turn the monitor on or turn up the brightness control to read what you've written, and then save or revise it as appropriate. Later, you may be able to transfer some of your freewriting into your draft.

ESL Invisible writing can be especially helpful if English is not your first language and you tend to worry about errors while writing: the blank computer screen leaves you no choice but to explore ideas without regard for their expression. If you choose to write with the monitor on, concentrate on *what* you want to say, not *how* you're saying it.

Focused freewriting

FOCUSED FREEWRITING is more concentrated: you start with your topic and write about it without stopping for, say, fifteen minutes or one full page. As in all freewriting, you push to bypass mental blocks and self-consciousness, not debating what to say or editing what you've written. With focused freewriting, though, you let the physical act of writing take you into and around your subject.

An example of focused freewriting can be found in the work of Sara Ling, whose journal entry appears on page 8. In a composition course Ling's instructor had distributed "Welcome to Cyberbia," an essay by M. Kadi about communication on the Internet. The instructor then gave the following assignment:

> M. Kadi's "Welcome to Cyberbia" holds that the Internet will do little to bridge differences among people because its users gravitate toward other users who are like themselves in most respects. In an essay of 500–700 words, respond to Kadi's essay with a limited and

well-supported opinion of your own: Can the Internet serve as a medium for positive change in the way people of diverse backgrounds relate to each other? If so, how? If not, why not? The first draft is due Monday, April 4, for class discussion.

On first reading Kadi's essay, Ling had been impressed with its tight logic but had found unconvincing its pessimistic view of the Internet's potential. She reread the essay and realized that some of Kadi's assertions did not correspond to her own Internet experiences. This discovery prompted the following focused freewriting:

> Kadi says we only meet people like ourselves on the Internet, but I've met lots with very different backgrounds and interests. Actually, "turned out to have" is more like it, since I didn't know anything about them at first. There's the anonymity thing, but Kadi ignores it. You can be anyone or no one. I can pose as a man if I want (probably should have, to avoid rejection on the snowboarding forum). No one has to know I'm female or Asian Canadian or a student. We're not stuck in our identities. Not hampered by them in expressing our views and getting those views accepted. Communication without set identity, especially physical appearance. This could make for more tolerance of others, of difference.

(An outline and drafts of Ling's paper appear on pp. 19–20, 23, 27–28, and 31–33.)

(2d) Brainstorming

A method similar to freewriting is BRAINSTORMING—focusing intently on a subject for a fixed period (say, fifteen minutes), pushing yourself to list every idea and detail that comes to mind. Like freewriting, brainstorming requires turning off your internal editor so that you keep moving ahead. (The technique of invisible writing on a computer, described on p. 9, can help you move forward.)

Here is an example of brainstorming by a student, Johanna Abrams, on what a summer job can teach:

> summer work teaches—
> how to look busy while doing nothing
> how to avoid the sun in summer
> seriously: discipline, budgeting money, value of money
> which job? Burger King cashier? baby sitter? mail-room clerk?
> mail room: how to sort mail into boxes: this is learning??
> how to survive getting fired—humiliation, outrage
> Mrs. King! the mail-room queen as learning experience
> the shock of getting fired: what to tell parents, friends?
> Mrs. K was so rigid—dumb procedures
> initials instead of names on the mail boxes—confusion!
> Mrs. K's anger, resentment: the disadvantages of being smarter than your boss

The odd thing about working in an office: a world with its own
rules for how to act
what Mr. D said about the pecking order—big chick (Mrs. K) pecks
on little chick (me)
a job can beat you down—make you be mean to other people

(A later phase of Abrams's writing process appears on pp. 18–19.)

Working on a computer makes it fairly easy to edit and shape a brainstorming list into a preliminary outline of your paper (see p. 18). With a few keystrokes, you can delete weak ideas, expand strong ones, and rearrange items. You can also freewrite from the list if you think some ideas are especially promising and deserve more thought.

2e Clustering

Like freewriting and brainstorming, CLUSTERING also draws on free association and rapid, unedited work. But it emphasizes the relations between ideas by combining writing and nonlinear drawing. When clustering, you radiate outward from a centre point— your topic. When an idea occurs, you pursue related ideas in a branching structure until they seem exhausted. Then you do the same with other ideas, staying open to connections, continuously branching out or drawing arrows.

The example of clustering below shows how Robert Benday used the technique for ten minutes to expand on the topic of writing as a means of disguise, an idea he arrived at through freewriting (see p. 8).

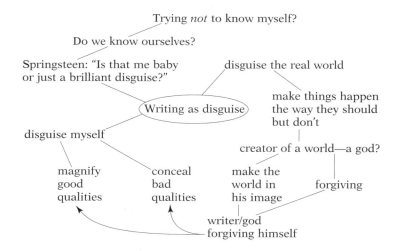

2g

2f Asking questions

Asking yourself a set of questions about your subject—and writing out the answers—can help you look at the topic objectively and see fresh possibilities in it.

1   Journalist's questions

A journalist with a story to report poses a set of questions:

Who was involved?
What happened, and what were the results?
When did it happen?
Where did it happen?
Why did it happen?
How did it happen?

These questions can also be useful in probing an essay subject, especially when you are telling a story or examining causes and effects.

2   Questions about patterns

We think about and understand a vast range of subjects through patterns such as narration, classification, and comparison and contrast. Asking questions based on the patterns can help you view your topic from many angles. Sometimes you may want to develop an entire essay using just one pattern.

How did it happen? (Narration)
How does it look, sound, feel, smell, taste? (Description)
What are examples of it or reasons for it? (Illustration or support)
What is it? What does it encompass, and what does it exclude? (Definition)
What are its parts or characteristics? (Division or analysis)
What groups or categories can it be sorted into? (Classification)
How is it like, or different from, other things? (Comparison and contrast)
Why did it happen? What results did or could it have? (Cause-and-effect analysis)
How do you do it, or how does it work? (Process analysis)

For more on these patterns, including paragraph-length examples, see pages 44–48.

2g Reading

Many assignments require reading. To respond to M. Kadi's essay about the Internet, for instance, Sara Ling had to digest Kadi's work. Essays on literary works as well as research papers also demand reading. But even when reading is not required by an assignment, it can help you locate or develop your topic by introducing you to ideas you didn't know or expanding on what you do know.

Say you were writing in favour of amateur athletics, a subject to which you had given a lot of thought. You might be inclined to proceed entirely on your own, drawing on facts, examples, and opinions already in your head. But a little digging in sources might open up more. For instance, an article in *Maclean's* magazine could introduce you to an old rule for amateur status, or a posting to an online newsgroup could suggest a pro-amateurism argument that hadn't occurred to you. (See pp. 308–22 for techniques of library and computer research that you can use to locate sources on a topic.)

People often read passively, absorbing content like blotters, not interacting with it. To read for ideas, you need to be more active, probing text and illustrations with your mind, nurturing any sparks they set off. Always write while you read so that you can keep notes on content and—just as important—on what the content makes you *think*. See pages 78–83 for specific guidelines on the process of active reading.

Note Whenever you use the information or ideas of others in your writing, you must acknowledge your sources in order to avoid the serious offence of plagiarism. (See p. 339–47.)

2h Thinking critically

Even if you do not read for information and ideas on your topic, you can still think critically about it. Critical thinking (discussed on pp. 78–87) can produce creative ideas by leading you to see what is not obvious. It can also lead you systematically to conclusions about your topic.

Sara Ling, writing about communication on the Internet, used the operations of critical thinking to explore her topic:

- *Analysis*: What are the subject's elements or characteristics? Ling looked at the ways Internet users can communicate because of their anonymity.
- *Interpretation*: What is the meaning or significance of the elements? Ling saw that the anonymity of Internet users could help them transcend their physical differences.
- *Synthesis*: How do the elements relate to each other, or how does this subject relate to another one? Ling perceived important and hopeful differences between anonymous Internet communication and face-to-face interaction.
- *Evaluation*: What is the value or significance of the subject? Ling concluded that by making people more tolerant of each other, the Internet could help build community out of diversity.

3 Thesis and Organization

Shaping your raw material helps you clear away unneeded ideas, spot possible gaps, and energize your topic. The two main operations in shaping material are focusing on a thesis (below) and organizing ideas (p. 16).

3a Conceiving a thesis statement

Your readers will expect your essay to be focused on and controlled by a main idea, or thesis. In your final draft you may express this idea in a thesis statement, often at the end of your introduction.

1 Functions of the thesis statement

As an expression of the thesis, the thesis statement serves three crucial functions and one optional one:

The thesis statement

- The thesis statement narrows your subject to a single, central idea that you want readers to gain from your essay.
- It claims something specific and significant about your subject, a claim that requires support.
- It conveys your purpose, your reason for writing.
- It often concisely previews the arrangement of ideas.

All of the following thesis statements fulfill the first three functions listed in the box (the nature of the assertion is highlighted in brackets). Examples 4 and 5 also fulfill the fourth function, previewing organization.

Subject	Thesis statement
1. The pecking order in an office	Two months working in a large agency taught me that an office's pecking order should be respected. [*Topic:* office's pecking order. *Assertion:* should be respected.]

2. The direct distribution to consumers via the World Wide Web

Because artists can now publish their music directly via the Web, consumers have many more choices than traditional distribution allows. [*Topic:* consumers. *Assertion:* have many more choices.]

3. Government aid to college and university students

To compete well in the global economy, Canada must make higher education affordable for any student who qualifies academically. [*Topic:* a competitive Canada. *Assertion:* must make higher education affordable.]

4. Preventing youth crime

Youth can be diverted from crime by active learning programs, full-time sports, and intervention by mentors and role models. [*Topic:* youth. *Assertion:* can be diverted from crime in three ways.]

5. The effects of strip-mining

Strip-mining should be tightly controlled in this region to reduce its pollution of water resources, its destruction of the land, and its devastating effects on people's lives. [*Topic:* strip-mining. *Assertion:* should be tightly controlled for three reasons.]

ESL In some cultures it is considered unnecessary or impolite for a writer to have an opinion or to state his or her main idea outright. But readers of English usually expect a clear and early idea of what a writer thinks.

2 Development of the thesis statement

A thesis will not usually leap fully formed into your head: you will have to develop and shape the idea as you develop and shape your essay. Still, trying to draft a thesis statement early can give you a point of reference when changes inevitably occur.

While you are developing your thesis statement, ask questions about each attempt:

Checklist for revising the thesis statement

- How well does the *subject* of your statement capture the subject of your paper?
- What *claim* does your statement make about your subject?
- What is the *significance* of the claim? How does it answer "So what?" and convey your purpose?
- How can the claim be *limited* or made more *specific*? Does it state a single idea and clarify the boundaries of the idea?
- How *unified* is the statement? How do each word and phrase contribute to a single idea?

3b

Here are examples of thesis statements revised to meet these requirements:

Original	Revised
This new product brought in over $300,000 last year. [A statement of fact, not an assertion: what is significant about the product's success?]	This new product succeeded because of its innovative marketing campaign, including widespread press coverage, in-store entertainment, and a consumer newsletter.
People should not go on fad diets. [A vague statement that needs limiting with one or more reasons: what's wrong with fad diets?]	Fad diets can be dangerous when they deprive the body of essential nutrients or rely on excessive quantities of potentially harmful foods.
Televised sports are different from live sports. [A general statement that needs to be made more specific: how are they different, and why is the difference significant?]	Although television cannot transmit all the excitement of being in a crowd during a game, its close-ups and slow-motion replays more than compensate.
Seat belts can save lives, but now carmakers are installing air bags. [Not unified: how do the two parts of the sentence relate to each other?]	If drivers had used lifesaving seat belts more often, carmakers might not have needed to install air bags.

3b   Organizing your ideas

Most essays share a basic pattern of introduction (states the subject), body (develops the subject), and conclusion (pulls the essay's ideas together). Introductions and conclusions are discussed on pages 48–52. Within the body, every paragraph develops some aspect of the essay's main idea, or thesis. See pages 32–33 for Sara Ling's essay, with annotations highlighting the body's pattern of support for the thesis statement.

ESL If English is not your native language, the pattern of introduction-body-conclusion and the particular schemes discussed here may differ from what you are used to. For instance, instead of focusing the introduction quickly on the topic and thesis, writers in your native culture may take an indirect approach. (See also p. 49.) And instead of arranging body paragraphs to emphasize general points and then support those points with specific details, examples, or reasons, writers in your native culture may leave the general points unsupported (assuming that readers will supply the evidence themselves) or may give only the specifics (assuming that readers will infer the general points). (See also p. 37.) When writing in English, you need to address readers' expectations for directness and for the statement and support of general points.

1 The general and the specific

To organize material for an essay, you need to distinguish between general and specific ideas and see the relations between ideas. GENERAL and SPECIFIC refer to the number of instances or objects included in a group signified by a word. The following "ladder" illustrates a general-to-specific hierarchy:

Most general

↑ life form
  plant
  rose
↓ Uncle Dan's prize-winning John Cabot rose

Most specific

As you arrange your material, pick out the general ideas and then the specific points that support them. Set aside points that seem irrelevant to your key ideas. On a computer, you can easily experiment with various arrangements of general ideas and supporting information: save the master list, duplicate it, and then use the Cut and Paste functions to move material around, or (a little quicker) drag selected text to where you want it.

2 Schemes for organizing essays

An essay's body paragraphs may be arranged in many ways that are familiar to readers. The choice depends on your subject, purpose, and audience.

- *Spatial:* In describing a person, place, or thing, move through space systematically from a starting point to other features— for instance, top to bottom, near to far, left to right.
- *Chronological:* In recounting a sequence of events, arrange the events as they actually occurred in time, first to last.
- *General to specific:* Begin with an overall discussion of the subject; then fill in details, facts, examples, and other support.
- *Specific to general:* First provide the support; then draw a conclusion from it.
- *Climactic:* Arrange ideas in order of increasing importance to your thesis or increasing interest to the reader.
- *Problem-solution:* First, outline a problem that needs solving; then propose a solution. (See pp. 100–103 for an example.)

3b

3   Outlines

It's not essential to craft a detailed outline before you begin drafting an essay; in fact, too detailed a plan could prevent you from discovering ideas while you draft. Still, even a rough scheme can show you patterns of general and specific, suggest proportions, and highlight gaps or overlaps in coverage.

There are several different kinds of outlines, some more flexible than others.

Scratch or informal outline

A scratch or informal outline includes key general points in the order they will be covered. It may also suggest the specific evidence for them.

Here is Sara Ling's scratch outline for her essay on Internet communication:

Thesis statement

By lowering the barriers of physical appearance in communication, the Internet's uniquely anonymous form of interaction could build diversity into community.

Scratch outline

No fear of prejudgment
    Physical attributes unknown—age, race, gender, etc.
    We won't be shut out because of appearance
Inability to prejudge others
    Assumptions based on appearance
    Meeting of minds only
    Finding shared interests and concerns

A scratch or informal outline may be all you need to begin drafting. Sometimes, though, it may prove too skimpy a guide, and you may want to use it as a preliminary to a more detailed outline. Indeed, Sara Ling used her scratch outline as a base for a detailed formal outline that gave her an even more definite sense of direction (see opposite page).

Tree diagram

In a tree diagram, ideas and details branch out in increasing specificity. Unlike more linear outlines, this diagram can be supplemented and extended indefinitely, so it is easy to alter. Johanna Abrams developed the following example from her brainstorming about a summer job (p. 10):

Thesis statement

Two months working in a large agency taught me that an office's pecking order should be respected.

Tree diagram

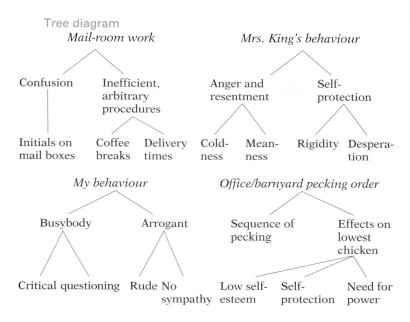

A tree diagram can be especially useful for planning a project for the World Wide Web. The diagram can help you lay out the organization of your project and its links and then later can serve as a site map for your readers. (For more on online writing, see pp. 106–07.)

Formal outline

A formal outline not only lays out main ideas and their support but also shows the relative importance of all the essay's elements. On the basis of her scratch outline (previous page), Sara Ling prepared this formal outline for her essay on the Internet:

Thesis statement

By lowering the barriers of physical appearance in communication, the Internet's uniquely anonymous form of interaction could build diversity into community.

Formal outline

I. No fear of being prejudged
    A. Unknown physical attributes
        1. Gender
        2. Age
        3. Race
        4. Style
    B. Freer communication
    C. No automatic rejection

3b

II. Inability to prejudge others
  A. No assumptions based on appearance
    1. Body type
    2. Physical disability
    3. Race
  B. Discovery of shared interests and concerns
    1. Sports and other activities
    2. Family values
    3. Political views
  C. Reduction of physical bias

This example illustrates several principles of outlining that can ensure completeness, balance, and clear relationships:

- All parts are systematically indented and labelled: Roman numerals (I, II) for primary divisions; indented capital letters (A, B) for secondary divisions; further indented Arabic numerals (1, 2) for supporting examples. (The next level down would be indented further still and labelled with small letters: a, b.)
- The outline divides the material into several groups. A long list of points at the same level should be broken up into groups.
- Topics of equal generality appear in parallel headings (with the same indention and numbering or lettering).
- All subdivided headings break into at least two parts because a topic cannot logically be divided into only one part.
- All headings are expressed in parallel grammatical form—in the example, as phrases using a noun plus modifiers. This is a topic outline; in a sentence outline all headings are expressed as full sentences.

Note Because of its structure, a formal outline can be an excellent tool for analyzing a draft before revising it. (See p. 24.)

4 Unity and coherence

Two qualities of effective writing relate to organization: unity and coherence. When you perceive that someone's writing "flows well," you are probably appreciating these qualities.

To check an outline or draft for unity, ask these questions:

- Is each section relevant to the main idea (thesis) of the essay?
- Within main sections, does each example or detail support the principal idea of that section?

To check your outline or draft for coherence, ask the following questions:

- Do the ideas follow a clear sequence?
- Are the parts of the essay logically connected?
- Are the connections clear and smooth?

See also pages 38–43 on unity and coherence in paragraphs.

4 Drafting

Drafting is an occasion for exploration. Don't expect to transcribe solid thoughts into polished prose: solidity and polish will come with revision and editing. Instead, while drafting, let the very act of writing help you find and form your meaning.

4a Starting to draft

Beginning a draft sometimes takes courage, even for seasoned professionals. Procrastination may actually help if you let ideas for writing simmer at the same time. At some point, though, you'll have to face the blank paper or computer screen. The following techniques can help you begin:

- Read over what you've already written—notes, outlines, and so on—and immediately start your draft with whatever comes to mind.
- Freewrite (see p. 8).
- Write scribbles or type nonsense until usable words start coming.
- Pretend you're writing to a friend about your topic.
- Conjure up an image that represents your topic—a physical object, a facial expression, two people arguing over something, a giant machine gouging the earth for a mine, whatever. Describe that image.
- Skip the opening and start in the middle. Or write the conclusion.
- Write a paragraph on what you think your essay will be about when you finish it.
- Using your outline, divide your essay into chunks—say, one for the introduction, another for the first point, and so on. Start writing the chunk that seems most eager to be written, the one you understand best or feel most strongly about.

4b Maintaining momentum

Drafting requires momentum: the forward movement opens you to fresh ideas and connections. To keep moving while drafting, try one or more of these techniques:

- Set aside enough time for yourself. (For a brief essay, a first draft is likely to take at least an hour or two.)

4c

- Work in a place where you won't be interrupted, and make yourself comfortable.
- If you must stop working, leave a note with the draft about what you expect to do next. Then you can pick up where you stopped with minimal disruption.
- Be as fluid as possible, and don't worry about mistakes. Spontaneity will allow your attitudes toward your subject to surface naturally in your sentences, and it will also make you receptive to ideas and relations you haven't seen before. Mistakes will be easier to find and correct later, when you're not also trying to create.
- Keep going. Skip over sticky spots; leave a blank if you can't find the right word; put alternative ideas or phrasings in brackets so that you can consider them later without bogging down. If an idea pops out of nowhere but doesn't seem to fit in, quickly jot it down on a separate sheet, or write it into the draft and bracket or boldface it for later attention. You can use an asterisk (*) or some other symbol to mark places where you feel blocked or uncertain. On a computer you can find these places later by using the Search command to locate the symbol.
- Resist self-criticism. Don't worry about your style, grammar, spelling, punctuation, and the like. Don't worry about what your readers will think. These are very important matters, but save them for revision. If you're writing on a computer, help yourself resist self-criticism by turning off automatic spelling or grammar checkers or by trying invisible writing as described on page 9.
- Use your thesis statement and outline to remind you of your planned purpose, organization, and content.
- But don't feel constrained by your thesis and outline. If your writing leads you in a more interesting direction, follow.

If you write on a computer, frequently save or file the text you're drafting—at least every fifteen minutes or every couple of pages and every time you leave the computer. In addition, back up your drafts on a separate disk, and perhaps even print paper copies (so-called hard copy) in case anything happens to your disks.

(4c) Examining a sample first draft

Sara Ling's first draft on Internet communication appears on the opposite page. (Her earlier work appears on pp. 8, 9–10, 18–19.)

Title?

In "Welcome to Cyberbia," M. Kadi says that the Internet will lead to more fragmentation in society because people just seek out others like themselves. But Kadi ignores the Internet's uniquely anonymous form of interaction could actually build diversity into community by lowering the barriers of physical appearance in communication.

Anonymity on the Internet. It's one of the best things about technology. No one knows your age or gender or race. Whether your fat or thin or neat or sloppy. What kind of clothes you wear. (Maybe your not wearing clothes at all). People who know you personally don't even know who you are with an invented screen name.

We can communicate freely without being prejudged because of our appearance. For example, I participate in a snowboarding forum that has mostly men. I didn't realize what I was getting into when I used my full name as my screen name. Before long, I was often being shouted down with such insults as "What does a girl know?" and "Why don't you go back to knitting?" Then a nice man I had been exchanging messages with wrote me a private e-mail, and he turned out to be a she! This woman had been wiser than me and hidden her gender with her screen name. She hadn't received any of the hostile responses I had, just because no one knew she was a woman. As this example shows, posing as people different from who they really are can enable people to make themselves heard in situations where normally (in the real world) they would be shut out.

We cannot prejudge others because of their appearance. Often in face-to-face interaction we assume we know things about people just because of the way they look. Assumptions prevent people from discovering their shared interests and concerns, and this is particularly true where race is concerned. The anonymity of the Internet makes physical barriers irrelevant, and only people's minds meet. Because of this, the Internet could create a world free of physical bias.

Logged on to the Internet we can become more tolerant of others. We can become a community.

5 Revising and Editing

During revision—literally "re-seeing"—you shift your focus outward from yourself and your subject toward your readers, concentrating on what will help them respond as you want. It's wise to revise in at least two stages, one devoted to fundamental meaning and structure (here called REVISING) and one devoted to word choice, grammar, punctuation, and other features of the surface (here called EDITING). Knowing that you will edit later gives you the freedom at first to look beyond the confines of the page or screen to the whole paper.

5a Revising

To revise your writing, you have to read it critically (see p. 78), and that means you have to create some distance between your draft and yourself. One of the following techniques may help you see your work objectively:

- Take a break after finishing the draft to pursue some other activity. A few hours may be enough; a whole night or day is preferable.
- Ask someone to read and react to your draft. If your instructor encourages collaboration among students, by all means take advantage of the opportunity to hear the responses of others. (See pp. 34–35 for more on collaboration.)
- If you compose your draft in handwriting, type it before revising it. The act of transcription can reveal gaps in content or problems in structure.
- Outline your draft. While reading it, highlight the main points supporting the thesis. Write these sentences down separately in outline form. (If you're working on a computer, you can copy and paste these sentences.) Then examine the outline you've made for logical order, gaps, and digressions. A formal outline can be especially illuminating because of its careful structure (see pp. 19–20).
- Listen to your draft: read it out loud to yourself or a friend or classmate, read it into a tape recorder and play the tape, or have someone read the draft to you.

Computerized word processing has removed the mechanical drudgery of revision, but writers disagree over whether it's better to consider revisions on a paper printout or on screen.

- Paper copy allows you to see the whole draft at once and may be easier to read accurately, but if your work is stored on a computer you then have to key in your changes.
- Working on a computer allows you to see changes as you make them and to experiment with different versions of the same passage, but it can prevent you from seeing your work as a whole.

Whatever your own preference, do take a couple of precautions. First, work on a duplicate of any draft you're revising so that the original remains intact until you're truly finished with it. (You may be able to do without the duplicate if your word processor has a function that shows, or "tracks," changes alongside the original text, allowing you later to accept or reject alterations.) And second, save successive drafts under their own file names in case you need to consult them for ideas or phrasings.

Set aside at least as much time to revise your essay as you took to draft it. Plan on going through the draft several times to answer the questions in the checklist below and to resolve any problems you uncover.

Checklist for revision

- *Purpose:* What is the essay's purpose? Does it conform to the assignment? Is it consistent throughout the paper? (See p. 6.)
- *Thesis:* What is the thesis of the essay? Where does it become clear? How well do thesis and paper match: Does the paper stray from the thesis? Does it fulfill the commitment of the thesis? (See pp. 14–16.)
- *Structure:* What are the main points of the paper? (List them.) How well does each support the thesis? How effective is their arrangement for the paper's purpose? (See pp. 16–21.)
- *Development:* How well do details, examples, and other evidence support each main point? Where, if at all, might readers find support skimpy or have trouble understanding the content? (See pp. 4–5, 38–43.)
- *Tone:* What is the tone of the paper? How do particular words and sentence structures create the tone? How appropriate is it for the purpose, topic, and intended readers? Where is it most and least successful? (See pp. 4–5.)
- *Unity:* What does each sentence and paragraph contribute to the thesis? Where, if at all, do digressions occur? Should these be cut, or can they be rewritten to support the thesis? (See pp. 20, 37–38.)

**rev
5a**

- *Coherence:* How clearly and smoothly does the paper flow? Where does it seem rough or awkward? Can any transitions be improved? (See pp. 20, 38–43.)
- *Title, introduction, conclusion:* How accurately and interestingly does the title reflect the essay's content? (See below.) How well does the introduction engage and focus readers' attention? (See pp. 48–50.) How effective is the conclusion in providing a sense of completion? (See pp. 50–52.)

A note on titling your essay

The revision stage is a good time to consider a title because attempting to sum up your essay in a phrase can focus your attention sharply on your topic, purpose, and audience.

Here are some suggestions for titling an essay:

- A DESCRIPTIVE TITLE is almost always appropriate and is usually expected for academic writing. It announces the topic clearly, accurately, and as briefly as possible. Sara Ling's final title—"The Internet: Fragmentation or Community?"—is an example. Other examples are "Images of Lost Identity in *North by Northwest*"; "An Experiment in Small-Group Dynamics"; "Why Alberta Hated the National Energy Policy"; "Food Poisoning Involving *E. coli* Bacteria: A Review of the Literature."
- A SUGGESTIVE TITLE—the kind often found in popular magazines—may be appropriate for more informal writing. Examples include "Making Peace" (for an essay on UN peacekeeping) and "Anyone for Soup?" (for an essay on working in a soup kitchen). For a more suggestive title, Ling might have chosen something like "What We Don't Know Can Help Us" or "Secrets of the Internet." Such a title conveys the writer's attitudes and hints at the topic, thereby pulling readers into the essay to learn more. A source for such a title may be a familiar phrase, a fresh image, or a significant expression from the essay itself.
- A title tells readers how big the topic is. For Ling's essay, the title "The Internet" or "Anonymity" would have been too broad, whereas "Lose Your Body" or "Discovering Common Ground" would have been too narrow because each deals with only part of the paper's content.
- A title should not restate the assignment or the thesis statement, as in "The Trouble with M. Kadi's Picture of the Internet" or "What I Think About Diversity on the Internet."

For more information on essay titles, see pages 411 (the format of a title in the final paper) and 291–92 (italicizing words in a title).

5b Examining a sample revision

In revising her first draft, Sara Ling had the help of her instructor and several of her classmates, to whom she showed the draft as part of her assignment. (See p. 34 for more on this kind of collaboration.) She revised thoroughly in response to others' comments and her own evaluation of the draft's strengths and weaknesses. The first half of the revision begins below. The main changes are explained below and keyed to the revision by numbers (some numbers are used more than once).

1. With a descriptive title, Ling named her topic and forecast how she would approach it.
2. Ling rewrote and expanded the previous abrupt introduction to draw readers into the question she would explore and to give a fuller summary of Kadi's essay.
3. Ling rewrote the transitions between paragraphs to make each paragraph relate clearly to her thesis statement and to make the essay flow more smoothly.
4. Ling added examples to support her general statements. This and the following two categories of changes occupied most of Ling's attention during revision.
5. Ling condensed the example from her experience. Some readers commented that it overwhelmed the paragraph, and Ling realized that she had given more background than needed.
6. In response to her classmates' comments, Ling qualified her ideas to acknowledge complexities she had previously ignored. (The qualification created an overlong paragraph, so Ling broke the paragraph in two.)

The Internet: Fragmentation or Community?   1

~~Title?~~

We hear all sorts of predictions about how the Internet will enrich our lives 2
and promote equality, tolerance, and thus community in our society. But are
these promises realistic? In her essay "Welcome to Cyberbia," M. Kadi argues
that they are not. Instead, she maintains,

~~In "Welcome to Cyberbia," M. Kadi~~ says that the Internet will lead
            , not community,   *users merely*
to more fragmentation, in society because ~~people just~~ seek out others
            with the same biases, needs, and concerns as their own. The
            point is an interesting one, but Kadi overlooks
~~like themselves. But Kadi ignores~~ the Internet's uniquely anonymous
            which
form of interaction, could actually build diversity into community by

lowering the barriers of physical appearance in communication.
            Writing on the Internet, you can be as anonymous as you like. Unless   3
            Anonymity on the Internet. It's one of the best things about tech-
you tell them, the people you communicate with do not   *you're*
~~nology. No one~~ knows your age or gender or race. Whether ~~your~~ fat or

thin or neat or sloppy. What kind of clothes you wear. (Maybe ~~your~~ *you're* not

Even p
wearing clothes at all). People who know you personally don't ~~even~~

if you conceal your identity
know who you are with an invented screen name.

Because of this anonymity, we
3   ~~We~~ can communicate freely without being prejudged because of

4   our appearance. For example, *a high school student can participate in a physics discussion group, and not be dismissed by professional physicists in the group just because of her age. An adult man can chat about music with teenagers, who might otherwise ignore or laugh at him.*

5   *A woman I know posed as a man on   and received none of the hostile*
~~I participate in a snowboarding forum that has mostly men. I didn't~~
responses such as "What does a girl know?" that I got when I revealed my
~~realize what I was getting into when I used my full name as my screen~~
gender on the same forum.
~~name. Before long, I was often being shouted down with such insults as~~

~~"What does a girl know?" and "Why don't you go back to knitting?"~~

~~Then a nice man I had been exchanging messages with wrote me a~~

~~private e-mail, and he turned out to be a she! This woman had been~~

~~wiser than me and hidden her gender with her screen name. She hadn't~~

~~received any of the hostile responses I had, just because no one knew~~

~~she was a woman.~~

6   *Granted, concealing or altering identities on the Internet can be a problem, as when adults pose as children to seduce or harm them. These well-publicized occurrences say a great deal about the need to monitor the use of the Internet by children, and being cautious about getting together with Internet correspondents. However, they do not undermine the value of*

~~As this example shows, posing as people different from who they really~~
being able
~~are can~~ enable people to make themselves heard in situations where

normally (in the real world) they would be shut out.

(5c) Editing and proofreading

Editing, like revision, is a two-step process. First, edit the revised draft for style, sense, and correctness; then format and proofread the final draft.

1   Editing

After you've revised your essay so that all the content is in place, turn to the important work of removing any surface problems that could interfere with a reader's understanding or enjoyment of your ideas.

Try these approaches to discover what needs editing:

- Take a break, even fifteen or twenty minutes, to clear your head.
- Read the draft *slowly,* and read what you *actually see.* Otherwise, you're likely to read what you intended to write but didn't.
- As you read the draft, imagine yourself encountering it for the first time, as a reader will.
- Have a friend or relative read your work. (If your native language is not English, you may find it especially helpful to have a native speaker read your revised drafts.) When you share your work in class, listen to the responses of your classmates or instructor. (See pp. 34–35.)
- As when revising, read the draft aloud, preferably into a tape recorder, listening for awkward rhythms, repetitive sentence patterns, and missing or clumsy transitions.
- Learn from your own experience. Keep a record of the problems that others have pointed out in your writing. When editing, check your work against this record.

If you write on a computer, consider these additional approaches to editing:

- Don't rely on your word processor's spelling, grammar, and style checkers to find what needs editing.
- If possible, work on a double-spaced paper copy. Most people find it much harder to spot errors on a computer screen than on paper.
- Use the Find command to locate and correct mistakes or stylistic problems that tend to crop up in your writing—certain misspellings, overuse of *there is,* wordy phrases such as *the fact that,* and so on.
- The ease of editing on a computer can lead to overediting and steal the life from your prose. Resist any temptation to rewrite sentences over and over. (If your computer's grammar and style checker contributes to the temptation, consider turning it off.)
- Inserting or deleting text on a computer requires special care not to omit needed words or leave in unneeded words.

In your editing, work first for clarity and a smooth movement among sentences and then for correctness. Use the questions in the checklist below to guide your editing, referring to the page numbers in parentheses as needed.

Checklist for editing

- *Clarity:* How well do words and sentences convey their intended meanings? Which if any words and sentences are confusing? Check the paper especially for these:

  Exact words (pp. 144–51)
  Parallelism (pp. 132–34)
  Clear modifiers (pp. 228–32)
  Clear reference of pronouns (pp. 211–18)
  Complete sentences (pp. 234–38)
  Sentences separated correctly (pp. 238–42)

- *Effectiveness:* How well do words and sentences engage and direct readers' attention? Where, if at all, does the writing seem wordy, choppy, or dull? Check the paper especially for these:

  Emphasis on main ideas (pp. 123–27)
  Smooth and informative transitions (pp. 42–43)
  Variety in sentence length and structure (pp. 135–38)
  Appropriate words (pp. 139–51)
  Concise sentences (pp. 152–57)

- *Correctness:* How little or how much do surface errors interfere with clarity and effectiveness? Check the paper especially for these:

  Spelling (pp. 281–86)
  Verb forms, especially *-s* and *-ed* endings and correct forms of irregular verbs (pp. 176–88)
  Verb tenses, especially consistency (pp. 189–92)
  Agreement between subjects and verbs, especially when words come between them or the subject is *each, everyone,* or a similar word (pp. 200–5)
  Pronoun forms (pp. 206–11)
  Agreement between pronouns and antecedents, especially when the antecedent contains *or,* or it is *everyone, person,* or a similar word (pp. 211–15)
  Sentence fragments (pp. 234–38)
  Commas, especially with comma splices (pp. 238–42), with *and* or *but* (p. 251), with introductory elements (pp. 251–52), with nonessential elements (pp. 252–56), and with series (pp. 256–57)
  Apostrophes in possessives but not plural nouns (*Dave's/witches,* pp. 267–69) and in contractions but not possessive personal pronouns (*it's/its,* p. 270)

2   Formatting and proofreading

After editing your essay, retype or print it one last time. Follow the wishes of your instructor in formatting your document. Two common formats are discussed and illustrated in this book: MLA on pages 380–421 and APA on pages 423–445. In addition, Chapter 7 treats principles and elements of document design.

Be sure to proofread the final essay several times to spot and correct errors. To increase the accuracy of your proofreading, you may need to experiment with ways to keep yourself from relaxing into the rhythm and the content of your prose. Here are a few tricks, including some used by professional proofreaders:

- Read printed copy, even if you will eventually submit the paper electronically. Most people proofread more accurately when reading type on paper than when reading it on a computer screen. (At the same time, don't view the printed copy as necessarily error-free just because it's clean. Clean-looking copy may still harbour errors.)
- Read the paper aloud, very slowly, and distinctly pronounce exactly what you see.
- Place a ruler under each line as you read it.
- Read "against copy," comparing your final draft one sentence at a time against the edited draft.
- Take steps to keep the content of your writing from distracting you while you proofread. Read the essay backward, end to beginning, examining each sentence as a separate unit. Or, taking advantage of a computer, isolate each paragraph from its context by printing it on a separate page. (Of course, reassemble the paragraphs before submitting the paper.)

(5d) Examining a sample editing and final draft

The second paragraph of Sara Ling's edited draft appears below. One change Ling made throughout the essay shows up here: she resolved an inconsistency in references to *you, people,* and *we,* settling on a consistent *we.* In addition, Ling corrected several sentence fragments in the middle of the paragraph.

                   we   *we*
Writing on the Internet, ~~you~~ can be as anonymous as ~~you~~ like.
    we   *we*
Unless ~~you~~ tell them, the people ~~you~~ communicate with do not know
our   *W*   *we're*
~~your~~ age or gender or race~~.~~ ~~W~~hether ~~you're~~ fat or thin or neat or
       W   *we*   *if we're*
sloppy~~.~~ ~~W~~hat kind of clothes ~~you~~ wear~~.~~ (~~Maybe you're not~~ wearing
                                us
clothes at all). Even people who know ~~you~~ personally don't know
    we   *we*   *our*   *ies*
who ~~you~~ are if ~~you~~ conceal ~~your~~ identit~~y~~ with ~~an~~ invented screen
      s
name~~.~~

Sara Ling's final essay appears on the next page, typed in MLA format except for page breaks. (See pp. 410–14.) Comments in the margins point out key features of the essay's content.

Sara Ling

Professor Nelson

English 120A

14 April 2008

The Internet: Fragmentation or Community?   Descriptive title

We hear all sorts of predictions about how the   Introduction
Internet will enrich our individual lives and promote
communication, tolerance, and thus community in
our society. But are these promises realistic? In her   1. Question to be
essay "Welcome to Cyberbia," M. Kadi argues that   addressed
they are not. Instead, she maintains, the Internet will   2. Summary of
lead to more fragmentation, not community, because   Kadi's essay
users merely seek out others with the same biases,
concerns, and needs as their own. The point is an
interesting one, but Kadi seems to overlook that the
Internet's uniquely anonymous form of interaction   3. Thesis statement
could actually build diversity into community by
lowering the barriers of physical appearance in
communication.

Writing on the Internet, we can be as anony-   Explanation of
mous as we like. Unless we tell them, the people we   Internet's
                                                              anonymity
communicate with do not know our age or gender or
race, whether we're fat or thin or neat or sloppy, or
what kind of clothes we wear (if we're wearing clothes
at all). Even people who know us personally don't
know who we are if we conceal our identities with invented screen names.

Because of this anonymity, we can communicate   First main point: We
freely on the Internet without being prejudged because   are not prejudged
                                                              by others.
of our physical attributes. For example, a high school   1. Examples
student can participate in a physics discussion group
without fear of being dismissed by the group's professional physicists just because of her age. Similarly, an
adult man can chat about music with teenagers who
might otherwise ignore or laugh at him. A woman I
know posed as a man on a snowboarding forum and

received none of the hostile responses—such as "What does a girl know?"—that I got when I innocently revealed my gender on the same forum.

Granted, concealing or altering identities on the Internet can be a problem, as when adults pose as children to seduce or harm them. These well-publicized occurrences say much about the need to monitor children's use of the Internet and be cautious about meeting Internet correspondents. However, they do not undermine the value of being able to make ourselves heard in situations where normally (in the real world) we would be shut out.

The Internet's anonymity has a flip side, too: just as we cannot be prejudged, so we cannot prejudge others because of their appearance. Often in face-to-face interaction, we assume we know things about people just because of the way they look. People with athletic builds must be unintelligent. Heavy people must be uninteresting. People in wheelchairs must be unapproachable or pathetic. Perhaps most significant, people of other races must have fixed and contrary views about all kinds of issues, from family values to crime to affirmative action. Assumptions like these prevent us from discovering the interests and concerns we share with people who merely look different. But with the anonymity of the Internet, such physical barriers to understanding are irrelevant.

A world without physical bias may be an unreachable ideal, but the more we communicate with just our minds, the more likely it is that our minds will find common ground. Logged on, we can become more accepted and more accepting, more tolerated and more tolerant. We can become a community.

Work Cited

Kadi, M. "Welcome to Cyberbia." *Utne Reader* Mar.–Apr. 1995: 57–59. Print.

Margin annotations:

2. Qualification of first main point

3. Conclusion of first main point

Second main point: We cannot prejudge others.

1. Clarification of second main point

2. Examples

3. Effects

4. Conclusion of second main point

Conclusion, summarizing essay

Work cited in MLA style

5e Revising collaboratively

In many writing courses students work together on writing, most often commenting on each other's work to help with revision. This collaborative writing gives experience in reading written work critically and in reaching others through writing. Collaboration may occur face to face in small groups, via drafts and comments on paper, or on computers.

Whether you collaborate in person, on paper, or on a computer, you will be more comfortable and helpful and will benefit more from others' comments if you follow a few guidelines.

Commenting on others' writing

- Be sure you know what the writer is saying. If necessary, summarize the paper to understand its content. (See pp. 74–76.)
- Unless you have other instructions, address only your most significant concerns with the work. (Use the revision checklist on p. 30 as a guide to what is significant.) Remember that you are the reader, not the writer. Resist the temptation to edit sentences, add details, or otherwise assume responsibility for the paper.
- Be specific. If something confuses you, say *why*. If you disagree with a conclusion, say *why*.
- Be supportive as well as honest. Tell the writer what you like about the paper. Phrase comments positively: instead of *This paragraph doesn't interest me*, say *You have an interesting detail here that I almost missed*. Question the writer in a way that emphasizes the effect of the work on you, the reader: *This paragraph confuses me because. . . .* And avoid measuring the work against a set of external standards: *This essay is poorly organized. Your thesis statement is inadequate.*
- While reading, make your comments in writing, even if you will be delivering them in person later on. Then you'll be able to recall what you thought.
- If you are reading the paper on a computer, not on paper, then be sure to specify what part of the paper each of your comments relates to. When you review papers using e-mail, you can embed your comments directly into the paper. You can do the same when you review papers in word-processor files, or you may be able to use your word processor's Comment function to insert your comments as annotations on the paper.
- If you are responding on paper or online, not face to face with the writer, remember that the writer won't be able to ask for immediate clarification or infer additional information from your gestures, facial expressions, and tone of voice. In these situations, word your comments carefully to avoid misunderstandings.

Benefiting from comments on your writing

- Think of your readers as counsellors or coaches who will help you see the virtues and flaws in your work and sharpen your awareness of readers' needs.
- Read or listen to comments closely.
- Make sure you know what the critic is saying. If you need more information, ask for it, or consult the appropriate section of this handbook.
- Don't become defensive. Letting comments offend you will only erect a barrier to improvement in your writing. As one writing teacher advises, "Leave your ego at the door."
- When comments seem appropriate, revise your work in response to them. You will learn more from the act of revision than from just thinking about changes.
- Though you should be open to suggestions, you are the final authority on your paper. You are free to decline advice when you think it is inappropriate.
- Keep track of both the strengths and weaknesses others identify. Then in following assignments you can build on your successes and give special attention to problem areas.

ESL In some cultures writers do not expect criticism from readers, or readers do not expect to think and speak critically about what they read. If critical responses are uncommon in your native culture, collaboration may at first be uncomfortable for you. Consider that many writers in English think of a draft or even a final paper as more an exploration of ideas than the last word on a subject, and they are interested in their readers' questions and suggestions. Readers of English, in turn, often approach a text in a skeptical frame of mind. Their tactful questions and suggestions are usually considered appropriate.

(5f) Preparing a writing portfolio

Your writing teacher may ask you to assemble samples of your writing into a portfolio, or folder, once or more during the course. Such a portfolio gives you a chance to consider all your writing over a period and to showcase your best work.

Although the requirements for portfolios vary, most teachers are looking for a range of writing that demonstrates your progress and strengths as a writer. You, in turn, see how you have advanced from one assignment to the next, as you've had time for new knowledge to sink in and time for practice. Teachers often allow students to revise papers before placing them in the portfolio, even if the papers have already been submitted earlier. In that case, every paper in the portfolio can benefit from all your learning.

¶
6

An assignment to assemble a writing portfolio will probably also provide guidelines for what to include, how the portfolio will be evaluated, and how (or whether) it will be weighted for a grade. Be sure you understand the purpose of the portfolio and who will read it. For instance, if your composition teacher will be the only reader and his or her guidelines encourage you to show evidence of progress, you might include a paper that took big risks but never entirely succeeded. In contrast, if a committee of teachers will read your work and the guidelines urge you to demonstrate your competence as a writer, you might include only papers that did succeed.

Unless the guidelines specify otherwise, provide error-free copies of your final drafts, label all your samples with your name, and assemble them all in a folder. Add a cover letter or memo that lists the samples, explains why you've included each one, and evaluates your progress as a writer. The self-evaluation involved should be a learning experience for you and will help your readers assess your development as a writer.

6 Paragraphs

1. topic sentence.
2. Explanation
3. Examples
4. Paralism.
Their, ~~actually~~ are still

A PARAGRAPH is a group of related sentences set off by a beginning indention or, sometimes, by extra space. Paragraphs give you and your readers a breather from long stretches of text, and they indicate key steps in the development of your thesis.

In the body of your essay, you may use paragraphs for any of these purposes:

- To introduce one of the main points supporting your essay's central idea (its thesis) and to develop the point with examples, facts, or other supporting evidence. (See pp. 14–16 for a discussion of an essay's thesis.)
- Within a group of paragraphs centring on one main point, to introduce and develop a key example or other important evidence.
- To shift approach—for instance, from pros to cons, from problem to solution, from questions to answers.
- To mark movement in a sequence, such as from one reason or step to another.

¶
6a

This chapter discusses the three qualities of an effective body paragraph: unity (see below), coherence (pp. 38–43), and development (pp. 44–48). In addition, the chapter discusses two special kinds of paragraphs: introductions and conclusions (pp. 48 and 50).

Checklist for revising paragraphs

- Is the paragraph unified? Does it adhere to one general idea that is either stated in a topic sentence or otherwise apparent? (See next page.)
- Is the paragraph coherent? Do the sentences follow a clear sequence (p. 39)? Are the sentences linked as needed by parallelism (p. 40), repetition or restatement (p. 40), pronouns (p. 40), consistency (p. 41), and transitional expressions (p. 42)?
- Is the paragraph developed? Is the general idea of the paragraph well supported with specific evidence such as details, facts, examples, and reasons? (See p. 44.)

ESL Not all languages share the conventions of English paragraphs. In some languages, for instance, writing moves differently from English—not from left to right, but from right to left or down rows from top to bottom. Even in languages that move as English does, writers may not use paragraphs at all. Or they may use paragraphs but not state the central ideas or provide transitional expressions to show readers how sentences relate. If your native language is not English and you have difficulty with paragraphs, don't worry about paragraphing during drafting. Instead, during a separate step of revision, divide your text into parts that develop your main points. Mark those parts with indentions.

(6a) Maintaining paragraph unity

An effective paragraph develops one central idea—in other words, it is UNIFIED. For example:

> All this beautiful scenery does, however, make for some interesting logistical challenges. Everywhere you go in Vancouver you have to get on a bridge to get somewhere else. The downtown core is in effect an island, with five of the six accesses to it by bridge or viaduct. This naturally shapes the traffic routes, the traffic mentality and, eventually, the personality of the city. One of the newspaper chains recently decided against establishing a third paper in Vancouver because its research showed a community chopped

up by water, creating pockets of tinier communities rather than a homogeneous whole.

—ALLAN FOTHERINGHAM

Fotheringham's paragraph works because it follows through on the central idea stated in the underlined first sentence, the TOPIC SENTENCE. But what if he had written it this way instead?

> All this beautiful scenery does, however, make for some interesting logistical challenges. Everywhere you go in Vancouver you have to get on a bridge to get somewhere else. The downtown core is in effect an island, with five of the six accesses to it by bridge or viaduct. They don't make bridges like they used to. Bridges used to define a city, gave it a style and a signature. Nor, for that matter, do they make viaducts like they used to. Toronto may be the only city with a signature viaduct. But, of course, Toronto doesn't have any famous bridges: they suffer from bridge envy.

In this altered version, the topic of Vancouver's geography is forgotten midway. In Fotheringham's original, by contrast, every sentence after the first develops the meaning of the topic sentence with examples.

A topic sentence need not always come first in the paragraph. For instance, it may come last, presenting your idea only after you have provided the evidence for it. Or it may not be stated at all, especially in narrative or descriptive writing in which the point becomes clear in the details. But always the idea should govern the paragraph's content as if it were standing guard at the opening.

6b Achieving paragraph coherence

When a paragraph is COHERENT, readers can see how it holds together: the sentences seem to flow logically and smoothly into one another. Exactly the opposite happens with this paragraph:

> The ancient Egyptians were masters of preserving dead people's bodies by making mummies of them. Mummies several thousand years old have been discovered nearly intact. The skin, hair, teeth, finger- and toenails, and facial features of the mummies were evident. It is possible to diagnose the diseases they suffered in life, such as smallpox, arthritis, and nutritional deficiencies. The process was remarkably effective. Sometimes apparent were the fatal afflictions of the dead people: a middle-aged king died from a blow on the head, and polio killed a child king. Mummification consisted of removing the internal organs, applying natural preservatives inside and out, and then wrapping the body in layers of bandages.

The paragraph is hard to read. The sentences lurch instead of gliding from point to point.

As it was actually written, the paragraph is much clearer (below). Not only did the writer arrange information differently but he also built links into his sentences so that they would flow smoothly. The highlighting on the actual paragraph emphasizes the techniques:

- After stating the central idea in a topic sentence, the writer moves to two more specific explanations and illustrates the sec-ond with four sentences of examples.
- Circled words repeat or restate key terms or concepts.
- Boxed words link sentences and clarify relationships.
- Underlined phrases are in parallel grammatical form to reflect their parallel content.

> Central idea
> The ancient Egyptians were masters of preserving dead people's bodies by making mummies of them. Basically, mummification consisted of removing the internal organs, applying natural preservatives inside and out, and then wrapping the body in layers of bandages. And the process was remarkably effective. Indeed, mummies several thousand years old have been discovered nearly intact. Their skin, hair, teeth, finger- and toenails, and facial features are still evident. Their diseases in life, such as smallpox, arthritis, and nutritional deficiencies, are still diagnosable. Even their fatal afflictions are still apparent: a middle-aged king died from a blow on the head; a child king died from polio.
>
> —MITCHELL ROSENBAUM (student), "Lost Arts of the Egyptians"

1 Paragraph organization

A coherent paragraph organizes information so that readers can easily follow along. These are common paragraph schemes:

- *General to specific:* Sentences downshift from more general statements to more specific ones. (See the paragraph above by Rosenbaum.)
- *Climactic:* Sentences increase in drama or interest, ending in a climax. (See the paragraph by Lawrence Mayer on the next page.)
- *Spatial:* Sentences scan a person, place, or object from top to bottom, from side to side, or in some other way that approximates the way people actually look at things. (See the paragraph by Virginia Woolf on p. 44.)
- *Chronological:* Sentences present events as they occurred in time, earlier to later. (See the paragraph by Kathleen LaFrank on p. 42.)

¶ coh
6b

2 Parallelism

Parallelism helps tie sentences together. In the following paragraph the underlined parallel structures of *She* and a verb link all sentences after the first one. Parallelism also appears *within* many of the sentences. Aphra Behn (1640–89) was the first Englishwoman to write professionally.

> In addition to her busy career as a writer, Aphra Behn also found time to briefly marry and spend a little while in debtors' prison. She found time to take up a career as a spy for the English in their war against the Dutch. She made the long and difficult voyage to Suriname [in South America] and became involved in a slave rebellion there. She plunged into political debate at Will's Coffee House and defended her position from the stage of the Drury Lane Theater. She actively argued for women's rights to be educated and to marry whom they pleased, or not at all. She defied the seventeenth-century dictum that ladies must be "modest" and wrote freely about sex.
>
> —Angeline Goreau, "Aphra Behn"

3 Repetition and restatement

Repeating or restating key words helps make a paragraph coherent and also reminds readers what the topic is. In the following paragraph note the underlined repetition of *sleep* and restatement of *adults:*

> Perhaps the simplest fact about sleep is that individual needs for it vary widely. Most adults sleep between seven and nine hours, but occasionally people turn up who need twelve hours or so, while some rare types can get by on three or four. Rarest of all are those legendary types who require almost no sleep at all; respected researchers have recently studied three such people. One of them—a healthy, happy woman in her seventies—sleeps about an hour every two or three days. The other two are men in early middle age, who get by on a few minutes a night. One of them complains about the daily fifteen minutes or so he's forced to "waste" in sleeping.
>
> —Lawrence A. Mayer, "The Confounding Enemy of Sleep"

4 Pronouns

Because pronouns refer to nouns, they can help relate sentences to each other. In the paragraph above by Angeline Goreau,

---

KEY TERM

Parallelism The use of similar grammatical structures for similar elements of meaning within or among sentences: *The book caused a stir in the media and aroused debate in Parliament.* (See also Chapter 16.)

the pronoun *she* works just this way by substituting for *Aphra Behn* in every sentence after the first.

5   Consistency

Consistency (or the lack of it) occurs primarily in the person and number of nouns and pronouns and in the tense of verbs. Any inconsistencies not required by meaning will interfere with a reader's ability to follow the development of ideas.

Note the underlined inconsistencies in the next paragraphs:

Shifts in tense

In the Hopi religion, water <u>is</u> the driving force. Since the Hopi <u>lived</u> in the Arizona desert, they <u>needed</u> water urgently for drinking, cooking, and irrigating crops. Their complex beliefs <u>are</u> focused in part on gaining the assistance of supernatural forces in obtaining water. Many of the Hopi kachinas, or spirit essences, <u>were</u> directly concerned with clouds, rain, and snow.

Shifts in number

<u>Kachinas</u> represent spiritually the things and events of the real world, such as cumulus clouds, mischief, cornmeal, and even death. A <u>kachina</u> is not worshipped as a god but regarded as an interested friend. <u>They</u> visit the Hopi from December through July in the form of men who dress in kachina costumes and perform dances and other rituals.

Shifts in person

Unlike the man, the Hopi <u>woman</u> does not keep contact with kachinas through costumes and dancing. Instead, <u>one</u> receives a tihu, or small effigy, of a kachina from the man impersonating the kachina. <u>You</u> are more likely to receive a tihu as a girl approaching marriage, though a child or older woman may receive one, too.

KEY TERMS

PRONOUN A word that refers to and functions as a noun, such as *I, you, he, she, it, we, they: The patient could not raise <u>her</u> arm.* (See p. 161.)

TENSE The form of a verb that indicates the time of its action, such as present (*I <u>run</u>*), past (*I <u>ran</u>*), or future (*I <u>will run</u>*). (See p. 189.)

NUMBER The form of a noun, pronoun, or verb that indicates whether it is singular (one) or plural (more than one): *boy, boys.*

PERSON The form of a pronoun that indicates whether the subject is speaking (first person: *I, we*), spoken to (second person: *you*), or spoken about (third person: *he, she, it, they*). All nouns are in the third person.

¶ coh

6b

The grammar checker on a word processor cannot help you locate shifts in tense, number, or person among sentences. Shifts are sometimes necessary (as when tenses change to reflect actual differences in time), and even a passage with needless shifts may still consist of sentences that are grammatically correct (as all the sentences are in the above examples). The only way to achieve consistency in your writing is to review it yourself.

6   Transitional expressions

Transitional expressions such as *therefore, in contrast,* or *meanwhile* can forge specific connections between sentences, as do the underlined expressions in this paragraph:

> Medical science has <u>thus</u> succeeded in identifying the hundreds of viruses that can cause the common cold. It has <u>also</u> discovered the most effective means of prevention. One person transmits the cold viruses to another most often by hand. <u>For instance,</u> an infected person covers his mouth to cough. He <u>then</u> picks up the telephone. <u>Half an hour later</u>, his daughter picks up the same telephone. <u>Immediately</u> afterward, she rubs her eyes. <u>Within a few days</u>, she, <u>too</u>, has a cold. <u>And thus</u> it spreads. To avoid colds, <u>therefore</u>, people should wash their hands often and keep their hands away from their faces.
>
> —KATHLEEN LaFRANK (student), "Colds: Myth and Science"

Note that you can use transitional expressions to link paragraphs as well as sentences. In the first sentence of LaFrank's paragraph, the word *thus* signals that the sentence refers to an effect discussed in the preceding paragraph.

The following box lists many transitional expressions by the functions they perform:

Transitional expressions

To add or show sequence

again, also, and, and then, besides, equally important, finally, first, further, furthermore, in addition, in the first place, last, moreover, next, second, still, too

To compare

also, in the same way, likewise, similarly

To contrast

although, and yet, but, but at the same time, despite, even so, even though, for all that, however, in contrast, in spite of, nevertheless, notwithstanding, on the contrary, on the other hand, regardless, still, though, yet

To give examples or intensify

after all, an illustration of, even, for example, for instance, indeed, in fact, it is true, of course, specifically, that is, to illustrate, truly

To indicate place

above, adjacent to, below, elsewhere, farther on, here, near, nearby, on the other side, opposite to, there, to the east, to the left

To indicate time

after a while, afterward, as long as, as soon as, at last, at length, at that time, before, earlier, formerly, immediately, in the meantime, in the past, lately, later, meanwhile, now, presently, shortly, simultaneously, since, so far, soon, subsequently, then, thereafter, until, until now, when

To repeat, summarize, or conclude

all in all, altogether, as has been said, in brief, in conclusion, in other words, in particular, in short, in simpler terms, in summary, on the whole, that is, therefore, to put it differently, to summarize

To show cause or effect

accordingly, as a result, because, consequently, for this purpose, hence, otherwise, since, then, therefore, thereupon, thus, to this end, with this object

Note Draw carefully on this list of transitional expressions because the ones in each group are not interchangeable. For instance, *besides*, *finally*, and *second* may all be used to add information, but each has its own distinct meaning.

ESL If transitional expressions are not common in your native language, you may be tempted to compensate when writing in English by adding them to the beginnings of most sentences. But such explicit transitions aren't needed everywhere, and in fact too many can be intrusive and awkward. When inserting transitional expressions, consider the reader's need for a signal: often the connection from sentence to sentence is already clear from the context or can be made clear by relating the content of sentences more closely (see pp. 38–43). When you do need transitional expressions, try varying their positions in your sentences, as illustrated in the sample paragraph on page 42.

6c Developing paragraphs

An effective, well-developed paragraph always provides the specific information that readers need and expect in order to understand you and to stay interested in what you say. Paragraph length can be a rough gauge of development: anything much shorter than 100 to 150 words may leave readers with a sense of incompleteness.

To develop or shape an idea in a paragraph, one or more of the following patterns may help. (These patterns may also be used to develop entire essays. See p. 12.)

1 Narration

Narration retells a significant sequence of events, usually in the order of their occurrence (that is, chronologically). A narrator is concerned not just with the sequence of events but also with their consequence, their importance to the whole.

> Jill's story is typical for "recruits" to religious cults. She was very lonely in college and appreciated the attention of the nice young men and women who lived in a house near campus. They persuaded her to share their meals and then to move in with them. Between intense bombardments of "love," they deprived her of sleep and sometimes threatened to throw her out. Jill became increasingly confused and dependent, losing touch with any reality besides the one in the group. She dropped out of school and refused to see or communicate with her family. Before long she, too, was preying on lonely college students.
>
> —HILLARY BEGAS (student), "The Love Bombers"

2 Description

Description details the sensory qualities of a person, scene, thing, or feeling, using concrete and specific words to convey a dominant mood, to illustrate an idea, or to achieve some other purpose.

> The sun struck straight upon the house, making the white walls glare between the dark windows. Their panes, woven thickly with green branches, held circles of impenetrable darkness. Sharp-edged wedges of light lay upon the window-sill and showed inside the room plates with blue rings, cups with curved handles, the bulge of a great bowl, the criss-cross pattern in the rug, and the formidable corners and lines of cabinets and bookcases. Behind their conglomeration hung a zone of shadow in which might be a further shape to be disencumbered of shadow or still denser depths of darkness.
>
> —VIRGINIA WOOLF, The Waves

3   Illustration or support

An idea may be developed with several specific examples, like those used by Allan Fotheringham on pages 37–38, or with a single extended example, as in the next paragraph:

> The language problem that I was attacking loomed larger and larger as I began to learn more. When I would describe in English certain concepts and objects enmeshed in Korean emotion and imagination, I became slowly aware of nuances, of differences between two languages even in simple expression. The remark "Kim entered the house" seems to be simple enough, yet, unless a reader has a clear visual image of a Korean house, his understanding of the sentence is not complete. When a Korean says he is "in the house," he may be in his courtyard, or on his porch, or in his small room! If I wanted to give a specific picture of entering the house in the Western sense, I had to say "room" instead of house—sometimes. I say "sometimes" because many Koreans entertain their guests on their porches and still are considered to be hospitable, and in the Korean sense, going into the "room" may be a more intimate act than it would be in the English sense. Such problems!
>
> —Kim Yong Ik, "A Book-Writing Venture"

Sometimes you can develop a paragraph by providing your reasons for stating a general idea. For instance:

> There are three reasons, quite apart from scientific considerations, that mankind needs to travel in space. The first reason is the need for garbage disposal: we need to transfer industrial processes into space, so that the earth may remain a green and pleasant place for our grandchildren to live in. The second reason is the need to escape material impoverishment: the resources of this planet are finite, and we shall not forgo forever the abundant solar energy and minerals and living space that are spread out all around us. The third reason is our spiritual need for an open frontier: the ultimate purpose of space travel is to bring to humanity not only scientific discoveries and an occasional spectacular show on television but a real expansion of our spirit.
>
> —Freeman Dyson, *Disturbing the Universe*

4   Definition

Defining a complicated, abstract, or controversial term often requires extended explanation. The following definition of the word *quality* comes from an essay asserting that "quality in product and effort has become a vanishing element of current civilization." Notice how the writer pins down her meaning by offering examples and by setting up contrasts with nonquality.

> In the hope of possibly reducing the hail of censure which is certain to greet this essay (I am thinking of going to Alaska or possibly Patagonia in the week it is published), let me say that quality,

as I understand it, means investment of the best skill and effort possible to produce the finest and most admirable result possible. Its presence or absence in some degree characterizes every man-made object, service, skilled or unskilled labor—laying bricks, painting a picture, ironing shirts, practicing medicine, shoemaking, scholarship, writing a book. You do it well or you do it half-well. Materials are sound and durable or they are sleazy; method is painstaking or whatever is easiest. Quality is achieving or reaching for the highest standard as against being satisfied with the sloppy or fraudulent. It is honesty of purpose as against catering to cheap or sensational sentiment. It does not allow compromise with the second-rate.

—BARBARA TUCHMAN, "The Decline of Quality"

5   Division or analysis

With division or analysis, you separate something into its elements to understand it better—for instance, you might divide a newspaper into its sections, such as national news, regional news, lifestyle, and so on. As in the paragraph below, you may also interpret the meaning and significance of the elements you identify.

The surface realism of the soap opera conjures up an illusion of "liveness." The domestic settings and easygoing rhythms encourage the viewer to believe that the drama, however ridiculous, is simply an extension of daily life. The conversation is so slow that some have called it "radio with pictures." (Advertisers have always assumed that busy housewives would listen, rather than watch.) Conversation is casual and colloquial, as though one were eavesdropping on neighbors. There is plenty of time to "read" the character's face; close-ups establish intimacy. The sets are comfortably familiar: well-lit interiors of living rooms, restaurants, offices, and hospitals. Daytime soaps have little of the glamour of their prime-time relations. The viewer easily imagines that the conversation is taking place in real time.

—RUTH ROSEN, "Search for Yesterday"

Analysis is a key skill in critical reading. See pages 81–82.

6   Classification

When you sort many items into groups, you classify the items to see their relations more clearly. The following paragraph identifies three groups, or classes, of parents:

In my experience, the parents who hire daytime sitters for their school-age children tend to fall into one of three groups. The first group includes parents who work and want someone to be at home when the children return from school. These parents are looking for an extension of themselves, someone who will give the care they would give if they were at home. The second group includes parents who may be home all day themselves but are too disorganized or too frazzled by their children's demands to handle child care alone. They are looking for an organizer and helpmate. The third and final group includes parents who do not want to be bothered by their children, whether they are home all day or not. Unlike the parents in the first two groups, who care for their children however they can, these parents seek a permanent substitute for themselves.

—NANCY WHITTLE (student), "Modern Parenting"

7 Comparison and contrast

Comparison and contrast may be used separately or together to develop an idea. The following paragraph illustrates one of two common ways of organizing a comparison and contrast: SUBJECT BY SUBJECT, first one subject and then the other.

Consider the differences also in the behaviour of rock and classical music audiences. At a rock concert, the audience members yell, whistle, sing along, and stamp their feet. They may even stand during the entire performance. The better the music, the more active they'll be. At a classical concert, in contrast, the better the performance, the more still the audience is. Members of the classical audience are so highly disciplined that they refrain from even clearing their throats or coughing. No matter what effect the powerful music has on their intellects and feelings, they sit on their hands.

—TONY NAHM (student), "Rock and Roll Is Here to Stay"

The next paragraph illustrates the other common organization: POINT BY POINT, with the two subjects discussed side by side and matched feature for feature:

The first electronic computer, ENIAC, went into operation just over fifty years ago, yet the differences between it and today's home computer are enormous. ENIAC was enormous itself, consisting of forty panels, each two feet wide and four feet deep. Today's PC or Macintosh, by contrast, can fit on one's desk or even lap. ENIAC had to be configured by hand, with its programmers taking up to two days to reset switches and cables. Today, the average home user can change programs in an instant. And for all its size and inconvenience, ENIAC was also slow. In its time, its operating speed of 100,000 pulses per second seemed amazingly fast. However, today's home machine can operate at 1 billion pulses per second or faster.

—SHIRLEY KAJIWARA (student), "The Computers We Deserve"

8 Cause-and-effect analysis

When you use analysis to explain why something happened or what did or may happen, then you are determining causes or effects. In the following paragraph the author looks at the cause of an effect—Japanese collectivism:

The shinkansen or "bullet train" speeds across the rural areas of Japan giving a quick view of cluster after cluster of farmhouses surrounded by rice paddies. This particular pattern did not develop purely by chance, but as a consequence of the technology peculiar to the growing of rice, the staple of the Japanese diet. The growing of rice requires the construction and maintenance of an irrigation system, something that takes many hands to build. More importantly, the planting and the harvesting of rice can only be done efficiently with the cooperation of twenty or more people. The "bottom line" is that a single family working alone cannot produce enough rice to survive, but a dozen families working together can produce a surplus. Thus the Japanese have had to develop the capacity to work together in harmony, no matter what the forces of disagreement or social disintegration, in order to survive.

—WILLIAM OUCHI, *Theory Z: How American Business Can Meet the Japanese Challenge*

9   Process analysis

When you analyze how to do something or how something works, you explain a process. The following example identifies the process, describes the equipment needed, and details the steps in the process:

As a car owner, you waste money when you pay a mechanic to change the engine oil. The job is not difficult, even if you know little about cars. All you need is a wrench to remove the drain plug, a large, flat pan to collect the draining oil, plastic bottles to dispose of the used oil, and fresh oil. First, warm up the car's engine so that the oil will flow more easily. When the engine is warm, shut it off and remove its oil-filler cap (the owner's manual shows where this cap is). Then locate the drain plug under the engine (again consulting the owner's manual for its location) and place the flat pan under the plug. Remove the plug with the wrench, letting the oil flow into the pan. When the oil stops flowing, replace the plug and, at the engine's filler hole, add the amount and kind of fresh oil specified by the owner's manual. Pour the used oil into the plastic bottles and take it to a waste-oil collector, which any garage mechanic can recommend.

—ANTHONY ANDREAS (student), "Do-It-Yourself Car Care"

6d   Writing introductory and concluding paragraphs

1   Introductions

An introduction draws readers from their world into your world.

- It focuses readers' attention on the topic and arouses their curiosity about what you have to say.

- It specifies your subject and implies your attitude.
- Often it includes your thesis statement. (See p. 14.)
- It is concise and sincere.

To focus readers' attention, you have a number of options:

Some strategies for introductions

- Ask a question.
- Relate an incident.
- Use a vivid quotation.
- Create a visual image that represents your subject.
- Offer a surprising statistic or other fact.
- State an opinion related to your thesis.
- Provide background.
- Outline the argument your thesis refutes.
- Make a historical comparison or contrast.
- Outline a problem or dilemma.
- Define a word central to your subject.
- In some business or technical writing, simply state your main idea.

ESL These options for an introduction may not be what you are used to if your native language is not English. In other cultures, readers may seek familiarity or reassurance from an author's introduction, or they may prefer an indirect approach to the subject. In English, however, writers and readers prefer originality and concise, direct expression.

Effective openings

A very common introduction opens with a statement of the essay's general subject, clarifies or limits the subject in one or more sentences, and then asserts the point of the essay in the thesis statement (underlined in the examples below):

> We Canadians love our doughnut shops. From coast to coast, in country and in city, you will find Canadians gathering in doughnut shops. We gather there not just to eat and drink but also to talk, to discuss, to see and be seen. <u>What the café is to French public life, what the pub is to the English neighbourhood, so the doughnut shop is to the Canadian strip mall.</u>
>
> —TERRY PELLETIER (student), "Doughnut Dominion"

> Can your home or office computer make you sterile? Can it strike you blind or dumb? The answer is: probably not. Nevertheless, reports of side effects relating to computer use should be examined, especially in the area of birth defects, eye complaints, and postural difficulties. <u>Although little conclusive evidence exists</u>

to establish a causal link between computer use and problems of this sort, the circumstantial evidence can be disturbing.

—THOMAS HARTMANN, "How Dangerous Is Your Computer?"

In much business writing, it's more important to tell readers immediately what your point is than to try to engage them. This introduction to a brief memo quickly outlines a problem and (in the thesis statement) suggests a way to solve it:

> Starting next month, the holiday rush and staff vacations will leave our department short-handed. We need to hire two or perhaps three temporary keyboarders to maintain our schedules for the month.

Additional examples of effective introductions appear in complete writing samples on pages 32, 100, 121, 363, 364, 415 and 441.

Openings to avoid

When writing and revising your introduction, avoid some approaches that are likely to bore readers or make them question your sincerity or control:

- Don't reach back too far with vague generalities or truths, such as those beginning "Throughout human history. . ." or "In today's world . . ." You may have needed a warm-up paragraph to start drafting, but your readers can do without it.
- Don't start with "The purpose of this essay is . . . ," "In this essay I will . . . ," or any similar flat announcement of your intention or topic.
- Don't refer to the title of the essay in the first sentence—for example, "This is my favourite activity" or "This is a big problem."
- Don't start with "According to Webster . . ." or a similar phrase leading to a dictionary definition. A definition can be an effective springboard to an essay, but this kind of lead-in has become dull with overuse.
- Don't apologize for your opinion or for inadequate knowledge with "I'm not sure if I'm right, but I think . . . ," "I don't know much about this, but . . . ," or similar lines.

2   Conclusions

Your conclusion finishes off your essay and tells readers where you think you have brought them. It answers the question "So what?"

Usually set off in its own paragraph, the conclusion may consist of a single sentence or a group of sentences. It may take one or more of the following approaches:

Some strategies for conclusions

- Strike a note of hope or despair.
- Give a symbolic or powerful fact or other detail.
- Give an especially compelling example.
- Create a visual image that represents your subject.
- Use a quotation.
- Recommend a course of action.
- Summarize the paper.
- Echo the approach of the introduction.
- Restate your thesis and reflect on its implications.

The following paragraph concludes the essay on doughnuts whose introduction is on page 49. The writer both summarizes his essay and echoes his introduction.

> Thus, the little circle of fried dough draws us together: police and citizen, senior and student, anglophone and francophone. By day and by night, through summer's heat and winter's snow, the doughnut shop is there for us, our second home, our national refuge.
>
> —TERRY PELLETIER (student), "Doughnut Dominion"

In the next paragraph the author concludes an essay on environmental protection with a call for action:

> Until we get the answers, I think we had better keep on building power plants and growing food with the help of fertilizers and such insect-controlling chemicals as we now have. The risks are well known, thanks to the environmentalists. If they had not created a widespread public awareness of the ecological crisis, we wouldn't stand a chance. But such awareness by itself is not enough. Flaming manifestos and prophecies of doom are no longer much help, and a search for scapegoats can only make matters worse. The time for sensations and manifestos is about over. Now we need rigorous analysis, united effort and very hard work.
>
> —PETER F. DRUCKER, "How Best to Protect the Environment"

Conclusions to avoid

Conclusions have several pitfalls you'll want to avoid:

- Don't simply restate your introduction—statement of subject, thesis statement, and all. Presumably the paragraphs in the body of your essay have contributed something to the opening statements, and it's that something you want to capture in your conclusion.
- Don't start off in a new direction, with a subject different from or broader than the one your essay has been about.

- Don't conclude more than you reasonably can from the evidence you have presented. If your essay is about your frustrating experience trying to clear a parking ticket, you cannot reasonably conclude that *all* local police forces are too tied up in red tape to be of service to the people.
- Don't apologize for your essay or otherwise cast doubt on it. Don't say, "Even though I'm no expert," or "This may not be convincing, but I believe it's true," or anything similar. Rather, to win your readers' confidence, display confidence.

7 Document Design

Imaginehowharditwouldbetoreadandwriteiftextlookedlikethis. To make reading and writing easier, we place spaces between words. This convention and many others—such as page margins, paragraph breaks, and headings—have evolved over time to help writers communicate clearly with readers.

This chapter looks at the principles and elements of design that can help you present any document effectively. Guidelines for specific kinds of documents appear elsewhere in this book:

- Designing pages for the World Wide Web, Chapter 12, page 104.
- Designing documents for business, Chapter 14, page 114.
- Formatting academic papers in MLA style, Chapter 58, page 380.
- Formatting academic papers in APA style, Chapter 59, page 423.

7a   Considering principles of design

Most of the principles of design respond to the ways we read. White space, for instance, relieves our eyes and helps to lead us through a document. Groupings or lists help to show relationships. Type sizes, images, and colour add variety and help to emphasize important elements.

As you begin to design your own documents, think about your purpose, the expectations of your readers, and how readers will move through your document. Also consider the general principles of design discussed below, noting how they overlap and support each other. The flyer on the following page illustrates some of these principles. An advertisement intended both to attract attention and to

Literacy Volunteers

ANNUAL

AWARDS

DINNER

Friday Night
February 25th
7:30-9:30
Suite 42
Springfield
VAC Hospital

✔ **Enjoy food and beverages provided by some of Springfield's finest restaurants.**

✔ **Celebrate the efforts and special accomplishments of our students.**

✔ **Congratulate our tutors for their wonderful service.**

For information, contact VAC Literacy Volunteers at (905) 555-9191

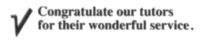

convey information, the flyer is at first glance visually appealing, but it also effectively organizes information and directs our attention.

Creating flow

Many of the other design principles work in concert with the larger goal of conducting the reader through a document by establishing flow, a pattern for the eye to follow. In some documents, such as reports, flow may be achieved mainly with headings, lists, and illustrations (see pp. 58–63). In other documents, such as the flyer on the previous page, flow will come from the arrangement and spacing of information as well as from headings.

Spacing

The white space on a page eases crowding and focuses readers' attention. On an otherwise full page, just the space indicating paragraphs (an indention or a line of extra space) gives readers a break and reassures them that ideas are divided into manageable chunks.

In papers, reports, and other formal documents, spacing appears mainly in paragraph breaks, in margins, and around headings and lists. In publicity documents, such as flyers and brochures, spacing is usually more generous between elements: helping boxes, headings, and the like pop off the page.

Grouping

Grouping information shows relationships visually, reinforcing the sense of the text itself. Here in this discussion, we group the various principles of design under visually identical headings to emphasize them and their similar importance. In the flyer on the previous page, a list set off with check marks itemizes the activities planned for the advertised event. The list covers *all* the activities and *only* the activities: details of date, time, and place, for instance, appear elsewhere on the page. Thinking of likely groups as you write can help you organize your material so that it makes sense to you and your readers.

Emphasizing

Part of a critical reader's task is to analyze and interpret the meaning of a document, and design helps the reader by stressing what's important. Type fonts and sizes, headings, indentions, colour, boxes, white space—all of these guide the reader's eye and establish hierarchies of information, so that the reader almost instinctively grasps what is crucial, what is less so, and what is merely supplementary. In the flyer on the previous page, for instance, colour and a box emphasize crucial information about the event being advertised. In this book, colour, size, and indention establish the relative importance of various headings: for instance, the coloured rule above heading 7b, opposite, indicates that it is a primary heading, more important than the numbered headings following it. As you design a document, considering where and how you want to emphasize elements can actually help you determine your document's priorities.

Standardizing

As we read a document, the design of its elements quickly creates expectations in us. We assume, for instance, that headings in the same size and colour signal information of the same importance or that a list contains items of parallel content. Just as the design creates expectations, so it should fulfill them, treating similar elements similarly. Anticipating design standards as you write a document can help you develop a consistent approach to its elements and then convey that approach to readers. Standardizing also creates clear, uncluttered documents.

Even if they are used consistently, too many variations in type fonts and sizes, colours, indentions, and the like overwhelm readers as they try to determine the significance of the parts. Many formal documents, such as papers and reports, need no more than a single type font for text and headings, with type size and highlighting (such as CAPITAL LETTERS, **boldface,** or *italics*) distinguishing the levels of headings. Publicity documents, such as flyers and brochures, generally employ more variation to arrest readers' attention. The flyer on page 53, for example, uses three type fonts: one for the organization's name, another for the event's title, and a third for everything else. Variations in the third font distinguish the box, the list, and the information along the bottom.

(7b)   Using the elements of design

Applying the preceding design principles involves seven main elements of document design: print quality, margins, and text (pp. 56–58); lists (p. 58); headings (pp. 58–59); tables, figures, and images (pp. 59–63); and colour (p. 63). You won't use all these elements for every project, however, and in many academic- and business-writing situations you will be required to follow a prescribed format.

Note Your word processor may provide wizards or templates for many kinds of documents, such as letters, memos, reports, agendas, résumés, and brochures. WIZARDS guide you through setting up and writing complicated documents. TEMPLATES are preset forms to which you add your own text, headings, and other elements. Wizards and templates can be helpful, but not if they lead you to create cookie-cutter documents no matter what the writing situation. Always keep in mind that a document should be appropriate for your subject, audience, and purpose.

1   Print quality

The cartridge on your printer should be fresh enough to produce a dark impression. A printer that forms characters out of tiny
dots may be acceptable for your academic papers, but make sure
the tails on letters such as *j*, *p*, and *y* fall below the line of type, as
they do here. For documents that are complex or that will be distributed to the public, use an inkjet or laser printer, which creates
characters more like the ones you see here. If you require colour,
varied type fonts, or illustrations and your printer is not up to the
job, you may be able to use more advanced equipment in your
school's computer lab.

2   Margins

Margins at the top, bottom, and sides of a page help to prevent
the page from overwhelming readers with unpleasant crowding.
Most academic and business documents use a minimum one-inch
margin on all sides. Publicity documents, such as the flyer on
page 53, often use narrower margins, compensating with white
space between elements.

3   Text

A document must be readable. You can make text readable by
attending to line spacing, type fonts and sizes, highlighting, word
spacing, and line breaks.

Line spacing

Most academic documents are double-spaced, with an initial
indention for paragraphs, and most business documents are single-
spaced, with an extra line of space between paragraphs. Double or
triple spacing sets off headings in both. Publicity documents, such
as flyers and brochures, tend to use more line spacing to separate
and group distinct parts of the content.

Type fonts and sizes

The readability of text also derives from the type fonts (or
faces) and their sizes. For academic and business documents,
choose a type size of 10 or 12 points, as in these samples:

```
10-point Courier      10-point Times New Roman
12-point Courier      12-point Times New Roman
```

For text, generally use a font with SERIFS—the small lines finishing
the letters in the samples above and in the font you're reading now.
SANS SERIF fonts (*sans* means "without" in French) include this one
found on many word processors:

10-point Arial   12-point Arial

Though fine for headings, sans serif type can be more difficult than serif type to read in extended text.

Your word processor probably offers many decorative fonts as well:

10-POINT COPPERPLATE

10-point Corvallis Sans

10-POINT STENCIL

10-point Lubalin Graph

10-point Comic

10-point Eras Demi

10-point Park Avenue

10-POINT TRAJAN

Such fonts often appear in publicity documents like the flyer on page 53, where they can attract attention, create motion, and reinforce a theme. (In publicity documents, too, font sizes are often much larger than 10 or 12 points, even for passages of text.) In academic and business writing, however, many decorative fonts are inappropriate: letter forms should be conventional and regular.

Note The point size of a type font is often an unreliable guide to its actual size, as the decorative fonts above illustrate: all the samples are 10 points, but they vary considerably. Before you use a font, print out a sample to be sure it is the size you want.

Highlighting

Within a document's text, underlined, *italic*, **boldface,** or even colour type can emphasize key words or sentences. Underlining is most common in academic writing situations, where instructors often prefer it to italics, especially for titles in source citations. (See p. 291.) Italics are more common in business writing and publicity documents. Both academic and business writing sometimes use boldface to give strong emphasis—for instance, to a term being defined—and publicity documents often rely extensively on boldface to draw the reader's eye. Neither academic nor business writing generally uses colour within passages of text. In publicity documents, however, colour may be effective if the colour is dark enough to be readable. (See p. 63 for more on colour in document design.)

No matter what your writing situation, use highlighting selectively to complement your meaning, not merely to decorate your work. Many readers consider type embellishments distracting.

Word spacing

In most writing situations, follow these guidelines for spacing within and between words:

- Leave one space between words.
- Leave one space after all punctuation, with these exceptions:

Dash (two hyphens or the so-called em-dash on a computer)	book--its	book—its
Hyphen	one-half	
Apostrophe within a word	book's	
Two or more adjacent marks	book.")	
Opening quotation mark, parenthesis, or bracket	("book	[book

- Generally, leave one space before and after an ellipsis mark, and use three spaced periods for the mark itself. (See pp. 277–79.)

book . . . in

Line breaks

Your word processor will generally insert appropriate breaks between lines of continuous text: it will not, for instance, automatically begin a line with a comma or period, and it will not end a line with an opening parenthesis or bracket. When you instruct it to do so (usually under the Tools menu), it will also automatically hyphenate words to prevent very short lines. However, you will have to prevent it from breaking a two-hyphen dash or a three-period ellipsis mark by spacing to push the beginning of each mark to the next line.

4   Lists

Lists give visual reinforcement to the relations between like items—for example, the steps in a process or the elements of a proposal. A list is easier to read than a paragraph and adds white space to the page.

When wording a list, work for parallelism among items—for instance, use all complete sentences or all phrases. (See also p. 134.) Set the list with space above and below and with numbering or bullets (centred dots or other devices, used in the list about headings on the next page).

5   Headings

Headings are signposts: they direct the reader's attention by focusing the eye on a document's most significant content. Most publicity documents, such as flyers and brochures, use headings both functionally, to direct readers' attention, and decoratively, to capture readers' attention. In contrast, most academic and business documents use headings only functionally, to divide text, orient readers, and create emphasis. Short academic and business documents, such as a three-page paper or a one-page letter, may not need headings at all. But for longer documents follow these guidelines:

- Use one, two, or three levels of headings depending on the needs of your material and the length of your document. Some level of heading every two or so pages will help keep readers on track.
- Create an outline of your document to plan where headings should go. Reserve the first level of heading for the main points (and sections) of your document. Use a second and perhaps a third level of heading to mark subsections of supporting information.
- Keep headings as short as possible while making them specific about the material that follows.
- Word headings consistently—for instance, all questions (*What Is the Scientific Method?*), all phrases with *-ing* words (*Understanding the Scientific Method*), or all phrases with nouns (*The Scientific Method*).
- Indicate the relative importance of headings with type size, positioning, and highlighting, such as capital letters, underlining, or boldface.

FIRST-LEVEL HEADING

Second-Level Heading

Third-Level Heading

First-Level Heading

Second-Level Heading

Third-Level Heading

- Generally, you can use the same type font and size for headings as for the text. For variety you may want to increase the heading size a bit and try a sans serif font like the one in the second example above. Avoid very decorative fonts like the Corvallis Sans or Stencil shown on page 57.
- Don't break a page immediately after a heading. Push the heading to the next page.

Note Document format in psychology and some other social sciences requires a particular treatment of headings. See pages 437–40.

6   Tables, figures, and images

Tables, figures, and images can often make a point for you more efficiently than words can. Tables present data. Figures (such as graphs and charts) usually recast data in visual form. Images (such as diagrams, drawings, photographs, and clip art) can explain processes, represent what something looks like, add emphasis, or convey a theme.

Academic and many business documents tend to use tables, figures, and images differently from publicity documents. In the latter, illustrations are generally intended to attract readers' attention, enliven the piece, or emphasize a point, and they may not be linked directly to the document's text. In academic and business writing, however, illustrations directly reinforce and amplify the text. Follow these guidelines when using tables, figures, or images in academic and most business writing:

- Focus on a purpose for your illustration—a reason for including it and a point you want it to make. Otherwise, readers may find it irrelevant or confusing.
- Provide a source note whenever the data or the entire illustration is someone else's independent material (see p. 335). Each discipline has a slightly different style for such source notes: those in the table and figures on pages 61–62 reflect the style of the social sciences. See also Chapters 59–62.
- Number figures and images together, and label them as figures: Figure 1, Figure 2, and so on. Number and label tables separately from figures: Table 1, Table 2, and so on.
- Refer to each illustration (for instance, "See Figure 2") at the point(s) in the text where readers will benefit by consulting it.
- Unless your document includes many illustrations, place each one on a page by itself immediately after the page that refers to it.

Note Many businesses and academic disciplines have preferred styles for illustrations that differ from those given here. When in doubt about how to prepare and place tables and figures, ask your instructor or supervisor.

Tables

Tables usually summarize raw data, displaying the data concisely and clearly.

- Above the table, provide a self-explanatory title. Readers should see what the table illustrates without having to refer to your text.
- Provide self-explanatory headings for horizontal rows and vertical columns. Use abbreviations only if you are certain readers will understand them.
- Lay out rows and columns for maximum clarity. In the sample below, lines divide the table into parts, headings align with their data, and numbers align vertically down columns.

Table 1

Canadian General Election, November 27, 2000

Party	Percentage of Votes	Actual Seats	Seats If under PR System
Liberal	40.8	172	123
Canadian Alliance	25.5	66	77
Progressive Conservative	12.2	12	37
Bloc Québécois	10.7	38	32
New Democratic	8.5	13	26
Green	0.8	0	2
Other	1.5	0	4

Source: Comparative Politics: An Institutional and Cross-National Approach, Canadian Edition (Table 7.10, p. 170), by Gregory S. Mahler and Donald J. MacInnis, 2002, Toronto: Prentice Hall.

Notes: Seats required for a majority government: 156. Turnout: 62.9 percent.

Figures

Figures represent data graphically. They include the three kinds presented on the next page: pie charts (showing percentages making up a whole), bar graphs (showing comparative data), and line graphs (showing change).

- Below the figure, provide a self-explanatory caption or legend. Readers should see what the figure represents without having to refer to the body of your document.
- Provide self-explanatory labels for all parts of the figure.
- Draw the figure to reflect its purpose and the visual effect you want it to have. For instance, shortening the horizontal date axis in Figure 3 on the next page emphasizes the dramatic upward movement of the line over time.
- When preparing a graph, generally make the width greater than the height. All graphs should have a zero point so that the values are clear.

Photographs, clip art, and other images

Images can either add substance to a document or simply enliven it. In a psychology paper, for instance, a photograph may illustrate a key experiment, while in a brochure a photograph may add the visual interest of, say, people working together. In academic and most business documents, images may include not only photographs but

des
7b

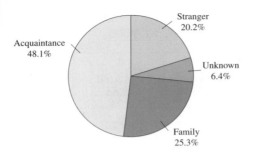

Figure 1. Violence against women, by relationship of accused to victim, 2002.
Source: Statistics Canada, Catalogue no. 85–205.

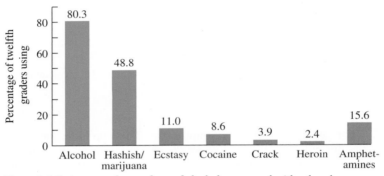

Figure 2. Lifetime prevalence of use of alcohol, compared with other drugs,
among twelfth graders in 2000.
Source: Data from Monitoring the Future, Institute for Social Research,
University of Michigan, published in Lloyd D. Johnston et al., Monitoring the
Future: National Survey Results on Drug Use, 1975–2000. Vol 1: Secondary
School Students. Bethesda, MD: National Institute on Drug Abuse, 2001.

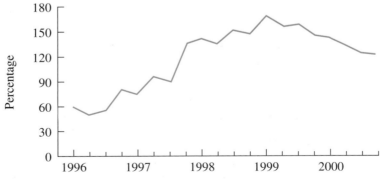

Figure 3. Five-year cumulative return for equities in Standard & Poor's 500
Index, 1996–2000.

also diagrams and drawings. They cannot represent your ideas by themselves: you need to consider carefully how they relate and add to your text, you need to explain their significance, and you need to label, number, and caption them (see p. 62).

One kind of image rarely appears in academic and business writing: CLIP ART, icons, and drawings such as the writing hand used in the flyer on page 53. Many word processors provide files of clip art, and they are also available from CD-ROMs and Web sites. But even in publicity documents you should be selective in using these resources: clip art is mostly decorative, and an overdecorated document is not only cluttered but unemphatic.

Note When using an image prepared by someone else—for instance, a photograph downloaded from the Web or an item of clip art from a CD-ROM—you must verify that the source permits reproduction of the image before you use it. In most documents but especially academic papers, you must also cite the source. See pages 344–45 on copyright issues with Internet sources.

7 Colour

With a colour printer, many word processors and most desktop publishers can produce documents that use colour for bullets, headings, borders, boxes, illustrations, and other elements. Publicity documents generally use colour, whereas academic and business documents consisting only of text and headings may not need colour. (Ask your instructor or supervisor for his or her preferences.) If you do use colour, follow these guidelines:

- Employ colour to clarify and highlight your content. Too much colour or too many colours on a page will distract rather than focus readers' attention.
- If you use colour for type, make sure the type is readable. For text, where type is likely to be relatively small, use only dark colours. For headings, lighter colours may be readable if the type is large and boldfaced.
- Stick to the same colour for all headings at the same level (for instance, red for main headings, black for secondary headings).
- For bullets, box backgrounds, lines, and other nontext elements, colour can be used more decoratively to enliven the page. Still, stick to no more than a few colours to keep pages clean.
- For illustrations, use colour to distinguish the segments of charts, the lines of graphs, and the parts of diagrams. Use only as many colours as you need to make your illustration clear.

2 Writing in and out of Post Secondary

2 Writing in and out of Post Secondary

8 Academic Writing

When you write in college or university, you work within a community of teachers and students who have specific aims and expectations. The basic aim of this community—whether in English, psychology, biology, or some other discipline—is to contribute to and build knowledge through questioning, research, and communication. The differences among disciplines lie mainly in the kinds of questions asked, the kinds of research done to find the answers, and the ways of communicating the answers.

Academic writers communicate using conventional forms, such as case studies, research reports, and reviews of others' writing on a particular subject. Both a discipline's concerns and the kind of writing create the writing situation, which in turn shapes a writer's choice of subject, conception of audience, definition of purpose, choice of structure and content, and even choice of language. This chapter introduces academic writing situations in general. See also pp. 351–74 on the specific goals and expectations of the humanities, the social sciences, and the natural and applied sciences.

8a Becoming an academic writer

As an academic writer, you participate in a discipline community first by studying a subject, acquiring its vocabulary, and learning to express yourself in its ways. As you gain experience and knowledge, you begin to contribute to the community by asking questions and communicating your answers. In any discipline, making the transition to academic writing will be easier if you practise the strategies outlined in the following box.

Tips for becoming an academic writer

- **Study the syllabus for each course.** This outline lays out the instructor's expectations as well as the course topics, assignments, and deadlines.
- **Do the assigned reading.** You'll gain experience with the discipline's terms and ideas, and you'll become familiar with the kinds of writing expected of you.

- **Attend and participate in class.** Make class attendance a priority, whether or not the instructor checks the roll. Listen carefully, take notes (see p. 72 for tips), ask questions, and join in discussions.
- **Ask questions.** Instructors, advisers, tutors, other students—all can help you.
- **Understand the writing situation posed by each assignment.** Knowing your audience, purpose, options for subjects, and other elements of the situation will help you meet the assignment's expectations. (See p. 3 on analyzing assignments.)

8b   Analyzing audience

Some of your writing assignments may specify an identifiable group of readers—for instance, fellow students, the city council, or the editors of a newspaper. Such readers' needs and expectations vary widely; the discussion on page 5 can help you discover what they might be. Many assignments will specify or assume an educated audience or an academic audience. This more general group of readers looks for writing that is clear, balanced, well organized, and well reasoned, among other qualities discussed on the next page. Still other assignments will specify or assume an audience of experts on your subject, readers who look in addition for writing that meets the subject's requirements for claims and evidence, organization, language, format, and other qualities.

Of course, much of your academic writing will have only one reader besides you: the instructor of the course for which you are writing. Instructors fill two main roles as readers:

- **They represent the audience you are addressing.** They may actually be members of the audience, as when you address academic readers or subject experts. Or they may imagine themselves as members of your audience—reading, for instance, as if they sat on the city council. In either case, they're interested in how effectively you write for the audience.
- **They serve as coaches,** guiding you toward achieving the goals of the course and, more broadly, toward the academic aims of building and communicating knowledge.

Like everyone else, instructors have preferences and peeves, but you'll waste time and energy trying to anticipate them. Do attend to written and spoken directions for assignments, of course. But otherwise view your instructors as representatives of the community you are writing for. Their responses will be guided by the community's aims and expectations and by a desire to teach you about them.

8c) Determining purpose

For most academic writing, your general purpose will be mainly explanatory or mainly argumentative. That is, you will aim to clarify your subject so that readers understand it as you do, or you will aim to gain readers' agreement with a debatable idea about the subject. (See p. 6 for more on general purposes and pp. 88–103 for more on argument.)

Your specific purpose—including your subject and how you hope readers will respond—depends on the kind of writing you're doing. In a biology lab report, for instance, you want your readers to understand why you conducted your study, how you conducted it, what the results were, and what their significance is. Not coincidentally, these topics correspond to the major sections of a biology lab report. In following the standard format, you both help to define your purpose and begin to meet the discipline's (and thus your instructor's) expectations.

Your specific purpose will be more complex as well. You take a course to learn about a subject and the ways experts think about it. Your writing, in return, contributes to the discipline through the knowledge you uncover and the lens of your perspective. At the same time, as a student you want to demonstrate your competence with research, evidence, format, and other requirements of the discipline.

8d

8d) Choosing structure and content

Many academic writing assignments will at least imply how you should organize your paper and even how you should develop your ideas. Like the biology lab report mentioned above, the type of paper required will break into discrete parts, each with its own requirements for content.

No matter what type of paper an assignment specifies, the broad academic aims of building and exchanging knowledge determine features that are common across disciplines. Follow these general guidelines for your academic writing, supplementing them as indicated with others elsewhere in this book:

- **Develop a central idea or claim, called a** *thesis.* Everything in the paper should relate clearly to this claim. For more on theses, see pages 14–16.
- **State the thesis,** usually near the beginning of the paper.
- **Support the thesis with evidence,** drawn usually from research and sometimes from your own experience. The kinds of evidence

will depend on the discipline you're writing in and the type of paper you're doing. For more on evidence in the disciplines, see pages 357–58 (literature), 366–67 (other humanities), 369–71 (social sciences), and 374 (natural and applied sciences).

- **Interact with sources.** Do not merely summarize sources but evaluate and synthesize them from your own perspective. For more on using sources, see pages 322–31.
- **Acknowledge sources fully,** using the documentation style appropriate to the discipline. For lists of disciplines' style guides, see pages 369, 373, and 377–78. For documentation guidelines and samples, see pages 380–94 (English and some other humanities), pages 423–40 (social sciences), pages 448–56 (history, philosophy, and other humanities), and pages 456–63 (natural and applied sciences) and pages 463–66 (engineering).
- **Balance your presentation.** Discuss evidence and opposing views fairly, and take a serious and impartial approach.
- **Organize clearly within the framework of the type of writing you're doing.** Develop your ideas as simply and directly as your purpose and content allow. Clearly relate sentences, paragraphs, and sections so that readers always know where they are in the paper's development.

ESL These features are far from universal. In other cultures, for instance, academic writers may be indirect or may not have to acknowledge well-known sources. Recognizing such differences between practices in your native culture and in Canada can help you adapt to Canadian academic writing.

8e Using academic language

Canadian academic writing relies on a dialect called standard English. The dialect is also used in business, the professions, government, the media, and other sites of social and economic power where people of diverse backgrounds must communicate with one another. It is "standard" not because it is better than other forms of English, but because it is accepted as the common language, much as the dollar coin is accepted as the common currency.

Standard English varies a lot, from the formal English of a parliamentary Throne Speech through the middle formality of this handbook to the informal chitchat between anchors on morning TV. Even in academic writing, standard English allows much room for the writer's own tone and voice, as these passages on the same topic show:

More formal

Using the technique of "colour engineering," manufacturers and advertisers can heighten the interest of consumers in a product by adding colour that does not contribute to the utility of the product but appeals more to emotions. In one example from the 1920s, manufacturers of fountain pens, which had previously been made of hard black rubber, dramatically increased sales simply by producing the pens in bright colours.

Two complicated sentences, one explaining the technique and one giving the example

Drawn-out phrasing, such as interest of consumers instead of consumers' interest

Formal vocabulary, such as heighten, contribute, and utility

8e

Less formal

A touch of "colour engineering" can sharpen the emotional appeal of a product or its ad. New colour can boost sales even when the colour serves no use. In the 1920s, for example, fountain-pen makers introduced brightly coloured pens along with the familiar ones of hard black rubber. Sales shot up.

Four sentences, two each for explaining the technique and giving the example

More informal phrasing, such as Sales shot up

More informal vocabulary, such as touch, boost, and ad

As different as they are, both examples illustrate several common features of academic language:

- **It follows the conventions of standard English for grammar and usage.** These conventions are described in guides to the dialect, such as this handbook.
- **It uses a standard vocabulary, not one that only some groups understand,** such as slang, an ethnic or regional dialect, or another language. (See pp. 139–41 for more on specialized vocabularies.)
- **It creates some distance between writer and reader with the third person** (*he, she, it, they*). The first person (*I, we*) is sometimes appropriate to express personal opinions or invite readers to think along, but not with a strongly explanatory purpose (*I discovered that "colour engineering" can heighten* . . .). The second person (*you*) is appropriate only in addressing readers directly (as in this handbook), and even then it may seem condescending or too chummy (*You should know that "colour engineering" can heighten* . . .).
- **It is authoritative and neutral.** In the preceding examples, the writers express themselves confidently, not timidly (as in *One possible example of colour engineering that might be considered in this case is* . . .). They also refrain from hostility (*Advertisers will stop at nothing to achieve their goals*) and enthusiasm (*Colour engineering is genius at work*).

At first, the diverse demands of academic writing may leave you groping for an appropriate voice. In an effort to sound fresh and confident, you may write too casually:

Too casual

"Colour engineering" is a great way to get at consumers' feelings. . . . When the guys jazzed up the colour, sales shot through the roof.

In an effort to sound "academic," you may produce wordy and awkward sentences:

Wordy and awkward

The emotions of consumers can be made more engaged by the technique known as "colour engineering." . . . A very large increase in the sales of fountain pens was achieved by the manufacturers of the pens as a result of this colour enhancement technique. [The passive voice in this example, such as *increase . . . was achieved* instead of *the manufacturers achieved,* adds to its wordiness and indirection. See pp. 198–200 for more on voice.]

A cure for writing too informally or too stiffly is to read academic writing so that the language and style become familiar and to edit your writing (see pp. 28–30).

ESL If your first language is not English or is an English dialect, you know well the power of communicating with others who share your language. Learning to write standard English in no way requires you to abandon your first language. Like most multilingual people, you are probably already adept at switching between languages as the situation demands—speaking one way with your relatives, say, and another way with an employer. As you practise academic writing, you'll develop the same flexibility with it.

9 Study Skills

Academic success depends on active, involved learning. If you haven't already, read the previous chapter on academic writing. Apply the principles there with this chapter's practical tips for managing your time, getting the most from your classes and your reading, and preparing for exams.

(9a) Managing your time

Planning and pacing your schoolwork and other activities will help you study more efficiently with less stress.

1 Scheduling your time

One way to organize your time is to use a calendar that divides each day into waking hours. Block out your activities that occur regularly and at specific times, such as commuting, attending classes, and working. Then fill in the other activities (such as exercise, eating, and studying) that do not necessarily occur at fixed times. Be sure to leave time for relaxing: an unrealistic schedule that assigns all available time to studying will quickly prove too difficult to live by.

9a

2 Organizing your workload

Use the syllabuses for your courses to estimate the amount of weekly study time required for each course. Generally, plan on two hours of studying for each hour in class—that is, about six hours for a typical course. Block out study periods using these guidelines:

- **Schedule study time close to class time.** You'll study more productively if you review notes, read assigned material, or work on projects shortly after each class period.
- **Pace assignments.** Plan to start early and work regularly on projects requiring extensive time, such as research papers, so that you will not be overwhelmed near the deadline. (See p. 299 for advice on scheduling research projects.)
- **Adjust the weekly plan as needed to accommodate changes in your workload.** Before each week begins, examine its schedule to be sure you've built in enough time to study for an exam, finish a paper, or meet other deadlines and commitments.

3 Making the most of study time

When you sit down to study, use your time efficiently:

- **Set realistic study goals.** Divide your study sessions into small chunks, each with a short-term goal, such as previewing a textbook chapter or drafting three paragraphs of a paper. Plan breaks, too, so that you can clear your mind, stretch, and re-focus on your goals.
- **Tackle difficult homework first.** Resist any urge to put off demanding jobs, such as working on papers, reading textbooks, or doing math problems. Save easy tasks for when you're less alert.
- **Evaluate how you use your study time.** At the end of each week, ask yourself whether you were as productive as you needed to be. If not, what changes can you make to accomplish your goals for the coming week?

9b) Listening and taking notes in class

When you begin each class, push aside other concerns so that you can focus and listen. Either on paper or on a computer, record what you hear as completely as possible while sorting out the main ideas from the secondary and supporting ones. (See the box below.) Such active note taking will help you understand the instructor's approach to the course and provide you with complete material for later study.

9c

Tips for taking class notes

- **Use your own words.** You will understand and retain the material better if you rephrase it. But use the speaker's words if necessary to catch everything.
- **Leave space in your notes if you miss something.** Ask someone for the missing information as soon as possible after the class.
- **Include any reading content mentioned by your instructor.** Use the notes to integrate all the components of the course—your instructor's views, your own thoughts, and the assigned reading, even if you've already read it.
- **Review your notes shortly after class.** Reinforce your new knowledge when it is fresh by underlining key words and ideas, adding headings and comments in the margins, converting your notes to questions, or outlining the lecture based on your notes.

9c) Reading for comprehension

The assigned reading you do for college or university courses—such as textbooks, journal articles, and works of literature—requires a greater focus on understanding and retention than does the reading you do for entertainment or for practical information. The process outlined below may seem time consuming, but with practice you'll become efficient at it.

Note The following process stresses ways of understanding what you read. In critical reading, covered in the next chapter, you extend this process to analyze and evaluate what you read and see.

1 Writing while reading

Reading for comprehension is an *active* process. Students often believe they are reading actively when they roll a highlighter over the important ideas in a text, but truly engaged reading requires more than that. If you take notes while reading, you "translate" the work into your own words and reconstruct it for yourself.

The substance of your reading notes will change as you preview, read, and summarize. At first, you may jot quick, short notes in the margins, on separate pages, or on a computer. (Use the last two for material you don't own or are reading online.) As you delve into the work, the notes should become more detailed, restating important points, asking questions, connecting ideas. (See pp. 79–80 for an example of a text annotated in this way by a student.) For some reading, you may want to keep a reading journal that records both what the work says and what you think about it.

2   Previewing

For most course reading, you should **skim** before reading word for word. Skimming gives you an overview of the material: its length and difficulty, organization, and principal ideas.

- **Gauge length and level.** Is the material brief and straightforward enough to read in one sitting, or do you need more time?
- **Examine the title and introduction.** The title and first couple of paragraphs will give you a sense of the topic, the author's approach, and the main ideas. As you read them, ask yourself what you already know about the subject so that you can integrate new information with old.
- **Move from heading to heading.** Viewing the headings as headlines or as the levels of an outline will give you a feeling for which ideas the author sees as primary and which subordinate.
- **Note highlighted words.** You will likely need to learn the meanings of terms in **bold**, *italic*, or colour.
- **Slow down for pictures, diagrams, tables, graphs, and other illustrations.** They often contain concentrated information.
- **Read the summary or conclusion.** These paragraphs often recap the main ideas.
- **Think over what you've skimmed.** Try to recall the central idea, or thesis, and the sequence of ideas.

3   Reading

After previewing a text, you can settle into it to learn what it has to say.

First reading

The first time through new material, read as steadily and smoothly as possible, trying to get the gist of what the author is saying.

- **Read in a place where you can concentrate.** Choose a quiet environment away from distractions such as music or talking.

9c

- **Give yourself time.** Rushing yourself or worrying about something else you have to do will prevent you from grasping what you read.
- **Try to enjoy the work.** Seek connections between it and what you already know. Appreciate new information, interesting relationships, forceful writing, humour, good examples.
- **Make notes sparingly during this first reading.** Mark major stumbling blocks—such as a paragraph you don't understand—so that you can try to resolve them before rereading.

ESL If English is not your first language and you come across unfamiliar words, don't stop and look up every one. You will lose more in concentration than you will gain in understanding. Instead, try to guess the meanings of unfamiliar words from their contexts, circle them, and look them up later.

Rereading

After the first reading, plan on at least one other. This time read *slowly*. Your main concern should be to grasp the content and how it is constructed. That means rereading a paragraph if you didn't get the point or using a dictionary to look up words you don't know.

Use your pen, pencil, or keyboard freely to highlight and distill the text:

- **Distinguish main ideas from supporting ideas.** Look for the central idea, or thesis, for the main idea of each paragraph or section, and for the evidence supporting ideas.
- **Learn key terms.** Understand both their meanings and their applications.
- **Discern the connections among ideas.** Be sure you see why the author moves from point A to point B to point C and how those points relate to support the central idea. It often helps to outline the text or summarize it (see below).
- **Add your own comments.** In the margins or separately, note links to other readings or to class discussions, questions to explore further, possible topics for your writing, points you find especially strong or weak. (This last category will occupy much of your time when you are expected to read critically. See pp. 78–83.)

4   Summarizing

A good way to master the content of a text is to **summarize** it: reduce it to its main points, in your own words.

Summarizing even a passage of text can be tricky. On the opposite page is material from an introductory biology textbook followed by one attempt to summarize the material

9c

Writing a summary

- **Understand the meaning.** Look up words or concepts you don't know so that you understand the author's sentences and how they relate to one another.
- **Understand the organization.** Work through the text to identify its sections—single paragraphs or groups of paragraphs focused on a single topic. To understand how parts of a work relate to one another, try drawing a tree diagram or creating an outline (pp. 18–19).
- **Distill each section.** Write a one- or two-sentence summary of each section you identify. Focus on the main point of the section, omitting examples, facts, and other supporting evidence.
- **State the main idea.** Write a sentence or two capturing the author's central idea.
- **Support the main idea.** Write a full paragraph (or more, if needed) that begins with the central idea and supports it with the sentences that summarize sections of the work. The paragraph should concisely and accurately state the thrust of the entire work.
- *Use your own words.* By writing, you re-create the meaning of the work in a way that makes sense for you.

9c

Original text

As astronomers study newly discovered planets orbiting distant stars, they hope to find evidence of water on these far-off celestial bodies, for water is the substance that makes possible life as we know it here on Earth. All organisms familiar to us are made mostly of water and live in an environment dominated by water. They require water more than any other substance. Human beings, for example, can survive for quite a few weeks without food, but only a week or so without water. Molecules of water participate in many chemical reactions necessary to sustain life. Most cells are surrounded by water, and cells themselves are about 70–95% water. Three-quarters of Earth's surface is submerged in water. Although most of this water is in liquid form, water is also present on Earth as ice and vapor. Water is the only common substance to exist in the natural environment in all three physical states of matter: solid, liquid, and gas.

—Neil A. Campbell and Jane B. Reece, *Biology*

Draft summary

Astronomers look for water in outer space because life depends on it. It is the most common substance on Earth and in living cells, and it can be a liquid, a solid (ice), or a gas (vapour).

This summary accurately restates ideas in the original, but it does not pare the passage to its essence. The work of astronomers and the three physical states of water add colour and texture to the original, but they are asides to the key concept that water sustains life because of its role in life. The following revision narrows the summary to this concept:

Revised summary

Water is the most essential support for life, the dominant substance on Earth and in living cells and a component of life-sustaining chemical processes.

Note Do not count on the AutoSummarize function on your word processor for summarizing texts that you may have copied onto your computer. The summaries are rarely accurate, and you will not gain the experience of interacting with the texts on your own.

(9d) Preparing for exams

Studying for an exam involves three main steps, each requiring about a third of the preparation time: reviewing the material, organizing summaries of the material, and testing yourself. Your main goals are to strengthen your understanding of the subject, making both its ideas and its details more memorable, and to increase the flexibility of your new knowledge so that you can apply it in new contexts.

Note Cramming for an exam is about the least effective way of preparing for one. It takes longer to learn under stress, and the learning is shallower, more difficult to apply, and more quickly forgotten. Information learned under stress is even harder to apply in stressful situations, such as taking an exam. And the lack of sleep that usually accompanies cramming makes a good performance even more unlikely. If you must cram for a test, face the fact that you can't learn everything. Spend your time reviewing main concepts and facts.

1   Reviewing and memorizing the material

Divide your class notes and reading assignments into manageable units. Reread the material, recite or write out the main ideas and selected supporting ideas and examples, and then skim for an overview. Proceed in this way through all the units of the course, returning to earlier ones as needed to refresh your memory or to relate ideas.

During this stage you should be memorizing what you don't already know by heart. Try these strategies for strengthening your memory:

- **Link new and known information.** For instance, to remember a sequence of four dates in twentieth-century African history, link the dates to simultaneous and more familiar events in the United States.

- **Create groups of ideas or facts that make sense to you.** For instance, memorize French vocabulary words in related groups, such as words for parts of the body or parts of a house. Keep the groups small: research has shown that we can easily memorize about seven items at a time but have trouble with more.
- **Create narratives and visual images.** You may recall a story or a picture more easily than words. For instance, to remember how the economic laws of supply and demand affect the market for rental housing, you could tie the principles to a narrative about the aftermath of the 1917 Halifax harbour explosion, when half the population was suddenly homeless. Or you could visualize a person who has dollar signs for eyes and is converting a spare room into a high-priced rental unit, as many did after the earthquake to meet the new demand for housing.
- **Use *mnemonic devices*, or tricks for remembering.** Say the history dates you want to remember are separated by five years, then four, then nine. By memorizing the first date and recalling 5 + 4 = 9, you'll have command of all four dates.

2   Organizing summaries of the material

Allow time to reorganize the material in your own way, creating categories that will help you apply the information in various contexts. For instance, in studying for a biology exam, work to understand a process, such as how a plant develops or how photosynthesis occurs. Or in studying for an American government test, explain the structures of the local, state, and federal levels of government. Other useful categories include advantages/disadvantages and causes/effects. Such analytical thinking will improve your mastery of the course material and may even prepare you directly for specific essay questions.

3   Testing yourself

Convert each heading in your lecture notes and course reading into a question. Answer in writing, going back to the course material to fill in what you don't yet know. Be sure you can define and explain all key terms. For subjects that require solving problems (such as mathematics, statistics, or physics), work out a difficult problem for every type on which you will be tested. For all subjects, focus on the main themes and questions of the course. In a psychology course, for example, be certain you understand principal theories and their implications. In a literature course, test your knowledge of literary movements and genres or the relations among specific works.

When you are satisfied with your preparation, stop studying and get a good night's sleep.

9d

10 Critical Thinking and Reading

Throughout college or university and beyond, you will be expected to think, read, and write critically. *Critical* here does not mean "negative" but "skeptical," "exacting," "creative." You already operate critically every day as you figure out why things happen to you or what your experiences mean. This chapter introduces more formal methods for thinking and reading critically (below) and the following chapter discusses a particular kind of critical writing: argument (p. 88).

10a Thinking and reading critically

In college, university, and work, much of your critical thinking will focus on written texts (a short story, a journal article, an Internet posting, a site on the World Wide Web) or on visual objects (a photograph, a chart, a film). Like all subjects worthy of critical consideration, such works operate on at least three levels: (1) what the creator actually says or shows, (2) what the creator does not say or show but builds into the work (intentionally or not), and (3) what you think. Discovering each level of the work, even if it is visual, involves four main steps: previewing the material, reading actively, summarizing, and forming a critical response.

ESL The idea of reading critically may require you to make some adjustments if readers in your native culture tend to seek understanding or agreement more than engagement from what they read. Readers of English use texts for all kinds of reasons, including pleasure, reinforcement, and information. But they also read skeptically, critically, to see the author's motives, test their own ideas, and arrive at new knowledge.

1 Previewing the material

When you're reading a work of literature, such as a short story or a poem, it's often best just to plunge right in (see p. 354). But for critical reading of other works, it's worthwhile to form some expectations and even some preliminary questions before you start reading word for word. Your reading will be more informed and fruitful.

Use the following questions as a previewing guide:

- *Length:* Is the material brief enough to read in one sitting, or do you need more time? To gauge the length of an online source such as a Web site, study any menus for an indication of the source's complexity. Then scroll through a couple of pages and follow a couple of links to estimate the overall length.

- *Facts of publication:* Does the date of publication suggest currency or datedness? Does the publisher or publication specialize in a particular kind of material—scholarly articles, say, or popular books? For a Web source, who or what sponsors the site: An individual? A nonprofit organization? An academic institution? A corporation? A government body? (See p. 325 on reading electronic addresses.)
- *Content cues:* What do the title, summary or abstract, headings, illustrations, and other features tell you? What questions do they raise in your mind?
- *Author:* What does the biographical information tell you about the author's publications, interests, biases, and reputation in the field? For an online message, which may be posted by an unfamiliar or anonymous author, what can you gather about the author from his or her words? If possible, trace unfamiliar authors to learn more about them. (See pp. 324–25.)
- *Yourself:* Do you anticipate particular difficulties with the content? What biases of your own may influence your response to the text—for instance, anxiety, curiosity, boredom, or an outlook similar or opposed to that of the author?

10a

2   Reading actively

Reading is itself more than a one-step process. Your primary goal is to understand the first level on which the text operates— what the author actually says.

The first time through new material, read as steadily and smoothly as possible, trying to get the gist of what the author is saying and a sense of his or her tone. Then reread the material *slowly* to grasp its content and how it is constructed. That means stopping to puzzle out a paragraph if you didn't get the point, looking up words in a dictionary, or following links at a Web site.

Use your pen, pencil, or keyboard freely to annotate the text or to make separate notes. In the following example, a student annotates the introductory paragraphs of "Student Loans," an essay by the economist and columnist Thomas Sowell:

> The first lesson of economics is scarcity: There is never enough of anything to fully satisfy all those who want it.
>
> The first lesson of politics is to disregard the first lesson of economics. When politicians discover some group that is being vocal about not having as much as they want, the "solution" is to give them more. Where do politicians get this "more"? They rob Peter to pay Paul.

Basic contradiction between economics and politics

← *biblical reference?*

After a while, <u>of course</u>, they discover that
Peter doesn't have <u>enough</u>. <u>Bursting with com-
passion</u>, politicians rush to <u>the rescue</u>. <u>Needless
to say</u>, they do not admit that robbing Peter to
pay Paul was a <u>dumb idea</u> in the first place. On
the contrary, they now rob Tom, Dick, and Harry
to help Peter.

*ironic and
dismissive
language*

The latest chapter in this <u>long-running saga</u>
is that politicians have now <u>suddenly discovered</u>
that many college students graduate heavily in
debt. To politicians it follows, as the night follows the day, that the government should come
to their rescue with the taxpayers' money.

*politicians =
fools? or
irresponsible?*

10a

(After this introduction, Sowell discusses several reasons why government student-loan programs should not be expanded: they benefit many who don't need financial help, they make college possible
for many who aren't serious about education, and they contribute
to rising tuitions.)

3 Summarizing

A good way to master the content of a text and see its strengths
and weaknesses is to summarize it: distill it to its main points, in
your own words. Here is one procedure for summarizing:

- Look up words or concepts you don't know so that you understand the author's sentences and how they relate to each other.
- Work through the text to identify its sections—single paragraphs or groups of paragraphs focused on a single topic,
  related pages or links in a Web site. To understand how parts of
  a work relate to each other, try drawing a tree diagram or creating an outline (pp. 18–19). Although both tools work well for
  straight text, the tree diagram may work better for nonlinear
  material such as a Web site.
- Write a one- or two-sentence summary of each section you
  identify. Focus on the main point of the section, omitting examples, facts, and other supporting evidence.

The following sentence summarizes the first four paragraphs of
Thomas Sowell's "Student Loans," on the previous page and continued at the top of this page:

As their support of the government's student loan program illustrates, politicians ignore the economic reality that using resources
to benefit one group (students in debt) involves taking the
resources from another group (taxpayers).

Note When you write a summary, using your own words will
ensure that you avoid plagiarism. Even when the summary is in
your own words, if you use it in something written for others you
must cite the source of the ideas. See Chapter 51.

4   Forming a critical response

Once you've grasped the content of what you're reading—what the author says—then you can turn to understanding what the author does not say outright but suggests or implies or even lets slip. At this stage you are concerned with the purpose or intention of the author and with how he or she carries it out.

Critical thinking and reading consist of four overlapping operations: analyzing, interpreting, synthesizing, and (often) evaluating.

Analyzing

ANALYSIS is the separation of something into its parts or elements, the better to understand it. To see these elements in what you are reading, begin with a question that reflects your purpose in analyzing the text: why you are curious about it or what you're trying to make out of it. This question will serve as a kind of lens that highlights some features and not others.

For an example, look at the screen shot below, showing the home page of a Web site that offers relief from student-loan debt. Analyzing this page, you might ask what kind of organization

10a

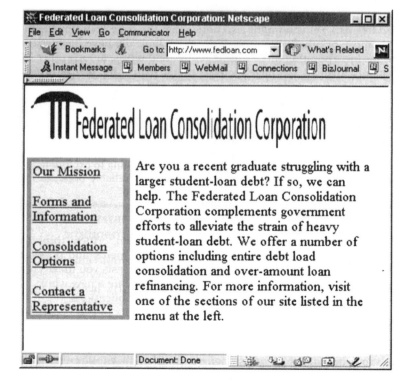

the Federated Loan Consolidation Corporation is or what its intentions are. Answering either question, you would examine the address of the site (in the field at the top of the page), the organization's name, the paragraph of text, and the design of the page—its use of type, colour, and decorative elements.

Interpreting

Identifying the elements of something is of course only the beginning: you also need to interpret the meaning or significance of the elements and of the whole. Interpretation usually requires you to infer the author's ASSUMPTIONS—that is, opinions or beliefs about what is or what could or should be. (*Infer* means to draw a conclusion based on evidence.)

Assumptions are pervasive: we all adhere to certain values, beliefs, and opinions. But assumptions are not always stated outright. Speakers and writers may judge that their audience already understands and accepts their assumptions; they may not even be aware of their assumptions; or they may deliberately refrain from stating their assumptions for fear that the audience will disagree. That is why your job as a critical thinker is to interpret what the assumptions are.

To discover assumptions of the Federated Loan Consolidation Corporation (previous page), you would look at the address of the Web site, where *com* indicates that the organization is a commercial entity. (See p. 325 for more on interpreting electronic addresses.) Yet you might also notice that the page does not resemble those of other corporate sites, which typically have flashier designs incorporating more images, colour, and boxes, among other elements. Instead, the page's look is rather plain— the sort of design you might expect from a government site. The prominent *Federated* in the organization's name and *complements government efforts* in the text reinforce the appearance of a government connection. These findings might lead you to infer the following:

> The Federated Loan Consolidation Corporation assumes that its readers (potential customers) will be more willing to explore its refinancing options if they believe that it is a reliable organization somehow affiliated with the government.

Synthesizing

If you stopped at analysis and interpretation, critical thinking and reading might leave you with a pile of elements and possible meanings but no vision of the whole. With SYNTHESIS you make connections among parts *or* among wholes. You create a new whole by drawing conclusions about relationships and implications.

The following conclusion draws on elements of the Federated Loan Consolidation Corporation home page and the inference above about the company's understanding of its readers:

> The Federated Loan Consolidation Corporation uses its name, a mention of the government, and a restrained design to appeal to potential customers who may be wary of commercial lending operations.

With synthesis, you create something different from what you started with. To the uncritical reader (perhaps someone burdened with student loans), the home page of the Federated Loan Consolidation Corporation might seem to offer government-backed relief from debt. To you—after analysis, interpretation, and synthesis—the official-looking page is a kind of mask worn by a commercial lender. The difference depends entirely on the critical reading.

Evaluating

Much critical reading and writing ends at synthesis: you form and explain your understanding of what the work says and doesn't say. If you are also expected to EVALUATE the work, however, you will go further to judge its quality and significance. You may be evaluating a source you've discovered in research (see pp. 323–29), or you may be completing an assignment to state and defend a judgment, a statement such as *The author does not summon the evidence to support her case* or *On the home page of the Federated Loan Consolidation Corporation, a commercial lender attempts to mislead vulnerable customers by wearing the reassuring costume of government*.

Evaluation takes a certain amount of confidence. You may think that you lack the expertise to cast judgment on another's work, especially if the work is difficult or the author well known. True, the more informed you are, the better a critical reader you are. But conscientious reading and analysis will give you the internal authority to judge a work *as it stands* and *as it seems to you*, against your own unique bundle of experiences, observations, and attitudes.

(10b) Viewing images critically

Every day we are bombarded with images—posters on walls or windows, pictures on billboards, commercials on television, to name just a few examples. Most images slide by without our noticing them, or so we think. But images, sometimes even more than text, can influence us covertly. Their creators have purposes, some worthy, some not, and understanding those purposes requires that we think critically.

10b

10b

The methods of viewing images critically parallel those for reading text critically: preview, analyze, interpret, synthesize, and (often) evaluate. In the next few pages, we'll apply these methods to the illustration above, an advertising poster for United Way Toronto.

1   Previewing

Look at the work as a whole:

- What can you tell about the source of the work? Who created it?
- What does the work show?
- What is the work's overall effect?
- What questions do you have about the work?

Most advertisements have two significant sources: the site where the ad appeared and the company or organization that produced the ad. In this instance, the sites would be multiple and variable, wherever United Way could place its poster. The producer of the ad in this case is a charitable organization, the Toronto chapter of the largest national umbrella organization for multiple individual charities.

The ad itself consists of three elements, two photographic, one textual: (1) a photograph of an older woman sleeping in an armchair in a cluttered apartment or private residence; (2) rising out of the sleeping woman is a photographic image of the same woman in an active, alert position; (3) the text of four sentences, the first in larger type, and the familiar rainbow-and-hand logo of United Way running across the bottom. The overall effect of the second image of the active woman rising out of her sleeping self is striking and dramatic. Because the advertiser is a well-known charitable organization, the questions raised are not about the producer's motivations, but about how the elements of the text combine to affect the viewer. Unlike a commercial advertiser, a charitable organization would not work to affect only the viewer's personal sense of interests and well-being, but his or her sense of the interests and well-being of others, including strangers. How, then, does this ad work to affect the viewer's sense of charity toward others? And how does the ad create links between the viewer and the well-being of strangers?

10b

2   Analyzing

Study the work closely to begin answering your questions about it. Look not just at the obvious content but at the features that may seem unimportant. Assume that everything in the work appears there for a reason.

- Which elements stand out the most? Which are less prominent?
- What do colour, composition, and similar features emphasize?
- If words accompany the image, what do they contribute in relation to the image?

In the United Way ad, the most prominent element is the photograph: the image of the active, alert woman rising out of her resting self. The setting or background of this striking juxtaposition or setting together of images is clearly the older woman's residence or apartment. Beside the chair, on the viewer's left, there are newspapers both in a magazine rack and piled on the floor with a telephone and what appears to be a photograph album. On our right appears a clock, a radio, a lamp, and a photograph of a man in uniform. In the right foreground are her tea things, her medication, and a doily.

The most striking element, however, is the active woman rising out of the resting woman. They are clearly the same woman, though the active woman is very different. In a computer generated effect familiar to contemporary audiences, she appears to be sloughing off her resting self as if rising out of or even ripping her way out of a second skin. She now is wide-awake, looking out of the photographic frame towards the upper right. She wears a large sun visor, and her pink suit contrasts warmly with the cooler blue of her sleeping image. Her face is fully lit, in contrast to the shadowed face of the rester.

3   Interpreting

Consider what the elements of the work convey about the assumptions and intentions of its creator.

- What do the various elements of the work say, in images or in words?
- What appeals do the elements make to viewers? Do they emphasize reason or feelings of a combination?
- What does the creator seem to assume about viewers' interests, beliefs, and needs?
- What seems to be the purpose of the work?

10b

The United Way ad appeals partly to reason: to the interest of viewers in directly affecting in a positive way one of the most vulnerable and helpless groups in any society. But this appeal to reason, though well based on a rational understanding of the effect of charitable donations on a society as a whole and the particular groups involved and on the donor, is only partial. The ad appeals most strongly to emotion. The startling image of a transformed, robust woman rising out of her weaker, wearier self would likely surprise and engage the viewer in the purpose of the ad.

The cluttered setting emphasizes the effects of time and age. The photograph album and newspapers on the left represent the media and technologies of the past, as does the radio and the pre-digital clock on the left. The soldier in the photograph must have fought in a war in the distant past. The medications in the foreground indicate the infirmities of old age. These seem to be the props of hopelessness or at least of a present dominated by the past. What really dominates the space, however, is the strikingly represented transformation of the woman from a sleeper caught in the past to the woman whose brightly lit face seems to be looking upwards and out to the future. From this motion outwards and up, the viewer's eye is drawn down to the text below which explains and enforces the purpose of this dramatic image.

4   Synthesizing

Consider how the work's elements mesh to achieve an overall meaning or effect.

- How do the elements relate to and reinforce one another?
- What point or points do the elements make together? What is the message?
- How does the work relate to similar works—for instance, works in the same medium or with the same purpose?

The United Way ad represents one of the largest and most visible charitable organization in Canada, and this particular ad represents United Way in Canada's largest city. The purpose of

United Way, as the public, it is fair to say, generally understands it, is to provide an umbrella or rainbow organization that can most effectively maximize and unify charitable appeals. So that each charity does not have to conduct its own campaign, United Way conducts a single campaign, though many charities still conduct their own campaigns. In other words, United Way is a large organization collecting millions of dollars that is entirely dependent, however, on individual donors and whose beneficial effect, moreover, is on the most vulnerable and often most hidden- away individuals.

The ultimate aim of the ad, then, would be to make clear this relation between donor, charitable organization, and the possible beneficiary. The effect of the photograph and the text is to show visually a way out that is confirmed by the two levels of text at the bottom. The first level, addressed in second person to the viewer, plays on the words "giving" and "way" to emphasize to each individual donor the ultimate purpose of their donations to the charitable organization. The second level names some specific services provided by the Way, directs the donor to the easiest donation site, and plays again on "way" to mobilize the viewer's charity: "Without you, there would be no way." Our donations help to give a way for seniors from the hopeless state of the sleeping woman to the hopeful state of her second and radiant image.

10b

5   Evaluating

Judge the reasonableness, significance, or value of the work.

- How accurate and fair is the work, or how distorted and biased?
- How successful is the work? Does it achieve its apparent purpose? Is its purpose worthwhile?
- How does the work affect you? Do you find it informative, inviting, dull, objectionable, or what?

All of the questions above should be asked by the reader of any advertisement. As works of persuasion, commercial advertising rarely meets high standards of reasonableness and accuracy. Its promotional purpose encourages one-sidedness and selective use of evidence, when evidence is offered. As noted above, a charitable organization like United Way can be assumed not to have those motivations; however, it must also work to persuade people to part with money in such an environment.

As an advertisement, the United Way ad is quite successful. The ad appeals to the sympathetic emotions of the viewer without overindulging or overtaxing those emotions. Through its photographic, visual, and written elements, the ad links the potential donor, the organization, and the human focus of the sympathy.

11 Argument

Argument is writing that attempts to solve a problem, open readers' minds to an opinion, change readers' own opinions, or move readers to action. Using a variety of techniques, you engage readers to find common ground and narrow the distance between your views and theirs.

11a

(11a) Understanding and using the elements of argument

An argument has four main elements: topic, claims, evidence, and assumptions. (The last three are adapted from the work of the British philosopher Stephen Toulmin.)

1 The topic

An argument starts with a topic and often with an opinion about the topic as well—that is, an idea that makes you want to write about the topic. (If you don't have a topic or you aren't sure what you think about it, try some of the invention techniques discussed on pp. 7–13.) Your initial opinion should meet several requirements:

- It can be disputed: reasonable people can disagree over it.
- It *will* be disputed: it is controversial.
- It is narrow enough to research and argue in the space and time available.

On the flip side of these requirements are several kinds of statements or views that will not work as the starting place of argument: indisputable facts, such as the functions of the human liver; personal preferences or beliefs, such as a moral commitment to vegetarianism; and ideas that few would disagree with, such as the virtues of a secure home.

2 Claims

CLAIMS are statements that require support. In an argument you refine your initial opinion into a central claim and assert it outright as the THESIS STATEMENT, or main idea: it is what the argument is about. For instance:

The college needs a new chemistry laboratory to replace the existing outdated lab.

Claims are usually statements of opinion, fact, or belief:

- An OPINION is a judgment that is based on facts and arguable on the basis of facts, such as the example above about a new chemistry lab.
- A FACT is potentially verifiable and thus not arguable—for example, *The cost of medical care is rising.*
- A BELIEF, while seemingly arguable, is not based on facts and so cannot be contested on the basis of facts—for example, *The primary goal of government should be to provide equality of opportunity for all.*

Only an opinion may serve as the thesis statement of an argument. A claim of fact or belief may serve as a secondary claim supporting the thesis but not as the thesis statement itself.

11a

3   Evidence

EVIDENCE demonstrates the validity of your claims. The evidence to support the claim above about the need for a new chemistry lab might include the present lab's age, an inventory of facilities and equipment, and the testimony of chemistry professors.

There are several kinds of evidence:

- FACTS, statements whose truth can be verified: *Poland is slightly smaller than Manitoba.*
- STATISTICS, facts expressed as numbers: *Of those polled, 62 percent prefer a flat tax.*
- EXAMPLES, specific instances of the point being made: *Many groups, such as the elderly and the disabled, would benefit from this policy.*
- EXPERT OPINIONS, the judgments formed by authorities on the basis of their own examination of the facts: *Affirmative action is necessary to right past injustices, a point argued by Alan Borovoy, the current director of the Canadian Civil Liberties Association.*
- APPEALS to readers' beliefs or needs, statements that ask readers to accept a claim in part because it states something they already accept as true without evidence: *The shabby, antiquated chemistry lab shames the school, making it seem a second-rate institution.*

Evidence must be reliable to be convincing. Ask these questions about your evidence:

- Is it accurate—trustworthy, exact, and undistorted?
- Is it relevant—authoritative, pertinent, and current?

- Is it representative—true to its context, neither under- nor over-representing any element of the sample it's drawn from?
- Is it adequate—plentiful and specific?

4   Assumptions

An ASSUMPTION is an opinion, a principle, or a belief that ties evidence to claims: the assumption explains why a particular piece of evidence is relevant to a particular claim. For instance:

Claim: The college needs a new chemistry laboratory.
Evidence (in part): The testimony of chemistry professors.
Assumption: Chemistry professors are the most capable of evaluating the present lab's quality.

Assumptions are not flaws in arguments but necessities: we all acquire beliefs and opinions that shape our views of the world. Just as interpreting a work's assumptions is a significant part of critical reading (see p. 86), so discovering your own assumptions is a significant part of argumentative critical writing. If your readers do not share your assumptions or perceive that you are not forthright about your biases, they will be less receptive to your argument. (See the following discussion of reasonableness.)

ESL The ways of conceiving and writing arguments described here may be initially uncomfortable to you if your native culture approaches such writing differently. In some cultures, for example, a writer is expected to begin indirectly, to avoid asserting his or her opinion outright, to rely for evidence on appeals to tradition, or to establish a compromise rather than argue a position. Writers of English, however, look or aim for a well-articulated opinion, evidence gathered from many sources, and a direct and concise argument for the opinion.

(11b) Writing reasonably

Reasonableness is essential if an argument is to establish common ground between you and your readers. Readers expect logical thinking, appropriate appeals, fairness toward the opposition, and, combining all of these, writing that is free of fallacies.

1   Logical thinking

The thesis of your argument is a conclusion you reach by reasoning about evidence. Two processes of reasoning, induction and deduction, are familiar to you even if you aren't familiar with their names.

Induction

When you're about to buy a used car, you consult friends, relatives, and consumer guides before deciding what kind of car to buy. Using INDUCTION, or INDUCTIVE REASONING, you make specific observations about cars (your evidence) and you induce, or infer, a GENERALIZATION that Car X is most reliable. The generalization is a claim supported by your observations.

You might also use inductive reasoning in a term paper on print advertising:

> Analyze advertisements in newspapers and magazines (evidence).
> Read comments by advertisers, publishers, and critics (more evidence).
> Form a conclusion about print advertising (generalization/claim).

11b

Reasoning inductively, you connect your evidence to your generalization by assuming that what is true in one set of circumstances (the ads you look at) is true in a similar set of circumstances (other ads). With induction you create new knowledge out of old.

The more evidence you accumulate, the more probable it is that your generalization is true. Note, however, that absolute certainty is not possible. At some point you must *assume* that your evidence justifies your generalization, for yourself and your readers. Most errors in inductive reasoning involve oversimplifying either the evidence or the generalization. See pages 93–94 on fallacies.

Deduction

You use DEDUCTION, or DEDUCTIVE REASONING, when you proceed from your generalization that Car X is the most reliable used car to your own specific circumstances (you want to buy a used car) to the conclusion that you should buy Car X. In deduction your assumption is a generalization, principle, or belief that you think is true. It links the evidence (new information) to the claim (the conclusion you draw). With deduction you apply old information to new.

Say that you want the school administration to postpone new room fees for one dormitory. You can base your argument on a deductive SYLLOGISM:

> *Premise:* The administration should not raise fees on dorm rooms in poor condition. [A generalization or belief that you assume to be true.]
> *Premise:* The rooms in Polk Hall are in poor condition. [New information: a specific case of the first premise.]
> *Conclusion:* The administration should not raise fees on the rooms in Polk Hall. [Your claim.]

As long as the premises of a syllogism are true, the conclusion derives logically and certainly from them. Errors in constructing syllogisms lie behind many of the fallacies discussed on pages 93–95.

2   Rational, emotional, and ethical appeals

In most arguments you will combine RATIONAL APPEALS to readers' capacities for logical reasoning with EMOTIONAL APPEALS to readers' beliefs and feelings. The following example illustrates both: the second sentence makes a rational appeal (to the logic of financial gain), and the third sentence makes an emotional appeal (to the sense of fairness and open-mindedness).

> Advertising should show more physically challenged people. The hundreds of thousands of disabled Canadians have considerable buying power, yet so far advertisers have made no attempt to tap that power. Further, by keeping the physically challenged out of the mainstream depicted in ads, advertisers encourage widespread prejudice against disability, prejudice that frightens and demeans those who hold it.

For an emotional appeal to be successful, it must be appropriate for the audience and the argument:

- It must not misjudge readers' actual feelings.
- It must not raise emotional issues that are irrelevant to the claims and the evidence. (See pp. 93–94 for a discussion of specific inappropriate appeals, such as bandwagon and *ad hominem*.)

A third kind of approach to readers, the ETHICAL APPEAL, is the sense you give of being a competent, fair person who is worth heeding. A rational appeal and an appropriate emotional appeal contribute to your ethical appeal, and so does your acknowledging opposing views (see below). An argument that is concisely written and correct in grammar, spelling, and other matters will underscore your competence. In addition, a sincere and even tone will assure readers that you are a balanced person who wants to reason with them.

A sincere and even tone need not exclude language with emotional appeal—words such as *frightens* and *demeans* at the end of the example about advertising. But avoid certain forms of expression that will mark you as unfair:

- Insulting words such as *idiotic* or *fascist*.
- Biased language such as *fags* or *broads*. (See pp. 142–44.)
- Sarcasm—for instance, using the sentence *What a brilliant idea* to indicate contempt for the idea and its originator.
- Exclamation points! They'll make you sound shrill!

3   Acknowledgment of opposing views

A good test of your fairness in argument is how you handle possible objections. Assuming your thesis is indeed arguable, then others can marshal their own evidence to support a different view or views. You need to find out what these other views are and what the support is for them. Then, in your argument, you need to take these views on, refute those you can, grant the validity of others, and demonstrate why, despite their validity, the opposing views are less compelling than your own. (See the sample essay on pp. 100–03 for examples.)

Before you draft your essay, list for yourself all the opposing views you can think of. You'll find them in your research, by talking to friends, and by critically thinking about your own ideas. Figure out which opposing views you can refute (do more research if necessary), and prepare to concede those views you can't refute. It's not a mark of weakness or failure to admit that the opposition has a point or two. Indeed, by showing yourself to be honest and fair, you strengthen your ethical appeal and thus your entire argument.

11b

4   Fallacies

FALLACIES—errors in argument—either evade the issue of the argument or treat the argument as if it were much simpler than it is.

Evasions

An effective argument squarely faces the central issue or question it addresses. An ineffective argument may dodge the issue in one of the following ways:

- BEGGING THE QUESTION: treating an opinion that is open to question as if it were already proved or disproved.

  The university library's expenses should be reduced by cutting subscriptions to useless periodicals. [Begged questions: Are some of the library's periodicals useless? Useless to whom?]

- NON SEQUITUR (Latin: "It does not follow"): linking two or more ideas that in fact have no logical connection.

  If high school English were easier, fewer students would have trouble with the college English requirement. [Presumably, if high school English were easier, students would have more trouble.]

- RED HERRING: introducing an irrelevant issue intended to distract readers from the relevant issues.

  A campus speech code is essential to protect students, who already have enough problems coping with rising tuition. [Tuition costs and speech codes are different subjects. What protections do students need that a speech code will provide?]

- APPEAL TO READERS' FEAR OR PITY: substituting emotions for reasoning.

  She should not have to pay taxes because she is an aged widow with no friends or relatives. [Appeals to people's pity. Should age and loneliness, rather than income, determine a person's tax obligation?]

- BANDWAGON: inviting readers to accept a claim because everyone else does.

  As everyone knows, marijuana use leads to heroin addiction. [What is the evidence?]

- AD HOMINEM (Latin: "to the man"): attacking the qualities of the people holding an opposing view rather than the substance of the view itself.

  One of the scientists has been treated for emotional problems, so his pessimism about nuclear waste merits no attention. [Do the scientist's previous emotional problems invalidate his current views?]

Oversimplifications

In a vain attempt to create something neatly convincing, an ineffective argument may conceal or ignore complexities in one of the following ways:

- HASTY GENERALIZATION: making a claim on the basis of inadequate evidence.

  It is disturbing that several of the youths who shot up schools were users of violent video games. Obviously, these games can breed violence, and they should be banned. [A few cases do not establish the relation between the games and violent behaviour. Most youths who play violent video games do not behave violently.]

- SWEEPING GENERALIZATION: making an insupportable statement. Many sweeping generalizations are absolute statements involving words such as *all, always, never,* and *no one* that allow no exceptions. Others are stereotypes, conventional and oversimplified characterizations of a group of people:

  People who live in cities are unfriendly.
  British Columbians are laid-back.
  Women are emotional.
  Men can't express their feelings.
  (See also pp. 142–144 on sexist and other biased language.)

- REDUCTIVE FALLACY: oversimplifying (reducing) the relation between causes and effects.

  Poverty causes crime. [If so, then why do people who are not poor commit crimes? And why aren't all poor people criminals?]

- POST HOC FALLACY (from Latin, *post hoc, ergo propter hoc:* "after this, therefore because of this"): assuming that because *A* preceded *B*, then *A* must have caused *B*.

  The town council erred in permitting the adult bookstore to open, for shortly afterward two women were assaulted. [It cannot be assumed without evidence that the women's assailants visited or were influenced by the bookstore.]

- EITHER/OR FALLACY: assuming that a complicated question has only two answers, one good and one bad, both good, or both bad. Either we permit mandatory drug testing in the workplace or productivity will continue to decline. [Productivity is not necessarily dependent on drug testing.]

(11c) Organizing an argument

All arguments include the same parts:

- The introduction establishes the significance of the subject and provides background. The introduction generally includes the thesis statement. However, if you think your readers may have difficulty accepting your thesis statement before they see at least some support for it, then it may come later in the paper. (See pp. 48–50 for more on introductions.)
- The body states the claims that support the thesis and, in one or more paragraphs, develops each claim with clearly relevant evidence. See below for more on organizing the body.
- The response to opposing views details those views and either demonstrates your argument's greater strengths or concedes the opponents' points. See below for more on organizing this response.
- The conclusion restates the thesis, summarizes the argument, and makes a final appeal to readers. (See pp. 50–52 for more on conclusions.)

The structure of the body and the response to opposing views depend on your subject, purpose, audience, and form of reasoning. Here are several possible arrangements:

The traditional scheme	The problem-solution scheme
Claim 1 and evidence	The problem: claims and evidence
Claim 2 and evidence	The solution: claims and evidence
Claim X and evidence	Response to opposing views
Response to opposing views	

Variations on the traditional scheme

Use a variation if you believe your readers will reject your argument without an early or intermittent response to opposing views.

Response to opposing views	Claim 1 and evidence
Claim 1 and evidence	Response to opposing views
Claim 2 and evidence	Claim 2 and evidence
Claim X and evidence	Response to opposing views
	Claim X and evidence
	Response to opposing views

11c

(11d) Using visual arguments

In a **visual argument** you use one or more images to engage and convince readers. Advertisements often provide the most vivid and memorable examples of visual arguments, but writers in almost every field—from medicine to music, from physics to physical education—support their claims with images. The main elements of written arguments discussed on pages 88–90—claims, evidence, and assumptions—appear also in visual arguments.

1 Claims

The claims in an image may be made by composition as well as by content, with or without accompanying words. For instance:

IMAGE   A photograph framing hundreds of chickens crammed into small cages, resembling familiar images of World War II concentration camps.

CLAIM   Commercial poultry-raising practices are cruel and unethical.

IMAGE   A chart with dramatically contrasting bars that represent the optimism, stress, and heart disease reported by people before and after they participated in a program of daily walking.

CLAIM   Daily exercise leads to a healthier and happier life.

On the next page is one of a series of advertisements featuring unnamed but well-known people as milk drinkers. The celebrity here is Oscar de la Hoya, a boxing champion. The ad makes several claims both in the photograph and in the text.

2 Evidence

The kinds of evidence offered by images parallel those found in written arguments:

- **Facts:** You might provide facts in the form of data, as in a graph showing a five-year rise in oil prices. Or you might draw an inference from data, as the ad on the next page does by stating that milk provides "high-quality protein for your muscles without the fat."
- **Examples:** Most often, you'll use examples to focus on an instance of your argument's claims, as Oscar de la Hoya represents milk drinkers in the ad on the following page.
- **Expert opinions:** You might present a chart from an expert showing a trend in unemployment among high school graduates.
- **Appeals to beliefs or needs:** You might depict how things clearly ought to be (an anti-drug brochure featuring a teenager who is confidently refusing peer pressure) or, in contrast, show

Claims in an image

Image claim: Cool, tough men drink milk.

Image claim: Attractive people drink milk.

Image claim: Athletes drink milk.

Text claim: Milk is a good source of nutrition, helping to build muscles.

What? Were you expecting Hercules or something? Listen, I've got three words for strong muscles. Fat free milk. We're talking high-quality protein for your muscles without the fat. And man, there ain't nothing uglier than an overweight lightweight.

got milk?

Advertisement by the Milk Processor Education Program

11d

how things clearly should not be (a Web site for an anti-hunger campaign featuring images of emaciated children).

To make an image work hard as evidence, be sure it relates directly to a point in your argument, adds to that point, and gives readers something to think about. Always include a caption that provides source information and that explicitly ties the image to your text, so that readers don't have to puzzle out your intentions. Number images in sequence (Fig. 1, Fig. 2, and so on), and refer to them by number at the appropriate points in your text. (See pp. 59–63 for more on captioning and numbering illustrations.)

The images on the next page illustrate the use of visual evidence in an argument with the following thesis: *Television shows focusing on cosmetic procedures are encouraging women to opt for such procedures in order to conform to a particular standard of beauty.*

Images as evidence

Before and after images show the effects of cosmetic procedures more emphatically than a description would

11d

Caption explaining the images and the woman's cosmetic treatments, tying the images to the text of the paper

Figure 1. Before and after images of a participant on the television show Extreme Makeover. In addition to the change in personal style implied by the change in clothes, hairdo, and body language, this participant also underwent nose surgery, a brow lift, eye surgery, dental work, liposuction, and breast augmentation. Photographs from Walt Disney Internet Group, ABC, Extreme Makeover, 2005, 30 May 2005 <http://abc.go.com/primetime/extrememakeover/index.html>.

Graph from a reputable source demonstrating the overall increase in cosmetic procedures

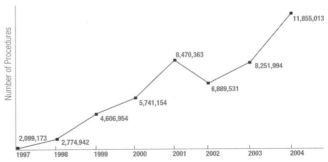

Cosmetic Surgery Trends
Surgical and Nonsurgical Cosmetic Procedures: Totals
Source: American Society for Aesthetic Plastic Surgery

Caption explaining the graph and highlighting the 2004 increase, the most relevant to the paper's claims

Figure 2. Numbers of cosmetic procedures performed in the United States, 1997–2004. In 2004 such procedures increased 44 percent. Graph from American Society for Aesthetic Plastic Surgery, 2004 Cosmetic Surgery National Data Bank: Statistics, 3 June 2005 <http://www.surgery.org/press/statistics-2004.php>.

3   Assumptions

Like a written argument, a visual argument is based on assumptions—your ideas about the relation between evidence and claims (p. 96). Look again at the milk ad featuring Oscar de la Hoya (p. 97). The advertiser seems to have assumed that simply stating the benefits of milk drinking would not be convincing and that a celebrity endorsement would strengthen the claims and evidence. In addition, the photograph of de la Hoya emphasizes qualities that the advertiser presumably thought would appeal to readers: toughness, directness, and, for the original American audience (in the robe draped over the boxer's shoulders), patriotism.

As in written arguments, the assumptions in visual arguments must be appropriate for your readers if the argument is to succeed with them. The milk ad originally appeared in sports magazines, so the advertiser could assume that readers knew of and admired de la Hoya. But to readers uninterested in sports or even opposed to boxing, the photograph might actually undermine the ad's effectiveness.

11d

4   Appeals

Images can help to strengthen the rational, emotional, and ethical appeals of your written argument (p. 92):

- **Images can contribute evidence,** as long as they come from reliable sources, present information accurately and fairly, and relate clearly to the argument's claims.
- **Images can appeal to a host of ideas and emotions,** including patriotism, curiosity, moral values, sympathy, and anger. Any such appeal should correctly gauge readers' beliefs and feelings, and it should be clearly relevant to the argument.
- **Images can show that you are a competent, fair, and trustworthy source of information,** largely through their relevance, reliability, and sensitivity to readers' needs and feelings.

5   Recognizing fallacies

When making a visual argument, you'll need to guard against all the fallacies discussed on pages 93–95. Here we'll focus on specific visual examples. The first, the milk ad on page 97, uses Oscar de la Hoya for snob appeal, inviting readers to be like someone they admire. If you drink milk, the ad says subtly, you too may become fit, skilful, and direct (notice that de la Hoya looks unguardedly into the camera). The ad does have some substance in its specific and verifiable claim that milk contains "high-quality protein for your muscles without the fat," but de la Hoya himself, with his milk moustache, makes a stronger claim.

6　Choice of images

You can wait until you've drafted an argument before concentrating on what images to include. This approach keeps your focus on the research and writing needed to craft the best argument from sources. But you can also begin thinking visually at the beginning of a project, as you might if your initial interest in the subject was sparked by a compelling image. Either way, ask yourself some basic questions as you consider visual options:

- **Which parts of your argument can use visual reinforcement?** What can be explained better visually than verbally? Can a graph or chart present data compactly and interestingly? Can a photograph appeal effectively to readers' beliefs and values?
- **What are the limitations or requirements of your writing situation?** What do the type of writing you're doing and its format allow? Look through examples of similar writing to gauge the kinds of illustrations readers will expect.
- **What kinds of visuals are readily available on your subject?** As you researched your subject, what images seemed especially effective? What sources have you not yet explored? what images can a standard search engine find for you?
- **Should you create original images tailored to your argument?** Instead of searching for existing images, would your time be better spent taking your own photographs or using computer software to compose visual explanations, such as charts, graphs, and diagrams?

Note Any image you include in a paper requires the same detailed citation as a written source. If you plan to publish your argument online, you will also need to seek permission from the author. See pages 339–47 on citing sources and obtaining permissions.

(11e)　Examining a sample argument

The following student essay illustrates the principles discussed in this chapter. As you read the essay, note especially the structure, the relation of claims and supporting evidence, the kinds of appeals the author makes, and the ways he addresses opposing views.

TV Can Be Good for You

Television wastes time, pollutes minds, destroys brain cells, and turns some viewers into murderers. Thus runs the prevailing talk

Introduction:

Identification of prevailing view

about the medium, supported by serious research as well as simple belief. But television has at least one strong virtue, too, which helps to explain its endurance as a cultural force. In an era when people often have little time to speak with one another, television provides replacement voices that ease loneliness, spark healthful laughter, and even educate young children.

Most people who have lived alone understand the curse of silence, when the only sound is the buzz of unhappiness or anxiety inside one's own head. Although people of all ages who live alone can experience intense loneliness, the elderly are especially vulnerable to solitude. For example, they may suffer increased confusion or depression when left alone for long periods but then rebound when they have steady companionship (Bondevik and Skogstad 329–30).

A study of elderly men and women in New Zealand found that television can actually serve as a companion by assuming "the role of social contact with the wider world," reducing "feelings of isolation and loneliness because it directs viewers' attention away from themselves" ("Television Programming"). Thus television's replacement voices can provide comfort because they distract from a focus on being alone.

The absence of real voices can be most damaging when it means a lack of laughter. Here, too, research shows that television can have a positive effect on health. Laughter is one of the most powerful calming forces available to human beings, proven in many studies to reduce heart rate, lower blood pressure, and ease other stress-related ailments (Burroughs, Mahoney, and Lippman 172; Griffiths 18). Television offers plenty of laughter for all kinds of viewers: the recent listings for a single Friday night included more than twenty comedy programs running on the networks and on basic cable between 6 and 9 PM.

A study reported in a health magazine found that laughter inspired by television and video is as healthful as the laughter generated by live comedy. Volunteers laughing at a video comedy routine "showed significant improvements in several immune functions, such as natural killer-cell activity" (Laliberte 78). Further, the effects of the comedy were so profound that "merely anticipating watching a funny video improved

Sidebar annotations:

Disagreement with prevailing view

Thesis statement making three claims for television

Background for claim 1: effects of loneliness

11e

Evidence for effects of loneliness

Evidence for effects of television on loneliness

Statement of claim 1

Background for claim 2: effects of laughter

Evidence for effects of laughter

Evidence for comedy on television

Evidence for effects of laughter in response to television

mood, depression, and anger as much as two days beforehand" (Laliberte 79). Even for people with plenty of companionship, television's replacement voices can have healthful effects by causing laughter.

Statement of claim 2

Television also provides information about the world. This service can be helpful to everyone but especially to children, whose natural curiosity can exhaust the knowledge and patience of their parents and caretakers. While the TV may be baby-sitting children, it can also enrich them. For example, educational programs such as those on the Discovery Channel, the Disney Channel, and PBS offer a steady stream of information at various cognitive levels. Even many cartoons, which are generally dismissed as mindless or worse, familiarize children with the material of literature, including strong characters enacting classic narratives.

Background for claim 3: educational effects

Evidence for educational programming on television

Two researchers studying children and television found that TV is a source of creative and psychological instruction, inspiring children "to play imaginatively and develop confidence and skills" (Colman and Colman 9). Instead of passively watching, children "interact with the programs and videos" and "sometimes include the fictional characters they've met into reality's play time" (Colman and Colman 8). Thus television's replacement voices both inform young viewers and encourage exchange.

Evidence for educational effects of television on children

Statement of claim 3

The value of these replacement voices should not be oversold. For one thing, almost everyone agrees that too much TV does no one any good and may cause much harm. Many studies show that excessive TV watching increases violent behaviour, especially in children, and can cause, rather than ease, other antisocial behaviours and depression (Reeks 114; Walsh 34). In addition, human beings require the give and take of actual interaction. Steven Pinker, an expert in children's language acquisition, warns that children cannot develop language properly by watching television. They need to interact with actual speakers who respond directly to their specific needs (282). Replacement voices are not real voices and in the end can do only limited good.

Anticipation of objections

1. Harm of television

2. Need for actual interaction

But even limited good is something, especially for those who are lonely, angry, or neglected. Television is not an entirely positive

Qualification of claims in response to objections

Conclusion

force, but neither is it an entirely negative one. Its voices stand by to provide company, laughter, and information whenever they're needed.

Works Cited

Bondevik, Margareth, and Anders Skogstad. "The Oldest Old, ADL, Social Network, and Loneliness." Western Journal of Nursing Research 20.3 (1998): 325–43.

Burroughs, W. Jeffrey, Diana L. Mahoney, and Louis G. Lippman. "Perceived Attributes of Health-Promoting Laughter: Cross-Generational Comparison." Journal of Psychology 136.2 (2002): 171–81.

Colman, Robyn, and Adrian Colman. "Inspirational Television." Youth Studies in Australia 21.3 (2002): 8–10.

Griffiths, Joan. "The Mirthful Brain." Omni Aug. 1996: 18–19.

Laliberte, Richard W. "The Benefits of Laughter." Shape Sept. 2002: 78–79.

Pinker, Steven. The Language Instinct: How the Mind Creates Language. New York: Harper, 1994.

Reeks, Anne. "Kids and TV: A Guide." Parenting Apr. 2002: 110–15.

"Television Programming for Older People, the Perspective of the Older Community: Summary Research Report." NZ on Air. 25 July 2001. 15 Oct. 2002 <http://www.nzonair.gov. nz/media/policyandresearch/oldpeoplesreport. pdf>.

Walsh, Teri. "Too Much TV Linked to Depression." Prevention Feb. 1999: 34–36.

—CRAIG HOLBROOK (student)

11e

12 Online Writing

This chapter provides advice for composing your own Web pages—whether for family and friends, a group you belong to, or projects for courses. The chapter notes some key differences between Web compositions and printed documents (below); gives sources for HTML editors, the software used to create Web compositions (p. 105); and discusses content and design issues for posting papers on the Web (p. 106) and creating original sites (p. 107).

(12a) Distinguishing Web compositions from printed documents

12a

We generally read printed documents LINEARLY—that is, straight through from first page to last. Reference aids such as indexes and cross-references can help us find material out of the linear order, but the text is usually intended to be read in sequence:

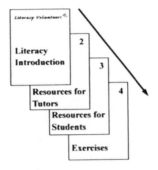

In contrast, a HYPERTEXT such as a Web site is intended to be examined in the order readers choose as they follow electronic links among the pages of the site and often to related sites.

The preceding illustration shows the structure of a fairly simple Web site: readers can move in any direction signalled by arrows or back to the home page with a single click of the mouse.

The main disadvantage of a hypertext is that it can disorient readers as they explore the various links. A Web site requires careful planning of the links between pages and thoughtful cues to help readers keep track of their location in the site.

Note It's easy to incorporate material from other sources into a Web site, but you have the same obligation to cite your sources as you do in a printed document (see pp. 344–45). Further, you may

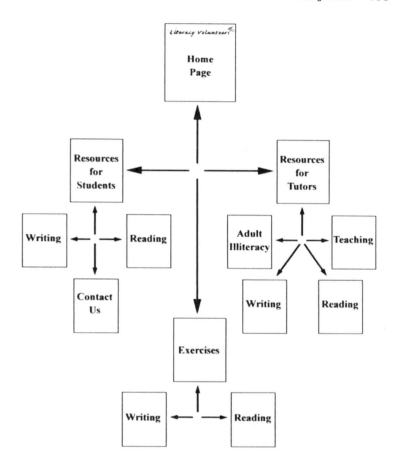

need to seek the copyright holder's permission before publishing the material on the Web. See page 345 for more on copyright.

(12b) Using HTML

Most Web pages are created using hypertext markup language, or HTML, and an HTML editor. The HTML editing program inserts command codes into your document that achieve the effects you want when the material appears on the Web.

From the user's point of view, most HTML editors work much as word processors do, with similar options for sizing, formatting, and highlighting copy and with a display that shows what you will see in the final version. Indeed, you can compose a Web page without bothering at all about the behind-the-scenes HTML coding. As you gain experience with Web building, however, you may want to create more sophisticated pages by editing the codes themselves, using the HTML editor or a basic text editor such as Notepad or SimpleText.

There are many HTML editors on the market. But your computer may already have a good HTML editor if it is fairly new or includes a popular Web browser. Students can also download free or low-cost editors from a number of Web sites.

12c

(12c)　Creating online papers

When you create a composition for the Web, it will likely fall into one of two categories: pages such as class papers that resemble printed documents in being linear and text-heavy and that call for familiar ways of writing and reading (discussed below); or "native" hypertext documents that you build from scratch, and that call for screen-oriented writing and reading (pp. 107–10).

If an instructor asks you to post a paper to a Web site, you can compose it on your word processor and then use the Save As HTML function available on most word processors to translate it into a Web page. After translating the paper, your word processor should allow you to modify some of the elements on the page, or you can open the translated document in an HTML editor.

The illustration below shows the opening screen of a student's project for a composition course. The project incorporates many of the design features that make any text-heavy document more accessible to Web readers:

- Use a simple white or cream-coloured background for your pages. It is more difficult to read text on a computer screen than on paper, and bright or dark background colours compound the problem.
- Use a standard type font for text (see p. 56), and use a type size that will be readable on various systems. With standard fonts, a size of at least 12 points should ensure that pages are readable on most systems.
- Web pages automatically run text the full width of the screen unless you give other instructions. To make reading easier, increase the margins so that lines run no more than seventy to eighty characters (including spaces).
- Use headings as signposts in documents that require scrolling through several screens. Otherwise, readers may lose their sense of the document's overall organization.

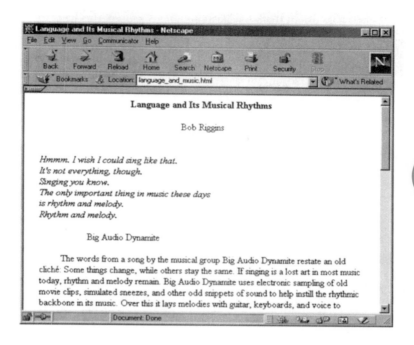

12d Creating original sites

When you create an original Web site, you need to be aware that Web readers generally alternate between skimming pages for highlights and focusing intently on sections of text. To facilitate this kind of reading, you'll want to consider the guidelines on the previous page for handling text and also your site's structure and content, flow, ease of navigation, and use of images, video, and sound.

1 Structure and content

Your site's organization should be easy to grasp so that it does not disorient readers.

- Sketch possible site plans before getting started. (See p. 105 for an example.) Your aim is to develop a sense of the major components of your project and to create a logical space for each component. As you conceive the organization of your site, consider how menus on the site's pages can provide overviews of the organization as well as direct access to the pages. (See pp. 108–09.)
- Treat the first few sentences on any page as a crucial get-acquainted space for you and your readers. In this opening, try to hook readers with an interesting question or a central concern,

and help orient them by clarifying the relation of this page to the others on the site.

- Create links among the pages of your own site to help readers move around easily. Create links to other sites that are strictly relevant to your own ideas: too many links or unrelated links will confuse and frustrate readers. For every link, indicate what's at the other location. Instead of just *Click here,* for instance, say *Click here for writing exercises* or *Further information about snowboarding.* When you provide a list of links to related sites, annotate each one with information about its contents.

- Distill your text so that it includes only essential information. Of course, concise prose is essential in any writing situation, but Web readers expect to scan text quickly and, in any event, have difficulty following long text passages on a computer screen. (See pp. 152–57 for advice on writing concisely.)

2   Flow

Beginning Web authors sometimes start at the top of the page and then add element upon element until information proceeds down the screen much as it would in a printed document. However, by thinking about how information will flow on a page, you can take better advantage of the Web's visual nature.

The screen shot below shows part of the opening page of the site mapped on page 105. Though simple in content and design, the page illustrates how the arrangement of elements can invite readers in and direct their attention. A large banner headline contains the

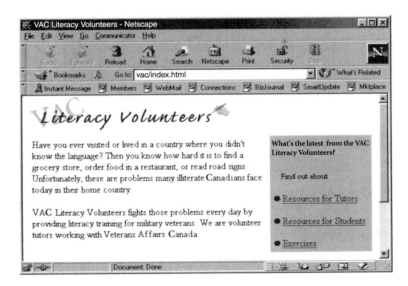

sponsoring organization's logo. The opening text is set in a readable font, is written to engage readers' interest, and is broken into short paragraphs. A text box to the right adds variety to the page and provides a menu of the site so that readers can quickly move to the information they seek.

To achieve flow on your Web pages, follow these guidelines:

- Standardize elements of your design to create expectations in readers and to fulfill those expectations. For instance, develop a uniform style for the main headings of pages, for headings within pages, and for menus. (For more on standardizing, see p. 55.)
- Make scanning easy for readers. Focus them on crucial text by adding space around it. Use icons and other images to emphasize text. (See below.) Add headings to break up text and to highlight content. Use lists to reinforce the parallel importance of items. (See pp. 58–59 for more on headings and lists.)
- Position boxes, illustrations, and other elements to help conduct readers through a page. Such elements can align in the centre or on the left or right of the page. Use space around the elements to keep them from interfering with text and to highlight them.

3   Ease of navigation

A Web site of more than a couple of pages requires a menu on every page that lists the features of the site, giving its plan at a glance. By clicking on any item in the menu, readers can go directly to a page that interests them. The menu can use just text to indicate links, as in the screen shot on the previous page, or it can include icons to catch the reader's eye, as in the following illustration. (Always supplement icons with verbal descriptions of the links to be sure readers understand where each link leads.)

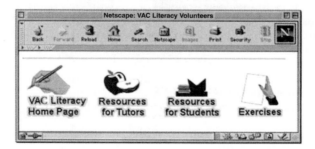

You can embed a menu at the top, side, or bottom of a page. Menus at the top or side are best on short pages because they will not scroll off the screen as readers move down the page. On longer pages menus at the bottom prevent readers from reaching a dead end, a point where they can't easily move forward or backward. You can also use a combination of menus—for instance, one near the top of a page and another at the bottom.

In designing a menu, keep it simple: the use of many different type fonts and colours will overwhelm readers instead of orienting them. And make the menus look the same from one page to the next so that readers recognize them easily.

13 Oral Presentations

Effective speakers use organization, voice, and other techniques to help their audiences follow and appreciate their presentations.

13a Organizing the presentation

Give your oral presentation a recognizable shape so that listeners can see how ideas and details relate to each other.

The introduction

The beginning of an oral presentation should try to accomplish three goals:

- **Gain the audience's attention and interest.** Begin with a question, an unusual example or statistic, or a short, relevant story.
- **Put yourself in the speech.** Demonstrate your expertise, experience, or concern to gain the interest and trust of your audience.
- **Introduce and preview your topic and purpose.** By the time your introduction is over, listeners should know what your subject is and the direction you'll take to develop your ideas.

Your introduction should prepare your audience for your main points but not give them away. Think of it as a sneak preview of your speech, not the place for an apology such as *I wish I'd had more time to prepare . . .* or a dull statement such as *My speech is about. . . .*

Supporting material

Just as you do when writing, you should use facts, statistics, examples, and expert opinions to support the main points of your oral presentation. In addition, you can make your points more memorable with vivid description, well-chosen quotations, true or fictional stories, and analogies.

The conclusion

You want your conclusion to be clear, of course, but you also want it to be memorable. Remind listeners of how your topic and main idea connect to their needs and interests. If your speech was motivational, tap an emotion that matches your message. If your speech was informational, give some tips on how to remember important details.

13b

(13b) Delivering the presentation

Methods of delivery

You can deliver an oral presentation in several ways:

- **Impromptu, without preparation:** Make a presentation without planning what you will say. Impromptu speaking requires confidence and excellent general preparation.
- **Extemporaneously:** Prepare notes to glance at but not read from. This method allows you to look and sound natural while ensuring that you don't forget anything.
- **Speaking from a text:** Read aloud from a written presentation. You won't lose your way, but you may lose your audience. Avoid reading for an entire presentation.
- **Speaking from memory:** Deliver a prepared presentation without notes. You can look at your audience every minute, but the stress of retrieving the next words may make you seem tense and unresponsive.

Vocal delivery

The sound of your voice will influence how listeners receive you. Rehearse your presentation several times until you are confident that you are speaking loudly, slowly, and clearly enough for your audience to understand you.

Physical delivery

You are more than your spoken words when you make an oral presentation. If you are able, stand up to deliver your presentation, moving your body toward one side of the room and the other, stepping out from behind any lectern or desk, and gesturing as appropriate. Above all, make eye contact with your audience as you speak. Looking directly in your listeners' eyes conveys your honesty, your confidence, and your control of the material.

Visual aids

You can supplement an oral presentation with visual aids such as posters, models, slides, or videos.

- **Use visual aids to underscore your points.** Short lists of key ideas, illustrations such as graphs or photographs, or objects such as models can make your presentation more interesting and memorable. But use visual aids judiciously: a battery of illustrations or objects will bury your message rather than amplify it.
- **Coordinate visual aids with your message.** Time each visual to reinforce a point you're making. Tell listeners what they're looking at. Give them enough viewing time so they don't mind turning their attention back to you.
- **Show visual aids only while they're needed.** To regain your audience's attention, remove or turn off any aid as soon as you have finished with it.

Many speakers use *PowerPoint* or other software to present visual aids. Preparing screens of brief points supported by data, images, or video, you can use such software to help listeners follow your main points. To use *PowerPoint* or other software effectively, follow the guidelines above and also the following:

- **Don't put your whole presentation on screen.** Select key points, and distill them to as few words as possible. Think of the slides as quick, easy-to-remember summaries.
- **Use a simple design.** Avoid turning your presentation into a show about the software's many capabilities.
- **Use a consistent design.** For optimal flow through the presentation, each slide should be formatted similarly.
- **Add only relevant illustrations.** Avoid loading the presentation with mere decoration.

Practice

Take time to rehearse your presentation out loud, with the notes you will be using. Gauge your performance by making an audio- or videotape of yourself or by practising in front of a mirror. Practising out loud will also tell you if your presentation is running too long or too short.

If you plan to use visual aids, you'll need to practise with them, too. Your goal is to eliminate hitches (upside-down slides, missing charts) and to weave the visuals seamlessly into your presentation.

Stage fright

Many people report that speaking in front of an audience is their number-one fear. Even many experienced and polished speakers have some anxiety about delivering an oral presentation, but they use this nervous energy to their advantage, letting it propel them into working hard on each presentation. Several techniques can help you reduce anxiety:

- **Use simple relaxation exercises.** Deep breathing or tensing and relaxing your stomach muscles can ease some of the physical symptoms of speech anxiety—stomachache, rapid heartbeat, and shaky hands, legs, and voice.
- **Think positively.** Instead of worrying about the mistakes you might make, concentrate on how well you've prepared and practised your presentation and how significant your ideas are.
- **Don't avoid opportunities to speak in public.** Practice and experience build speaking skills and offer the best insurance for success.

13b

PowerPoint **slides**

First slide, introducing the project and presentation

Simple, consistent slide design focusing viewers' attention on information, not *PowerPoint* features

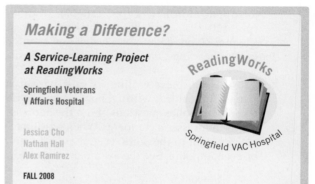

Later slide, using brief, bulleted points to be explained by the speaker

Photographs reinforcing the project's activities

14 Public Writing

Writing outside school, such as for business or for community work, resembles academic writing in many ways. It usually involves the same basic writing process, discussed on pages 1–36: assessing the writing situation, developing what you want to say, freely working out your meaning in a draft, and editing and revising so that your writing will achieve your purpose with readers. It often involves research, as discussed on pages 299–348. And it involves the standards of conciseness, appropriate and exact language, and correct grammar and usage discussed in Chapters 15 through 49.

But public writing has its own conventions, too. They vary widely, depending on what you're writing and why, whether it's a proposal for your job or a flyer for a community group. This chapter covers several types of public writing: business letter format (below), job-application letters (pp. 116–17), résumés (pp. 117–20), memos (pp. 120–121), and electronic communication (pp. 121–22). See Chapter 7 on document design for pointers on type fonts, page layout, headings, and other elements of business documents.

ESL Business writing in your native culture may differ from Canadian business writing. For instance, writers may be expected to begin with polite questions about the addressee or with compliments for the addressee's company. When writing to Canadian businesspeople, get right to the point, even if at first your opening sounds abrupt or even impolite. See the examples opposite and on page 121.

(14a) Writing business letters and résumés

1 Business letter format

For any business letter, use either unlined white paper measuring 8½″ x 11″ or what is called letterhead stationery with your address printed at the top of the sheet. Type the letter single-spaced (with double space between elements) on only one side of a sheet.

A common form for business letters is illustrated on the facing page.

- The RETURN-ADDRESS HEADING gives your address (but not your name) and the date. (If you are using stationery with a printed heading, you need only give the date.) Place your heading at least an inch from the top of the page. Align the heading at the left margin.

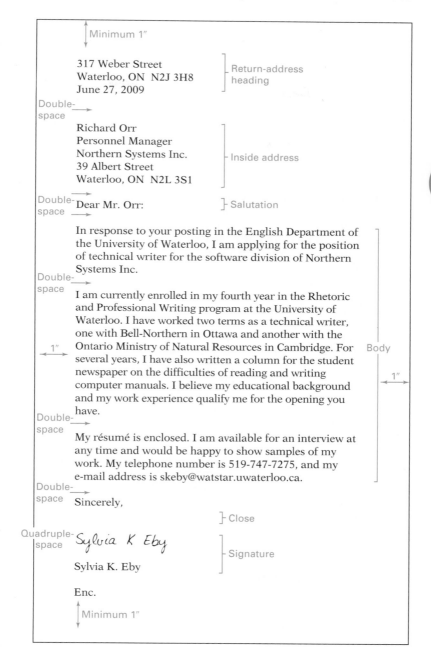

Minimum 1"

317 Weber Street
Waterloo, ON N2J 3H8
June 27, 2009

Return-address heading

Double-space

Richard Orr
Personnel Manager
Northern Systems Inc.
39 Albert Street
Waterloo, ON N2L 3S1

Inside address

14a

Double-space Dear Mr. Orr:

Salutation

In response to your posting in the English Department of
the University of Waterloo, I am applying for the position
of technical writer for the software division of Northern
Systems Inc.

Double-space

I am currently enrolled in my fourth year in the Rhetoric
and Professional Writing program at the University of
Waterloo. I have worked two terms as a technical writer,
one with Bell-Northern in Ottawa and another with the
Ontario Ministry of Natural Resources in Cambridge. For
several years, I have also written a column for the student
newspaper on the difficulties of reading and writing
computer manuals. I believe my educational background
and my work experience qualify me for the opening you
have.

Body

1"

1"

Double-space

My résumé is enclosed. I am available for an interview at
any time and would be happy to show samples of my
work. My telephone number is 519-747-7275, and my
e-mail address is skeby@watstar.uwaterloo.ca.

Double-space Sincerely,

Close

Quadruple-space Sylvia K Eby

Sylvia K. Eby

Signature

Enc.

Minimum 1"

- The INSIDE ADDRESS shows the name, title, and complete address of the person you are writing to. Place the address at least two lines below the return-address heading.
- The SALUTATION greets the addressee. Position it at the left margin, two lines below the inside address and two lines above the body of the letter. Follow it with a colon. Whenever possible, address your letter to a specific person. (Call the company or department to ask whom to address your letter to.) If you can't find a person's name, then use a job title (*Dear Human Resources Manager, Dear Customer Service Manager*) or use a general salutation (*Dear Smythe Shoes*). Use *Ms.* as the title for a woman when she has no other title, when you don't know how she prefers to be addressed, or when you know that she prefers *Ms.*
- The BODY of the letter, containing its substance, begins at the left margin. Instead of indenting the first line of each paragraph, insert an extra line of space between paragraphs.
- The letter's CLOSE begins two lines below the last line of the body and aligns at the left margin. The close should reflect the level of formality in the salutation: *Respectfully, Cordially, Yours truly,* and *Sincerely* are more formal closes; *Regards* and *Best wishes* are less formal. Capitalize only the first word, and follow the close with a comma.
- The SIGNATURE falls below the close and has two parts: your name typed four lines below the close, and your handwritten signature in the space between. Give your name as you sign cheques and other documents.
- Below the signature at the left margin, you may want to include additional information such as *Enc.* (indicating an enclosure with the letter) or *cc: Margaret Zusky* (indicating that a copy is being sent to the person named).

Use an envelope that will accommodate the letter once it is folded horizontally in thirds. The envelope should show your name and address in the upper left corner and the addressee's name, title, and address in the centre. For easy machine reading, Canada Post recommends all capital letters and no punctuation (spaces separate the elements on a line, with two spaces before the postal code), as in this address:

RICHARD ORR
PERSONNEL MANAGER
NORTHERN SYSTEMS INC
39 ALBERT ST
WATERLOO ON N2L 3S1

2   Job-application letter

The sample on the previous page illustrates the key features of a job-application letter:

14a

- The letter should be an interpretation of your résumé for a particular job, not a detailed account of the entire résumé. Instead of reciting your job history, highlight and reshape only the relevant parts.
- Announce at the outset what job you seek and how you heard about it.
- Include any special reason you have for applying, such as a specific career goal.
- Summarize your qualifications for this particular job, including relevant facts about education and employment history and emphasizing notable accomplishments. Mention that additional information appears in an accompanying résumé.
- At the end of the letter, mention that you are available for an interview at the convenience of the addressee, or specify when you will be available (for instance, when your current job or classes leave you free, or when you could travel to the employer's city).

14a

3   Résumé

For the résumé that accompanies your letter of application, you can use the guidelines below and the samples on the next two pages. (The samples illustrate only one possible organization; another, for instance, arranges employment history not by job but by functions and skills).

- Provide the following, in table form: your name, postal address, phone number, and e-mail address; career objective; education; employment history; any special skills or awards; and information about how to obtain your references. (See the sample on the next page.)
- Use headings to mark the various sections of the résumé, spacing around them and within sections so that important information stands out.
- Usage varies on capital letters in résumés. Keep in mind that passages with many capitals can be hard to read. Definitely use capitals for proper nouns (pp. 288–89), but consider dropping them for job titles, course names, department names, and the like.
- Limit your résumé to one page so that it can be quickly reviewed. However, if your experience and education are extensive, a two-page résumé is preferable to a single cramped, unreadable page.
- If you are submitting a printed résumé, you may want to use some of the techniques of document design discussed on pages 52–63. On the next two pages, the sample résumé appears both in a traditional format and in a more contemporary design.

14a

Sylvia K. Eby
317 Weber Street
Waterloo, Ontario N2J 3H8
519-747-7275
skeby@watstar.uwaterloo.ca

Position desired
Technical writer.

Education
University of Waterloo, 2005 to present.
Year: fourth.
Major: English (Rhetoric and Professional Writing).

Kitchener Collegiate Institute, 2000–2005.
Graduated with OAC standing.

Employment history
The Imprint, student newspaper of University of Waterloo,
2006 to present. Responsibilities include writing weekly
column.

Bell-Northern, Ottawa, summer 2007. Responsibilities
included writing manuals for telephone equipment.

Ontario Ministry of Natural Resources, Cambridge,
summer 2006. Responsibilities included designing and
writing pamphlets on conservation.

Special skills
Fluent in French.
Proficient in Internet research and Web design.

References
Available upon request: Placement Office
                               University of Waterloo
                               Waterloo, ON N2L 3G1

Sylvia K. Eby   317 Weber Street
                                    Waterloo, Ontario N2J 3H8
                                             519-747-7275
                                    skeby@watstar.uwaterloo.ca

---

**Position
desired**   Technical writer

Education   *University of Waterloo*, 2005 to present
                  Current standing: fourth year
                  Major: English (Rhetoric and Professional Writing)
                  Technical writing courses: writing online, arts
                  writing, the rhetoric of Web design, the rhetoric
                  of text and image

                  Kitchener Collegiate Institute, 2000–2005
                  Graduated with OAC standing

Employment   2006 to present. Reporter, The Imprint, student
                  newspaper of the University of Waterloo. Write
                  regular column on Internet and online issues.

                  Summer 2007. Technical writer. Bell-Northern,
                  Ottawa. Wrote manuals for telephone equipment.

                  Summer 2006. Technical writer. Ontario Ministry of
                  Natural Resources, Cambridge. Wrote and
                  designed pamphlets on conservation.

Special skills Fluent in French.
                    Proficient in Internet research and Web design.

References   Available on request:

                  Placement Office
                  University of Waterloo
                  Waterloo, ON N2L 3G1

14a

Employers often want an electronic version of a résumé so that they can add it to a computerized database of applicants. The employers may scan your printed résumé to convert it to an electronic file, or they may request electronic copy from you in the first place. If you think a potential employer may use an electronic version of your résumé, follow these additional guidelines:

- Keep the design simple so that the résumé can be read accurately by a scanner or transmitted accurately by electronic mail. Avoid images, unusual type, more than one column, vertical or horizontal lines, and highlighting (boldface, italic, or underlining). If its highlighting was removed, the traditionally designed sample on page 118 could probably be scanned or transmitted electronically. The two-column sample on page 119 perhaps could not.
- Use concise, specific words to describe your skills and experience. The employer's computer may use keywords (often nouns) to identify the résumés of suitable job candidates, and you want to ensure that your résumé includes the appropriate keywords. Name your specific skills—for example, the computer programs you can operate—and write concretely with words like *manager* (not *person with responsibility for*) and *reporter* (not *staff member who reports*). Look for likely keywords in the employer's description of the job you seek.

(14b) Writing business memos

Business memorandums (memos, for short) address people within the same organization. A memo can be quite long, but more often it deals briefly with a specific topic, such as an answer to a question, a progress report, or an evaluation.

Both the form and the structure of a memo are designed to get to the point and dispose of it quickly (see the sample on the facing page). State your reason for writing in the first sentence. Devote the first paragraph to a concise presentation of your answer, conclusion, or evaluation. In the rest of the memo explain your reasoning or evidence. Use headings or lists as appropriate to highlight key information.

Most companies have their own conventions for memo formats. The heading usually consists of the company name, the addressee's name, the writer's name (initialled in handwriting), the date, and a subject description or title. (See the sample.) The body of the memo is usually single-spaced, with double spacing between paragraphs and no paragraph indentions. An indication of who receives copies of the memo can be given two spaces below the last line of the body.

Bigelow Wax Company

TO: Aileen Rosen, Director of Sales
FROM: Patricia Phillips, Territory 12 *PP*
DATE: March 17, 2009
SUBJECT: 2008 sales of Quick Wax in Territory 12

Since it was introduced in January of 2008, Quick Wax has been unsuccessful in Territory 12 and has not affected the sales of our Easy Shine. Discussions with customers and my own analysis of Quick Wax suggest three reasons for its failure to compete with our product.

1. Quick Wax has not received the promotion necessary for a new product. Advertising—primarily on radio—has been sporadic and has not developed a clear, consistent image for the product. In addition, the Quick Wax sales representative in Territory 12 is new and inexperienced; he is not known to customers, and his sales pitch (which I once overheard) is weak. As far as I can tell, his efforts are not supported by phone calls or mailings from his home office.

2. When Quick Wax does make it to the store shelves, buyers do not choose it over our product. Though priced competitively with our product, Quick Wax is poorly packaged. The container seems smaller than ours, though in fact it holds the same eight ounces. The lettering on the Quick Wax package (red on blue) is difficult to read, in contrast to the white-on-green lettering on the Easy Shine package.

3. Our special purchase offers and my increased efforts to serve existing customers have had the intended effect of keeping customers satisfied with our product and reducing their inclination to stock something new.

Copies: L. Mendes, Director of Marketing
         L. MacGregor, Customer Service Manager

14c

(14c) Communicating electronically

Communicating via electronic devices, especially electronic mail and fax machines, speeds up correspondence but also creates new challenges. These challenges can be addressed by understanding that electronic communication is much the same as any other form of more traditional communication. Generally, the standards for business e-mail are the same as for other business correspondence.

Faxes follow closely the formats of print documents, whether letters (p. 115) or memos (pp. 120–21). But there are some key differences:

- Small type, photographs, horizontal lines, and other elements that look fine on your copy may not be legible to the addressee.
- Most faxes require a cover sheet with fax-specific information: the addressee's name, company, and fax number; the date, time, and subject; your own name and fax and telephone numbers (the telephone number is important in case something goes wrong with the transmission); and the total number of pages (including the cover sheet) in the fax.
- Because fax transmissions can go astray, it's often wise to advise your addressee to expect a fax. Such advice is essential if the fax is confidential, because the machine is often shared.
- Transmission by fax can imply that the correspondence is urgent. If yours isn't, consider using the mail. (Swamping your correspondents with needless faxes can make you the child who cried wolf when you really have an urgent message to transmit.)

14c

3 Clarity and Style

3 Clarity and Style

15 Emphasis

Emphatic writing leads readers to see your main ideas both within and among sentences. You can achieve emphasis by attending to your subjects and verbs (below), using sentence beginnings and endings (p. 125), coordinating equally important ideas (p. 127), and subordinating less important ideas (p. 129). In addition, emphatic writing is concise writing, the subject of Chapter 20.

Note Many computerized grammar and style checkers can spot some problems with emphasis, such as nouns made from verbs, passive voice, wordy phrases, and long sentences that may also be flabby and unemphatic. However, the checkers cannot help you identify the important ideas in your sentences or whether those ideas receive appropriate emphasis.

(15a) Using subjects and verbs effectively

The heart of every sentence is its subject, which usually names the actor, and its verb, which usually specifies the subject's action: *Children* [subject] *grow* [verb]. When these elements do not identify the key actor and action in the sentence, readers must find that information elsewhere and the sentence may be wordy and unemphatic.

In the following sentences, the subjects and verbs are underlined.

UNEMPHATIC   The intention of the company was to expand its workforce. A proposal was also made to diversify the backgrounds and abilities of employees.

These sentences are unemphatic because their key ideas (the company's intending and proposing) do not appear in their subjects and verbs. Revised, the sentences are not only clearer but more concise:

_KEY TERMS_____

SUBJECT Who or what a sentence is about: *Biologists often study animals.* (See p. 167.)

VERB The part of a sentence that asserts something about the subject: *Biologists often study animals.* (See p. 162.)

REVISED   The <u>company intended</u> to expand its workforce.
               It also <u>proposed</u> to diversify the backgrounds
               and abilities of employees.

Several constructions can drain meaning from a sentence's
subject and verb:

- Nouns made from verbs can obscure the key actions of
  sentences and add words. These nouns include *intention* (from
  intend), *proposal* (from *propose*), *decision* (from *decide*),
  expectation (from *expect*), *persistence* (from *persist*), *argument*
  (from *argue*), and *inclusion* (from *include*).

  UNEMPHATIC   After the company made a <u>decision</u> to hire more
                 disabled workers, its next step was the <u>construc-</u>
                 <u>tion</u> of wheelchair ramps and other facilities.
  REVISED   After the company <u>decided</u> to hire more dis-
                 abled workers, it next <u>constructed</u> wheelchair
                 ramps and other facilities.

- Weak verbs, such as *made* and *was* in the unemphatic sentence
  above, tend to stall sentences just where they should be moving
  and often bury key actions:

  UNEMPHATIC   The company <u>is</u> now the leader among busi-
                 nesses in complying with the 2001 Disabilities
                 Act. Its officers <u>make</u> frequent speeches on the
                 Act to business groups.
  REVISED   The company now <u>leads</u> other businesses in
                 complying with the 2001 Disabilities Act. Its
                 officers frequently <u>speak</u> on the Act to business
                 groups.

- Don't try to eliminate every use of *be, have,* or *make: be* and
  have are essential as helping verbs (*is going, has written*); *be*
  links subjects and words describing them (*Planes are noisy*);
  and *have* and *make* have independent meanings (among them
  "possess" and "force," respectively). But do consider replacing
  forms of *be, have,* and *make* when one of the words following
  the verb could be made into a strong verb itself, as in these
  examples:

emph
15a

___ KEY TERMS _____

NOUN A word that names a person, thing, quality, place, or idea:
student, desk, happiness, city, democracy. (See pp. 160–61.)

HELPING VERB A verb used with another verb to convey time, obliga-
tion, and other meanings: <u>*was* drilling</u>, <u>*would have been* drilling</u>. (See
p. 163.)

Unemphatic	Emphatic
was influential	influenced
is a glorification	glorifies
have a preference	prefer
had the appearance	appeared, seemed
made a claim	claimed

- Verbs in the passive voice state actions received by, not performed by, their subjects. Thus the passive de-emphasizes the true actor of the sentence, sometimes omitting it entirely. Generally, prefer the active voice, in which the subject performs the verb's action. (See also p. 199.)

UNEMPHATIC   The 2001 law is seen by most businesses as fair, but the costs of complying have sometimes been exaggerated.

REVISED   Most businesses see the 2001 law as fair, but some opponents have exaggerated the costs of complying.

(15b)   Using sentence beginnings and endings

emph
15b

Readers automatically seek a writer's principal meaning in the main clause of a sentence—essentially, in the subject that names the actor and the verb that usually specifies the action. (See p. 123.) Thus you can help readers understand your intended meaning by controlling the information in your subjects and the relation of the main clause to any modifiers attached to it.

Old and new information

Generally, readers expect the beginning of a sentence to contain information that they already know or that you have already introduced. They then look to the ending for new information. In the

_ KEY TERMS _____

PASSIVE VOICE The verb form when the subject names the *receiver* of the verb's action: *The house was destroyed by the tornado.*

ACTIVE VOICE The verb form when the subject names the *performer* of the verb's action: *The tornado destroyed the house.*

MAIN CLAUSE A word group that can stand alone as a sentence, containing a subject and a verb and not beginning with a subordinating word: *The books were expensive.* (See pp. 174–75.)

MODIFIER A word or word group that describes another word or word group—for example, *sweet* candy, *running in the park*. (See pp. 164 and 171–72.)

unemphatic passage below, the subjects of the second and third sentences both begin with new topics (underlined) while the old topics (the controversy and education) appear at the ends of the sentences:

> UNEMPHATIC   Education almost means controversy these days, with rising costs and constant complaints about its inadequacies. But the value of schooling should not be obscured by the controversy. The single best means of economic advancement, despite its shortcomings, remains education.

In the more emphatic revision, the underlined old information begins each sentence and new information ends the sentence. The passage follows the pattern A→B. B→C. C→D.

> REVISED   Education almost means controversy these days, with rising costs and constant complaints about its inadequacies. But the controversy should not obscure the value of schooling. Education remains, despite its shortcomings, the single best means of economic advancement.

emph
15b

Cumulative and periodic sentences

You can call attention to information by placing it first or last in a sentence, reserving the middle for incidentals:

> UNEMPHATIC   Education remains the single best means of economic advancement, despite its shortcomings. [Emphasizes shortcomings.]
>
> REVISED   Despite its shortcomings, education remains the single best means of economic advancement. [Emphasizes advancement more than shortcomings.]
>
> REVISED   Education remains, despite its shortcomings, the single best means of economic advancement. [De-emphasizes shortcomings.]

A sentence that begins with the main clause and then adds modifiers is called CUMULATIVE because it accumulates information as it proceeds:

> CUMULATIVE   Education has no equal in opening minds, instilling values, and creating opportunities.

CUMULATIVE   Most of the Great American Desert is made up
of bare rock, rugged cliffs, mesas, canyons,
mountains, separated from one another by
broad flat basins covered with sun-baked mud
and alkali, supporting a sparse and measured
growth of sagebrush or creosote or saltbush,
depending on location and elevation.
—EDWARD ABBEY

The opposite kind of sentence, called PERIODIC, saves the main clause until just before the end (the period) of the sentence. Everything before the main clause points toward it:

PERIODIC   In opening minds, instilling values, and creating
opportunities, education has no equal.
PERIODIC   With people from all over the world—Koreans,
Jamaicans, Vietnamese, Haitians, and
Chinese—the Canadian mosaic is continually
changing.

The periodic sentence creates suspense for readers by reserving important information for the end. But readers should already have an idea of the sentence's subject—because it was discussed or introduced in the preceding sentence—so that they know what the opening modifiers describe.

coord

15c

(15c) Using coordination

Use COORDINATION to show that two or more elements in a sentence are equally important in meaning.

- Link two main clauses with a comma and a coordinating conjunction, such as *and* or *but*:

  The Parliament Buildings in Ottawa were almost completely destroyed by fire in 1916, <u>but</u> they were rebuilt shortly after.

KEY TERMS

COORDINATING CONJUNCTIONS *And, but, or, nor,* and sometimes *for, so, yet.* (See p. 166.)

CONJUNCTIVE ADVERBS Modifiers that describe the relation of the ideas in two clauses, such as *hence, however, indeed,* and *thus.* (See pp. 241–42.)

- Link two main clauses with a semicolon alone or a semicolon and a conjunctive adverb, such as *however*:

  The general structure of the building remained the same; <u>however</u>, the scale was slightly modified.

- Within clauses, link words and phrases with a coordinating conjunction, such as *and* or *or*:

  The gothic arches <u>and</u> the central tower were sharpened <u>or</u> given more prominence in the new design.

Note Computerized grammar and style checkers may spot some errors in punctuating coordinated elements, and they can flag long sentences that may contain excessive coordination. But otherwise they provide little help with coordination because they cannot recognize the relations among ideas in sentences. You'll need to weigh and clarify those relations yourself.

1   Coordinating to relate equal ideas

coord

15c

Coordination shows the equality between elements, as illustrated above. At the same time as it clarifies meaning, it can also help smooth choppy sentences:

CHOPPY
SENTENCES
We should not rely so heavily on oil. Coal and uranium are also overused. We have a substantial energy resource in the moving waters of our rivers. Smaller streams add to the total volume of water. The resource renews itself. Coal and oil are irreplaceable. Uranium is also irreplaceable. The cost of water does not increase much over time. The costs of coal, oil, and uranium rise dramatically.

The revision groups coal, oil, and uranium and clearly opposes them to water (the connecting words are underlined):

IDEAS
COORDINATED
We should not rely so heavily on coal, oil, <u>and</u> uranium, <u>for</u> we have a substantial energy resource in the moving waters of our rivers <u>and</u> streams. Coal, oil, <u>and</u> uranium are irreplaceable <u>and</u> thus subject to dramatic cost increases; water, <u>however</u>, is self-renewing <u>and</u> more stable in cost.

___ KEY TERM _____

CORRELATIVE CONJUNCTIONS Pairs of connecting words, such as *both . . . and, either . . . or, not only . . . but also.* (See p. 166.)

2 Coordinating effectively

Use coordination only to express the *equality* of ideas or details. A string of coordinated elements—especially main clauses—implies that all points are equally important:

EXCESSIVE COORDINATION   We were near the end of the trip, and the storm kept getting worse, and the snow and ice covered the windshield, and I could hardly see the road ahead, and I knew I should stop, but I kept on driving, and once I barely missed a truck.

Such a passage needs editing to stress the important points (underlined below) and to de-emphasize the less important information:

REVISED   As we neared the end of the trip, <u>the storm kept getting worse</u>, covering the windshield with snow and ice until I could barely see the road ahead. Even though I knew I should stop, <u>I kept on driving</u>, once barely missing a truck. [The revision uses main clauses only for the main ideas, underlined.]

Even within a single sentence, coordination should express a logical equality between ideas:

FAULTY   John Stuart Mill was a nineteenth-century utilitarian, and he believed that actions should be judged by their usefulness or by the happiness they cause. [The two clauses are not separate and equal: the second expands on the first by explaining what a utilitarian such as Mill believed.]

REVISED   John Stuart Mill, <u>a nineteenth-century utilitarian</u>, believed that actions should be judged by their usefulness or by the happiness they cause.

sub

15d

15d Using subordination

Use SUBORDINATION to indicate that some elements in a sentence are less important than others for your meaning. Usually, the main idea appears in the main clause, and supporting details appear in subordinate structures:

• Use a subordinate clause beginning with *although, because, if, who* (*whom*), *that, which,* or another subordinating word:

┌──── less important (subordinate clause) ────┐ more important
                                                ┌── (main clause) ──┐
Although production costs have declined, they are still high.

less important
(subordinate clause)

Costs, which include labour and facilities, are difficult to control.

more important (main clause)

- Use a phrase:

less important   more important
(phrase)   (main clause)

Despite some decline, production costs are still high.

less important (phrase)

Costs, including labour and facilities, are difficult to control.

more important (main clause)

- Use a single word:

Declining costs have not matched prices.
Labour costs are difficult to control.

Note Computerized grammar and style checkers may spot some errors in punctuating subordinated elements, and they can flag long sentences that may contain excessive subordination. But otherwise they provide little help with subordination because they cannot recognize the relations among ideas in sentences. You'll need to weigh and clarify those relations yourself.

sub
15d

1   Subordinating to emphasize main ideas

A string of main clauses can make everything in a passage seem equally important:

STRING OF   In recent years computer prices have dropped,
MAIN CLAUSES and production costs have dropped more slowly,
             and computer manufacturers have had to strug-
             gle, for their profits have been shrinking.

Emphasis comes from keeping the truly important information in the main clause (underlined) and subordinating the less important details:

REVISED   Because production costs have dropped more
           slowly than prices in recent years, computer
           manufacturers have had to struggle with shrink-
           ing profits.

___KEY TERMS___

SUBORDINATE CLAUSE A word group that contains a subject and a verb, begins with a subordinating word such as *because* or *who,* and is not a question: *Words can do damage when they hurt feelings.* (See pp. 173–74.)

PHRASE A word group that lacks a subject or verb or both: *Words can do damage by hurting feelings.* (See p. 170.)

2 Subordinating effectively

Use subordination only for the less important information in a sentence.

FAULTY   Ms. Angelo was in her first year of teaching, although she was a better instructor than others with many years of experience.

The sentence above suggests that Angelo's inexperience is the main idea, whereas the writer intended to stress her skill *despite* her inexperience. Subordinating the inexperience and elevating the skill to the main clause (underlined) gives appropriate emphasis:

REVISED   Although Ms. Angelo was in her first year of teaching, <u>she was a better instructor than others with many years of experience.</u>

Subordination loses its power to organize and emphasize when too much loosely related detail crowds into one long sentence:

OVERLOADED The boats that were moored at the dock when the hurricane, which was one of the worst in three decades, struck were ripped from their moorings, because the owners had not been adequately prepared, since the weather service had predicted the storm would blow out to sea, which they do at this time of year.

The revision stresses important information in the main clauses (underlined):

REVISED   Struck by one of the worst hurricanes in three decades, <u>the boats at the dock were ripped from their moorings. The owners were unprepared</u> because the weather service had said that hurricanes at this time of year blow out to sea.

sub

15d

16 Parallelism

PARALLELISM is a similarity of grammatical form for similar elements of meaning within a sentence or among sentences.

> The air is dirtied by <u>factories belching smoke</u>
> and
> <u>cars spewing exhaust</u>.

In this example the two underlined phrases have the same function and importance (both specify sources of air pollution), so they also have the same grammatical construction. Parallelism makes form follow meaning.

Note A computerized grammar and style checker cannot recognize faulty parallelism because it cannot recognize the relations among ideas. You will need to find and revise problems with parallelism on your own.

// 16a

16a Using parallelism with *and, but, or, nor, yet*

The coordinating conjunctions *and, but, or, nor,* and *yet* always signal a need for parallelism:

> The industrial base was <u>shifting</u> and <u>shrinking</u>. [Parallel words.]
>
> Politicians rarely <u>acknowledged the problem</u> or <u>proposed alternatives</u>. [Parallel phrases.]
>
> Industrial workers were understandably disturbed <u>that they were losing their jobs</u> and <u>that no one seemed to care</u>. [Parallel clauses.]

When sentence elements linked by coordinating conjunctions are not parallel in structure, the sentence is awkward and distracting:

> NONPARALLEL   Three reasons why steel companies kept losing money were that their plants were inefficient, high labour costs, and foreign competition was increasing.

KEY TERM

COORDINATING CONJUNCTIONS Words that connect elements of the same kind and importance: *and, but, or, nor,* and sometimes *for, so, yet*. (See p. 166.)

REVISED	Three reasons why steel companies kept losing money were <u>inefficient plants</u>, high labour costs, and <u>increasing foreign competition</u>.
NONPARALLEL	Success was difficult even for efficient companies because of the shift away from all manufacturing in Canada and the fact that steel production was shifting toward emerging nations.
REVISED	Success was difficult even for efficient companies because of the shift away from all manufacturing in Canada and <u>toward steel production in emerging nations</u>.

All the words required by idiom or grammar must be stated in compound constructions (see also p. 151):

| FAULTY | Given training, workers can acquire the skills and interest in other jobs. [Idiom dictates different prepositions with *skills* and *interest*.] |
| REVISED | Given training, workers can acquire the skills <u>for</u> and interest <u>in</u> other jobs. |

(16b) Using parallelism with *both . . . and, not . . . but*, or another correlative conjunction

Correlative conjunctions stress equality and balance between elements. Parallelism confirms the equality.

> It is not <u>a tax bill</u> but <u>a tax relief bill</u>, providing relief not <u>for the needy</u> but <u>for the greedy</u>.
> —FRANKLIN DELANO ROOSEVELT

With correlative conjunctions, the element after the second connector must match the element after the first connector:

| NONPARALLEL | Huck Finn learns not only that human beings have an enormous capacity for folly but also enormous dignity. [The first element includes *that human beings have;* the second element does not.] |
| REVISED | Huck Finn learns <u>that human beings have</u> not only an enormous capacity for folly but also enormous dignity. [Repositioning *that human beings have* makes the two elements parallel.] |

KEY TERM

CORRELATIVE CONJUNCTIONS Pairs of words that connect elements of the same kind and importance, such as *both . . . and, either . . . or, neither . . . nor, not . . . but, not only . . . but also.* (See p. 166.)

//
16b

(16c) Using parallelism in comparisons

Parallelism confirms the likeness or difference between two elements being compared using *than* or *as:*

NONPARALLEL   Huck Finn proves less a bad boy than to be an independent spirit. In the end he is every bit as determined in rejecting help as he is to leave for "the territory."

REVISED   Huck Finn proves less a bad boy than <u>an independent spirit</u>. In the end he is every bit as determined <u>to reject help</u> as he is to leave for "the territory."

(See also p. 222 on making comparisons logical.)

(16d) Using parallelism with lists, headings, and outlines

The items in a list or outline are coordinate and should be parallel. Parallelism is essential in the headings that divide a paper into sections (see pp. 58–59) and in a formal topic outline (p. 19).

Nonparallel	Revised
Changes in Renaissance England	Changes in Renaissance England
1. Extension of trade routes	1. Extension of trade routes
2. Merchant class became more powerful	2. <u>Increased power</u> of the merchant class
3. The death of feudalism	3. <u>Death</u> of feudalism
4. Upsurging of the arts	4. <u>Upsurge</u> of the arts
5. Religious quarrels began	5. <u>Rise</u> of religious quarrels

//
16d

17 Variety and Details

Writing that's interesting as well as clear has at least two features: the sentences vary in length and structure, and they are well textured with details.

Note Some computerized grammar and style checkers will flag long sentences, and you can check for appropriate variety in a series of such sentences. But generally these programs cannot help you see where variety may be needed because they cannot recognize the relative importance and complexity of your ideas. Nor can they suggest where you should add details. To edit for variety and detail, you need to listen to your sentences and determine whether they clarify your meaning.

17a Varying sentence length

In most contemporary writing, sentences tend to vary from about ten to about forty words, with an average of between fifteen and twenty-five words. If your sentences are all at one extreme or the other, your readers may have difficulty focusing on main ideas and seeing the relations among them:

- If most of your sentences contain thirty-five words or more, your main ideas may not stand out from the details that support them. Break some of the long sentences into shorter, simpler ones.
- If most of your sentences contain fewer than ten or fifteen words, all your ideas may seem equally important and the links between them may not be clear. Try combining them with coordination (p. 127) and subordination (p. 129) to show relationships and stress main ideas over supporting information.

___ KEY TERM ___

MAIN CLAUSE A word group that contains a subject and a verb and does not begin with a subordinating word: *Tourism is an industry. It brings in over $2 billion a year.* (See p. 173.)

(17b) Varying sentence structure

A passage will be monotonous if all its sentences follow the same pattern, like soldiers marching in a parade. Try these techniques for varying structure.

1   Subordination

A string of main clauses in simple or compound sentences can be especially plodding:

> MONOTONOUS The moon is now drifting away from the earth. It moves away at the rate of about one inch a year. This movement is lengthening our days. They increase a thousandth of a second every century. Forty-seven of our present days will someday make up a month. We might eventually lose the moon altogether. Such great planetary movement rightly concerns astronomers, but it need not worry us. It will take 50 million years.

Enliven such writing—and make the main ideas stand out—by expressing the less important information in subordinate clauses and phrases. In the revision below, underlining indicates subordinate structures that used to be main clauses:

> REVISED The moon is now drifting away from the earth about one inch a year. At a thousandth of a second every century, this movement is lengthening our days. Forty-seven of our present days will someday make up a month, if we don't eventually lose the moon altogether. Such great planetary movement rightly concerns astronomers, but it need not worry us. It will take 50 million years.

2   Sentence combining

As the preceding example shows, subordinating to achieve variety often involves combining short, choppy sentences into longer units that link related information and stress main ideas. On the following page is another unvaried passage:

___ KEY TERMS _____

SUBORDINATE CLAUSE A word group that contains a subject and verb, begins with a subordinating word such as *because* or *who,* and is not a question: *Tourism is an industry that brings in over $2 billion a year.* (See p. 173.)

PHRASE A word group that lacks a subject or verb or both: *Tourism is an industry valued at over $2 billion a year.* (See p. 170.)

MONOTONOUS   Astronomy may seem a remote science. It may
seem to have little to do with people's daily
lives. Many astronomers find otherwise. They
see their science as soothing. It gives perspective to everyday routines and problems.

Combining five sentences into one, the revision is both clearer and
easier to read. Underlining highlights the many changes:

REVISED   Astronomy may seem a remote science having
little to do with people's daily lives, but many
astronomers find their science soothing because
it gives perspective to everyday routines and
problems.

3   Varied sentence beginnings

An English sentence often begins with its subject, which generally
captures old information from a preceding sentence (see p. 125–26):

The defendant's lawyer was determined to break the prosecution's
witness. He relentlessly cross-examined the stubborn witness for a
week.

However, an unbroken sequence of sentences beginning with the
subject quickly becomes monotonous:

var
17b

MONOTONOUS   The defendant's lawyer was determined to break
the prosecution's witness. He relentlessly cross-
examined the witness for a week. The witness
had expected to be dismissed within an hour
and was visibly irritated. She did not cooperate.
She was reprimanded by the judge.

Beginning some of these sentences with other expressions improves
readability and clarity:

REVISED   The defendant's lawyer was determined to break
the prosecution's witness. For a week he relentlessly cross-examined the witness. Expecting to
be dismissed within an hour, the witness was
visibly irritated. She did not cooperate. Indeed,
she was reprimanded by the judge.

The underlined expressions on the next page represent the most
common choices for varying sentence beginnings:

- Adverb modifiers, such as *For a week* (modifies the verb *cross-examined*).
- Adjective modifiers, such as *Expecting to be dismissed within an hour* (modifies *witness*).
- Transitional expressions, such as *Indeed*. (See pp. 42–43 for a list.)

KEY TERMS

ADVERB A word or word group that describes a verb, an adjective, another adverb, or a whole sentence: *dressed sharply*, *clearly unhappy*, *soaring from the mountain*. (See p. 164.)

ADJECTIVE A word or word group that describes a noun or pronoun: *sweet smile*, *certain someone*. (See p. 164.)

ESL   Placing certain adverb modifiers at the beginning of a sentence requires you to change the normal subject–verb order as well. The most common of these modifiers are negatives, including *seldom, rarely, in no case, not since,* and *not until.*

adverb   noun   verb phrase

FAULTY   Seldom a speaker has held the floor so long.

adverb   helping   main
verb   subject   verb

REVISED   Seldom has a speaker held the floor so long.

4   Varied word order

Occasionally, you can vary a sentence and emphasize it at the same time by inverting the usual order of parts:

A dozen witnesses testified for the prosecution, and the defence lawyer barely questioned eleven of them. The twelfth, however, he grilled. [Normal word order: *He grilled the twelfth, however.*]

Inverted sentences used without need are artificial. Use them only when emphasis demands.

(17c) Adding details

Relevant details such as facts and examples create the texture and life that keep readers awake and help them grasp your meaning. For instance:

FLAT   Created in 1885, Banff National Park stretches along the Continental Divide. Its mountains and valleys are home to thick forests and to herds of mammals and their predators.

DETAILED   Created in 1885, Banff National Park stretches for 240 kilometres along the eastern slope of the Continental Divide. Its mountains and valleys are home to thick forests of lodgepole pine, alpine fir, and blue spruce and to herds of elk, mule deer, and bighorn sheep and their predators, the wolf pack, the cougar, and the dangerous and unpredictable grizzly.

18 Appropriate and Exact Words

The clarity and effectiveness of your writing will depend greatly on the use of words that are appropriate for your writing situation (below) and that express your meaning exactly (p. 144).

18a Choosing the appropriate words

Appropriate words suit your writing situation—your subject, purpose, and audience. In most academic and career writing you should rely on what's called STANDARD ENGLISH, the written English normally expected and used in schools, businesses, government, and other places where people of diverse backgrounds must communicate with one another. Standard English is "standard" not because it is better than other forms of English but because it is accepted as the common language, much as dimes and quarters are accepted as the common currency.

The vocabulary of standard English is huge, allowing expression of an infinite range of ideas and feelings; but it does exclude words that only some groups of people use, understand, or find inoffensive. Some of these more limited vocabularies should be avoided altogether; others should be used cautiously and in relevant situations, as when aiming for a special effect with an audience you know will appreciate it. Whenever you doubt a word's status, consult a dictionary. (See p. 145.)

Note Many computerized grammar and style checkers can be set to flag potentially inappropriate words, such as nonstandard language, slang, colloquialisms, and gender-specific terms (*manmade, mailman*). However, the checker can flag only words listed in its dictionary. And you'll need to determine whether a flagged word is or is not appropriate for your writing situation, as explained on the following pages.

1 Dialect and nonstandard language

Like many countries, Canada includes scores of regional, social, or ethnic groups with their own distinct DIALECTS, or versions of English: standard English, Newfoundland English, Jamaican English, and the dialect of the Ottawa Valley are examples. All the dialects of English share many features, but each also has its own vocabulary, pronunciation, and grammar.

appr
18a

If you speak a dialect of English besides standard English, you need to be careful about using your dialect in situations where standard English is the norm, such as in academic or business writing. Otherwise, your readers may not understand your meaning, or they may perceive your usage as incorrect. (Dialects are not wrong in themselves, but forms imported from one dialect into another may still be perceived as wrong.)

Your participation in the community of standard English does not mean you should abandon your own dialect. Of course, you will want to use it with others who speak it. You may want to quote it in an academic paper (as when analyzing or reporting conversation in dialect). And you may want to use it in writing you do for yourself, such as notes and drafts, which should be composed as freely as possible. But edit your drafts carefully to eliminate dialect expressions, especially those that dictionaries label "nonstandard," such as *eh, inn't, them books, this here rink, right smart, such smart, rink rat, knowed, throwed, could of, ought of, snuck, after saying, didn't never, haven't no, I done, I seen, yous*.

2 Slang

appr
18a

SLANG is the language used by a group, such as musicians or computer programmers, to reflect common experiences and to make technical references efficient. The following example is from an essay on the slang of "skaters" (skateboarders):

> Curtis slashed ultra-punk crunchers on his longboard, while the Rube-man flailed his usual Gumbyness on tweaked frontsides and lofty fakie ollies.
>
> —MILES ORKIN, "Mucho Slingage by the Pool"

Among those who understand it, slang may be vivid and forceful. It often occurs in dialogue, and an occasional slang expression can enliven an informal essay. But most slang is too flippant and imprecise for effective communication, and it is generally inappropriate for college or business writing. Notice the gain in seriousness and precision achieved in the following revision:

SLANG	Many students start out <u>pretty together</u> but then <u>get weird</u>.
REVISED	Many students start out <u>with clear goals</u> but then <u>lose their direction</u>.

3 Colloquial language

COLLOQUIAL LANGUAGE is the everyday spoken language, including expressions such as *get together, go crazy, do the dirty work,* and *get along.*

When you write informally, colloquial language may be appropriate to achieve the casual, relaxed effect of conversation. An occasional colloquial word dropped into otherwise more formal writing can also help you achieve a desired emphasis. But most colloquial language is not precise enough for college or career writing. In such writing you should generally avoid any words and expressions labelled "informal" or "colloquial" in your dictionary.

COLLOQUIAL   According to a Native American myth, the Great Creator had a dog hanging around with him when he created the earth.

REVISED   According to a Native American myth, the Great Creator was accompanied by a dog when he created the earth.

4 Technical words

All disciplines and professions rely on specialized language that allows the members to communicate precisely and efficiently with each other. Chemists, for instance, have their *phosphatides*, and literary critics have their *motifs* and *subtexts*. Without explanation technical words are meaningless to nonspecialists. When you are writing for nonspecialists, avoid unnecessary technical terms and carefully define terms you must use.

5 Indirect and pretentious writing

Small, plain, and direct words are almost always preferable to big, showy, or evasive words. Take special care to avoid euphemisms, double-talk, and pretentious writing.

A EUPHEMISM is a presumably inoffensive word that a writer or speaker substitutes for a word deemed potentially offensive or too blunt, such as *passed away* for *died* or *misspeak* for *lie*. Use euphemisms only when you know that blunt, truthful words would needlessly hurt or offend members of your audience.

A kind of euphemism that deliberately evades the truth is DOUBLE-TALK (also called DOUBLESPEAK): language intended to confuse or to be misunderstood. Today double-talk is unfortunately common in politics and advertising—the *revenue enhancement* that is really a tax, the *peacekeeping function* that is really war making, the *biodegradable* bags that last decades. Double-talk has no place in honest writing.

Euphemism and sometimes double-talk seem to keep company with PRETENTIOUS WRITING, fancy language that is more elaborate than its subject requires. Choose your words for their exactness and economy. The big, ornate word may be tempting, but pass it up. Your readers will be grateful.

PRETENTIOUS   To perpetuate our endeavour of providing funds for our retired citizens as we do at the present moment, we will face the exigency of enhanced contributions from all our citizens.

REVISED   We cannot continue to fund the Canada Pension Plan for retired citizens unless we raise taxes.

appr

18a

6   Sexist and other biased language

Even when we do not mean it to, our language can reflect and perpetuate hurtful prejudices toward groups of people. Such biased language can be obvious—words such as *nigger, frog, mick, kike, fag, dyke,* or *broad*. But it can also be subtle, generalizing about groups in ways that may be familiar but that are also inaccurate or unfair.

Biased language reflects poorly on the user, not on the person or persons whom it mischaracterizes or insults. Unbiased language does not submit to false generalizations. It treats people respectfully as individuals and labels groups as they wish to be labelled.

Stereotypes of race, ethnicity, religion, age, and other characteristics

A STEREOTYPE is a generalization based on poor evidence, a kind of formula for understanding and judging people simply because of their membership in a group:

Men are uncommunicative.
Women are emotional.
Liberals want to raise taxes.
Conservatives are affluent.

appr
18a

At best, stereotypes betray a noncritical writer, one who is not thinking beyond notions received from others. In your writing, be alert for statements that characterize whole groups of people:

STEREOTYPE   Elderly drivers should have their licences limited to daytime driving only. [Asserts that all elderly people are poor night drivers.]
REVISED   Drivers with impaired night vision should have their licences limited to daytime driving only.

Some stereotypes have become part of the language, but they are still potentially offensive:

STEREOTYPE   The administrators are too blind to see the need for a new gymnasium.
REVISED   The administrators do not understand the need for a new gymnasium.

Sexist language

Among the most subtle and persistent biased language is that expressing narrow ideas about men's and women's roles, position, and value in society. Like other stereotypes, this SEXIST LANGUAGE can wound or irritate readers, and it indicates the writer's thoughtlessness or unfairness. The following box suggests some ways of eliminating sexist language:

Eliminating sexist language

- Avoid demeaning and patronizing language:

  SEXIST   Dr. Keith Kim and Lydia Hawkins co-authored the article.

  REVISED   Dr. Keith Kim and Dr. Lydia Hawkins co-authored the article.

  REVISED   Keith Kim and Lydia Hawkins co-authored the article.

  SEXIST   Ladies are entering almost every occupation formerly filled by men.

  REVISED   Women are entering almost every occupation formerly filled by men.

- Avoid occupational or social stereotypes:

  SEXIST   The considerate doctor commends a nurse when she provides his patients with good care.

  REVISED   The considerate doctor commends a nurse who provides good care for patients.

  SEXIST   The grocery shopper should save her coupons.

  REVISED   Grocery shoppers should save their coupons.

- Avoid referring needlessly to gender:

  SEXIST   Marie Curie, a woman chemist, discovered radium.

  REVISED   Marie Curie, a chemist, discovered radium.

  SEXIST   The patients were tended by a male nurse.

  REVISED   The patients were tended by a nurse.

- Avoid using *man* or words containing *man* to refer to all human beings. Here are a few alternatives:

businessman	businessperson
chairman	chair, chairperson
craftsman	craftsperson, artisan
layman	layperson
mankind	humankind, humanity, human beings, humans
manmade	handmade, manufactured, synthetic, artificial
manpower	personnel, human resources
policeman	police officer
salesman	salesperson, sales representative

  SEXIST   Man has not reached the limits of social justice.

  REVISED   Humankind [or Humanity] has not reached the limits of social justice.

  SEXIST   The furniture consists of manmade materials.

  REVISED   The furniture consists of synthetic materials.

- Avoid the GENERIC *HE*, the male pronoun used to refer to both genders. (See also pp. 213–214.)

  SEXIST   The newborn child explores his world.

  REVISED   Newborn children explore their world. [Use the plural for the pronoun and the word it refers to.]

appr
18a

REVISED	The newborn <u>child</u> explores <u>the</u> world. [Avoid the pronoun altogether.]
REVISED	The newborn <u>child</u> explores <u>his or her</u> world. [Substitute male and female pronouns.]

Use the last option sparingly—only once in a group of sentences and only to stress the singular individual.

Appropriate labels

We often need to label groups: *swimmers, politicians, mothers, Christians, Westerners, students.* But labels can be shorthand stereotypes, slighting the person labelled and ignoring the preferences of the group members themselves. Although sometimes dismissed as "political correctness," showing sensitivity about labels hurts no one and helps gain your readers' trust and respect.

- Be careful to avoid labels that (intentionally or not) disparage the person or group you refer to. A person with emotional problems is not a *mental patient.* A person with cancer is not a *cancer victim.* A person using a wheelchair is not *wheelchair-bound.*
- Use names for racial, ethnic, and other groups that reflect the preferences of each group's members, or at least many of them. Examples of current preferences include *Asian Canadian, Latino/Latina* (for Americans or Canadians of Spanish-speaking descent), and *disabled* (rather than *handicapped*). But labels change often. To learn how a group's members wish to be labelled, ask them directly, attend to usage in reputable periodicals, or check a recent dictionary. A helpful reference is Marilyn Schwartz's *Guidelines for Bias-Free Writing* (1995).

exact
18b

(18b) Choosing the exact words

To write clearly and effectively, you will want to find the words that fit your meaning exactly and convey your attitude precisely.

Note A computerized grammar and style checker can provide some help with inexact language. For instance, you can set it to flag commonly confused words (such as *continuous/continual*), misused prepositions in idioms (such as *accuse for* instead of *accuse of*), and clichés. But the checker can flag only words stored in its dictionary. It can't help you at all in using words with appropriate connotations, making abstract words concrete, or solving other problems discussed in this section. You'll need to read your work carefully on your own.

1   Word meanings and synonyms

For writing exactly, a dictionary is essential and a thesaurus can be helpful.

Desk dictionaries

A desk dictionary defines about 150,000 to 200,000 words and provides pronunciation, grammatical functions, history, and other information. Here is a sample from *Merriam-Webster's Collegiate Dictionary:*

Spelling and word division — Pronunciation

reck•on \'re-kən\ *vb* **reck•oned; reck•on•ing** \'re-kə-niŋ, 'rek-niŋ\ — Etymology
[ME *rekenen,* fr. OE *-recenian* (as in *gerecenian* to narrate); akin to OE *reccan*] *vt* (13c) **1 a :** COUNT ⟨~ the days till Christmas⟩ **b :** ESTI-MATE, COMPUTE ⟨~ the height of a building⟩ **c :** to determine by refer-ence to a fixed basis ⟨the existence of the U.S. is ~*ed* from the Declara- — Meanings
tion of Independence⟩ **2 :** to regard or think of as : CONSIDER **3** *chiefly dial :* THINK, SUPPOSE ⟨I ~ I've outlived my time —Ellen Glas- — Quotation and source
gow⟩ ~ *vi* **1 :** to settle accounts **2 :** to make a calculation **3 a :** JUDGE **b** *chiefly dial :* SUPPOSE, THINK **4 :** to accept something as certain : place reliance ⟨I ~ on your promise to help⟩ — **reckon with :** — Idioms
to take into consideration — **reckon without :** to fail to consider : IGNORE

Grammatical functions and forms   Label (*dial=* *dialect*)   Synonym

exact
18b

Good desk dictionaries, in addition to *Merriam-Webster's*, include the *Canadian Oxford Dictionary*, the *Gage Canadian Dictionary*, and *Webster's New World Dictionary*. Most of these are available in both print and electronic form (CD-ROM or online). In addition, the following Web sites provide online dictionaries or links to online dictionaries:

Encyberpedia
http://www.encyberpedia.com/glossary.htm

Internet Public Library
http://www.ipl.org/div/subject/browse/ref28.05.00.html

iTools
http://www.itools.com/lang/

ESL   If English is not your first language, you probably should have a dictionary prepared especially for ESL students, containing special information on prepositions, count versus noncount nouns, and many other matters. Reliable ESL dictionaries include

COBUILD English Language Dictionary, Longman Dictionary of Contemporary English, and *Oxford Advanced Learner's Dictionary.*

Thesauruses

To find a word with the exact shade of meaning you intend, you may want to consult a thesaurus, or book of SYNONYMS—words with approximately the same meaning. A thesaurus such as *Roget's International Thesaurus* lists most imaginable synonyms for thousands of words. The word *news,* for instance, has half a page of synonyms in *Roget's International,* including *tidings, dispatch, gossip,* and *journalism.*

Since a thesaurus aims to open up possibilities, its lists of synonyms include approximate as well as precise matches. The thesaurus does not define synonyms or distinguish among them, however, so you need a dictionary to discover exact meanings. In general, don't use a word from a thesaurus—even one you like the sound of—until you are sure of its appropriateness for your meaning.

Note The Web sites given above for online dictionaries contain links to thesauruses as well. Your word processor may also include a thesaurus, making it easy to look up synonyms and insert the chosen word into your text. But still you should consult a dictionary unless you are certain of the word's meaning.

exact
18b

2   The right word for your meaning

All words have one or more basic meanings (called DENOTATIONS)—the meanings listed in the dictionary, without reference to emotional associations. If readers are to understand you, you must use words according to their established meanings.

- Consult a dictionary whenever you are unsure of a word's meaning.
- Distinguish between similar-sounding words that have widely different denotations:

  INEXACT   Older people often suffer <u>infirmaries</u> [places for the sick].

  EXACT   Older people often suffer <u>infirmities</u> [disabilities].

- Some words, called *homonyms,* sound exactly alike but differ in meaning: for example, *principal/principle* or *rain/reign/rein.* (See pp. 281–82 for a list of commonly confused homonyms.)
- Distinguish between words with related but distinct meanings:

  INEXACT   Television commercials <u>continuously</u> [unceasingly] interrupt programming.

  EXACT   Television commercials <u>continually</u> [regularly] interrupt programming.

In addition to their emotion-free meanings, many words also carry associations with specific feelings. These CONNOTATIONS can shape readers' responses and are thus a powerful tool for writers. The following word pairs have related denotations but very different connotations:

pride: sense of self-worth
vanity: excessive regard for oneself

firm: steady, unchanging, unyielding
stubborn: unreasonable, bullheaded

lasting: long-lived, enduring
endless: without limit, eternal

enthusiasm: excitement
mania: excessive interest or desire

A dictionary can help you track down words with the exact connotations you want. Besides providing meanings, your dictionary may also list and distinguish synonyms to guide your choices. A thesaurus can also help if you use it carefully, as discussed on the previous page.

3   Concrete and specific words

Clear, exact writing balances abstract and general words, which outline ideas and objects, with concrete and specific words, which sharpen and solidify.

exact

18b

- ABSTRACT WORDS name qualities and ideas: *beauty, inflation, management, culture, liberal.* CONCRETE WORDS name things we can know by our five senses of sight, hearing, touch, taste, and smell: *sleek, humming, brick, bitter, musty.*
- GENERAL WORDS name classes or groups of things, such as *buildings, weather,* or *birds,* and include all the varieties of the class. SPECIFIC WORDS limit a general class, such as *buildings,* by naming one of its varieties, such as *skyscraper, Victorian courthouse,* or *hut.*

Abstract and general words are useful in the broad statements that set the course for your writing.

The wild horse in North America has a <u>romantic</u> history.

<u>Relations</u> between the sexes today are more <u>relaxed</u> than they were in the past.

But such statements need development with concrete and specific detail. Detail can turn a vague sentence into an exact one:

VAGUE   The size of his hands made his smallness real. [How big were his hands? How small was he?]

EXACT   Not until I saw his delicate, doll-like hands did I realize that he stood a full head shorter than most other men.

If you write on a computer, you can use its Find function to help you find and revise abstract and general words that you tend to overuse. Examples of such words include *nice, interesting, things, very, good, a lot, a little,* and *some.*

4   Idioms

Idioms are expressions in any language that do not fit the rules for meaning or grammar—for instance, *put up with, plug away at, make off with.*

Idiomatic combinations of verbs or adjectives and prepositions can be confusing for both native and nonnative speakers of English. A number of these pairings are listed below and opposite. (More appear on pp. 187–88.)

ESL Those learning English as a second language are justified in stumbling over its prepositions because their meanings can shift depending on context and because they have so many idiomatic uses. In mastering English prepositions, you probably can't avoid memorization. But you can help yourself by memorizing related groups, such as those below:

- *At/in/on* in expressions of time: Use *at* before actual clock time: *at 8:30.* Use *in* before a month, year, century, or period: *in April, in 1985, in the twenty-first century, in the next month.* Use *on* before a day or date: *on Tuesday, on August 31.*
- *At/in/on* in expressions of place: Use *at* before a specific place or address: *at the school, at 511 Iris Street.* Use *in* before a place with limits or before a city, province, country, or continent: *in the house, in a box, in Winnipeg, in China.* Use *on* to mean "supported by" or "touching the surface of": *on the table, on Iris Street, on page 150.*
- *For/since* in expressions of time: Use *for* before a period of time: *for an hour, for two years.* Use *since* before a specific point in time: *since 1995, since yesterday.*

An ESL dictionary is the best source for the meanings of prepositions; see the recommendations on page 146. In addition, some references focus on prepositions. One is the *Oxford Dictionary of Current Idiomatic English, volume 1: Verbs with Prepositions and Particles.*

exact
18b

Idioms with prepositions

abide by a rule	accuse of a crime
abide in a place or state	accustomed to
according to	adapt from a source
accords with	adapt to a situation

afraid of

agree on a plan
agree to a proposal
agree with a person

angry with

aware of

based on

capable of

certain of

charge for a purchase
charge with a crime

concur in an opinion
concur with a person

contend for a principle
contend with a person

dependent on

differ about or over a question
differ from in some quality
differ with a person

disappointed by or in a person
disappointed in or with a thing

familiar with

identical with or to

impatient at her conduct
impatient for a raise
impatient of restraint
impatient with a person

independent of

infer from

inferior to

involved in a task
involved with a person

oblivious of or to one's
   surroundings
oblivious of something
   forgotten

occupied by a person
occupied in study
occupied with a thing

opposed to

part from a person
part with a possession

prior to

proud of

related to

rewarded by the judge
rewarded for something done
rewarded with a gift

similar to

superior to

wait at a place
wait for a train, a person
wait in a room
wait on a customer

exact

18b

5   Figurative language

FIGURATIVE LANGUAGE (or a FIGURE OF SPEECH) departs from the literal meanings of words, usually by comparing very different ideas or objects:

LITERAL   As I try to write, I can think of nothing to say.
FIGURATIVE   As I try to write, my mind is a slab of black slate.

Imaginatively and carefully used, figurative language can capture meaning more precisely and feelingly than literal language. Here is a figure of speech at work in technical writing (paraphrasing the physicist Edward Andrade):

The molecules in a liquid move continuously like couples on an overcrowded dance floor, jostling each other.

The two most common figures of speech are the simile and the metaphor. Both compare two things of different classes, often one abstract and the other concrete. A SIMILE makes the comparison explicit and usually begins with *like* or *as:*

> The march of social progress is <u>like</u> a large and struggling parade, with the seers and prophets at its head and a smug minority bringing up the rear.
>
> —PIERRE BERTON

A METAPHOR claims that the two things are identical, omitting such words as *like* and *as:*

> Literature is not only a mirror; it is also a map, a geography of the mind.
>
> —MARGARET ATWOOD

To be successful, figurative language must be fresh and unstrained, calling attention not to itself but to the writer's meaning. Be especially wary of mixed metaphors, which combine two or more incompatible figures:

MIXED	Various thorny problems that we try to sweep under the rug continue to bob up all the same.
IMPROVED	Various thorny problems that we try to weed out continue to thrive all the same.

exact
18b

6   Trite expressions

TRITE EXPRESSIONS, or CLICHÉS, are phrases so old and so often repeated that they have become stale. They include the following:

add insult to injury	a needle in a haystack
better late than never	point with pride
cool, calm, and collected	pride and joy
crushing blow	ripe old age
easier said than done	rude awakening
face the music	sadder but wiser
few and far between	shoulder the burden
green with envy	shoulder to cry on
hard as a rock	sneaking suspicion
heavy as lead	stand in awe
hit the nail on the head	strong as an ox
hour of need	thin as a rail
ladder of success	tried and true
moving experience	wise as an owl

Clichés may slide into your drafts while you are trying to find the words for your meaning. To edit clichés, listen to your writing for any expressions that you have heard or used before. You can also supplement your efforts with a computerized style checker, which may include a cliché detector. No such program can flag all possible clichés, though, so you'll have to rely on your own editing as well. When you find a cliché, substitute fresh words of your own or restate the idea in plain language.

19 Completeness

The most serious kind of incomplete sentence is the sentence fragment (see Chapter 35). But sentences are also incomplete when they omit one or more words needed for clarity.

Note Computerized grammar and style checkers will not flag most kinds of incomplete sentences discussed in this section. Only your own careful proofreading can ensure that sentences are complete.

inc
19a

19a Writing complete compounds

You may omit words from a compound construction when the omission will not confuse readers:

> Environmentalists have hopes for alternative fuels and [for] public transportation.
> Some cars will run on electricity and some [will run] on methane.

Such omissions are possible only when the words omitted are common to all the parts of a compound construction. When the parts differ in any way, all words must be included in all parts.

> Our new car gets twenty kilometres per litre; some old cars get as little as five kilometres per litre. [One verb is singular, the other plural.]

___ KEY TERM ___

COMPOUND CONSTRUCTION Two or more elements (words, phrases, clauses) that are equal in importance and that function as a unit: *Rain fell; streams overflowed* (clauses); *dogs and cats* (words).

(19b) Adding needed words

In haste or carelessness, do not omit small words that are needed for clarity:

INCOMPLETE	Regular payroll deductions are a type painless savings. You hardly notice missing amounts, and after period of years the contributions can add a large total.
REVISED	Regular payroll deductions are a type of painless savings. You hardly notice the missing amounts, and after a period of years the contributions can add up to a large total.

Attentive proofreading is the only insurance against this kind of omission. *Proofread all your papers carefully.* See pages 30–31 for tips.

ESL If your native language is not English, you may have difficulty knowing when to use the English articles *a, an,* and *the.* For guidelines on using articles, see pages 225–26.

con
20

20 Conciseness

Concise writing makes every word count. Conciseness is not the same as mere brevity: detail and originality should not be cut along with needless words. Rather, the length of an expression should be appropriate to the thought.

You may find yourself writing wordily when you are unsure of your subject or when your thoughts are tangled. It's fine, even necessary, to stumble and grope while drafting. But you should straighten out your ideas and eliminate wordiness during revision and editing.

Note Any computerized grammar and style checker will identify at least some wordy structures, such as repeated words, weak verbs, passive voice, and *there is* and *it is* constructions. No checker can identify all these structures, however; nor can it tell you whether the structure is appropriate for your ideas. In short, a checker can't substitute for your own careful reading and editing.

ESL As you'll see in the examples that follow, wordiness is not a problem of incorrect grammar. A sentence may be perfectly grammatical but still contain unneeded words that interfere with the clarity and force of your idea.

(20a) Focusing on the subject and verb

Using the subjects and verbs of your sentences for the key actors and actions will reduce words and emphasize important ideas. (See pp. 123–25 for more on this topic.)

> **WORDY**   The <u>reason</u> why most of the country shifts to daylight saving time <u>is</u> that winter days are much shorter than summer days.
>
> **CONCISE**   Most of the <u>country</u> <u>shifts</u> to daylight saving time because winter days are much shorter than summer days.

Ways to achieve conciseness

con
20a

Wordy (87 words)

The highly pressured <u>nature</u> of critical-care nursing is <u>due to the fact</u> that the patients have life-threatening illnesses. Critical-care nurses must have possession of steady nerves to care for patients who are critically ill and very sick. The nurses must also have possession of interpersonal skills. They must also have medical skills. It is considered by most health-care professionals that these nurses are essential if there is to be improvement of patients who are now in critical care from that status to the status of intermediate care.

— Focus on subject and verb (p. 153), and cut or shorten empty words and phrases (p. 154).

— Avoid nouns made from verbs (p. 154).

— Cut unneeded repetition (p. 155).

— Combine sentences (p. 156).

— Change passive voice to active voice (p. 154).

— Eliminate *there is* constructions (p. 156).

— Cut unneeded repetition (155), and reduce clauses and phrases (p. 156).

Concise (37 words)

Critical-care nursing is highly pressured because the patients have life-threatening illnesses. Critical-care nurses must possess steady nerves and interpersonal and medical skills. Most health-care professionals consider these nurses essential if patients are to improve to intermediate care.

Focusing on subjects and verbs will also help you avoid several other causes of wordiness discussed further on pages 123–25:

Nouns made from verbs

WORDY   The <u>occurrence</u> of the winter solstice, the shortest day of the year, <u>is</u> an event occurring about December 22.

CONCISE The winter <u>solstice</u>, the shortest day of the year, <u>occurs</u> about December 22.

Weak verbs

WORDY   The earth's axis <u>has</u> a tilt as the planet <u>is</u> in orbit around the sun so that the northern and southern hemispheres <u>are</u> alternately in alignment toward the sun.

CONCISE The earth's axis <u>tilts</u> as the planet <u>orbits</u> around the sun so that the northern and southern hemispheres alternately <u>align</u> toward the sun.

Passive voice

WORDY   During its winter the northern hemisphere <u>is tilted</u> farthest away from the sun, so the nights <u>are made</u> longer and the days <u>are made</u> shorter.

CONCISE During its winter the northern hemisphere <u>tilts</u> away from the sun, <u>making</u> the nights longer and the days shorter.

See also pages 198–99 on changing the passive voice to the active voice, as in the example above.

(20b) Cutting empty words

Empty words walk in place, gaining little or nothing in meaning. Many can be cut entirely. The following are just a few examples:

all things considered	in a manner of speaking
as far as I'm concerned	in my opinion
for all intents and purposes	last but not least
for the most part	more or less

Other empty words can also be cut, usually along with some of the words around them:

area	element	kind	situation
aspect	factor	manner	thing
case	field	nature	type

Still others can be reduced from several words to a single word:

For	Substitute
at all times	always
at the present time	now, yet

because of the fact that	because
by virtue of the fact that	because
due to the fact that	because
for the purpose of	for
in order to	to
in the event that	if
in the final analysis	finally

Cutting or reducing such words and phrases will make your writing move faster and work harder:

WORDY   As far as I am concerned, because of the fact that a situation of discrimination continues to exist in the field of medicine, women have not at the present time achieved equality with men.

CONCISE   Because of continuing discrimination in medicine, women have not yet achieved equality with men.

(20c) Cutting unnecessary repetition

Unnecessary repetition weakens sentences:

WORDY   Many unskilled workers without training in a particular job are unemployed and do not have any work.

CONCISE   Many unskilled workers are unemployed.

con
20c

Be especially alert to phrases that say the same thing twice. In the examples below, the unneeded words are underlined:

circle around	important [basic] essentials
consensus of opinion	puzzling in nature
continue on	repeat again
cooperate together	return again
final completion	revert back
frank and honest exchange	square [round] in shape
the future to come	surrounding circumstances

ESL The preceding phrases are redundant because the main word already implies the underlined word or words. A dictionary will tell you what meanings a word implies. *Assassinate*, for instance, means "murder someone well known," so the following sentence is redundant: *Julius Caesar was assassinated and killed.*

_KEY TERMS_____

PASSIVE VOICE The verb form when the subject names the *receiver* of the verb's action: *The house was destroyed by the tornado.* (See pp. 198–99.)

ACTIVE VOICE The verb form when the subject names the *performer* of the verb's action: *The tornado destroyed the house.* (See pp. 198–99.)

(20d) Reducing clauses and phrases

Modifiers—subordinate clauses, phrases, and single words—
can be expanded or contracted depending on the emphasis you want
to achieve. (Generally, the longer a construction, the more emphasis
it has.) When editing your sentences, consider whether any modifiers can be reduced without loss of emphasis or clarity:

WORDY   The Channel Tunnel, which runs between Britain
         and France, bores through a bed of solid chalk that
         is thirty-seven kilometres across.

CONCISE The Channel Tunnel between Britain and France
         bores through thirty-seven kilometres of solid chalk.

(20e) Cutting *there is* or *it is*

You can postpone the sentence subject with the words *there is*
(*there are, there was, there were*) and *it is* (*it was*): *There is* reason for
voting. *It is your vote that counts.* These EXPLETIVE CONSTRUCTIONS can
be useful to emphasize the subject (as when introducing it for the first
time) or to indicate a change in direction. But often they just add
words and create limp substitutes for more vigorous sentences:

WORDY   There were delays and cost overruns that plagued
         the tunnel's builders. It was a fear of investors that
         they would not earn profits once the tunnel opened.

CONCISE Delays and cost overruns plagued the tunnel's
         builders. Investors feared that they would not earn
         profits once the tunnel opened.

ESL When you must use an expletive construction, be careful
to include *there* or *it*. Only commands and some questions can
begin with verbs.

(20f) Combining sentences

Often the information in two or more sentences can be combined into one tight sentence:

WORDY   So far, business has been disappointing. Fewer trav-
         ellers than were expected have boarded the tunnel
         train. The train runs between London and Paris.

CONCISE So far, business has been disappointing, with fewer
         travellers than expected boarding the tunnel train
         that runs between London and Paris.

(See also pp. 136–37 on combining sentences to achieve variety.)

con
20f

(20g) Rewriting jargon

JARGON can refer to the special vocabulary of any discipline or profession. (See p. 141.) But it has also come to describe vague, inflated language that is overcomplicated, even incomprehensible. When it comes from government or business, we call it *bureaucratese*. It sounds almost as if the writer deliberately ignored every suggestion for clear, concise writing:

JARGON — In order to enable achievement of curricular standards, students will engage together in cooperative learning in an authentic assessment that is to involve obtaining accessing skills.

TRANSLATION — This term, students will work on group projects dealing with real-world situations. During these projects, they will learn how to find information.

con 20g

KEY TERMS

MODIFIER A word or word group that limits or qualifies another word: *slippery* road.

SUBORDINATE CLAUSE A word group that contains a subject and a verb, begins with a subordinating word such as *because* or *who*, and is not a question. Most subordinate clauses serve as modifiers: *Two accidents occurred on the road, which was unusually slippery.* (See pp. 173–74.)

PHRASE A word group that lacks a subject or a verb or both. Many phrases serve as modifiers: *road with a slippery surface.* (See p. 170.)

4 Sentence Parts and Patterns

4 Sentence Parts and Patterns

Basic Grammar

Grammar describes how language works, and understanding it can help you create clear and accurate sentences. This section explains the kinds of words in sentences (Chapter 21) and how to build basic sentences (22), expand them (23), and classify them (24).

Note Computerized grammar and style checkers can both offer assistance and cause problems as you compose correct sentences. Look for the cautions and tips for using such checkers in this and the next part of this book.

21 Parts of Speech

All English words fall into eight groups, called PARTS OF SPEECH: nouns, pronouns, verbs, adjectives, adverbs, prepositions, conjunctions, and interjections.

Note In different sentences a word may serve as different parts of speech. For example:

The government sent <u>aid</u> to the city. [*Aid* is a noun.]
Governments <u>aid</u> citizens. [*Aid* is a verb.]

The *function* of a word in a sentence always determines its part of speech in that sentence.

gr
21a

(21a) Recognizing nouns

Nouns name. They may name a person (*Sidney Crosby, Sarah Polley, astronaut*), a thing (*chair, book, Mt. Tremblant*), a quality (*pain, mystery, simplicity*), a place (*city, Vancouver, ocean, Red Sea*), or an idea (*reality, peace, success*).

The forms of nouns depend partly on where they fit in certain groups. As the examples indicate, the same noun may appear in more than one group.

- COMMON NOUNS name general classes of things and do not begin with capital letters: *earthquake, citizen, earth, fortitude, army.*
- PROPER NOUNS name specific people, places, and things and begin with capital letters: *Nellie Furtado, St. John's, Quebec City, Supreme Court of Canada.*
- COUNT NOUNS name things considered countable in English. Most add *-s* or *-es* to distinguish between singular (one) and plural (more than one): *citizen, citizens; city, cities.* Some count nouns form irregular plurals: *woman, women; child, children.*
- NONCOUNT NOUNS name things that aren't considered countable in English (*earth, sugar*), or they name qualities (*chaos, fortitude*). Noncount nouns do not form plurals.
- COLLECTIVE NOUNS are singular in form but name groups: *army, family, herd, U.S. Congress.*

In addition, most nouns form the possessive by adding -*'s* to show ownership (*Nadia's books, citizen's rights*), source (*Auden's poems*), and some other relationships.

21b Recognizing pronouns

Most PRONOUNS substitute for nouns and function in sentences as nouns do: *Susanne Simard enlisted in the Coast Guard when she graduated.*

Pronouns fall into several subclasses depending on their form or function:

- PERSONAL PRONOUNS refer to a specific individual or to individuals: *I, you, he, she, it, we,* and *they.*
- INDEFINITE PRONOUNS, such as *everybody* and *some,* do not substitute for any specific nouns, though they function as nouns (*Everybody speaks*).
- RELATIVE PRONOUNS—*who, whoever, which, that*—relate groups of words to nouns or other pronouns (*The book that won is a novel*).
- INTERROGATIVE PRONOUNS, such as *who, which,* and *what,* introduce questions (*Who will contribute?*).
- DEMONSTRATIVE PRONOUNS, including *this, that,* and *such,* identify or point to nouns (*This is the problem*).
- INTENSIVE PRONOUNS—a personal pronoun plus *-self* or *-selves* (*himself, ourselves*)—emphasize a noun or other pronoun (*He himself asked that question*).

gr
21b

- REFLEXIVE PRONOUNS have the same form as intensive pronouns but indicate that the sentence subject also receives the action of the verb (*They injured themselves*).

The personal pronouns *I, he, she, we,* and *they* and the relative pronouns *who* and *whoever* change form depending on their function in the sentence. (See Chapter 30.)

(21c) Recognizing verbs

Verbs express an action (*bring, change, grow, consider*), an occurrence (*become, happen, occur*), or a state of being (*be, seem, remain*).

1 Forms of verbs

Verbs have five distinctive forms. If the form can change as described here, the word is a verb:

- The PLAIN FORM is the dictionary form of the verb. When the subject is a plural noun or the pronoun *I, we, you,* or *they,* the plain form indicates action that occurs in the present, occurs habitually, or is generally true.

  A few artists live in town today.
  They hold classes downtown.

- The -S FORM ends in *-s* or *-es*. When the subject is a singular noun, a pronoun such as *everyone,* or the personal pronoun *he, she,* or *it,* the -s form indicates action that occurs in the present, occurs habitually, or is generally true.

  The artist lives in town today.
  She holds classes downtown.

- The PAST-TENSE FORM indicates that the action of the verb occurred before now. It usually adds *-d* or *-ed* to the plain form, although most irregular verbs create it in different ways. (See pp. 176–178.)

  Many artists lived in town before this year.
  They held classes downtown. [Irregular verb.]

- The PAST PARTICIPLE is usually the same as the past-tense form, except in most irregular verbs. It combines with forms of *have* or *be* (*has climbed, was created*), or by itself it modifies nouns and pronouns (*the sliced apples*).

gr
21c

Artists have <u>lived</u> in town for decades.
They have <u>held</u> classes downtown. [Irregular verb.]

* The PRESENT PARTICIPLE adds *-ing* to the verb's plain form. It combines with forms of *be* (*is <u>buying</u>*), modifies nouns and pronouns (*the <u>boiling</u> water*), or functions as a noun (*<u>Running</u> exhausts me*).

A few artists are <u>living</u> in town today.
They are <u>holding</u> classes downtown.

The verb *be* has eight forms rather than the five forms of most other verbs:

PLAIN FORM	be		
PRESENT PARTICIPLE	being		
PAST PARTICIPLE	been		

	I	*he, she, it*	*we, you, they*
PRESENT TENSE	am	is	are
PAST TENSE	was	was	were

2   Helping verbs

Some verb forms combine with HELPING VERBS to indicate time, possibility, obligation, necessity, and other kinds of meaning: *can run*, *<u>was</u> sleeping*, *<u>had been</u> working*. In these VERB PHRASES *run*, *sleeping*, and *working* are MAIN VERBS—they carry the principal meaning.

Verb phrase

Helping   *Main*

Artists <u>can</u>   <u>train</u> others to draw.
The techniques <u>have</u>   <u>changed</u> little.

These are the most common helping verbs:

be able to	had better	must	used to
be supposed to	have to	ought to	will
can	may	shall	would
could	might	should	

Forms of *be:* be, am, is, are, was, were, been, being
Forms of *have:* have, has, had, having
Forms of *do:* do, does, did

See pages 180–85 for more on helping verbs.

gr
21c

21d   Recognizing adjectives and adverbs

ADJECTIVES describe or modify nouns and pronouns. They specify which one, what quality, or how many.

old   city
adjective noun

generous   one
adjective pronoun

two   pears
adjective noun

ADVERBS describe or modify verbs, adjectives, other adverbs, and whole groups of words. They specify when, where, how, and to what extent.

nearly destroyed
adverb verb

too quickly
adverb adverb

very   generous
adverb adjective

Unfortunately, taxes will rise.
adverb   word group

An *-ly* ending often signals an adverb, but not always: *friendly* is an adjective; *never, not,* and *always* are adverbs. The only way to tell whether a word is an adjective or an adverb is to determine what it modifies.

Adjectives and adverbs appear in three forms: POSITIVE (*green, angrily*), COMPARATIVE (*greener, more angrily*), and SUPERLATIVE (*greenest, most angrily*).

See Chapter 33 for more on adjectives and adverbs.

21e   Recognizing connecting words: Prepositions and conjunctions

gr
21e

Connecting words are mostly small words that link parts of sentences. They never change form.

1   Prepositions

PREPOSITIONS form nouns or pronouns (plus any modifiers) into word groups called PREPOSITIONAL PHRASES: *about love, down the stairs*. These phrases usually serve as modifiers in sentences, as in *The plants trailed down the stairs*. (See p. 170 for more on prepositional phrases.)

ESL The meanings and uses of English prepositions can be difficult to master. See pages 148–49 for a discussion of prepositions in idioms. See pages 187–88 for uses of prepositions in two-word verbs such as *look after* or *look up*.

Common prepositions

about	before	except for	of	throughout
above	behind	excepting	off	till
according to	below	for	on	to
across	beneath	from	onto	toward
after	beside	in	on top of	under
against	between	in addition to	out	underneath
along	beyond	inside	out of	unlike
along with	by	inside of	outside	until
among	concerning	in spite of	over	up
around	despite	instead of	past	upon
as	down	into	regarding	up to
aside from	due to	like	round	with
at	during	near	since	within
because of	except	next to	through	without

2   Subordinating conjunctions

SUBORDINATING CONJUNCTIONS form sentences into word groups called SUBORDINATE CLAUSES, such as *when the meeting ended*. These clauses serve as parts of sentences: *Everyone was relieved when the meeting ended.* (See p. 173 for more on subordinate clauses.)

Common subordinating conjunctions

after	even if	rather than	until
although	even though	since	when
as	if	so that	whenever
as if	if only	than	where
as long as	in order that	that	whereas
as though	now that	though	wherever
because	once	till	whether
before	provided	unless	while

ESL Subordinating conjunctions convey meaning without help from other function words, such as the coordinating conjunctions *and, but, for,* or *so:*

FAULTY Even though the parents are illiterate, but their children may read well. [*Even though* and *but* have the same meaning, so only one is needed.]

REVISED Even though the parents are illiterate, their children may read well.

gr

21e

3   Coordinating and correlative conjunctions

Coordinating and correlative conjunctions connect words or word groups of the same kind, such as nouns, adjectives, or sentences.

Coordinating conjunctions consist of a single word:

Coordinating conjunctions

and	nor	for	yet
but	or	so	

Biofeedback or simple relaxation can relieve headaches.

Relaxation works well, and it is inexpensive.

Correlative conjunctions are combinations of coordinating conjunctions and other words:

Common correlative conjunctions

both . . . and   neither . . . nor
not only . . . but also whether . . . or
not . . . but   as . . . as
either . . . or

Both biofeedback and relaxation can relieve headaches.

The headache sufferer learns not only to recognize the causes of headaches but also to control those causes.

gr
21f

(21f) Recognizing interjections

Interjections express feeling or command attention. They are rarely used in academic or business writing.

Oh, the meeting went fine.

They won seven thousand dollars! Wow!

22 The Sentence

The SENTENCE is the basic unit of expression. It is grammatically complete and independent: it does not serve as an adjective, adverb, or other single part of speech.

(22a) Recognizing subjects and predicates

Most sentences make statements. First the subject names something; then the PREDICATE makes an assertion about the subject or describes an action by the subject.

Subject	Predicate
Art	thrives.

The SIMPLE SUBJECT consists of one or more nouns or pronouns, whereas the COMPLETE SUBJECT also includes any modifiers. The SIMPLE PREDICATE consists of one or more verbs, whereas the COMPLETE PREDICATE adds any words needed to complete the meaning of the verb plus any modifiers.

Sometimes, as in the short example *Art thrives,* the simple and complete subject and predicate are the same. More often, they are different:

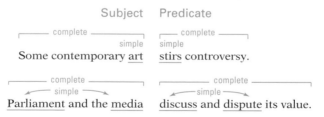

Subject · Predicate

complete · simple
Some contemporary <u>art</u> · <u>stirs</u> controversy.

complete · simple
<u>Parliament</u> and the <u>media</u> · <u>discuss</u> and <u>dispute</u> its value.

In the second example, the simple subject and simple predicate are both compound: in each, two words joined by a coordinating conjunction (*and*) serve the same function.

ESL The subject of an English sentence may be a noun (*art*) or a pronoun that refers to the noun (*it*), but not both. (See p. 244.)

FAULTY Some <u>art</u> <u>it</u> stirs controversy.
REVISED Some <u>art</u> stirs controversy.

(22b) Recognizing predicate patterns

All English sentences are based on five patterns, each differing in the complete predicate (the verb and any words following it).

ESL The word order in English sentences may not correspond to word order in the sentences of your native language. English, for instance, strongly prefers subject first, then verb, then any other words, whereas some other languages prefer the verb first.

Pattern 1: The earth trembled.

In the simplest pattern the predicate consists only of an INTRANSITIVE VERB, a verb that does not require a following word to complete its meaning.

Subject	Predicate
	Intransitive verb
The earth	trembled.
The hospital	may close.

Pattern 2: The earthquake destroyed the city.

In pattern 2 the verb is followed by a DIRECT OBJECT, a noun or pronoun that identifies who or what receives the action of the verb. A verb that requires a direct object to complete its meaning is called TRANSITIVE.

Subject	Predicate	
	Transitive verb	*Direct object*
The earthquake	destroyed	the city.
Education	opens	doors.

ESL Only transitive verbs can be used in the passive voice: *The city was destroyed*. Your dictionary will indicate whether a verb is transitive or intransitive. For some verbs (*begin, learn, read, write,* and others), it will indicate both uses.

gr
22b

_KEY TERM _____

PASSIVE VOICE The verb form in which the subject names the receiver of the verb's action: *Bad weather was predicted*. (See pp. 198–200.)

Pattern 3: The result was chaos.

In pattern 3 the verb is followed by a SUBJECT COMPLEMENT, a word that renames or describes the subject. A verb in this pattern is called a LINKING VERB because it links its subject to the description following. The linking verbs include *be, seem, appear, become, grow, remain, stay, prove, feel, look, smell, sound,* and *taste.* Subject complements are usually nouns or adjectives.

Subject	Predicate	
	Linking verb	*Subject complement*
The result	was	chaos.
The man	became	an accountant.

Pattern 4: The government sent the city aid.

In pattern 4 the verb is followed by a direct object and an INDIRECT OBJECT, a word identifying to or for whom the action of the verb is performed. The direct object and indirect object refer to different things, people, or places.

Subject	Predicate		
	Transitive verb	*Indirect object*	*Direct object*
The government	sent	the city	aid.
One company	offered	its employees	bonuses.

A number of verbs can take indirect objects, including those above and *allow, bring, buy, deny, find, get, give, leave, make, pay, read, sell, show, teach,* and *write.*

ESL   Some verbs are never followed by an indirect object—*admit, announce, demonstrate, explain, introduce, mention, prove, recommend, say,* and some others. However, the direct objects of these verbs may be followed by *to* or *for* and a noun or pronoun that specifies to or for whom the action was done: *The manual explains the new procedure to workers. A video demonstrates the procedure for us.*

gr
22b

Pattern 5: The citizens considered the earthquake a disaster.

In pattern 5 the verb is followed by a direct object and an OBJECT COMPLEMENT, a word that renames or describes the direct object. Object complements may be nouns or adjectives.

Subject	Predicate		
	Transitive verb	*Direct object*	*Object complement*
The citizens	considered	the earthquake	a disaster.
Success	makes	some people	nervous.

23 Phrases and Subordinate Clauses

Most sentences contain word groups that serve as adjectives, adverbs, or nouns and thus cannot stand alone as sentences.

- A *phrase* lacks either a subject or a predicate or both: *fearing an accident; in a panic.*
- A *subordinate clause* contains a subject and a predicate (like a sentence) but begins with a subordinating word: <u>when</u> *prices rise;* <u>whoever</u> *laughs.*

(23a) Recognizing phrases

1 Prepositional phrases

A PREPOSITIONAL PHRASE consists of a preposition plus a noun, a pronoun, or a word group serving as a noun, called the OBJECT OF THE PREPOSITION. A list of prepositions appears on page 165.

Preposition	Object
of	spaghetti
on	the surface
with	great satisfaction
upon	entering the room
from	where you are standing

Prepositional phrases usually function as adjectives or adverbs:

Life <u>on a raft</u> was an opportunity <u>for adventure</u>.
   adjective phrase   adjective phrase

Huck Finn rode the raft <u>by choice</u>.
                        adverb phrase

<u>With his companion</u>, Jim, Huck met many types <u>of people</u>.
 adverb phrase   adjective phrase

gr
23a

2   Verbal phrases

Certain forms of verbs, called VERBALS, can serve as modifiers or nouns. Often these verbals appear with their own modifiers and objects in VERBAL PHRASES.

Note Verbals cannot serve as verbs in sentences. *The sun rises over the dump* is a sentence; *The sun rising over the dump* is a sentence fragment. (See pp. 235–37.)

Participial phrases

Phrases made from present participles (ending in *-ing*) or past participles (usually ending in *-d* or *-ed*) serve as adjectives.

Strolling shoppers fill the malls.
    adjective

They make selections determined by personal taste.
                              adjective phrase

Note With irregular verbs, the past participle may have a different ending—for instance, *hidden funds*. (See pp. 176–78.)

ESL   For verbs expressing feeling, the present and past participles have different meanings: *It was a boring lecture. The bored students slept.* (See pp. 223–24.)

Gerund phrases

A GERUND is the *-ing* form of a verb when it serves as a noun. Gerunds and gerund phrases can do whatever nouns can do.

    sentence
    subject
Shopping satisfies personal needs.
    noun

                        object of preposition
Malls are good at creating such needs.
                        noun phrase

Infinitive phrases

An INFINITIVE is the plain form of a verb plus *to*: *to hide*. Infinitives and infinitive phrases serve as adjectives, adverbs, or nouns.

        sentence   subject
    — subject —   — complement —
To design a mall is to create an artificial environment.
    noun phrase   noun phrase

gr
23a

Malls are designed to make shoppers feel safe.
　　　　　　　　　　　adverb phrase

The environment supports the impulse to shop.
　　　　　　　　　　　　　　　　adjective

ESL Infinitives and gerunds may follow some verbs and not others and may differ in meaning after a verb: *The singer stopped to sing. The singer stopped singing.* (See pp. 185–87.)

3　Absolute phrases

An ABSOLUTE PHRASE consists of a noun or pronoun and a participle, plus any modifiers. It modifies the entire rest of the sentence it appears in.

|————— absolute phrase —————|
Their own place established, many ethnic groups are making way

for new arrivals.

Unlike a participial phrase (previous page), an absolute phrase always contains a noun that serves as a subject.

participial
|—— phrase ——|
Learning English, many immigrants discover Canadian culture.

|————— absolute phrase —————|
Immigrants having learned English, their opportunities widen.

4　Appositive phrases

An APPOSITIVE is usually a noun that renames another noun. An appositive phrase includes modifiers as well.

|—— appositive phrase
Bizen ware, a dark stoneware, is produced in Japan.

Appositives and appositive phrases sometimes begin with *that is, such as, for example,* or *in other words.*

|—— appositive phrase
Bizen ware is used in the Japanese tea ceremony: that is, the Zen

Buddhist observance that links meditation and art.

gr
23a

(23b) Recognizing subordinate clauses

A CLAUSE is any group of words that contains both a subject and a predicate. There are two kinds of clauses, and the distinction between them is important.

- A MAIN CLAUSE makes a complete statement and can stand alone as a sentence: *The sky darkened.*
- A SUBORDINATE CLAUSE is just like a main clause *except* that it begins with a subordinating word: *when the sky darkened*; *whoever calls.* The subordinating word reduces the clause from a complete statement to a single part of speech: an adjective, adverb, or noun.

Note A subordinate clause punctuated as a sentence is a sentence fragment. (See pp. 236–37.)

Adjective clauses

An ADJECTIVE CLAUSE modifies a noun or pronoun. It usually begins with the relative pronoun *who, whom, whose, which,* or *that.* The relative pronoun is the subject or object of the clause it begins. The clause ordinarily falls immediately after the word it modifies.

adjective clause
Parents who are illiterate may have bad memories of school.

adjective clause
One school, which is open year-round, helps parents learn to read.

Adverb clauses

An ADVERB CLAUSE modifies a verb, an adjective, another adverb, or a whole word group. It always begins with a subordinating conjunction, such as *although, because, if,* or *when.* (See p. 165 for a list.)

adverb clause
The school began teaching parents when adult illiteracy gained national attention.

adverb clause   main clause
Because it was directed at people who could not read, advertising had to be inventive.

gr
23b

Noun clauses

A NOUN CLAUSE replaces a noun in a sentence and serves as a subject, object, or complement. It begins with *that, what, whatever, who, whom, whoever, whomever, when, where, whether, why,* or *how.*

> ┌─────── sentence subject ───────┐
> <u>Whether the program would succeed</u> depended on door-to-door
>   noun clause
> advertising.

> ┌─────── direct object ───────┐
> Teachers explained in person <u>how the program would work</u>.
>   noun clause

24 Sentence Types

The four basic sentence structures vary in the number of main and coordinate clauses.

(24a) Recognizing simple sentences

A SIMPLE SENTENCE consists of a single main clause and no subordinate clause:

> ┌─────── main clause ───────┐
> Last summer was unusually hot.

> ┌─────────────── main clause ───────────────┐
> The summer made many farmers leave the area for good or
> reduced them to bare subsistence.

24b Recognizing compound sentences

A COMPOUND SENTENCE consists of two or more main clauses and no subordinate clause:

┌── main clause ──┐   ┌────── main clause ──────┐
Last July was hot, but August was even hotter.

┌──────── main clause ────────┐   ┌────── main clause ──────┐
The hot sun scorched the earth, and the lack of rain killed many

┌──┐
crops.

24c Recognizing complex sentences

A COMPLEX SENTENCE consists of one main clause and one or more subordinate clauses:

┌── main clause ──┐ ┌──────── subordinate clause ────────┐
Rain finally came, although many had left the area by then.

┌──────── main clause ────────┐ ┌── subordinate clause ──┐
Those who remained were able to start anew because the govern-
     subordinate clause

┌──────────────────────┐
ment came to their aid.

24d Recognizing compound-complex sentences

gr
24d

A COMPOUND-COMPLEX SENTENCE has the characteristics of both the compound sentence (two or more main clauses) and the complex sentence (at least one subordinate clause):

┌──────── subordinate clause ────────┐ ┌── main clause ──┐
Even though government aid finally came, many people had
┌────────────────────────────────┐ ┌──── main clause ────┐
already been reduced to poverty, and others had been forced to
┌──┐
move.

Verbs

VERBS express actions, conditions, and states of being. The basic uses and forms of verbs are described on pages 162–63. This section explains and solves the most common problems with verbs' forms (Chapter 25), tenses (26), mood (27), and voice (28) and shows how to make verbs match their subjects (29).

25 Verb Forms

(25a) Use the correct forms of *sing/sang/sung* and other irregular verbs.

Most verbs are REGULAR: they form their past tense and past participle by adding -*d* or -*ed* to the plain form.

Plain form	Past tense	Past participle
live	lived	lived
act	acted	acted

About 200 English verbs are IRREGULAR: they form their past tense and past participle in some irregular way. Check a dictionary under the verb's plain form if you have any doubt about its other forms. If the verb is irregular, the dictionary will list the plain form, the past tense, and the past participle in that order (*go, went, gone*). If the dictionary gives only two forms (as in *think, thought*), then the past tense and the past participle are the same.

vb
25a

___ KEY TERMS ___

PLAIN FORM The dictionary form of the verb: *I walk. You forget.* (See p. 162.)

PAST-TENSE FORM The verb form indicating action that occurred in the past: *I walked. You forgot.* (See p. 162.)

PAST PARTICIPLE The verb form used with *have, has,* or *had: I have walked.* It may also serve as a modifier: *This is a forgotten book.* (See p. 162.)

Common irregular verbs

Plain form	Past tense	Past participle
arise	arose	arisen
become	became	become
begin	began	begun
bid	bid	bid
bite	bit	bitten, bit
blow	blew	blown
break	broke	broken
bring	brought	brought
burst	burst	burst
buy	bought	bought
catch	caught	caught
choose	chose	chosen
come	came	come
cut	cut	cut
dive	dived, dove	dived
do	did	done
draw	drew	drawn
dream	dreamed, dreamt	dreamed, dreamt
drink	drank	drunk
drive	drove	driven
eat	ate	eaten
fall	fell	fallen
find	found	found
flee	fled	fled
fly	flew	flown
forget	forgot	forgotten, forgot
freeze	froze	frozen
get	got	got, gotten
give	gave	given
go	went	gone
grow	grew	grown
hang (suspend)	hung	hung
hang (execute)	hanged	hanged
hear	heard	heard
hide	hid	hidden
hold	held	held
keep	kept	kept
know	knew	known
lay	laid	laid
lead	led	led
leave	left	left
lend	lent	lent
let	let	let
lie	lay	lain
lose	lost	lost
pay	paid	paid

vb

25a

prove	proved	proved, proven
ride	rode	ridden
ring	rang	rung
rise	rose	risen
run	ran	run
say	said	said
see	saw	seen
set	set	set
shake	shook	shaken
shrink	shrank, shrunk	shrunk, shrunken
sing	sang	sung
sink	sank	sunk
sit	sat	sat
sleep	slept	slept
slide	slid	slid
speak	spoke	spoken
spring	sprang, sprung	sprung
stand	stood	stood
steal	stole	stolen
swim	swam	swum
swing	swung	swung
take	took	taken
tear	tore	torn
throw	threw	thrown
wear	wore	worn
write	wrote	written

The list on page 177 and above includes the most common irregular verbs. (When two forms are possible, as in *dove* and *dived*, both are included.)

vb

25b

Note A computerized grammar and style checker may flag incorrect forms of irregular verbs, but it may also fail to do so. When in doubt about the forms of irregular verbs, refer to the list above or consult a dictionary.

(25b) Distinguish between *sit* and *set, lie* and *lay,* and *rise* and *raise*.

The forms of *sit* and *set, lie* and *lay,* and *rise* and *raise* are easy to confuse.

Plain form	Past tense	Past participle
sit	sat	sat
set	set	set
lie	lay	lain

lay	laid	laid
rise	rose	risen
raise	raised	raised

In each of these confusing pairs, one verb is intransitive (it does not take an object) and one is transitive (it does take an object). (See pp. 168–69 for more on this distinction.)

Intransitive

The patients lie in their beds. [*Lie* means "recline" and takes no object.]

Visitors sit with them. [*Sit* means "be seated" or "be located" and takes no object.]

Patients' temperatures rise. [*Rise* means "increase" or "get up" and takes no object.]

Transitive

Orderlies lay the dinner trays on tables. [*Lay* means "place" and takes an object, here *trays.*]

Orderlies set the trays down. [*Set* means "place" and takes an object, here *trays.*]

Nursing aides raise the shades. [*Raise* means "lift" or "bring up" and takes an object, here *shades.*]

(25c) ## Use the *-s* and *-ed* forms of the verb when they are required.

Speakers of some English dialects and nonnative speakers of English sometimes omit verb endings required by standard English. One is the *-s* form of a verb, which is required when *both* of these situations hold:

* The subject is a singular noun (*boy*), an indefinite pronoun (*everyone*), or *he, she,* or *it.*
* The verb's action occurs in the present.

The letter asks [not ask] for a quick response.
Delay is [not be] costly.

Watch especially for the *-s* forms *has, does,* and *doesn't* (for *does not*).

The company has [not have] delayed responding.
It doesn't [not don't] have the needed data.
The contract does [not do] depend on the response.

Another ending sometimes omitted is *-d* or *-ed,* as in *we bagged* or *used cars.* The ending is particularly easy to omit if it isn't pronounced clearly in speech, as in *asked, discussed, fixed, mixed,*

vb

25c

supposed, walked, and *used.* Use the ending for a regular verb in *any* of these situations:

- The verb's action occurred in the past:

  The company <u>asked</u> [not <u>ask</u>] for more time.

- The verb form functions as a modifier:

  The data <u>concerned</u> [not <u>concern</u>] should be retrievable.

- The verb form combines with a form of *be* or *have:*

  The company is <u>supposed</u> [not <u>suppose</u>] to be the best.
  It has <u>developed</u> [not <u>develop</u>] an excellent reputation.

Note A computerized grammar and style checker will flag many omitted *-s* and *-ed* endings from verbs, such as in *he ask* or *was ask.* But it will miss many omissions, too. You'll need to proofread your papers carefully on your own to catch missing endings.

ESL Some languages do not require endings equivalent to the *-s* or *-ed* in English. If English is not your native language and you find you omit one or both of these endings, you may need to edit your drafts just for them.

(25d) Use helping verbs with main verbs appropriately. **ESL**

Helping verbs combine with main verbs in verb phrases: *The line <u>should have been cut</u>. Who <u>was calling</u>?*

Note Computerized grammar and style checkers often spot omitted helping verbs and incorrect main verbs with helping verbs, but sometimes they do not. A checker flagged *Many been fortunate, She working,* and *Her ideas are grow more complex* but overlooked other examples on the following pages, such as *The conference will be occurred.* Careful proofreading is the only insurance against missing helping verbs and incorrect main verbs.

vb
25d

1   Required helping verbs

Some English dialects omit helping verbs required by standard English. In the sentences below, the underlined helping verbs are essential:

Archaeologists <u>are</u> conducting fieldwork all over the world. [Not *Archaeologists conducting . . .*]
Many <u>have</u> been fortunate in their discoveries. [Not *Many been . . .*]
Some <u>could</u> be real-life Indiana Joneses. [Not *Some be . . .*]

The omission of a helping verb may create an incomplete sentence, or SENTENCE FRAGMENT, because a present participle (*conducting*), an irregular past participle (*been*), or the infinitive (*be*) cannot stand alone as the only verb in a sentence (see p. 235). To work as sentence verbs, these verb forms need helping verbs.

2   Combination of helping verb + main verb ESL

Helping verbs and main verbs combine into verb phrases in specific ways.

Note The main verb in a verb phrase (the one carrying the main meaning) does not change to show a change in subject or time: *she has sung, you had sung*. Only the helping verb may change, as in these examples.

Form of *be* + present participle

The PROGRESSIVE TENSES indicate action in progress. Create them with *be, am, is, are, was, were,* or *been* followed by the main verb's present participle, as in the following example.

She is working on a new book.

Be and *been* require additional helping verbs to form progressive tenses:

can	might	should			have	
could	must	will	}	be working	has	} been working
may	shall	would			had	

_ KEY TERMS _____

vb

25d

HELPING VERB A verb such as *can, may, be, have,* or *do* that forms a verb phrase with another verb to show time, permission, and other meanings. (See p. 163.)

MAIN VERB The verb that carries the principal meaning in a verb phrase: *has walked, could be happening.* (See p. 163.)

VERB PHRASE A helping verb plus a main verb: *will be singing, would speak.* (See p. 163.)

PRESENT PARTICIPLE The *-ing* form of the verb: *flying, writing.* (See p. 163.)

PROGRESSIVE TENSES Verb tenses expressing action in progress— for instance, *I am flying* (present progressive), *I was flying* (past progressive), *I will be flying* (future progressive). (See pp. 191–92.)

When forming the progressive tenses, be sure to use the *-ing* form of the main verb:

FAULTY   Her ideas are grow more complex. She is developed a new approach to ethics.

REVISED   Her ideas are growing more complex. She is developing a new approach to ethics.

Form of *be* + past participle

The PASSIVE VOICE of the verb indicates that the subject *receives* the action of the verb. Create the passive voice with *be, am, is, are, was, were, being,* or *been* followed by the main verb's past participle:

Her latest book was completed in four months.

Be, being, and *been* require additional helping verbs to form the passive voice:

have ⎤
has ⎬ been completed
had ⎦

will be completed

am   was ⎤
is   were ⎬ being completed
are ⎦

Be sure to use the main verb's past participle for the passive voice:

FAULTY   Her next book will be publish soon.
REVISED   Her next book will be published soon.

Note Use only transitive verbs to form the passive voice:

FAULTY   A philosophy conference will be occurred in the same week. [*Occur* is not a transitive verb.]
REVISED   A philosophy conference will occur in the same week.

vb
25d

See pages 198–99 for advice on when to use and when to avoid the passive voice.

KEY TERMS

PAST PARTICIPLE The *-d* or *-ed* form of a regular verb: *hedged, walked.* Most irregular verbs have distinctive past participles: *eaten, swum.* (See p. 162.)

PASSIVE VOICE The verb form when the subject names the receiver of the verb's action: *An essay was written by every student.* (See p. 198.)

TRANSITIVE VERB A verb that requires an object to complete its meaning: *Every student completed an essay* (*essay* is the object of *completed*). (See p. 168.)

Forms of *have*

Four forms of *have* serve as helping verbs: *have, has, had, having.* One of these forms plus the main verb's past participle creates one of the perfect tenses, those expressing action completed before another specific time or action:

Some students <u>have complained</u> about the laboratory.

Others <u>had complained</u> before.

Will and other helping verbs sometimes accompany forms of *have* in the perfect tenses:

Several more students <u>will have complained</u> by the end of the week.

Forms of *do*

Do, does, and *did* have three uses as helping verbs, always with the plain form of the main verb:

- To pose a question: *How <u>did</u> the trial <u>end</u>?*
- To emphasize the main verb: *It <u>did end</u> eventually.*
- To negate the main verb, along with *not* or *never: The judge <u>did not withdraw</u>.*

Be sure to use the main verb's plain form with any form of *do:*

FAULTY   The judge did <u>remained</u> in court.
REVISED   The judge did <u>remain</u> in court.

Modals

The modal helping verbs include *can, could, may,* and *might,* along with several two- and three-word combinations, such as *have to* and *be able to.*

Modals convey various meanings, with these being most common:

- Ability: *can, could, be able to*

The equipment <u>can detect</u> small vibrations. [Present.]

The equipment <u>could detect</u> small vibrations. [Past.]

The equipment <u>is able to detect</u> small vibrations. [Present. Past: *was able to.* Future: *will be able to.*]

vb
25d

_ KEY TERM _____

PERFECT TENSES Verb tenses expressing an action completed before another specific time or action: *We have eaten* (present perfect), *We had eaten* (past perfect), *We will have eaten* (future perfect). (See p. 191.)

- Possibility: *could, may, might, could/may/might have* + past participle

  The equipment could fail. [Present.]
  The equipment may fail. [Present and future.]
  The equipment might fail. [Present and future.]
  The equipment may have failed. [Past.]

- Necessity or obligation: *must, have to, be supposed to*

  The lab must purchase a backup. [Present or future.]
  The lab has to purchase a backup. [Present or future. Past: *had to*.]
  The lab will have to purchase a backup. [Future.]
  The lab is supposed to purchase a backup. [Present. Past: *was supposed to*.]

- Permission: *may, can, could*

  The lab may spend the money. [Present or future.]
  The lab can spend the money. [Present or future.]
  The lab could spend the money. [Present or future, more tentative.]
  The school then announced that the lab could spend the money. [Past.]

- Intention: *will, shall, would*

  The lab will spend the money. [Future.]
  Shall we offer advice? [Future. Use *shall* for questions requesting opinion or consent.]
  We knew we would offer advice. [Past.]

- Request: *could, can, would*

  Could [or can or would] you please obtain a bid? [Present or future.]

- Advisability: *should, had better, ought to, should have* + past participle

  You should obtain three bids. [Present or future.]
  You had better obtain three bids. [Present or future.]
  You ought to obtain three bids. [Present or future.]
  You should have obtained three bids. [Past.]

- Past habit: *would, used to*

  In years past we would obtain five bids.
  We used to obtain five bids.

The following conventions govern the combination of modals and main verbs shown in the examples:

- One-word modals do not change form to show a change in subject: *I could run, she could run.* Most two- and three-word modals do change form, like other helping verbs: *I have to run,* *she has to run.*

- Modals can sometimes indicate past, present, or future time, occasionally with a word change (*can* to *could,* for instance), with a form change in a two- or three-word modal (such as *is/was able to*), or with *have* before the past participle of the main verb (*might have driven*).
- Don't use *to* between a one-word modal and the main verb: *can drive,* not *can to drive.* (Most of the two- and three-word modals do include *to: ought to drive.*)
- Don't use two one-word modals together: *I will be able to drive,* not *I will can drive.*

(25e) Use a gerund or an infinitive after a verb as appropriate. ESL

Gerunds and infinitives may follow certain verbs but not others. And sometimes the use of a gerund or infinitive with the same verb changes the meaning of the verb.

Note A computerized grammar and style checker will spot some but not all errors in matching gerunds or infinitives with verbs. Use the lists given here and an ESL dictionary (see p. 145–46) to determine whether an infinitive or a gerund is appropriate.

1 Either gerund or infinitive

A gerund or an infinitive may come after the following verbs with no significant difference in meaning:

begin	continue	intend	prefer
can't bear	forget	like	remember
can't stand	hate	love	start

The pump began <u>working</u>. The pump began to <u>work</u>.

vb

25e

--- KEY TERMS ---

GERUND The *-ing* form of the verb used as a noun: <u>Smoking</u> *is unhealthful.* (See p. 171.)

INFINITIVE The plain form of the verb usually preceded by *to: to smoke.* An infinitive may serve as an adjective, adverb, or noun. (See pp. 171–72.)

2   Meaning change with gerund or infinitive

With four verbs, a gerund has quite a different meaning from an infinitive:

forget	stop
remember	try

The engineer stopped <u>eating</u>. [He no longer ate.]
The engineer stopped <u>to eat</u>. [He stopped in order to eat.]

3   Gerund, not infinitive

Do not use an infinitive after these verbs:

admit	discuss	mind	recollect
adore	dislike	miss	resent
appreciate	enjoy	postpone	resist
avoid	escape	practise	risk
consider	finish	put off	suggest
deny	imagine	quit	tolerate
detest	keep	recall	understand

FAULTY   He finished <u>to eat</u> lunch.
REVISED   He finished <u>eating</u> lunch.

4   Infinitive, not gerund

Do not use a gerund after these verbs:

agree	claim	manage	promise
appear	consent	mean	refuse
arrange	decide	offer	say
ask	expect	plan	wait
assent	have	prepare	want
beg	hope	pretend	wish

FAULTY   He decided <u>checking</u> the pump.
REVISED   He decided <u>to check</u> the pump.

5   Noun or pronoun + infinitive

Some verbs may be followed by an infinitive alone or by a noun or pronoun and an infinitive. The presence of a noun or pronoun changes the meaning.

ask	dare	need	wish
beg	expect	promise	would like
choose	help	want	

He expected <u>to watch</u>.
He expected <u>his workers to watch</u>.

vb
25e

Some verbs *must* be followed by a noun or pronoun before an infinitive:

admonish	encourage	oblige	require
advise	forbid	order	teach
allow	force	permit	tell
cause	hire	persuade	train
challenge	instruct	remind	urge
command	invite	request	warn
convince			

He instructed <u>his workers to watch</u>.

Do not use *to* before the infinitive when it follows one of these verbs and a noun or pronoun:

feel	make ("force")
have	see
hear	watch
let	

He let his workers <u>learn</u> by observation.

(25f) Use the appropriate particles with two-word verbs. ESL

Some verbs consist of two words: the verb itself and a PARTICLE, a preposition or adverb that affects the meaning of the verb. For example:

<u>Look up</u> the answer. [Research the answer.]

<u>Look over</u> the answer. [Examine the answer.]

The meanings of these two-word verbs are often quite different from the meanings of the individual words that make them up. (There are some three-word verbs, too, such as *put up with* and *run out of.*) An ESL dictionary, such as one of those mentioned on page 146, will define two-word verbs for you. It will also tell you whether

vb

25f

KEY TERMS

PREPOSITION A word such as *about, for,* or *to* that takes a noun or pronoun as its object: <u>at</u> *the house,* <u>in</u> *the woods.* (See p. 165 for a list of prepositions.)

ADVERB A word that modifies a verb (*went <u>down</u>*), adjective (*<u>very</u> pretty*), another adverb (*<u>too</u> sweetly*), or a whole word group (*<u>Eventually</u>, the fire died*). (See p. 164.)

the verbs may be separated in a sentence, as explained below. A computerized grammar and style checker will recognize few if any misuses of two-word verbs. You'll need to proofread on your own to catch and correct errors.

Note Many two-word verbs are more common in speech than in more formal academic or business writing. For formal writing, consider using *research* instead of *look up; examine* or *inspect* instead of *look over.*

1   Inseparable two-word verbs

Verbs and particles that may not be separated by any other words include the following:

catch on	go over	play around	stay away
come across	grow up	run into	stay up
get along	keep on	run out of	take care of
give in	look into	speak up	turn up at

FAULTY   Children <u>grow</u> quickly <u>up</u>.
REVISED   Children <u>grow up</u> quickly.

2   Separable two-word verbs

Most two-word verbs that take direct objects may be separated by the object.

Parents <u>help out</u> their children.
Parents <u>help</u> their children <u>out</u>.

If the direct object is a pronoun, the pronoun *must* separate the verb from the particle.

FAULTY   Parents <u>help out</u> them.
REVISED   Parents <u>help</u> them <u>out</u>.

vb
25f

The separable two-word verbs include the following:

bring up	give back	make up	throw out
call off	hand in	point out	try on
call up	hand out	put away	try out
drop off	help out	put back	turn down
fill out	leave out	put off	turn on
fill up	look over	take out	turn up
give away	look up	take over	wrap up

26 Verb Tenses

TENSE shows the time of a verb's action. The table on the next page illustrates the tense forms for a regular verb. (Irregular verbs have different past-tense and past-participle forms. See pp. 176–78.)

Note Computerized grammar and style checkers can provide little help with incorrect verb tenses and tense sequences because correctness is usually dependent on meaning. Proofread carefully yourself to catch errors in tense or tense sequence.

 26a Observe the special uses of the present tense (*sing*).

Most academic and business writing uses the past tense (*the rebellion occurred*), but the present tense has several distinctive uses.

Action occurring now
She <u>understands</u> the problem.
We <u>define</u> the problem differently.

Habitual or recurring action
Banks regularly <u>undergo</u> audits.
The audits <u>monitor</u> the banks' activities.

A general truth
The mills of the gods <u>grind</u> slowly.
The earth <u>is</u> round.

Discussion of literature, film, and so on
Huckleberry Finn <u>has</u> adventures we all envy.
In that article the author <u>examines</u> several causes of crime.

Future time
Next week we <u>draft</u> a new budget.
Funding <u>ends</u> in less than a year.

(Future time is really indicated here by *Next week* and *in less than a year*.)

t
26a

Tenses of a regular verb (active voice)

Present Action that is occurring now, occurs habitually, or is generally true

Simple present Plain form or *-s* form

I walk.
You/we/they walk.
He/she/it walks.

Present progressive *Am, is,* or *are* plus *-ing* form

I am walking.
You/we/they are walking.
He/she/it is walking.

Past Action that occurred before now

Simple past Past-tense form (*-d* or *-ed*)

I/he/she/it walked.
You/we/they walked.

Past progressive *Was* or *were* plus *-ing* form

I/he/she/it was walking.
You/we/they were walking.

Future Action that will occur in the future

Simple future Plain form plus *will*

I/you/he/she/it/we/they will walk.

Future progressive *Will be* plus *-ing* form

I/you/he/she/it/we/they will be walking.

Present perfect Action that began in the past and is linked to the present

Present perfect *Have* or *has* plus past participle (*-d* or *-ed*)

I/you/we/they have walked.
He/she/it has walked.

Present perfect progressive *Have been* or *has been* plus *-ing* form

I/you/we/they have been walking.
He/she/it has been walking.

Past perfect Action that was completed before another past action

Past perfect *Had* plus past participle (*-d* or *-ed*)

I/you/he/she/it/we/they had walked.

Past perfect progressive *Had been* plus *-ing* form

I/you/he/she/it/we/they had been walking.

Future perfect Action that will be completed before another future action

Future perfect *Will have* plus past participle (*-d* or *-ed*)

I/you/he/she/it/we/they will have walked.

Future perfect progressive *Will have been* plus *-ing* form

I/you/he/she/it/we/they will have been walking.

t
26a

(26b) Observe the uses of the perfect tenses (*have/had/will have sung*).

The perfect tenses consist of a form of *have* plus the verb's past participle (*closed, hidden*). They indicate an action completed before another specific time or action. The present perfect tense also indicates action begun in the past and continued into the present.

present perfect
The dancer has performed here only once. [The action is completed at the time of the statement.]

present perfect
Critics have written about the performance ever since. [The action began in the past and continues now.]

past perfect
The dancer had trained in Asia before his performance. [The action was completed before another past action.]

future perfect
He will have performed here again by next month. [The action begins now or in the future and will be completed by a specified time in the future.]

ESL With the present perfect tense, the words *since* and *for* are followed by different information. After *since,* give a specific point in time: *The United States has been a member of the United Nations since 1945.* After *for,* give a span of time: *The United States has been a member of the United Nations for half a century.*

(26c) Observe the uses of the progressive tenses (*is/was/will be singing*). **ESL**

t
26c

The progressive tenses indicate continuing (therefore progressive) action. They consist of a form of *be* plus the verb's *-ing* form (present participle). (The words *be* and *been* must be combined with other helping verbs. See pp. 180–81.)

present progressive
The economy is improving.

past progressive
Last year the economy was stagnating.

future progressive
Economists will be watching for signs of growth.

present perfect progressive
The government has been expecting an upturn.

past perfect progressive

Various indicators had been suggesting improvement.

future perfect progressive

By the end of this year, investors will have been watching interest rates nervously for nearly a decade.

Note Verbs that express unchanging states (especially mental states) rather than physical actions do not usually appear in the progressive tenses. These verbs include *adore, appear, believe, belong, care, hate, have, hear, know, like, love, mean, need, own, prefer, remember, see, sound, taste, think, understand,* and *want.*

FAULTY	She is wanting to study ethics.
REVISED	She wants to study ethics.

26d   Keep tenses consistent.

Within a sentence, the tenses of verbs and verb forms need not be identical as long as they reflect actual changes in time: *Hoi will graduate thirty years after his father arrived in Canada.* But needless shifts in tense will confuse or distract readers:

INCONSISTENT	Immediately after Hoi received his degree, his father laughed with happiness. But his little brother shouts his nickname and embarrasses him.
REVISED	Immediately after Hoi received his degree, his father laughed with happiness. But his little brother shouted his nickname and embarrassed him.

INCONSISTENT	The main character in the novel suffers psychologically because he has a clubfoot, but he eventually triumphed over his disability.
REVISED	The main character in the novel suffers psychologically because he has a clubfoot, but he eventually triumphs over his disability. [Use the present tense when discussing the content of literature, film, and so on.]

t seq
26e

26e   Use the appropriate sequence of verb tenses.

The SEQUENCE OF TENSES is the relation between the verb tense in a main clause and the verb tense in a subordinate clause. The tenses are often different, as in the following sentence:

Hoi's father <u>arrived</u> in Canada thirty years ago, after he <u>had married</u>, and now Hoi <u>has decided</u> that he <u>will return</u> to his father's homeland.

English tense sequence can be tricky for native speakers and especially challenging for nonnative speakers. The main difficulties are discussed below.

1   Past or past perfect tense in main clause

When the verb in the main clause is in the past or past perfect tense, the verb in the subordinate clause must also be past or past perfect:

main clause: subordinate clause:
past   past

The researchers <u>discovered</u> that people <u>varied</u> widely in their knowledge of public events.

main clause: subordinate clause:
past   past perfect

The variation <u>occurred</u> because respondents <u>had been born</u> in different decades.

main clause: subordinate clause:
past perfect   past

None of them <u>had been born</u> when John Diefenbaker <u>was</u> Prime Minister.

Exception Always use the present tense for a general truth, such as *The earth is round:*

main clause: subordinate clause:
past   present

Most <u>understood</u> that popular politicians <u>are</u> not necessarily good politicians.

2   Conditional sentences ESL

A CONDITIONAL SENTENCE states a factual relation between cause and effect, makes a prediction, or speculates about what might happen. Such a sentence usually consists of a subordinate clause beginning with *if, when,* or *unless* and a main clause stating the result. The three kinds of conditional sentences use distinctive verbs.

t seq

26e

__ KEY TERMS _____

MAIN CLAUSE A word group that contains a subject and a verb and does not begin with a subordinating word: *Books are valuable.* (See p. 173.)

SUBORDINATE CLAUSE A word group that contains a subject and a verb, begins with a subordinating word such as *because* or *who,* and is not a question: *Books are valuable <u>when they enlighten</u>.* (See p. 172.)

Factual relation

For statements asserting that something always or usually happens whenever something else happens, use the present tense in both clauses:

subordinate clause: main clause:
present   present

When a voter <u>casts</u> a ballot, he or she <u>has</u> complete privacy.

If the linked events occurred in the past, use the past tense in both clauses:

subordinate clause: main clause:
past   past

When voters <u>were enumerated</u>, they <u>had</u> to identify their occupation.

Prediction

For a prediction, generally use the present tense in the subordinate clause and the future tense in the main clause:

subordinate clause: main clause:
present   future

Unless citizens <u>regain</u> faith in politics, they <u>will</u> not <u>vote</u>.

Sometimes the verb in the main clause consists of *may, can, should,* or *might* plus the verb's plain form: *If citizens <u>regain</u> faith, they <u>may vote</u>.*

Speculation

Speculations are mainly of two kinds, each with its own verb pattern. For events that are possible in the present but unlikely, use the past tense in the subordinate clause and *would, could,* or *might* plus the verb's plain form in the main clause:

subordinate clause: main clause:
past   *would* + verb

If voters <u>had</u> more confidence, they <u>would vote</u> more often.

Use *were* instead of *was* when the subject is *I, he, she, it,* or a singular noun. (See pp. 196–97 for more on this distinctive verb form.)

subordinate clause: main clause:
past   *would* + verb

If the voter <u>were</u> more confident, he or she <u>would vote</u> more often.

For events that are impossible now, that are contrary to fact, use the same forms as above (including the distinctive *were* when applicable):

t seq
26e

subordinate clause:
past
main clause:
past

If Sir John A. Macdonald <u>were</u> available, he <u>might inspire</u> enthusiasm.

For events that were impossible in the past, use the past perfect tense in the subordinate clause and *would, could,* or *might* plus the present perfect tense in the main clause:

subordinate clause:
past perfect
main clause:
might + present perfect

If Sir Wilfrid Laurier <u>had lived</u> longer, he <u>might have helped</u> unify the country.

3   Indirect quotations ESL

An INDIRECT QUOTATION reports what someone said or wrote but not in the exact words and not in quotation marks: *Pierre Trudeau said that reason had made him* (quotation: "Reason made me"). Indirect quotations generally appear in a subordinate clause (underlined above), with certain conventions governing verb tense in most cases:

- When the verb in the main clause is in the present tense, the verb in the indirect quotation (subordinate clause) is in the same tense as the original quotation:

  main clause:
  present
  subordinate clause:
  present

  Ericson <u>says</u> that Macdonald <u>is</u> our preeminent national figure. [Quotation: "Macdonald <u>is</u> our preeminent national figure."]

  main clause:
  present
  subordinate clause:
  past

  He <u>says</u> that Macdonald <u>was</u> a brilliant motivator. [Quotation: "Macdonald <u>was</u> a brilliant motivator."]

- When the verb in the main clause is in the past tense, the verb in the indirect quotation usually changes tense from the original quotation. Present tense changes to past tense:

  main clause:
  past
  subordinate clause:
  past

  An adviser to Laurier <u>said</u> that the Prime Minister <u>was</u> always thoughtful. [Quotation: "The Prime Minister <u>is</u> always thoughtful."]

- Past tense and present perfect tense change to past perfect tense. (Past perfect tense does not change.)

  main clause:
  past
  subordinate clause:
  past perfect

  Trudeau <u>said</u> that reason <u>had made</u> him. [Quotation: "Reason <u>made</u> me."]

t seq

26e

- When the direct quotation states a general truth or reports a situation that is still true, use the present tense in the indirect quotation regardless of the verb in the main clause:

  main clause: subordinate clause:
  past   present
  Trudeau <u>said</u> that a lack of power <u>corrupts</u>. [Quotation: "Lack of power <u>corrupts</u>."]

Note As several of the examples show, an indirect quotation differs in at least two additional ways from the original quotation: (1) the indirect quotation is usually preceded by *that*, and (2) the indirect quotation changes pronouns, especially from forms of *I* or *we* to forms of *he, she,* or *they*.

27 Verb Mood

MOOD in grammar is a verb form that indicates the writer's or speaker's attitude toward what he or she is saying. The INDICATIVE MOOD states a fact or opinion or asks a question: *The theatre <u>needs</u> help*. The IMPERATIVE MOOD expresses a command or gives a direction. It omits the subject of the sentence, *you*: <u>Help</u> *the theatre*.

The SUBJUNCTIVE MOOD is trickier and requires distinctive verb forms described below.

Note A computerized grammar and style checker may spot some errors in the subjunctive mood, but it may miss others. Instead of relying on the checker to find and correct problems, proofread your work looking for appropriate uses of subjunctive verbs.

vb
27a

27a   Use the subjunctive verb forms appropriately, as in *I wish I were*.

The subjunctive mood expresses a suggestion, requirement, or desire, or it states a condition that is contrary to fact (that is, imaginary or hypothetical).

- Verbs such as *ask, insist, urge, require, recommend,* and *suggest* indicate request or requirement. They often precede a subordinate clause beginning with *that* and containing the substance of the request or requirement. For all subjects, the verb in the *that* clause is the plain form:

  plain
form
  Rules require that every donation <u>be</u> mailed.

- Contrary-to-fact clauses state imaginary or hypothetical conditions and usually begin with *if* or *unless* or follow *wish.* For present contrary-to-fact clauses, use the verb's past-tense form (for *be,* use the past-tense form *were*):

  past   past
  If the theatre <u>were</u> in better shape and <u>had</u> more money, its future would be assured.

  past
  I wish I <u>were</u> able to donate money.

- For past contrary-to-fact clauses, use the verb's past perfect form (*had* + past participle):

  past perfect
  The theatre would be better funded if it <u>had been</u> better managed.

  Note Do not use the helping verb *would* or *could* in a contrary-to-fact clause beginning with *if*:

NOT	Many people would have helped if they <u>would have</u> known.
BUT	Many people would have helped if they <u>had</u> known.

See also pages 193–95 for more on verb tenses in sentences like these.

vb
27b

(27b) Keep mood consistent.

Shifts in mood within a sentence or among related sentences can be confusing. Such shifts occur most frequently in directions.

INCONSISTENT	<u>Cook</u> the mixture slowly, and <u>you should stir</u> it until the sugar is dissolved. [Mood shifts from imperative to indicative.]
REVISED	<u>Cook</u> the mixture slowly, and <u>stir</u> it until the sugar is dissolved. [Consistently imperative.]

28 Verb Voice

The VOICE of a verb tells whether the subject of the sentence performs the action (ACTIVE) or is acted upon (PASSIVE). The actor in a passive sentence may be named in a prepositional phrase (as in the first passive example in the box below), or the actor may be omitted (as in the second passive example).

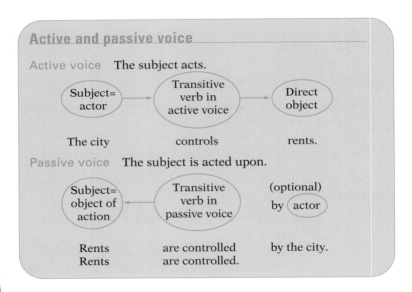

Active and passive voice

Active voice   The subject acts.

| Subject= actor | → | Transitive verb in active voice | → | Direct object |

The city   controls   rents.

Passive voice   The subject is acted upon.

| Subject= object of action | ← | Transitive verb in passive voice | (optional) by actor |

Rents   are controlled   by the city.
Rents   are controlled.

pass
28

ESL A passive verb always consists of a form of *be* plus the past participle of the main verb: *rents are controlled, people were inspired.* Other helping verbs must also be used with the words *be, being,* and *been: rents have been controlled, people would have been inspired.* Only a transitive verb (one that takes an object) may be used in the passive voice. (See p. 168.)

(28a) Generally, prefer the active voice.
Use the passive voice when the actor
is unknown or unimportant.

The active voice is usually clearer, more concise, and more forthright than the passive voice.

> WEAK PASSIVE The Internet is used for research by many schol-ars, and its expansion to the general public has been criticized by some.
>
> STRONG ACTIVE Many scholars use the Internet for research, and some have criticized its expansion to the general public.

The passive voice is useful in two situations: when the actor is unknown and when the actor is unimportant or less important than the object of the action.

> The Internet was established in 1969 by the U.S. Department of Defense. The network has now been extended internationally to governments, universities, foundations, corporations, and private individuals. [In the first sentence the writer wishes to stress the Internet rather than the Department of Defense. In the second sentence the actor is unknown or too complicated to name.]
>
> After the solution had been cooled to 10°C, the acid was added. [The person who cooled and added, perhaps the writer, is less important than the facts that the solution was cooled and acid was added. Passive sentences are common in scientific writing.]

Note Most computerized grammar and style checkers can be set to spot the passive voice. But they will then flag every instance, both appropriate (such as when the actor is unknown) and ineffective. And they will flag as passive some unobjectionable phrases that are actually a form of *be* plus a verb form serving as an adjective, such as the underlined words in this sentence: *We were delighted.* You'll need to decide for yourself whether flagged phrases really are passive and whether they are appropriate.

pass
28b

(28b) Keep voice consistent.

Shifts in voice that involve shifts in subject are usually unnecessary and confusing.

> INCONSISTENT Internet newsgroups cover an enormous range of topics for discussion. Forums for meeting people with like interests are provided in these groups.

REVISED   Internet <u>newsgroups cover</u> an enormous range of topics for discussion <u>and provide</u> forums for meeting people with like interests.

A shift in voice is appropriate when it helps focus the reader's attention on a single subject, as in *The <u>candidate campaigned</u> vigorously and <u>was nominated</u>* on the first ballot.

29 Agreement of Subject and Verb

A subject and its verb should agree in number and person.

More <u>Acadians live</u> in New Brunswick than in any other province.
subject   verb

<u>Acadia was</u> the name of the first French colony in Canada.
subject   verb

Most problems of subject–verb agreement arise when endings are omitted from subjects or verbs or when the relation between sentence parts is uncertain.

Note A computerized grammar and style checker will look for problems with subject–verb agreement. Most checkers also allow you to customize settings so that you can turn off other options and look just for agreement problems. However, a checker may mistakenly flag correct agreement and may then suggest "corrections" that are wrong. In addition, a checker may fail to spot actual errors. Do not automatically accept a checker's pointers, and proofread your work carefully on your own.

vb agr
29a

29a   The *-s* and *-es* endings work differently for nouns and verbs.

An *-s* or *-es* ending does opposite things to nouns and verbs: it usually makes a noun *plural*, but it always makes a present-tense verb *singular*. Thus if the subject noun is plural, it will end in *-s* or *-es* and the verb will not. If the subject is singular, it will not end in *-s* and the verb will.

Singular	Plural
The boy plays.	The boys play.
The bird soars.	The birds soar.

The only exceptions to these rules involve the nouns that form irregular plurals, such as *child/children, woman/women.* The irregular plural still requires a plural verb: *The children play. The women read.*

ESL Most noncount nouns—those that do not form plurals—take singular verbs: *That information is helpful.* (See p. 203 on collective nouns.)

(29b) Subject and verb should agree even when other words come between them.

The catalogue of course requirements often baffles [not baffle] students.

The requirements stated in the catalogue are [not is] unclear.

Note Phrases beginning with *as well as, together with, along with,* and *in addition to* do not change the number of the subject:

The president, as well as the deans, has [not have] agreed to revise the catalogue.

(29c) Subjects joined by *and* usually take plural verbs.

Gretzky and Coffey were teammates.

Exceptions When the parts of the subject form a single idea or refer to a single person or thing, they take a singular verb:

Avocado and bean sprouts is a California sandwich.

vb agr
29c

_ KEY TERMS _

PERSON	SINGULAR	PLURAL
First	I eat.	We eat.
Second	You eat.	You eat.
Third	He/she/it eats.	They eat.
	The bird eats.	Birds eat.

When a compound subject is preceded by the adjective *each* or *every*, the verb is usually singular:

Each man, woman, and child <u>has</u> a right to be heard.

29d When parts of a subject are joined by *or* or *nor*, the verb agrees with the nearer part.

Either the painter or the carpenter <u>knows</u> the cost.

The cabinets or the bookcases <u>are</u> too costly.

When one part of the subject is singular and the other plural, avoid awkwardness by placing the plural part closer to the verb so that the verb is plural:

AWKWARD   Neither the owners nor the contractor <u>agrees</u>.

REVISED   Neither the contractor nor the owners <u>agree</u>.

29e With *everyone* and other indefinite pronouns, use a singular or plural verb as appropriate.

Most indefinite pronouns are singular in meaning (they refer to a single unspecified person or thing), and they take a singular verb:

Something <u>smells</u>.   Neither <u>is</u> right.

vb agr

29e

KEY TERM _____

INDEFINITE PRONOUN A pronoun that does not refer to a specific person or thing:

			Singular or plural	*Plural*
Singular				
anybody	everyone	no one	all	both
anyone	everything	nothing	any	few
anything	much	one	more	many
each	neither	somebody	most	several
either	nobody	someone	some	
everybody	none	something		

The plural indefinite pronouns refer to more than one unspecified thing, and they take a plural verb:

Both are correct. Several were invited.

The other indefinite pronouns take a singular or a plural verb depending on whether the word they refer to is singular or plural:

All of the money is reserved for emergencies.

All of the funds are reserved for emergencies.

ESL See page 227 for the distinction between *few* ("not many") and *a few* ("some").

(29f) ## Collective nouns such as *team* take singular or plural verbs depending on meaning.

Use a singular verb with a collective noun when the group acts as a unit:

The group agrees that action is necessary.

But when the group's members act separately, not together, use a plural verb:

The old group have gone their separate ways.

The collective noun *number* may be singular or plural. Preceded by *a,* it is plural; preceded by *the,* it is singular:

A number of people are in debt.

The number of people in debt is very large.

vb agr
29f

ESL Some noncount nouns (nouns that don't form plurals) are collective nouns because they name groups: for instance, *furniture, clothing, mail.* These noncount nouns usually take singular verbs: *Mail arrives daily.* But some of these nouns take plural verbs, including *clergy, military, people, police,* and any collective noun that comes from an adjective, such as *the poor, the rich, the young, the elderly.* If you mean one representative of the group, use a singular noun such as *police officer* or *poor person.*

29g   *Who, which,* and *that* take verbs that agree with their antecedents.

When used as subjects, *who, which,* and *that* refer to another word in the sentence, called the ANTECEDENT. The verb agrees with the antecedent.

Mayor Garber ought to listen to the people who work for her.

Bardini is the only aide who has her ear.

Agreement problems often occur with relative pronouns when the sentence includes *one of the* or *the only one of the*:

Bardini is one of the aides who work unpaid. [Of the aides who work unpaid, Bardini is one.]

Bardini is the only one of the aides who knows the community. [Of the aides, only one, Bardini, knows the community.]

ESL In phrases like those above beginning with *one of the*, be sure the noun is plural: *Bardini is one of the aides [not aide] who work unpaid.*

29h   *News* and other singular nouns ending in *-s* take singular verbs.

Singular nouns ending in *-s* include *athletics, economics, linguistics, mathematics, measles, mumps, news, physics, politics,* and *statistics,* as well as place names such as *Athens, Wales,* and *United States.*

After so long a wait, the news has to be good.

Statistics is required of psychology majors.

A few of these words also take plural verbs, but only when they describe individual items rather than whole bodies of activity or knowledge: *The statistics prove him wrong.*

vb agr
29h

_ KEY TERM _

COLLECTIVE NOUN A noun with singular form that names a group of individuals or things—for instance, *army, audience, committee, crowd, family, group, team.*

Measurements and figures ending in *-s* may also be singular when the quantity they refer to is a unit.

Three years is a long time to wait.

Three-fourths of the library consists of reference books.

29i   The verb agrees with the subject even when the normal word order is inverted.

Inverted subject-verb order occurs mainly in questions and in constructions beginning with *there* or *it* and a form of *be*.

Is voting a right or a privilege?

Are a right and a privilege the same thing?

There are differences between them.

29j   *Is*, *are*, and other linking verbs agree with their subjects, not subject complements.

Make a linking verb agree with its subject, usually the first element in the sentence, not with the noun or pronoun serving as a subject complement.

The child's sole support is her court-appointed guardians.

Her court-appointed guardians are the child's sole support.

29k   Use singular verbs with titles and with words being described or defined.

vb agr
29k

Hakada Associates is a new firm.

Dream Days remains a favourite book.

Folks is a down-home word for *people*.

KEY TERMS

LINKING VERB A verb that connects or equates the subject and subject complement: for example, *seem, become,* and forms of *be*. (See p. 169.)

SUBJECT COMPLEMENT A word that describes or renames the subject: *They became chemists*. (See pp. 168–69.)

Pronouns

PRONOUNS—words such as *she* and *who* that refer to nouns—merit special care because all their meaning comes from the other words they refer to. This section discusses pronoun case (Chapter 30), matching pronouns and the words they refer to (31), and making sure pronouns refer to the right nouns (32).

30 Pronoun Case

CASE is the form of a noun or pronoun that shows the reader how that noun or pronoun functions in a sentence.

- The *subjective case* indicates that the word is a subject or subject complement.
- The *objective case* indicates that the word is an object of a verb or preposition.
- The *possessive case* indicates that the word owns or is the source of a noun in the sentence.

case

30

--- KEY TERMS ---

SUBJECT Who or what a sentence is about: *Biologists often study animals. They often work in laboratories.* (See p. 167.)

SUBJECT COMPLEMENT A word that renames or describes the sentence subject: *Biologists are scientists. The best biologists are she and Scoggins.* (See p. 169.)

OBJECT OF VERB The receiver of the verb's action (DIRECT OBJECT): *Many biologists study animals. The animals teach them.* Or the person or thing the action is performed for (INDIRECT OBJECT): *Some biologists give animals homes. The animals give them pleasure.* (See p. 168.)

OBJECT OF PREPOSITION The word linked by *with, for,* or another preposition to the rest of the sentence: *Many biologists work in a laboratory. For them the lab often provides a second home.* (See p. 170.)

Nouns change form only to show possession: *teacher's*. (See pp. 267–69.) The following pronouns change much more frequently:

Subjective	Objective	Possessive
I	me	my, mine
you	you	your, yours
he	him	his
she	her	her, hers
it	it	its
we	us	our, ours
you	you	your, yours
they	them	their, theirs
who	whom	whose
whoever	whomever	—

Note Computerized grammar and style checkers have difficulty with pronoun cases: they may flag as incorrect many appropriate uses of pronouns and yet miss others that are incorrect. Carefully consider any flagged pronoun and review your sentences on your own as well, deciding for yourself which are correct.

 30a Distinguish between compound subjects and compound objects: *she and I* vs. *her and me*.

Compound subjects or objects—those consisting of two or more nouns or pronouns—have the same case forms as they would if one noun or pronoun stood alone:

compound
subject
She and Novick discussed the proposal.

compound
object
The proposal disappointed her and him.

If you are in doubt about the correct form, try the test below:

A test for case forms in compound constructions

- Identify a compound construction (one connected by *and, but, or, nor*):

[He, Him] and [I, me] won the prize.
The prize went to [he, him] and [I, me].

case
30a

- Write a separate sentence for each part of the compound:

  [He, Him] won the prize. [I, Me] won the prize.
  The prize went to [he, him]. The prize went to [I, me].

- Choose the pronouns that sound correct:

  He won the prize. I won the prize. [Subjective.]
  The prize went to him. The prize went to me. [Objective.]

- Put the separate sentences back together:

  He and I won the prize.
  The prize went to him and me.

(30b) Use the subjective case for subject complements: *It was she*.

After a linking verb, a pronoun renaming the subject (a subject complement) should be in the subjective case:

                                    subject
                                 complement
The ones who care most are she and Novick.

        subject
     complement
It was they whom the mayor appointed.

If this construction sounds stilted to you, use the more natural order: *She and Novick are the ones who care most. The mayor appointed them.*

---

case

30c

(30c) The use of *who* vs. *whom* depends on the pronoun's function in its clause.

1   Questions

At the beginning of a question use *who* for a subject and *whom* for an object:

subject ⟶   object ⟵
Who wrote the policy?   Whom does it affect?

___ KEY TERM _____

LINKING VERB A verb, such as a form of *be*, that connects a subject and a word that renames or describes the subject (subject complement): *They are biologists.* (See p. 169.)

To find the correct case of *who* in a question, follow the steps below.

- Pose the question:

  [Who, Whom] makes that decision?
  [Who, Whom] does one ask?

- Answer the question, using a personal pronoun. Choose the pronoun that sounds correct, and note its case:

  [She, Her] makes that decision. <u>She</u> makes that decision. [Subjective.]
  One asks [she, her]. One asks <u>her</u>. [Objective.]

- Use the same case (*who* or *whom*) in the question:

  <u>Who</u> makes that decision? [Subjective.]
  <u>Whom</u> does one ask? [Objective.]

2   Subordinate clauses

In subordinate clauses use *who* and *whoever* for all subjects, *whom* and *whomever* for all objects.

subject ⟶
Give old clothes to <u>whoever</u> needs them.

object ⟵
I don't know <u>whom</u> the mayor appointed.

To determine which form to use, try the test below:

- Locate the subordinate clause:

  Few people know [<u>who, whom</u>] they should ask.
  They are unsure [<u>who, whom</u>] makes the decision.

- Rewrite the subordinate clause as a separate sentence, substituting a personal pronoun for *who, whom.* Choose the pronoun that sounds correct, and note its case:

  They should ask [she, her]. They should ask <u>her</u>. [Objective.]
  [She, her] usually makes the decision. <u>She</u> usually makes the decision. [Subjective.]

- Use the same case (*who* or *whom*) in the subordinate clause:

  Few people know <u>whom</u> they should ask. [Objective.]
  They are unsure <u>who</u> makes the decision. [Subjective.]

case

30c

___ KEY TERM ___

SUBORDINATE CLAUSE A word group that contains a subject and a verb and also begins with a subordinating word, such as *who, whom,* or *because.* (See p. 173.)

Note Don't let expressions such as *I think* and *she says* mislead you into using *whom* rather than *who* for the subject of a clause.

subject ⟶
He is the one who I think is best qualified.

To choose between who and whom in such constructions, delete the interrupting phrase so that you can see the true relation between parts: He is the one who is best qualified.

(30d) Use the appropriate case in other constructions.

1   *We* or *us* with a noun

The choice of *we* or *us* before a noun depends on the use of the noun:

object of preposition ⟶
Freezing weather is welcomed by us skaters.

subject ⟶
We skaters welcome freezing weather.

2   Pronoun in an appositive

In an appositive the case of a pronoun depends on the function of the word the appositive describes or identifies:

appositive identifies object
The class elected two representatives, DeShawn and me.

appositive identifies subject
Two representatives, DeShawn and I, were elected.

3   Pronoun after *than* or *as*

When a pronoun follows *than* or *as* in a comparison, the case of the pronoun indicates what words may have been omitted. A subjective pronoun must be the subject of the omitted verb:

subject
Some critics like Glass more than he [does].

An objective pronoun must be the object of the omitted verb:

object
Some critics like Glass more than [they like] him.

case
30d

_ KEY TERM _____

APPOSITIVE A noun or noun substitute that renames another noun immediately before it. (See p. 172.)

4   Subject and object of infinitive

Both the object *and* the subject of an infinitive are in the objective case:

subject of infinitive
The school asked <u>him</u> to speak.

object of infinitive
Students chose to invite <u>him</u>.

5   Case before a gerund

Ordinarily, use the possessive form of a pronoun or noun immediately before a gerund:

The coach disapproved of <u>their</u> lifting weights.

The <u>coach's</u> disapproving was a surprise.

31 Agreement of Pronoun and Antecedent

The ANTECEDENT of a pronoun is the noun or other pronoun to which the pronoun refers:

<u>Homeowners</u> fret over <u>their</u> tax bills.
antecedent   pronoun

pn agr
31

<u>Its</u> constant increases make the tax <u>bill</u> a dreaded document.
pronoun   antecedent

For clarity, a pronoun should agree with its antecedent in person, number, and gender.

Note A computerized grammar and style checker cannot help you with agreement between pronoun and antecedent. You'll need to check for errors on your own.

_KEY TERMS_____

INFINITIVE The plain form of the verb plus *to*: *to run*. (See p. 171.)

GERUND The *-ing* form of a verb used as a noun: <u>Running</u> *is fun*. (See p. 171.)

ESL The gender of a pronoun should match its antecedent, not a noun that the pronoun may modify: *Sara Young invited her* [not *his*] *son to join the company's staff.* Also, nouns in English have only neuter gender unless they specifically refer to males or females. Thus nouns such as *book*, *table*, *sun*, and *earth* take the pronoun *it*.

31a Antecedents joined by *and* usually take plural pronouns.

Mr. Bartos and I cannot settle our dispute.

The dean and my adviser have offered their help.

Exceptions When the compound antecedent refers to a single idea, person, or thing, then the pronoun is singular.

My friend and adviser offered her help.

When the compound antecedent follows *each* or *every*, the pronoun is singular.

Every girl and woman took her seat.

31b When parts of an antecedent are joined by *or* or *nor*, the pronoun agrees with the nearer part.

Tenants or owners must present their grievances.

Either the tenant or the owner will have her way.

pn agr
31b

_KEY TERMS_____

PERSON	SINGULAR	PLURAL
FIRST	*I*	*we*
SECOND	*you*	*you*
THIRD	*he, she, it*	*they*
	indefinite pronouns, singular nouns	plural nouns
GENDER		
MASCULINE	*he*, nouns naming males	
FEMININE	*she*, nouns naming females	
NEUTER	*it*, all other nouns	

When one subject is plural and the other singular, the sentence will be awkward unless you put the plural subject second.

> **AWKWARD**   Neither the tenants nor the owner has yet made <u>her</u> case.

> **REVISED**   Neither the owner nor the tenants have yet made <u>their</u> case.

(31c)   With ***everyone, person,*** and other indefinite words, use a singular or plural pronoun as appropriate.

Indefinite words—indefinite pronouns and generic nouns—do not refer to any specific person or thing. Most indefinite pronouns and all generic nouns are singular in meaning. When they serve as antecedents of pronouns, the pronouns should be singular:

> Everyone on the women's team now has <u>her</u> own locker.
> indefinite
pronoun

> Every person on the women's team now has <u>her</u> own locker.
> generic
noun

Five indefinite pronouns—*all, any, more, most, some*—may be singular or plural in meaning depending on what they refer to:

> Few women athletes had changing spaces, so most had to change
>
> in <u>their</u> rooms.

KEY TERMS

INDEFINITE PRONOUN A pronoun that does not refer to a specific person or thing:

Singular			*Singular or plural*	*Plural*
anybody	everyone	no one	all	both
anyone	everything	nothing	any	few
anything	much	one	more	many
each	neither	somebody	most	several
either	nobody	someone	some	
everybody	none	something		

GENERIC NOUN A singular noun such as *person, individual,* and *student* when it refers to a typical member of a group, not to a particular individual: *The <u>individual</u> has rights.*

pn agr

31c

Most of the changing space was dismal, its colour a drab olive green.

Four indefinite pronouns—*both, few, many, several*—are always plural in meaning:

Few realize how their athletic facilities have changed.

Most agreement problems arise with the singular indefinite words. We often use these words to mean something like "many" or "all" rather than "one" and then refer to them with plural pronouns, as in *Everyone has their own locker* or *A person can padlock their locker.* Often, too, we mean indefinite words to include both masculine and feminine genders and thus resort to *they* instead of the generic *he*—the masculine pronoun referring to both genders, as in *Everyone has his own locker.* (For more on the generic *he*, which many readers view as sexist, see pp. 142–44.) To achieve agreement in such cases, you have several options:

- Change the indefinite word to a plural, and use a plural pronoun to match:

  Athletes deserve their privacy.

  All athletes are entitled to their own lockers. [Notice that *locker* also changes to *lockers*.]

- Rewrite the sentence to omit the pronoun:

  The athlete deserves privacy.
  Everyone is entitled to a locker.

- Use *he or she* (*him or her, his or her*) to refer to the indefinite word:

  The athlete deserves his or her privacy.

pn agr
31d

However, used more than once in several sentences, *he or she* quickly becomes awkward. (Many readers do not accept the alternative *he/she.*) In most cases, using the plural or rewriting the sentence will not only correct an agreement problem but create a more readable sentence.

(31d) Collective nouns such as *team* take singular or plural pronouns depending on meaning.

Use a singular pronoun with a collective noun when referring to the group as a unit:

The committee voted to disband itself.

When referring to the individual members of the group, use a plural pronoun:

The old group have gone <u>their</u> separate ways.

ESL Collective nouns that are noncount nouns (they don't form plurals) usually take singular pronouns: *The mail sits in <u>its</u> own basket.* A few noncount nouns take plural pronouns, including *clergy, military, police, the rich,* and *the poor: The police support <u>their</u> unions.*

32 Reference of Pronoun to Antecedent

A pronoun should refer clearly to its ANTECEDENT, the noun it substitutes for. Otherwise, readers will have difficulty grasping the pronoun's meaning.

Note Computerized grammar and style checkers are not sophisticated enough to recognize unclear pronoun reference. For instance, a checker did not flag any of the confusing examples on this page or pages 216–18. You must proofread your work to spot unclear pronoun reference.

ref
32

ESL A pronoun needs a clear antecedent nearby, but don't use both a pronoun and its antecedent as the subject of the same clause: *<u>Jim</u>* [not *Jim he*] *told Mark to go alone.* (See also p. 244.)

_ KEY TERM _

COLLECTIVE NOUN A noun with singular form that names a group of individuals or things—for instance, *army, committee, family.*

32a   Make a pronoun refer clearly to one antecedent.

When either of two nouns can be a pronoun's antecedent, the reference will not be clear.

CONFUSING   Emily Dickinson is sometimes compared with Jane
Austen, but she was quite different.

Revise such a sentence in one of two ways:

* Replace the pronoun with the appropriate noun.

    CLEAR   Emily Dickinson is sometimes compared with
    Jane Austen, but Dickinson [or Austen] was quite
    different.

* Avoid repetition by rewriting the sentence. If you use the pronoun, make sure it has only one possible antecedent.

    CLEAR   Despite occasional comparison, Emily
    Dickinson and Jane Austen were quite different.

    CLEAR   Though sometimes compared with her, Emily
    Dickinson was quite different from Jane Austen.

32b   Place a pronoun close enough to its antecedent to ensure clarity.

A clause beginning with *who, which,* or *that* should generally fall immediately after the word to which it refers:

CONFUSING   Jody found a dress in the attic that her aunt had
worn.

CLEAR   In the attic Jody found a dress that her aunt had
worn.

32c   Make a pronoun refer to a specific antecedent, not an implied one.

A pronoun should refer to a specific noun or other pronoun. A reader can only guess at the meaning of a pronoun when its antecedent is implied by the context, not stated outright.

1   Vague *this, that, which,* or *it*

This, that, which, or *it* should refer to a specific noun, not to a whole word group expressing an idea or situation.

CONFUSING	The faculty agreed on changing the requirements, but it took time.
CLEAR	The faculty agreed on changing the requirements, but the agreement took time.
CLEAR	The faculty agreed on changing the requirements, but the change took time.
CONFUSING	The voyageurs interacted freely with the Natives and travelled wherever furs and the waterways took them. This gave the voyageurs a great advantage.
CLEAR	The voyageurs interacted freely with the Natives and travelled wherever furs and the waterways took them. This freedom and mobility gave the voyageurs a great advantage.

2   Implied nouns

A noun may be implied in some other word or phrase, such as an adjective (*happiness* implied in *happy*), a verb (*driver* implied in *drive*), or a possessive (*mother* implied in *mother's*). But a pronoun cannot refer clearly to an implied noun, only to a specific, stated one.

CONFUSING	Cohen's report brought her a lawsuit.
CLEAR	Cohen was sued over her report.
CONFUSING	Her reports on psychological development generally go unnoticed outside it.
CLEAR	Her reports on psychological development generally go unnoticed outside the field.

ref
32c

3   Indefinite *it, they,* or *you*

It, they, and *you* should have definite antecedents—nouns for *it* and *they,* an actual reader being addressed for *you*. Rewrite the sentence if the antecedent is missing.

CONFUSING	In Chapter 4 of this book it describes the seigneurial system of New France.

CLEAR   Chapter 4 of this book describes the seigneurial
             system of New France.

CONFUSING   In the average television drama they present a
             false picture of life.

CLEAR   The average television drama presents a false
             picture of life.

In all but very formal writing, *you* is acceptable when the
meaning is clearly "you, the reader." But the context must be appropriate for such a meaning.

INAPPROPRIATE In the fourteenth century you had to struggle
             simply to survive.
REVISED   In the fourteenth century one [or a person or
             people] had to struggle simply to survive.

(32d) Keep pronouns consistent.

Within a sentence or a group of related sentences, pronouns
should be consistent. Partly, consistency comes from making pronouns and their antecedents agree (see Chapter 31). In addition, the
pronouns within a passage should match each other.

INCONSISTENT One finds when reading that your concentration
             improves with practice, so that I now compre-
             hend more in less time.
REVISED   I find when reading that my concentration
             improves with practice, so that I now compre-
             hend more in less time.

ref
32d

Modifiers

MODIFIERS describe or limit other words in a sentence. They are adjectives, adverbs, or word groups serving as adjectives or adverbs. This section shows you how to identify and solve problems in the forms of modifiers (Chapter 33) and in their relation to the rest of the sentence (34).

33 Adjectives and Adverbs

ADJECTIVES modify nouns (*happy child*) and pronouns (*special someone*). ADVERBS modify verbs (*almost see*), adjectives (*very happy*), other adverbs (*not very*), and whole word groups (*Otherwise, the room was empty*). The only way to tell whether a modifier should be an adjective or an adverb is to determine its function in the sentence.

Note Computerized grammar and style checkers will spot some but not all problems with misused adjectives and adverbs. For instance, a checker flagged *Some children suffer bad* and *Chang was the most wisest person in town* and *Jenny did not feel nothing*. But it did not flag *Educating children good is everyone's focus* or *He was the most unique teacher we had*. You'll need to proofread your work on your own to be sure you've used adjectives and adverbs appropriately.

ESL In English an adjective does not change along with the noun it modifies to show plural number: *white* [not *whites*] *shoes*, *square* [not *squares*] *spaces*, *better* [not *betters*] *chances*. Only nouns form plurals.

(33a) Use adjectives only to modify nouns and pronouns.

Using adjectives instead of adverbs to modify verbs, adverbs, or other adjectives is nonstandard:

NONSTANDARD Educating children good is everyone's focus.

STANDARD   Educating children well is everyone's focus.

NONSTANDARD Some children suffer bad.

STANDARD   Some children suffer badly.

ESL To negate a verb or an adjective, use the adverb *not*:

They are not learning. They are not stupid.

To negate a noun, use the adjective *no*:

No child should fail to read.

(33b) Use an adjective after a linking verb to modify the subject. Use an adverb to modify a verb.

Some verbs may or may not be linking verbs, depending on their meaning in the sentence. When the word after the verb modifies the subject, the verb is linking and the word should be an adjective: *He looked happy.* When the word modifies the verb, however, it should be an adverb: *He looked carefully.*

Two word pairs are especially tricky. One is *bad* and *badly*:

ad
33b

The weather grew bad.   She felt bad.
        linking adjective   linking adjective
        verb   verb

Flowers grow badly in such soil.
        verb   adverb

KEY TERM

LINKING VERB A verb that connects a subject and a word that describes the subject: *They are golfers.* Linking verbs are forms of *be*, the verbs of our five senses (*look, sound, smell, feel, taste*), and *appear, seem, become, grow, turn, prove, remain, stay.* (See p. 169.)

The other is *good* and *well*. *Good* serves only as an adjective. *Well* may serve as an adverb with a host of meanings or as an adjective meaning only "fit" or "healthy."

Decker trained <u>well</u>.
verb   adverb

She felt <u>well</u>.
linking adjective
verb

Her health was <u>good</u>.
linking adjective
verb

(33c)   Use the comparative and superlative forms of adjectives and adverbs appropriately.

Adjectives and adverbs can show degrees of quality or amount with the endings *-er* and *-est* or with the words *more* and *most* or *less* and *least*. Most modifiers have three forms:

	Adjectives	Adverbs
Positive The basic form listed in the dictionary	red awful	soon quickly
Comparative A greater or lesser degree of the quality named	redder more/less awful	sooner more/less quickly
Superlative The greatest or least degree of the quality named	reddest most/least awful	soonest most/least quickly

If sound alone does not tell you whether to use *-er/-est* or *more/most*, consult a dictionary. If the endings can be used, the dictionary will list them. Otherwise, use *more* or *most*.

1   Irregular adjectives and adverbs

The irregular modifiers change the spelling of their positive form to show comparative and superlative degrees.

Positive	Comparative	Superlative
Adjectives		
good	better	best
bad	worse	worst
little	littler, less	littlest, least
many some much	more	most
Adverbs		
well	better	best
badly	worse	worst

ad

33c

2   Double comparisons

A double comparative or double superlative combines the *-er* or *-est* ending with the word *more* or *most*. It is redundant.

Chang was the <u>wisest</u> [not <u>most wisest</u>] person in town.
He was <u>smarter</u> [not <u>more smarter</u>] than anyone else.

3   Logical comparisons

Absolute modifiers

Some adjectives and adverbs cannot logically be compared—for instance, *perfect, unique, dead, impossible, infinite*. These absolute words can be preceded by adverbs like *nearly* or *almost* that mean "approaching," but they cannot logically be modified by *more* or *most* (as in *most perfect*).

NOT   He was the <u>most unique</u> teacher we had.
BUT   He was a <u>unique</u> teacher.

Completeness

To be logical, a comparison must also be complete in the following ways:

- The comparison must state a relation fully enough for clarity.

UNCLEAR Carmakers worry about their industry more than
         environmentalists.
CLEAR   Carmakers worry about their industry more than
         environmentalists <u>do</u>.
CLEAR   Carmakers worry about their industry more than
         <u>they worry about</u> environmentalists.

- The items being compared should in fact be comparable.

ILLOGICAL The cost of an electric car is greater than a gasoline-
          powered car. [Illogically compares a cost and a car.]
REVISED   The cost of an electric car is greater than <u>the cost of</u>
          [or <u>that of</u>] a gasoline-powered car.

See also pages 132–34 on parallelism with comparisons.

Any versus *any other*

Use *any other* when comparing something with others in the same group. Use *any* when comparing something with others in a different group.

ILLOGICAL Los Angeles is larger than <u>any</u> city in California.
          [Since Los Angeles is itself a city in California, the
          sentence seems to say that Los Angeles is larger
          than itself.]
REVISED   Los Angeles is larger than <u>any other</u> city in California.

ILLOGICAL Los Angeles is larger than <u>any other</u> city in Canada.
[The cities in Canada constitute a group to which
Los Angeles does not belong.]
REVISED Los Angeles is larger than <u>any</u> city in Canada.

(33d) Watch for double negatives.

A DOUBLE NEGATIVE is a nonstandard construction in which two negative words such as *no, none, neither, barely, hardly,* or *scarcely* cancel each other out. Some double negatives are intentional: for instance, *She was <u>not unhappy</u>* indicates with understatement that she was indeed happy. But most double negatives say the opposite of what is intended: *Jenny did <u>not</u> feel <u>nothing</u>* asserts that Jenny felt other than nothing, or something. For the opposite meaning, one of the negatives must be eliminated (*She felt <u>nothing</u>*) or one of them must be changed to a positive (*She did not feel <u>anything</u>*).

FAULTY   Canada Revenue <u>cannot hardly</u> audit all tax returns.
<u>None</u> of its audits <u>never</u> touch many cheaters.
REVISED Canada Revenue <u>cannot</u> audit all tax returns. Its
audits <u>never</u> touch many cheaters.

(33e) Distinguish between present and past participles as adjectives. ESL

Both present participles and past participles may serve as adjectives: *a <u>burning</u> building, a <u>burned</u> building.* As in the examples, the two participles usually differ in the time they indicate.

But some present and past participles—those derived from verbs expressing feeling—can have altogether different meanings. The present participle refers to something that causes the feeling: *That was a <u>frightening</u> storm.* The past participle refers to something that experiences the feeling: *They quieted the <u>frightened</u> horses.*

The following participles are among those likely to be confused:

amazing/amazed   annoying/annoyed
amusing/amused   astonishing/astonished

ad
33e

KEY TERMS

PRESENT PARTICIPLE The *-ing* form of a verb: *flying, writing.* (See p. 163.)

PAST PARTICIPLE The *-d* or *-ed* form of a regular verb: *slipped, walked.* Most irregular verbs have distinctive past participles, such as *eaten* or *swum.* (See pp. 162–63.)

boring/bored
confusing/confused
depressing/depressed
embarrassing/embarrassed
exciting/excited
exhausting/exhausted
fascinating/fascinated
frightening/frightened

frustrating/frustrated
interesting/interested
pleasing/pleased
satisfying/satisfied
shocking/shocked
surprising/surprised
tiring/tired
worrying/worried

(33f) Use *a, an, the*, and other determiners appropriately. ESL

DETERMINERS are special kinds of adjectives that mark nouns because they always precede nouns. Some common determiners are *a, an,* and *the* (called ARTICLES) and *my, their, whose, this, these, those, one, some,* and *any.*

Native speakers of English can rely on their intuition when using determiners, but nonnative speakers often have difficulty with them because many other languages use them quite differently or not at all. In English the use of determiners depends on the context they appear in and the kind of nouns they precede:

- A PROPER NOUN names a particular person, place, or thing and begins with a capital letter: *February, Joe Allen, Red River.* Most proper nouns are not preceded by determiners.
- A COUNT NOUN names something that is countable in English and can form a plural: *girl/girls, apple/apples, child/children.* A singular count noun is always preceded by a determiner; a plural count noun sometimes is.
- A NONCOUNT NOUN names something not usually considered countable in English, and so it does not form a plural. A noncount noun is sometimes preceded by a determiner. Here is a sample of noncount nouns, sorted into groups by meaning:

Abstractions: confidence, democracy, education, equality, evidence, health, information, intelligence, knowledge, luxury, peace, pollution, research, success, supervision, truth, wealth, work
Food and drink: bread, candy, cereal, flour, meat, milk, salt, water, wine
Emotions: anger, courage, happiness, hate, joy, love, respect, satisfaction
Natural events and substances: air, blood, dirt, gasoline, gold, hair, heat, ice, oil, oxygen, rain, silver, smoke, weather, wood
Groups: clergy, clothing, equipment, furniture, garbage, jewellery, junk, legislation, machinery, mail, military, money, police, vocabulary

Fields of study: accounting, architecture, biology, business, chemistry, engineering, literature, psychology, science

An ESL dictionary will tell you whether a noun is a count noun, a noncount noun, or both. (See pp. 145–146 for recommended dictionaries.)

Note Many nouns are sometimes count nouns and sometimes noncount nouns:

The library has a <u>room</u> for readers. [*Room* is a count noun meaning "walled area."]
The library has <u>room</u> for reading. [*Room* is a noncount noun meaning "space."]

Partly because the same noun may fall into different groups, computerized grammar and style checkers are unreliable guides to missing or misused articles and other determiners. For instance, a checker flagged the omitted *a* before *Scientist* in *Scientist developed new processes;* it did not flag the omitted *a* before *new* in *A scientist developed new process;* and it mistakenly flagged the correctly omitted article *the* before *Vegetation* in *Vegetation suffers from drought.* To correct omitted or misused articles, you'll need to proofread carefully on your own.

1 *A, an,* and ***the***

With singular count nouns

A or *an* precedes a singular count noun when the reader does not already know its identity, usually because you have not mentioned it before:

<u>A</u> scientist in our chemistry department developed <u>a</u> process to strengthen metals. [*Scientist* and *process* are being introduced for the first time.]

The precedes a singular count noun that has a specific identity for the reader, usually because (1) you have mentioned it before, (2) you identify it immediately before or after you state it, (3) it is unique (the only one in existence), or (4) it refers to an institution or facility that is shared by a community:

A scientist in our chemistry department developed a process to strengthen metals. <u>The</u> scientist patented <u>the</u> process. [*Scientist* and *process* were identified in the preceding sentence.]

<u>The</u> most productive laboratory is <u>the</u> research centre in <u>the</u> chemistry department. [*Most productive* identifies *laboratory. In the chemistry department* identifies *research centre.* And *chemistry department* is a shared facility.]

det
33f

The sun rises in the east. [*Sun* and *east* are unique.]

Many men and women aspire to the presidency. [*Presidency* is a shared institution.]

The fax machine has changed business communication. [*Fax machine* is a shared facility.]

The is not used before a singular noun that names a general category:

Wordsworth's poetry shows his love of nature [not the nature].

General Sherman said that war is hell. [*War* names a general category.]

The war in Croatia left many dead. [*War* names a specific war.]

With plural count nouns

A or *an* never precedes a plural noun. *The* does not precede a plural noun that names a general category. *The* does precede a plural noun that names specific representatives of a category.

Men and women are different. [*Men* and *women* name general categories.]

The women formed a team. [*Women* refers to specific people.]

With noncount nouns

A or *an* never precedes a noncount noun. *The* does precede a noncount noun that names specific representatives of a general category.

Vegetation suffers from drought. [*Vegetation* names a general category.]

The vegetation in the park withered or died. [*Vegetation* refers to specific plants.]

With proper nouns

det
33f

A or *an* never precedes a proper noun. *The* generally does not precede proper nouns.

Sanjay lives in Flin Flon.

There are exceptions, however. For instance, we generally use *the* before plural proper nouns (*the* Murphys, *the* Edmonton Oilers) and before the names of groups and organizations (*the* Board of Education, *the* Hot Stove League), ships (*the* Lusitania), oceans (*the* Pacific), mountain ranges (*the* Alps), regions (*the* Middle East), rivers (*the* Thompson), and some countries (*the* Philippines, *the* Netherlands).

2   Other determiners

The uses of English determiners besides articles also depend on context and kind of noun. The following determiners may be used as indicated with singular count nouns, plural count nouns, or non-count nouns.

With any kind of noun (singular count, plural count, noncount)

my, our, your, his, her, its, their, possessive nouns (*boy's, boys'*)
whose, which(ever), what(ever)
some, any, the other
no

Their account is overdrawn. [Singular count.]
Their funds are low. [Plural count.]
Their money is running out. [Noncount.]

Only with singular nouns (count and noncount)

this, that
This account has some money. [Count.]
That information may help. [Noncount.]

Only with noncount nouns and plural count nouns

most, enough, other, such, all, all of the, a lot of
Most funds are committed. [Plural count.]
Most money is needed elsewhere. [Noncount.]

Only with singular count nouns

one, every, each, either, neither, another
One car must be sold. [Singular count.]

Only with plural count nouns

these, those
both, many, few, a few, fewer, fewest, several
two, three, and so forth
Two cars are unnecessary. [Plural count.]

det
33f

Note *Few* means "not many" or "not enough." *A few* means "some" or "a small but sufficient quantity."

Few committee members came to the meeting.
A few members can keep the committee going.

Do not use *much* with a plural count noun.

Many [not much] members want to help.

Only with noncount nouns

much, more, little, a little, less, least, a large amount of
<u>Less</u> luxury is in order. [Noncount.]

Note *Little* means "not many" or "not enough." *A little* means "some" or "a small but sufficient quantity."

<u>Little</u> time remains before the conference.
The members need <u>a little</u> help from their colleagues.

Do not use *many* with a noncount noun.
<u>Much</u> [not <u>many</u>] work remains.

34 Misplaced and Dangling Modifiers

The arrangement of words in a sentence is an important clue to their relationships. Modifiers will be unclear if readers can't connect them to the words they modify.

Note Computerized grammar and style checkers do not recognize many problems with modifiers. For instance, a checker failed to flag the misplaced modifiers in *Gasoline high prices affect usually car sales* or the dangling modifier in *The vandalism was visible passing the building.* Proofread your work on your own to find and correct problems with modifiers.

mm
34a

34a Reposition misplaced modifiers.

A MISPLACED MODIFIER falls in the wrong place in a sentence. It is usually awkward or confusing. It may even be unintentionally funny.

1 Clear placement

Readers tend to link a modifier to the nearest word it could modify. Any other placement can link the modifier to the wrong word.

CONFUSING   He served steak to the men on paper plates.

CLEAR   He served the men steak on paper plates.

CONFUSING   According to the police, many dogs are killed by auto-
             mobiles and trucks roaming unleashed.

CLEAR   According to the police, many dogs roaming unleashed
             are killed by automobiles and trucks.

2   *Only* and other limiting modifiers

LIMITING MODIFIERS include *almost, even, exactly, hardly, just, merely, nearly, only, scarcely,* and *simply.* For clarity place such a modifier immediately before the word or word group you intend it to limit.

UNCLEAR   The archaeologist only found the skull on her last dig.

CLEAR   The archaeologist found only the skull on her last dig.

CLEAR   The archaeologist found the skull only on her last dig.

3   Adverbs with grammatical units

Adverbs can often move around in sentences, but some will be awkward if they interrupt certain grammatical units:

- A single-word adverb can interrupt subject and verb: *Bo gladly accepted.* But a longer adverb stops the flow of the sentence:

                   subject _____ adverb _____ verb
AWKWARD   Kuwait, after the Gulf War ended in 1991, began
             returning to normal.

             _____ adverb _____ subject verb
REVISED   After the Gulf War ended in 1991, Kuwait began
             returning to normal.

- Any adverb is awkward between a verb and its direct object:

                   ___ verb ___ adverb object
AWKWARD   The war had damaged badly many of Kuwait's oil fields.

                   ___ verb ___ object
REVISED   The war had badly damaged many of Kuwait's oil fields.
                   adverb

- A SPLIT INFINITIVE—an adverb placed between *to* and the verb— annoys many readers:

                                        ▼ infinitive ▼
AWKWARD   Environment Canada expected temperatures to not rise.

mm
34a

infinitive

REVISED   Environment Canada expected temperatures not to rise.

A split infinitive may sometimes be natural and preferable, though it may still bother some readers.

infinitive

Several Canadian industries expect to more than triple their use of robots.

Here the split infinitive is more economical than the alternatives, such as *Several Canadian industries expect to increase their use of robots by more than three times.*

- A single-word adverb may interrupt a verb phrase after the first helping verb: *Scientists have lately been using spacecraft to study the sun.* But a longer adverb is usually awkward inside a verb phrase:

helping   adverb
verb

AWKWARD   The spacecraft Ulysses will after travelling near the sun
main verb
report on the sun's energy fields.

adverb

REVISED   After travelling near the sun, the spacecraft Ulysses
verb phrase
will report on the sun's energy fields.

ESL In a question, place a one-word adverb after the first helping verb and subject:

helping   rest of
verb   subject   adverb   verb phrase
Will spacecraft ever be able to leave the solar system?

mm
34a

KEY TERMS

ADVERB A word or word group that describes a verb, adjective, other adverb, or whole word group, specifying how, when, where, or to what extent: *quickly* see, *solid like a boulder.*

DIRECT OBJECT The receiver of the verb's action: *The car hit a tree.* (See p. 168.)

INFINITIVE A verb form consisting of *to* plus the verb's plain (or dictionary) form: *to produce, to enjoy.* (See p. 171.)

4   Other adverb positions ESL

A few adverbs are subject to special conventions for placement:

- Adverbs of frequency include *always, never, often, rarely, seldom, sometimes,* and *usually*. They generally appear at the beginning of a sentence, before a one-word verb, or after the helping verb in a verb phrase:

helping
verb   adverb   main
verb

Robots have <u>sometimes</u> put humans out of work.

adverb   verb phrase

<u>Sometimes</u> robots have put humans out of work.

- Adverbs of frequency always follow the verb *be*.

verb adverb

Robots are <u>often</u> helpful to workers.

- Adverbs of degree include *absolutely, almost, certainly, completely, definitely, especially, extremely, hardly,* and *only*. They fall just before the word modified (an adjective, another adverb, sometimes a verb):

adverb   adjective

Robots have been <u>especially</u> useful in making cars.

- Adverbs of manner include *badly, beautifully, openly, sweetly, tightly, well,* and others that describe how something is done. They usually fall after the verb:

verb   adverb

Robots work <u>smoothly</u> on assembly lines.

- The position of the adverb *not* depends on what it modifies. When it modifies a verb, place it after the helping verb (or the first helping verb if more than one):

helping   main
verb   verb

Robots do <u>not</u> think.

When *not* modifies another adverb or an adjective, place it before the other modifier:

adjective

Robots are <u>not</u> sleek machines.

5   Order of adjectives ESL

English follows distinctive rules for arranging two or three adjectives before a noun. (A string of more than three adjectives before a noun is rare.) The adjectives follow this order:

> **KEY TERM**
>
> VERB PHRASE A verb consisting of a helping verb and a main verb that carries the principal meaning: *will have begun, can see*. (See p. 163.)

mm

34a

Determiner	Opinion	Size or shape	Age	Colour	Origin	Material	Noun used as adjective	Noun
many			new				city	by-laws
	lovely			green	Thai			birds
a		square				wooden		table
all			recent				business	reports
the				blue	litmus			paper

See pages 257–58 on punctuating adjectives before a noun.

(34b) Connect dangling modifiers to their sentences.

A DANGLING MODIFIER does not sensibly modify anything in its sentence.

DANGLING Passing the building, the vandalism became visible. [The modifying phrase seems to describe *vandalism,* but vandalism does not pass buildings. Who was passing the building? Who saw the vandalism?]

Dangling modifiers usually introduce sentences, contain a verb form, and imply but do not name a subject: in the example above, the implied subject is the someone or something passing the building. Readers assume that this implied subject is the same as the subject of the sentence (*vandalism* in the example). When it is not, the modifier "dangles" unconnected to the rest of the sentence. Here is another example:

DANGLING Although intact, graffiti covered every inch of the walls and windows. [The walls and windows, not the graffiti, were intact.]

To revise a dangling modifier, you have to recast the sentence it appears in. (Revising just by moving the modifier will leave it

dm
34b

_ KEY TERM _____

ADJECTIVE A word that describes a noun or pronoun, specifying which one, what quality, or how many: *good* one, *three* cars. (See p. 219.)

dangling: *The vandalism became visible passing the building.*) Choose a revision method depending on what you want to emphasize in the sentence.

Identifying and revising dangling modifiers

- If the modifier lacks a subject of its own (e.g., *when in diapers*), identify what it describes.
- Verify that what the modifier describes is in fact the subject of the main clause. If it is not, the modifier is probably dangling:

  DANGLING   When in diapers, my mother remarried.
  (modifier) (subject)

- Revise a dangling modifier (*a*) by recasting it with a subject of its own or (*b*) by changing the subject of the main clause:

  REVISION A When I was in diapers, my mother remarried.
  REVISION B When in diapers, I attended my mother's second wedding.

- Rewrite the dangling modifier as a complete clause with its own stated subject and verb. Readers can accept that the new subject and the sentence subject are different.

  DANGLING   Passing the building, the vandalism became visible.

  REVISED   As we passed the building, the vandalism became visible.

- Change the subject of the sentence to a word the modifier properly describes.

  DANGLING   Trying to understand the causes, vandalism has been extensively studied.

  REVISED   Trying to understand the causes, researchers have extensively studied vandalism.

dm
34b

Sentence Faults

A word group punctuated as a sentence will confuse or annoy readers if it lacks needed parts, has too many parts, or has parts that don't fit together.

35 Sentence Fragments

A SENTENCE FRAGMENT is part of a sentence that is set off as if it were a whole sentence. A sentence fragment can be set off by an initial capital letter and a final period or other end punctuation. Although writers occasionally use fragments deliberately and effectively (see p. 238), readers perceive most fragments as serious errors.

Note Computerized grammar and style checkers can spot many but not all sentence fragments. For instance, a checker flagged *The network growing* as a fragment but failed to flag *Thousands of new sites on the Web*. Repair any fragments that your checker does find, but proofread your work yourself to ensure that it's fragment-free.

frag

35

Complete sentence versus sentence fragment

A complete sentence or main clause

1. contains a subject and a verb (*The wind blows*)
2. and is not a subordinate clause (beginning with a word such as *because* or *who*).

A sentence fragment

1. lacks a verb (*The wind blowing*),
2. or lacks a subject (*And blows*),
3. or is a subordinate clause not attached to a complete sentence (*Because the wind blows*).

(35a) Test your sentences for completeness.

A word group punctuated as a sentence should pass *all three* of the following tests. If it does not, it is a fragment and needs to be revised.

Test 1: Find the verb.

Look for a verb in the group of words:

FRAGMENT   Thousands of new sites on the World Wide Web. [Compare a complete sentence: *Thousands of new sites have appeared on the World Wide Web*.]

Any verb form you find must be a FINITE VERB, one that changes form as indicated below. A verbal does not change; it cannot serve as a sentence verb without the aid of a helping verb.

	Finite verbs in complete sentences	Verbals in sentence fragments
Singular	The network grows.	The network growing.
Plural	Networks grow.	Networks growing.
Present	The network grows.	
Past	The network grew.	The network growing.
Future	The network will grow.	

ESL Some languages allow forms of *be* to be omitted as helping verbs or linking verbs. But English requires stating forms of *be*:

FRAGMENTS   The network growing. It already larger than its developers anticipated. [Compare complete sentences: *The network is growing. It is already larger than its developers anticipated*.]

Test 2: Find the subject.

The subject of the sentence will usually come before the verb. If there is no subject, the word group is probably a fragment:

frag

35a

 KEY TERMS

VERB The part of a sentence that asserts something about the subject: *Ducks swim*. Also called PREDICATE. (See p. 162.)

VERBAL A verb form that can serve as a noun, a modifier, or a part of a sentence verb, but not alone as the only verb of a sentence: *drawing, to draw, drawn*. (See p. 171.)

HELPING VERB A verb such as *is, were, have, might,* and *could* that combines with various verb forms to indicate time and other kinds of meaning: for instance, *were drawing, might draw*. (See p. 163.)

FRAGMENT   And has enormous popular appeal. [Compare a complete sentence: *And the Web has enormous popular appeal.*]

In one kind of complete sentence, a command, the subject *you* is understood: [*You*] *Experiment with the Web.*

ESL Some languages allow the omission of the sentence subject, especially when it is a pronoun. But in English, except in commands, the subject is always stated:

FRAGMENT   Web commerce is expanding dramatically. Is threatening traditional stores. [Compare a complete sentence: *It is threatening traditional stores.*]

Test 3: Make sure the clause is not subordinate.

A subordinate clause usually begins with a subordinating word, such as one of the following:

Subordinating conjunctions			Relative pronouns	
after	once	until	that	who/whom
although	since	when	which	whoever/whomever
as	than	where		
because	that	whereas		
if	unless	while		

Subordinate clauses serve as parts of sentences (nouns or modifiers), not as whole sentences:

FRAGMENT   When the government devised the Internet. [Compare a complete sentence: *The government devised the Internet.* Or: *When the government devised the Internet, no expansive computer network existed.*]

FRAGMENT   The reason that the government devised the Internet. [This fragment is a noun (*reason*) plus its modifier (*that . . . Internet*). Compare a

frag

35a

_ KEY TERMS _____

SUBJECT The part of a sentence that names who or what performs the action or makes the assertion of the verb: *Ducks swim.* (See p. 167.)

SUBORDINATE CLAUSE A word group that contains a subject and a verb, begins with a subordinating word such as *because* or *who,* and is not a question: *Ducks can swim when they are young.* A subordinate clause may serve as a modifier or as a noun. (See p. 173.)

complete sentence: *The reason that the government devised the Internet was to provide secure
links among departments and defence contractors.*]

Note Questions beginning with *how, what, when, where, which,
who, whom, whose,* and *why* are not sentence fragments: *Who was
responsible? When did it happen?*

(35b) ## Revise sentence fragments.

Correct sentence fragments in one of two ways depending on
the importance of the information in the fragment and thus how
much you want to stress it:

- Rewrite the fragment as a complete sentence. The information
  in the fragment will then have the same importance as that in
  other complete sentences.

FRAGMENT	A major improvement of the Internet occurred with the Web. Which allows users to move easily between sites.
REVISED	A major improvement of the Internet occurred with the Web. It allows users to move easily between sites.
FRAGMENT	The Web is a boon to researchers. A vast and accessible library.
REVISED	The Web is a boon to researchers. It forms a vast and accessible library.

- Combine the fragment with the appropriate main clause. The
  information in the fragment will then be subordinated to that
  in the main clause.

FRAGMENT	The Web is easy to use. Loaded with links and graphics.
REVISED	The Web, loaded with links and graphics, is easy to use.
FRAGMENT	With the links, users can move to other Web sites. That they want to consult.
REVISED	With the links, users can move to other Web sites that they want to consult.

frag

35b

(35c) Be aware of the acceptable uses of incomplete sentences.

A few word groups lacking the usual subject-predicate combination are incomplete sentences, but they are not fragments because they conform to the expectations of most readers. They include exclamations (*Oh no!*); questions and answers (*Where next? To Winnipeg.*); and commands (*Move along. Shut the window.*).

Experienced writers sometimes use sentence fragments when they want to achieve a special effect. Such fragments appear more in informal than in formal writing. Unless you are experienced and thoroughly secure in your own writing, you should avoid all fragments and concentrate on writing clear, well-formed sentences.

36 Comma Splices and Fused Sentences

cs/fs

36

When a sentence contains two main clauses in a row, readers need a signal that one main clause is ending and another beginning. The usual signal is a comma with coordinating conjunction (*The ship was huge, and its mast stood twenty metres high*) or a semicolon (*The ship was huge; its mast stood twenty metres high*).

Two problems in punctuating main clauses deprive readers of this signal. One is the COMMA SPLICE, in which the clauses are joined (or spliced) *only* with a comma:

> COMMA SPLICE The ship was huge, its mast stood twenty metres high.

____ KEY TERMS ____

MAIN CLAUSE A word group that contains a subject and a verb and does not begin with a subordinating word: *A dictionary is essential.*

COORDINATING CONJUNCTION *And, but, or, nor, for, so, yet.* (See p. 166.)

The other is the FUSED SENTENCE (or RUN-ON SENTENCE), in which no punctuation or conjunction appears between the clauses.

> FUSED SENTENCE   The ship was huge its mast stood twenty
> metres high.

Note Computerized grammar and style checkers can detect many comma splices, but they will not recognize every fused sentence and may flag errors in sentences that are complex but actually correct. Verify that revision is actually needed on any flagged sentence, and read your work carefully on your own to be sure it is correct.

ESL An English sentence may not include more than one main clause unless the clauses are separated by a comma and a coordinating conjunction or by a semicolon. If your native language does not have such a rule or has accustomed you to writing long sentences, you may need to edit your English writing especially for comma splices and fused sentences.

36a   **Separate main clauses not joined by *and, but*, or another coordinating conjunction.**

If your readers point out comma splices or fused sentences in your writing, you're not creating enough separation between main clauses in your sentences. The following guidelines can help you repair the problem:

Revision of comma splices and fused sentences

1. Underline the main clauses in your draft.
2. When two main clauses fall in the same sentence, check the connection between them.
3. If nothing falls between the clauses or only a comma does, revise in one of the following ways, depending on the relation you want to establish between the clauses. (See the text discussion for examples.)
- Make the clauses into separate sentences.
- Insert a comma followed by *and, but*, or another coordinating conjunction. Or, if the comma is already present, insert just the coordinating conjunction.
- Insert a semicolon between clauses.
- Subordinate one clause to the other.

cs/fs
36a

Separate sentences

Make the clauses into separate sentences when the ideas expressed are only loosely related:

> COMMA SPLICE Chemistry has contributed much to our understanding of foods, many foods such as wheat and beans can be produced in the laboratory.
>
> REVISED Chemistry has contributed much to our understanding of foods. Many foods such as wheat and beans can be produced in the laboratory.

ESL Making separate sentences may be the best option if you are used to writing very long sentences in your native language but often write comma splices in English.

Coordinating conjunction

Insert a coordinating conjunction in a comma splice when the ideas in the main clauses are closely related and equally important:

> COMMA SPLICE Some laboratory-grown foods taste good, they are nutritious.
>
> REVISED Some laboratory-grown foods taste good, and they are nutritious.

In a fused sentence insert a comma and a coordinating conjunction:

> FUSED Chemists have made much progress they still have a way to go.
>
> REVISED Chemists have made much progress, but they still have a way to go.

Semicolon

Insert a semicolon between clauses if the relation between the ideas is very close and obvious without a conjunction:

> COMMA SPLICE Good taste is rare in laboratory-grown vegetables, they are usually bland.
>
> REVISED Good taste is rare in laboratory-grown vegetables; they are usually bland.

Subordination

Subordinate one clause to the other when one idea is less important than the other:

> COMMA SPLICE The vitamins are adequate, the flavour is deficient.
>
> REVISED Even though the vitamins are adequate, the flavour is deficient.

cs/fs
36a

(36b) Separate main clauses related by *however, for example,* and so on.

Two groups of words that are not conjunctions describe how one main clause relates to another: CONJUNCTIVE ADVERBS and other TRANSITIONAL EXPRESSIONS. (See pp. 42–43 for a longer list of transitional expressions.)

Common conjunctive adverbs and transitional expressions

accordingly	for instance	in the meantime	otherwise
anyway	further	in the past	similarly
as a result	furthermore	likewise	so far
at last	hence	meanwhile	still
at length	however	moreover	that is
besides	incidentally	namely	then
certainly	in contrast	nevertheless	thereafter
consequently	indeed	nonetheless	therefore
even so	in fact	now	thus
finally	in other words	of course	to this end
for all that	in short	on the contrary	undoubtedly
for example	instead	on the whole	until now

When two clauses are related by a conjunctive adverb or another transitional expression, they must be separated by a period or by a semicolon. The adverb or expression is also generally set off by a comma or commas.

> COMMA SPLICE   Most Canadians refuse to give up unhealthful habits, consequently our medical costs are higher than those of many other countries.
>
> REVISED   Most Canadians refuse to give up unhealthful habits. Consequently, our medical costs are higher than those of many other countries.
>
> REVISED   Most Canadians refuse to give up unhealthful habits; consequently, our medical costs are higher than those of many other countries.

Conjunctive adverbs and transitional expressions are different from coordinating conjunctions (*and, but,* and so on) and subordinating conjunctions (*although, because,* and so on):

- Unlike conjunctions, conjunctive adverbs and transitional expressions do not join two clauses into a grammatical unit but merely describe the way two clauses relate in meaning.

cs/fs

36b

- Thus, unlike conjunctions, conjunctive adverbs and transitional expressions can be moved from one place to another in a clause. No matter where in the clause an adverb or expression falls, though, the clause must be separated from another main clause by a period or semicolon:

Most Canadians refuse to give up unhealthful habits; our medical costs, consequently, are higher than those of many other countries.

37 Mixed Sentences

A MIXED SENTENCE contains parts that do not fit together. The misfit may be in grammar or in meaning.

Note Computerized grammar and style checkers are not sophisticated enough to recognize most mixed sentences. Proofread your own work carefully to locate and revise problem sentences.

(37a) Match subjects and predicates in meaning.

In a sentence with mixed meaning, the subject is said to do or be something illogical. Such a mixture is sometimes called FAULTY PREDICATION because the predicate conflicts with the subject.

1   Illogical equation with *be*

When a form of *be* connects a subject and a word that describes the subject (a complement), the subject and complement must be logically related:

mixed

37a

KEY TERMS _____

SUBJECT The part of a sentence that names who or what performs the action or makes the assertion of the verb: *Geese fly*. (See p. 167.)

PREDICATE The part of a sentence containing the verb and asserting something about the subject: *Geese fly*. (See pp. 167–69.)

MIXED   A <u>compromise</u> between the city and the country

would be the ideal <u>place</u> to live.

REVISED   A <u>community</u> that offered the best qualities of both

city and country would be the ideal <u>place</u> to live.

2   *Is when, is where*

Definitions require nouns on both sides of *be*. Clauses that define and begin with *when* or *where* are common in speech but should be avoided in writing:

MIXED   An <u>examination</u> is <u>when you are tested</u> on what you know.

REVISED   An <u>examination</u> is a <u>test</u> of what you know.

3   *Reason is because*

The commonly heard construction *reason is because* is redundant since *because* means "for the reason that":

MIXED   The <u>reason</u> the temple requests donations <u>is because</u> the school needs expansion.

REVISED   The <u>reason</u> the temple requests donations is that the school needs expansion.

REVISED   The temple requests donations <u>because</u> the school needs expansion.

4   Other mixed meanings

Faulty predications are not confined to sentences with *be*:

MIXED   The <u>use</u> of emission controls <u>was created</u> to reduce air pollution.

REVISED   Emission <u>controls</u> <u>were created</u> to reduce air pollution.

mixed
37b

(37b)   Untangle sentences that are mixed
        in grammar.

Many mixed sentences start with one grammatical plan or construction but end with a different one:

                            modifier (prepositional phrase)
MIXED   By paying more attention to impressions than facts
         verb
         leads us to misjudge others.

This mixed sentence makes a prepositional phrase work as the subject of *leads*, but prepositional phrases function as modifiers, not as nouns, and thus not as sentence subjects.

```
                    ┌──────── modifier (prepositional phrase) ────────┐
```
REVISED   By paying more attention to impressions than facts,
          subject + verb
          we misjudge others.

Mixed sentences are especially likely on a word processor when you connect parts of two sentences or rewrite half a sentence but not the other half. Mixed sentences may also occur when you don't make the subject and verb of a sentence carry the principal meaning. (See pp. 123–25.) Here is another example:

```
              subject ┌──────── modifier (prepositional phrase) ────────┐
```
MIXED   The fact that someone may be considered guilty just
          for associating with someone guilty.

          subject + verb
REVISED   The fact is that someone may be considered guilty just for associating with someone guilty.

(37c)   State parts of sentences, such as subjects, only once. ESL

In some languages other than English, certain parts of sentences may be repeated. These include the subject in any kind of clause or an object or adverb in an adjective clause. In English, however, these parts are stated only once in a clause.

1   Repetition of subject

You may be tempted to restate a subject as a pronoun before the verb. But the subject needs stating only once in its clause:

FAULTY   The liquid it reached a temperature of 82°C.
REVISED   The liquid reached a temperature of 82°C.

FAULTY   Gases in the liquid they escaped.
REVISED   Gases in the liquid escaped.

2   Repetition in an adjective clause

ADJECTIVE CLAUSES begin with *who, whom, whose, which, that, where,* and *when.* (See also p. 173.) The beginning word replaces another word: the subject (*He is the person who called*), an object of a verb or preposition (*He is the person whom I mentioned*), or a preposition and pronoun (*He knows the office where [in which] the conference will occur*).

mixed
37c

Do not state the word being replaced in an adjective clause:

FAULTY   The technician <u>whom</u> the test depended on her was
burned. [*Whom* should replace *her*.]

REVISED   The technician <u>whom</u> the test depended on was
burned.

Adjective clauses beginning with *where* or *when* do not need an adverb such as *there* or *then:*

FAULTY   Gases escaped at a moment <u>when</u> the technician
was unprepared <u>then</u>.

REVISED   Gases escaped at a moment <u>when</u> the technician
was unprepared.

Note *Whom, which,* and similar words are sometimes omitted but are still understood by the reader. Thus the word being replaced should not be stated.

FAULTY   Accidents rarely happen to technicians the lab has
trained <u>*them*</u>. [*Whom* is understood: . . . *technicians*
<u>*whom*</u> *the lab has trained*.]

REVISED   Accidents rarely happen to technicians the lab has
trained.

mixed
37c

5 Punctuation

5 Punctuation

38 End Punctuation

End a sentence with one of three punctuation marks: a period (.), a question mark (?), or an exclamation point (!).

Note Do not rely on a computerized grammar and spelling checker to identify missing or misused end punctuation. Although a checker may flag missing question marks after direct questions or incorrect combinations of marks (such as a question mark and a period at the end of a sentence), it cannot do much else.

(38a) Use a period after most sentences and in many abbreviations.

1 Statements, mild commands, and indirect questions

Statement

The airline went bankrupt.   It no longer flies.

Mild command

Think of the possibilities.   Please consider others.

Indirect question

An INDIRECT QUESTION reports what someone asked but not in the exact form or words of the original question:

The judge asked why I had been driving with my lights off.
No one asked how we got home.

ESL Unlike a direct question, an indirect question uses the wording and subject-verb order of a statement: *The reporter asked why the negotiations failed* [not *why did the negotiations fail*].

2 Abbreviations

Use periods with most abbreviations involving small letters:

p.	Mrs.	e.g.	Ont.
Dr.	Mr.	i.e.	Feb.
Ph.D.	Ms.	a.m., p.m.	ft.

. ? !

38a

247

Note When an abbreviation falls at the end of a sentence, use only one period: *The school offers a Ph.D.*

Many abbreviations of two or more words using all-capital letters may be written with or without periods. Just be consistent.

BA or B.A.   US or U.S.   BC or B.C.   AM or A.M.

Omit periods from these abbreviations:

- The initials of a well-known person: *JFK, PET*
- The initials of an organization, corporation, or government agency: *CBC, RCMP*
- A postal abbreviation: *ON, AVE*
- An *acronym*, a pronounceable word formed from initials: *UNESCO, NAFTA*

(38b)   Use a question mark after a direct question and sometimes to indicate doubt.

1   Direct questions

Who will follow her?
What is the difference between these two people?

After indirect questions, use a period: *We wondered who would follow her.* (See the preceding page.)

Questions in a series are each followed by a question mark:

The officer asked how many times the suspect had been arrested. Three times? Four times? More than that?

2   Doubt

A question mark within parentheses can indicate doubt about a number or date.

The Greek philosopher Socrates was born in 470 (?) BC and died in 399 BC from drinking poison. [Socrates's birthdate is not known for sure.]

Use sentence structure and words, not a question mark, to express sarcasm or irony.

Not   Stern's friendliness (?) bothered Crane.
But   Stern's insincerity bothered Crane.

(38c) Use an exclamation point after an emphatic statement, interjection, or command.

No! We must not lose this election!
Come here immediately!

Follow mild interjections and commands with commas or periods, as appropriate: *Oh, call whenever you can.*

Note Use exclamation points sparingly, even in informal writing. Overused, they'll fail to impress readers, and they may make you sound overemphatic.

39 The Comma

The comma (,) is the most common punctuation mark inside sentences. Its main uses are shown in the box on the next page.

Note Computerized grammar and style checkers will recognize only some comma errors, ignoring others. Revise any errors that your checker points out, but you'll have to proofread your work on your own to find and correct most errors.

___ KEY TERMS ___

INTERJECTION A word that expresses feeling or commands attention, either alone or within a sentence: *Oh! Hey! Wow!* (See p. 166.)

COORDINATING CONJUNCTIONS *And, but, or, nor,* and sometimes *for, so, yet.* (See p. 166.)

MAIN CLAUSE A word group that contains a subject and a verb and does not begin with a subordinating word: *Water freezes at temperatures below 0°C.* (See p. 167.)

39

Main uses of the comma

- To separate main clauses linked by a coordinating conjunction (p. 251).

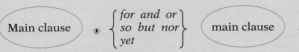

$$\text{Main clause} \quad , \quad \begin{cases} for \ and \ or \\ so \ but \ nor \\ yet \end{cases} \quad \text{main clause} \quad .$$

The building is finished, but it has no tenants.

- To set off most introductory elements (pp. 251–52).

$$\text{Introductory element} \quad , \quad \text{main clause} \quad .$$

Unfortunately, the only tenant pulled out.

- To set off nonessential elements (pp. 252–56).

$$\text{Main clause} \quad , \quad \text{nonessential element} \quad .$$

The empty building symbolizes a weak local economy, which affects everyone.

$$\text{Beginning of main clause} \quad , \quad \text{nonessential element} \quad , \quad \text{end of main clause} \quad .$$

The primary cause, the decline of local industry, is not news.

- To separate items in a series (pp. 259–57).

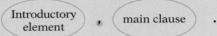

$$\ldots \quad \text{item 1} \quad , \quad \text{item 2} \quad , \quad \begin{cases} and \\ or \end{cases} \quad \text{item 3} \quad \ldots$$

The city needs healthier businesses, new schools, and improved housing.

- To separate coordinate adjectives (pp. 257–58).

$$\ldots \quad \text{first adjective} \quad , \quad \text{second adjective} \quad \text{word modified} \quad \ldots$$

A tall, sleek skyscraper is not needed.

Other uses of the comma:
    To separate parts of dates, addresses, long numbers (p. 258).
    To separate quotations and signal phrases (p. 259).

See also pages 260–62 for when *not* to use the comma.

39

39a Use a comma before ***and, but,*** or another coordinating conjunction linking main clauses.

When a coordinating conjunction links words or phrases, do not use a comma: *Dugain plays and sings Irish and English folk songs.* However, *do* use a comma when a coordinating conjunction joins main clauses, as in the next examples.

> Caffeine can keep coffee drinkers alert, and it may elevate their mood.
> Caffeine was once thought to be safe, but now researchers warn of harmful effects.
> Coffee drinkers may suffer sleeplessness, for the drug acts as a stimulant to the nervous system.

Note The comma goes *before,* not after, the coordinating conjunction: *Caffeine increases heart rate, and it* [not *and, it*] *constricts blood vessels.*

Exception Some writers omit the comma between main clauses that are very short and closely related in meaning: *Caffeine helps but it also hurts.* If you are in doubt about whether to use the comma in such a sentence, use it. It will always be correct.

 39b Use a comma to set off most introductory elements.

An INTRODUCTORY ELEMENT begins a sentence and modifies a word or words in the main clause that follows. It is usually followed by a comma.

Subordinate clause

Even when identical twins are raised apart, they grow up very like each other.

Verbal or verbal phrase

Explaining the similarity, some researchers claim that one's genes are one's destiny.

Concerned, other researchers deny the claim.

Prepositional phrase

In a debate that has lasted centuries, scientists use identical twins to argue for or against genetic destiny.

39b

Transitional expression

<u>Of course</u>, scientists can now look directly at the genes themselves to answer questions.

You may omit the comma after a short subordinate clause or prepositional phrase if its omission does not create confusion: *When snow falls the city collapses. By the year 2000 the world population had topped 6 billion.* But the comma is never wrong.

Note Take care to distinguish *-ing* words used as modifiers from *-ing* words used as subjects. The former almost always take a comma; the latter never do.

```
       ┌──── modifier ────┐      subject    verb
```
<u>Studying identical twins</u>, geneticists learn about inheritance.

```
       ┌──── subject ────┐     verb
```
<u>Studying identical twins</u> helps geneticists learn about inheritance.

(39c) Use a comma or commas to set off nonessential elements.

Commas around part of a sentence often signal that the element is not essential to the meaning. This NONESSENTIAL ELEMENT may modify or rename the word it refers to, but it does not limit the word to a particular individual or group. The meaning of the word would still be clear if the element were deleted:

Nonessential element

The company, <u>which is located in Newfoundland</u>, has an excellent reputation.

KEY TERMS

SUBORDINATE CLAUSE A word group that contains a subject and a verb, begins with a subordinating word such as *because* or *who*, and is not a question: *When water freezes, crystals form.* (See p. 173.)

VERBAL A verb form used as an adjective, adverb, or noun. A verbal plus any object or modifier is a VERBAL PHRASE: *frozen water, ready to freeze, rapid freezing.* (See p. 171.)

PREPOSITIONAL PHRASE A word group consisting of a preposition, such as *for* or *in,* followed by a noun or pronoun plus any modifiers: *in a jar, with a spoon.* (See p. 170.)

TRANSITIONAL EXPRESSION A word or phrase that shows the relationship between sentences: *for example, however, in fact, of course.* (See p. 42.)

(Because it does not restrict meaning, a nonessential element is also called a NONRESTRICTIVE ELEMENT.)

In contrast, an ESSENTIAL (or RESTRICTIVE) ELEMENT *does* limit the word it refers to: the element cannot be omitted without leaving the meaning too general. Because it is essential, such an element is *not* set off with commas.

A test for nonessential and essential elements

1. Identify the element:

   Hai Nguyen <u>who emigrated from Vietnam</u> lives in Calgary.

   Those <u>who emigrated with him</u> live elsewhere.

2. Remove the element. Does the fundamental meaning of the sentence change?

   Hai Nguyen lives in Calgary.   No.

   Those live elsewhere.   YES. [Who are *Those*?]

3. If NO, the element is nonessential and should be set off with punctuation:

   Hai Nguyen, <u>who emigrated from Vietnam,</u> lives in Calgary.

   If YES, the element is essential and should not be set off with punctuation:

   Those <u>who emigrated with him</u> live elsewhere.

Essential element

The company rewards employees <u>who work hard</u>.

Omitting the underlined words would distort the meaning: the company doesn't necessarily reward *all* employees, only the hardworking ones.

The same element in the same sentence may be essential or nonessential, depending on your intended meaning and the context in which the sentence appears.

Essential

Not all the bands were equally well received, however. The band <u>playing old music</u> held the audience's attention. The other groups created much less excitement. [*Playing old music* identifies a particular band.]

Nonessential

A new band called Fats made its debut on Saturday night. The band, <u>playing old music,</u> held the audience's attention. If this

39c

performance is typical, the group has a bright future. [*Playing old music* adds information about a band already named.]

Note When a nonessential element falls in the middle of a sentence, be sure to set it off with a pair of commas, one *before* and one *after* the element.

1   Nonessential phrases and clauses

Most nonessential phrases and subordinate clauses function as adjectives to modify nouns or pronouns. In each of the following examples, the underlined words could be omitted with no loss of clarity:

Emily Stowe was the first Canadian woman to receive a licence to practise medicine, in 1880. [Phrase.]

She was a medical pioneer, helping to found the first Canadian medical college for women. [Phrase.]

She taught at the school, which was situated in Toronto. [Clause.]

Stowe, who also published on women's rights, founded Canada's first suffrage group. [Clause.]

Note Use *that* only in an essential clause, never in a nonessential clause: . . . *school, which* [not *that*] *was affiliated. . . .* Many writers reserve *which* for nonessential clauses.

2   Nonessential appositives

Appositives may also be essential or nonessential, depending on meaning and context. A nonessential appositive merely adds information about the word it refers to:

Michael Ondaatje's fourth novel, *The English Patient*, won the Booker Prize. [The word *fourth* identifies the novel, while the title adds a detail.]

In contrast, an essential appositive limits or defines the word it refers to:

KEY TERMS

PHRASE A word group lacking a subject or a verb or both: *in Sarnia, carrying water.* (See p. 170.)

SUBORDINATE CLAUSE A word group that contains a subject and a verb, begins with a subordinating word such as *who* or *although,* and is not a question: *Samson, who won a gold medal, coaches in Utah.* (See p. 173.)

APPOSITIVE A noun that renames another noun immediately before it: *His wife, Kyra Sedgwick, is also an actor.* (See p. 172.)

39c

Ondaatje's novel *In the Skin of a Lion* is about the construction of the Bloor Viaduct in Toronto. [Ondaatje has written more than one novel, so the title is essential to identify the intended one.]

3   Other nonessential elements

Like nonessential modifiers or appositives, many other elements contribute to texture, tone, or overall clarity but are not essential to the meaning. Unlike nonessential modifiers or appositives, these other nonessential elements generally do not refer to any specific word in the sentence.

Note Use a pair of commas—one before, one after—when any of these elements falls in the middle of a sentence.

Absolute phrases

Domestic recycling having succeeded, the city now wants to extend the program to businesses.

Many businesses, their profits already squeezed, resist recycling.

Parenthetical and transitional expressions

Generally, set off parenthetical and transitional expressions with commas:

The world's most celebrated holiday is, perhaps surprisingly, New Year's Day. [Parenthetical expression.]

Interestingly, Canadians have relatively few holidays. [Parenthetical expression.]

Canadian workers, for example, receive fewer holidays than European workers do. [Transitional expression.]

(Dashes and parentheses may also set off parenthetical expressions. See pp. 275–77.)

When a transitional expression links main clauses, precede it with a semicolon and follow it with a comma (see p. 263):

KEY TERMS

ABSOLUTE PHRASE A phrase modifying a whole main clause and consisting of a participle and its subject: *Their homework completed, the children watched TV.* (See p. 172.)

PARENTHETICAL EXPRESSION An explanatory or supplemental word or phrase, such as *all things considered, to be frank,* or a brief example or fact. (See p. 277.)

TRANSITIONAL EXPRESSION A word or phrase that shows the relationship between sentences: *for example, however, in fact, of course.* (See p. 42.)

39c

European workers often have long paid vacations; indeed, they may receive a full month after just a few years with a company.

Note The conjunctions *and* and *but,* sometimes used as transitional expressions, are not followed by commas. (See p. 261.) Nor are commas required after some transitional expressions that we read without pauses, such as *also, hence, next, now,* and *thus.* A few transitional expressions, notably *therefore* and *instead,* do not need commas when they fall inside or at the ends of clauses.

Canadian workers thus put in more work days. But the days themselves may be shorter.

Phrases of contrast
The substance, not the style, is important.
Substance, unlike style, cannot be faked.

Tag questions
Jones should be allowed to vote, should he not?
They don't stop to consider others, do they?

Yes and no
Yes, the editorial did have a point.
No, that can never be.

Words of direct address
Cody, please bring me the newspaper.
With all due respect, sir, I will not.

Mild interjections
Well, you will never know who did it.
Oh, they forgot all about the baby.

(39d)   Use commas between items in a series.

A SERIES consists of three or more items of equal importance. The items may be words, phrases, or clauses.

___ KEY TERMS ___

TAG QUESTION A question at the end of a statement, consisting of a pronoun, a helping verb, and sometimes *not*: *It isn't wet, is it?*

INTERJECTION A word that expresses feeling or commands attention: *Oh, must we?*

Anna Spingle <u>married at the age of seventeen,</u> <u>had three children by twenty-one,</u> and <u>divorced at twenty-two.</u>

She worked as a <u>cook,</u> a <u>babysitter,</u> and a <u>crossing guard.</u>

Some writers omit the comma before the coordinating conjunction in a series (*Breakfast consisted of coffee, eggs and kippers*). But the final comma is never wrong, and it always helps the reader see the last two items as separate.

(39e) Use commas between two or more adjectives that equally modify the same word.

Adjectives that equally modify the same word—COORDINATE ADJECTIVES—may be separated either by *and* or by a comma.

Spingle's <u>scratched and dented</u> car is an eyesore, but it gets her to work.

She has dreams of a <u>sleek, shiny</u> car.

Tests for commas with adjectives

1. Identify the adjectives:
    She was a <u>faithful sincere</u> friend.
    They are <u>dedicated medical</u> students.

2. Can the adjectives be reversed without changing meaning?
    She was a <u>sincere faithful</u> friend.   YES.
    They are <u>medical dedicated</u> students.   No.

3. Can the word *and* be inserted between the adjectives without changing meaning?
    She was a <u>faithful and sincere</u> friend.   YES
    They are <u>dedicated and medical</u> students. No.

4. If yes to both questions, the adjectives should be separated by a comma:
    She was a <u>faithful, sincere</u> friend.

5. If no to both questions, the adjectives should not be separated by a comma:
    They are <u>dedicated medical</u> students.

39e

Adjectives are not coordinate—and should not be separated by commas—when the one nearer the noun is more closely related to the noun in meaning.

Spingle's children work at various odd jobs.
They all expect to go to a nearby community college.

39f   Use commas in dates, addresses, place names, and long numbers.

When they appear within sentences, dates, addresses, and place names punctuated with commas are also ended with commas.

Dates

July 1, 1867, was the birthday of the Confederation.
The signing of the armistice on Monday, November 11, 1918, ended the First World War.

Do not use commas between the parts of a date in inverted order (*15 December 1992*) or in dates consisting of a month or season and a year (*December 1941*).

Addresses and place names

Use the address 72 Douglas Drive, Saskatoon, Saskatchewan, for all correspondence.
Halifax, Nova Scotia, is the location of Dalhousie University.

Do not use a comma between a province name and a postal code.

Long numbers

Use the comma to separate the figures in long numbers into groups of three, counting from the right. With numbers of four digits, the comma is optional.

The new assembly plant cost $7,525,000.
A kilometre is 3,281 feet [*or* 3281 feet].

ESL Usage in English differs from that in some other languages, which use a period, not a comma, to separate the figures in long numbers.

(39g) Use commas with quotations according to standard practice.

The words *she said, he writes,* and so on identify the source of a quotation. These SIGNAL PHRASES should be separated from the quotation by punctuation, usually a comma or commas.

> Eleanor Roosevelt said, "You must do the thing you think you cannot do."
>
> "Knowledge is power," wrote Francis Bacon.
>
> "The shore has a dual nature," observes Rachel Carson, "changing with the swing of the tides." [The signal phrase interrupts the quotation at a comma and thus ends with a comma.]

Exceptions When a signal phrase interrupts a quotation between main clauses, follow the signal phrase with a semicolon or a period. The choice depends on the punctuation of the original.

> NOT   "That part of my life was over," she wrote, "his words had sealed it shut."
>
> BUT   "That part of my life was over," she wrote. "His words had sealed it shut." [*She wrote* interrupts the quotation at a period.]
>
> OR   "That part of my life was over," she wrote; "his words had sealed it shut." [*She wrote* interrupts the quotation at a semicolon.]

Do not use a comma when a signal phrase follows a quotation ending in an exclamation point or a question mark:

> "Claude!" Mrs. Harrison called.
>
> "Why must I come home?" he asked.

Do not use a comma with a quotation that is integrated into your sentence structure, including one introduced by *that:*

> James Baldwin insists that "one must never, in one's life, accept . . . injustices as commonplace."
>
> Baldwin thought that the violence of a riot "had been devised as a corrective" to his own violence.

Do not use a comma with a quoted title unless it is a nonessential appositive (p. 254):

> The Beatles recorded "She Loves Me" in the early 1960s.

39g

(39h) Delete commas where they are not required.

Commas can make sentences choppy and even confusing if they are used more often than needed or in violation of rules 39a–39g. The most common spots for misused commas are discussed below.

1   Not between subject and verb, verb and object, or preposition and object

NOT   The returning <u>soldiers, received</u> a warm welcome. [Separated subject and verb.]

BUT   The returning <u>soldiers received</u> a warm welcome.

NOT   They had <u>chosen, to fight</u> for their country <u>despite, the risks.</u> [Separated verb *chosen* and its object; separated preposition *despite* and its object.]

BUT   They had <u>chosen to fight</u> for their country <u>despite the risks.</u>

2   Not in most compound constructions

Compound constructions consisting of two elements almost never require a comma. The only exception is the sentence consisting of two main clauses linked by a coordinating conjunction: *The computer failed, but employees kept working.* (See p. 251.)

　　　　　　　┌──── compound subject ────┐
NOT   <u>Banks, and other financial institutions</u> have helped older
　　　　　　┌──── compound object of preposition ────┐
people with <u>money management, and investment.</u>

BUT   <u>Banks and other financial institutions</u> have helped older people with <u>money management and investment.</u>

　　　　　　　┌──── compound predicate ────┐
NOT   One bank <u>created</u> special accounts for older people, and
　　　┌── compound object of verb ──┐
held <u>classes, and workshops.</u>

KEY TERMS

NONESSENTIAL APPOSITIVE A word or words that rename an immediately preceding noun but do not limit or define the noun: *The author's first story, "Medicine Hat," won a prize.* (See p. 254.)

COMPOUND CONSTRUCTION Two or more words, phrases, or clauses connected by a coordinating conjunction, usually *and, but, or, nor*: *man and woman, old or young, leaking oil and spewing steam.*

39h

BUT   One bank <u>created</u> special accounts for older people and held <u>classes and workshops</u>.

3 Not after a conjunction

NOT   Parents of adolescents notice increased conflict at puberty, <u>and,</u> they complain of bickering.

BUT   Parents of adolescents notice increased conflict at puberty, <u>and</u> they complain of bickering.

NOT   <u>Although,</u> other primates leave the family at adolescence, humans do not.

BUT   <u>Although</u> other primates leave the family at adolescence, humans do not.

4 Not around essential elements

NOT   Margaret Laurence's work, *The Diviners,* is set in her mythical Manitoba town of Manawaka. [The title is essential to distinguish the novel from the rest of Laurence's work.]

BUT   Margaret Laurence's work *The Diviners* is set in her mythical Manitoba town of Manawaka.

NOT   The prose style, <u>that Laurence used,</u> influenced other novelists. [The clause identifies the prose style.]

BUT   The prose style <u>that Laurence used</u> influenced other novelists.

5 Not around a series

Commas separate the items *within* a series (p. 256) but do not separate the series from the rest of the sentence.

NOT   The skills of, <u>hunting, herding, and agriculture,</u> sustained the Natives.

BUT   The skills of <u>hunting, herding, and agriculture</u> sustained the Natives.

_ KEY TERMS _____

CONJUNCTION A connecting word such as a COORDINATING CONJUNCTION (*and, but, or,* and so on) or a SUBORDINATING CONJUNCTION (*although, because, when,* and so on). (See pp. 165–66.)

ESSENTIAL ELEMENT Limits the word it refers to and thus can't be omitted without leaving the meaning too general. (See p. 253.)

39h

6　Not before an indirect quotation

NOT　The report <u>concluded, that</u> dieting could be more
dangerous than overeating.

BUT　The report <u>concluded that</u> dieting could be more
dangerous than overeating.

40 The Semicolon

The semicolon (;) separates equal and balanced sentence elements—usually main clauses (below) and occasionally items in series (p. 264).

Note A computerized grammar and style checker can spot few errors in the use of semicolons and may suggest adding them incorrectly. To find semicolon errors, you'll need to proofread on your own.

40a　Use a semicolon between main clauses not joined by **and, but,** or another coordinating conjunction.

When no coordinating conjunction links two main clauses, the clauses should be separated by a semicolon.

A new ulcer drug arrived on the market with a mixed reputation; doctors find that the drug works but worry about its side effects.

KEY TERMS

MAIN CLAUSE A word group that contains a subject and a verb and does not begin with a subordinating word: *Parks help cities breathe.* (See p. 167.)

COORDINATING CONJUNCTIONS *And, but, or, nor,* and sometimes *for, so, yet.*

;
40a

The side effects are not minor; some leave the patient quite uncomfortable or even ill.

Note This rule prevents the errors known as comma splice and fused sentence. (See pp. 238–42.)

(40b) Use a semicolon between main clauses related by *however, for example,* and so on.

When a conjunctive adverb or another transitional expression relates two main clauses in a single sentence, the clauses should be separated with a semicolon:

An American immigrant, Levi Strauss, invented blue jeans in the 1860s; eventually, his product clothed working men throughout the West.

The position of the semicolon between main clauses never changes, but the conjunctive adverb or transitional expression may move around within the second clause. Wherever the adverb or expression falls, it is usually set off with a comma or commas. (See p. 260.)

Blue jeans have become fashionable all over the world; however, the American originators still wear more jeans than anyone else.

Blue jeans have become fashionable all over the world; the American originators, however, still wear more jeans than anyone else.

Blue jeans have become fashionable all over the world; the American originators still wear more jeans than anyone else, however.

Note This rule prevents the errors known as comma splice and fused sentence. (See pp. 238–42.)

KEY TERMS

Conjunctive adverb A modifier that describes the relation of the ideas in two clauses, such as *consequently, hence, however, indeed, instead, nonetheless, otherwise, still, then, therefore, thus.* (See pp. 241–42.)

Transitional expression A word or phrase that shows the relationship between ideas. Transitional expressions include conjunctive adverbs as well as *for example, in fact, of course,* and many other words and phrases. (See p. 42.)

;
40b

(40c)   Use semicolons between main clauses or series items containing commas.

Normally, commas separate main clauses linked by coordinating conjunctions (*and, but, or, nor*) and items in a series. But when the clauses or series items contain commas, a semicolon between them makes the sentence easier to read.

> Lewis and Clark led the men of their party with consummate skill, inspiring and encouraging them, doctoring and caring for them; and they kept voluminous journals.
>
> —PAGE SMITH

> The custody case involved Amy Dalton, the child; Ellen and Mark Dalton, the parents; and Ruth and Hal Blum, the grandparents.

(40d)   Delete or replace unneeded semicolons.

Too many semicolons can make writing choppy. And semicolons are often misused in certain constructions that call for other punctuation or no punctuation.

1   Not between a main clause and subordinate clause or phrase

The semicolon does not separate unequal parts, such as main clauses and subordinate clauses or phrases.

> NOT   Pygmies are in danger of extinction; because of encroaching development.
> BUT   Pygmies are in danger of extinction because of encroaching development.

> NOT   According to African authorities; only about 35,000 Pygmies exist today.
> BUT   According to African authorities, only about 35,000 Pygmies exist today.

2   Not before a series or explanation

Colons and dashes, not semicolons, introduce series, explanations, and so forth. (See pp. 265 and 275.)

> NOT   Teachers have heard all sorts of reasons why students do poorly; psychological problems, family illness, too much work, too little time.
> BUT   Teachers have heard all sorts of reasons why students do poorly: psychological problems, family illness, too much work, too little time.

;
40d

41 The Colon

The colon (:) is mainly a mark of introduction: it signals that the words following will explain or amplify (below). The colon also has several conventional uses, such as in expressions of time.

Note Most computerized grammar and style checkers cannot recognize missing or misused colons. You'll have to check for errors yourself.

(41a) Use a colon to introduce a concluding explanation, series, appositive, or long or formal quotation.

As an introducer, a colon is always preceded by a complete main clause. It may or may not be followed by a main clause. This is one way the colon differs from the semicolon, which generally separates main clauses only. (See pp. 263–64.)

Explanation

<u>Hydrology</u> has a deceptively simple definition: the study of water.

Sometimes a concluding explanation is preceded by *the following* or *as follows* and a colon:

A more precise definition might be <u>the following</u>: the study of the movement of water on or over land, its flows and gatherings, its evaporations and condensations, its interactions with landforms like deltas and coastlines.

KEY TERM

MAIN CLAUSE A word group that contains a subject and a verb and does not begin with a subordinating word: *Soul food is varied.* (See p. 167.)

:
41a

Note A complete sentence *after* a colon may begin with a capital letter or a small letter (as in the example above). Just be consistent throughout an essay.

Series

Canada has long coastal boundaries on three oceans: the Pacific, the Arctic, and the Atlantic.

Appositive

Canada has one salient feature: the longest coastline.

Namely, that is, and other expressions that introduce appositives *follow* the colon: *Canada has one salient feature: namely, the longest coastline.*

Long or formal quotation

One hydrologist has remarked on the importance of the study of this coastline: "We have to know as much as possible about this ecology in order to preserve and protect the immense resources of our coasts."

(41b) Use a colon after the salutation of a business letter, between a title and subtitle, and between divisions of time.

Salutation of business letter

Dear Ms. Burak:

Title and subtitle

Charles Dickens: An Introduction to His Novels

Time

12:26 AM   6:00 PM

KEY TERMS

APPOSITIVE A noun or noun substitute that renames another noun immediately before it: *my brother, Jack.* (See p. 172.)

PREPOSITION *In, on, outside,* or another word that takes a noun or pronoun as its object: *in the house.* (See p. 164.)

:
41b

41c Delete or replace unneeded colons.

Use the colon only at the end of a main clause. Do not use it inside a main clause, especially after *such as* or a verb:

NOT The most celebrated seafood is: the lobster. Seafood lovers also treasure delicacies such as: crab, scallops, shrimp, and mussels.

BUT The most celebrated seafood is the lobster. Seafood lovers also treasure delicacies such as crab, scallops, shrimp, and mussels.

42 The Apostrophe

The apostrophe (') appears as part of a word to indicate possession (below), the omission of one or more letters (p. 270), or (in a few cases) plurals (pp. 269–71).

Note Computerized grammar and style checkers have mixed results in recognizing apostrophe errors. For instance, most flag missing apostrophes in contractions (as in *isnt*), but many cannot distinguish between *its* and *it's*, *their* and *they're*, *your* and *you're*, *whose* and *who's*. The checkers can identify some apostrophe errors in possessives but will overlook others and may flag correct plurals. Instead of relying on your checker, try using your word processor's Search or Find function to hunt for all words you have ended in *-s*. Then check them to ensure that they correctly omit or include apostrophes and that needed apostrophes are correctly positioned.

42a Use the apostrophe and sometimes **-s** to form possessive nouns and indefinite pronouns.

A noun or indefinite pronoun shows possession with an apostrophe and, usually, an *-s: the dog's hair, everyone's hope.*

ˇ
42a

Note Apostrophes are easy to misuse. For safety's sake, check your drafts to be sure that all words ending in *-s* neither omit needed apostrophes nor add unneeded ones. Also, remember that the apostrophe or apostrophe-plus-*s* is an *addition*. Before this addition, always spell the name of the owner or owners without dropping or adding letters.

1   Singular words: Add *-'s.*

Bill Boughton's skilful card tricks amaze children.
Anyone's eyes would widen.
Most tricks will pique an adult's curiosity, too.

The *-'s* ending for singular words pertains also to singular words ending in *-s,* as the next examples show.

Henry James's novels reward the patient reader.
The business's customers filed suit.

Exception An apostrophe alone may be added to a singular word ending in *-s* when another *s* would make the word difficult to say: *Moses' mother, Joan Rivers' jokes.* But the added *-s* is never wrong (*Moses's, Rivers's*).

2   Plural words ending in *-s:* Add *-'* only.

Workers' incomes have fallen slightly over the past year.
Many students benefit from several years' work after high school.
The Jameses' talents are extraordinary.

Note the difference in the possessives of singular and plural words ending in *-s.* The singular form usually takes *-s: James's.* The plural takes only the apostrophe: *Jameses'.*

3   Plural words not ending in *-s:* Add *-'s.*

Children's educations are at stake.
We need to attract the media's attention.

4   Compound words: Add *-'s* only to the last word.

The brother-in-law's business failed.
Taxes are always somebody else's fault.

___ KEY TERM _____

> INDEFINITE PRONOUN A pronoun that does not refer to a specific person or thing, such as *anyone, each, everybody, no one,* or *something.* (See p. 202.)

Uses and misuses of the apostrophe

Uses	Misuses

Possessives of nouns and indefinite pronouns (p. 267)

Singular	Plural
Ms. Park's	the Parks'
everyone's	two weeks'

Contractions (p. 270)

it's a girl	shouldn't
you're	won't

Optional: Plurals of abbreviations, dates, and words or characters named as words (p. 270)

MA's or MAs	C's or Cs
1960's or 1960s	if's or ifs

Singular, not plural, possessives (p. 268)

Not	But
the Kim's car	the Kims' car
boy's fathers	boys' fathers

Plurals of nouns (p. 269)

Not	But
book's are	books are
the Freed's	the Freeds

Third-person singulars of verbs (p. 270)

Not	But
swim's	swims

Possessives of personal pronouns (p. 270)

Not	But
it's toes	its toes
your's	yours

5   Two or more owners: Add -'s depending on possession.

Individual possession

Zimbale's and Mason's comedy techniques are similar. [Each comedian has his own technique.]

Joint possession

The child recovered despite her mother and father's neglect. [The mother and father were jointly neglectful.]

(42b)   Delete or replace any apostrophe in a plural noun, a singular verb, or a possessive personal pronoun.

1   Plural nouns

The plurals of nouns are generally formed by adding -s or -es, or changing *y* to *i* and adding -es: *boys, families, Joneses, Murphys*. Don't add an apostrophe to form the plural:

42b

NOT   The Jones' controlled the firm's until 2004.
BUT   The Joneses controlled the firms until 2004.

2   Singular verbs

Verbs ending in *-s never* take an apostrophe:

NOT   The subway break's down less often now.
BUT   The subway breaks down less often now.

3   Possessives of personal pronouns

His, hers, its, ours, yours, theirs, and *whose* are possessive forms of *he, she, it, we, you, they,* and *who.* They do not take apostrophes:

NOT   The house is her's. It's roof leaks.
BUT   The house is hers. Its roof leaks.

Don't confuse possessive pronouns with contractions. See below.

(42c)   Use the apostrophe to form contractions.

A CONTRACTION replaces one or more letters, numbers, or words with an apostrophe, as in the following examples:

it is	it's	cannot	can't
they are	they're	does not	doesn't
you are	you're	were not	weren't
who is	who's	class of 1997	class of '97

Note Don't confuse contractions with personal pronouns:

Contractions	Personal pronouns
It's a book.	Its cover is green.
They're coming.	Their car broke down.
You're right.	Your idea is good.
Who's coming?	Whose party is it?

(42d)   Increasingly, the apostrophe does not mark plural abbreviations, dates, and words or characters named as words.

You'll sometimes see apostrophes used to form the plurals of abbreviations (BA's), dates (1900's), and words or characters named as words (*but*'s). However, most current style guides recommend against the apostrophe in these cases.

ˇ
42d

BAs   PhDs
1990s   2000s

The sentence has too many <u>buts</u> [or *buts*].
Two <u>3</u>s [or *3s*] end the zip code.

Note Underline or italicize a word or character named as a word (see p. 293), but not the added -*s*.

43 Quotation Marks

Quotation marks—either double (" ") or single (' ')—mainly enclose direct quotations from speech or writing, enclose certain titles, and highlight words used in a special sense. These are the uses covered in this chapter, along with placing quotation marks outside or inside other punctuation marks. Additional issues with quotations are discussed elsewhere in this book:

- Punctuating *she said* and other signal phrases with quotations (p. 259).
- Altering quotations using the ellipsis mark (pp. 277–79) or brackets (p. 279).
- Quoting sources versus paraphrasing or summarizing them (pp. 331–35).
- Avoiding plagiarism when quoting (pp. 342–43).
- Integrating quotations into your text (pp. 335–336).
- Formatting long prose quotations, dialogue, and poetry quotations in MLA style (p. 412) or in APA style (p. 440).

Note Always use quotation marks in pairs, one at the beginning of a quotation and one at the end. Most computerized grammar and style checkers will help you use quotation marks in pairs by flagging a lone mark, and many will identify where other punctuation falls incorrectly inside or outside quotation marks. However, the checkers cannot recognize other possible errors in punctuating quotations. You'll need to proofread carefully yourself.

" "
43

(43a) Use double quotation marks to enclose direct quotations.

A DIRECT QUOTATION reports what someone said or wrote, in the exact words of the original:

"Life," said the psychoanalyst Karen Horney, "remains a very efficient therapist."

Do not use quotation marks with an indirect quotation, which reports what someone said or wrote but not in the exact words.

The psychoanalyst Karen Horney claimed that life is a good therapist.

(43b) Use single quotation marks to enclose a quotation within a quotation.

"In formulating any philosophy," Woody Allen writes, "the first consideration must always be: What can we know? Descartes hinted at the problem when he wrote, 'My mind can never know my body, although it has become quite friendly with my leg.'"

Notice that two different quotation marks appear at the end of the sentence—one single (to finish the interior quotation) and one double (to finish the main quotation).

(43c) Put quotation marks around the titles of works that are parts of other works.

Use quotation marks to enclose the titles of works that are published or released within larger works. (See the box on the next page.) Use single quotation marks for a quotation within a quoted title, as in the article title and essay title in the box. And enclose all punctuation in the title within the quotation marks, as in the article title.

Note Some academic disciplines do not require quotation marks for titles within source citations. See pages 427–37 (APA style), 450–56 (Chicago), and 458–63 (CSE style).

" "

43c

Titles to be enclosed in quotation marks

Other titles should be underlined or italicized. (See pp. 291–92.)

Song
"Lucy in the Sky with Diamonds"

Short story
"Who Do You Think You Are?"

Short poem
"Stone Hammer Poem"

Article in a periodical
"Does 'Scaring' Work?"

Essay
"Joey: A 'Mechanical Boy'"

Episode of a television or radio program
"Numbered Swiss Accounts" (on The Fifth Estate)

Subdivision of a book
"The Mast Head" (Chapter 35 of Moby-Dick)

(43d) Quotation marks may enclose words being used in a special sense.

On movie sets movable "wild walls" make a one-walled room seem four-walled on film.

Note Use underlining or italics for defined words. (See p. 293.)

(43e) Delete quotation marks where they are not required.

Title of your paper
NOT "Native and Settler in One Poem by Robert Kroetsch"
BUT Native and Settler in One Poem by Robert Kroetsch
OR Native and Settler in "Stone Hammer Poem"

Common nickname
NOT "Gordie" Howe still prefers his nickname to his given name.
BUT Gordie Howe still prefers his nickname to his given name.

43e

Slang or trite expression

Quotation marks will not excuse slang or a trite expression that is inappropriate to your writing. If slang is appropriate, use it without quotation marks.

> Not His election campaign is "dead in the water" and needs a "jump start."
>
> But His election campaign has lost momentum and needs to be revived.

(43f) **Place other punctuation marks inside or outside quotation marks according to standard practice.**

1   Commas and periods: inside quotation marks

Swift uses irony in his essay "A Modest Proposal."

Many first-time readers are shocked to see infants described as "delicious."

"'A Modest Proposal,'" wrote one critic, "is so outrageous that it cannot be believed."

Exception When a parenthetical source citation immediately follows a quotation, place any period or comma *after* the citation.

One critic calls the essay "outrageous" (Olms 26).

Partly because of "the cool calculation of its delivery" (Olms 27), Swift's satire still chills a modern reader.

2   Colons and semicolons: outside quotation marks

A few years ago the slogan in elementary education was "learning by playing"; now educators are concerned with teaching basic skills.

We all know the meaning of "basic skills": reading, writing, and arithmetic.

3   Dashes, question marks, and exclamation points: inside quotation marks only if part of the quotation

When a dash, question mark, or exclamation point is part of the quotation, place it *inside* quotation marks. Don't use any other punctuation, such as a period or comma:

"But must you—" Marcia hesitated, afraid of the answer.

"Go away!" I yelled.

Did you say, "Who is she?" [When both your sentence and the quotation would end in a question mark or exclamation point, use only the mark in the quotation.]

When a dash, question mark, or exclamation point applies only to the larger sentence, not to the quotation, place it *outside* quotation marks—again, with no other punctuation:

> One evocative line in English poetry—"After many a summer dies the swan"—was written by Alfred, Lord Tennyson.
> Who said, "Now cracks a noble heart"?
> The woman called me "stupid"!

44 Other Marks

The other marks of punctuation are the dash (below), parentheses (p. 277), the ellipsis mark (p. 277), brackets (p. 279), and the slash (p. 280).

Note Some computerized grammar and style checkers will flag a lone parenthesis or bracket so that you can match it with another parenthesis or bracket. But most checkers cannot recognize other misuses of the marks covered here. You'll need to proofread your papers carefully for errors.

44a Use the dash or dashes to indicate shifts and to set off some sentence elements.

The dash (—) is mainly a mark of interruption: it signals a shift, insertion, or break. In your papers, form a dash with two hyphens (--) or use the character called an em dash on your word processor. Do not add extra space around or between the hyphens or around the em dash.

Note When an interrupting element starting with a dash falls in the middle of a sentence, be sure to add the closing dash to signal the end of the interruption. See the first example on the next page.

44a

1   Shifts in tone or thought

The novel—if one can call it that—appeared in 1994.
If the book had a plot—but a plot would be conventional.

2   Nonessential elements

Dashes may be used instead of commas to set off and emphasize modifiers, parenthetical expressions, and other nonessential elements, especially when these elements are internally punctuated:

The qualities Monet painted—sunlight, rich shadows, deep colours—abounded near the rivers and gardens he used as subjects.

Though they are close together—separated by only a few blocks—the two neighbourhoods could be in different countries.

3   Introductory series and concluding series and explanations

Shortness of breath, skin discolouration, or the sudden appearance of moles, persistent indigestion, the presence of a small lump—all these may signify cancer. [Introductory series.]

The patient undergoes a battery of tests—CAT scan, bronchoscopy, perhaps even biopsy. [Concluding series.]

Many patients are disturbed by the CAT scan—by the need to keep still for long periods in an exceedingly small space. [Concluding explanation.]

A colon could be used instead of a dash in the last two examples. The dash is more informal.

4   Overuse

Too many dashes can make writing jumpy or breathy:

NOT   In all his life—eighty-seven years—my great-grandfather never allowed his picture to be taken—not even once. He claimed the "black box"—the camera—would steal his soul.

BUT   In all his eighty-seven years, my great-grandfather did not allow his picture to be taken even once. He claimed the "black box"—the camera—would steal his soul.

—

44a

KEY TERM

NONESSENTIAL ELEMENT Gives added information but does not limit the word it refers to. (See pp. 252–56.)

44b Use parentheses to enclose parenthetical expressions and labels for lists within sentences.

Note Parentheses *always* come in pairs, one before and one after the punctuated material.

1 Parenthetical expressions

PARENTHETICAL EXPRESSIONS include explanations, facts, digressions, and examples that may be helpful or interesting but are not essential to meaning. Parentheses de-emphasize parenthetical expressions. (Commas emphasize them more and dashes still more.)

> The population of Vancouver (now about 1.7 million) has grown dramatically since 1960.

Note Don't put a comma before a parenthetical expression enclosed in parentheses. Punctuation after the parenthetical expression should be placed outside the closing parenthesis.

> NOT Vancouver's population compares with Houston's, (just over 2 million.)
>
> BUT Vancouver's population compares with Houston's (just over 2 million).

When it falls between other complete sentences, a complete sentence enclosed in parentheses begins with a capital letter and ends with a period.

> In general, coaches will tell you that scouts are just guys who can't coach. (But then, so are brain surgeons.)   —ROY BLOUNT

2 Labels for lists within sentences

> Outside the Middle East, the countries with the largest oil reserves are (1) Venezuela (63 billion barrels), (2) Russia (57 billion barrels), and (3) Mexico (51 billion barrels).

When you set a list off from your text, do not enclose such labels in parentheses.

44c Use the ellipsis mark to indicate omissions from quotations.

The ellipsis mark, consisting of three spaced periods (. . .), generally indicates an omission from a quotation. All academic

44c

disciplines now use the ellipsis in the style demonstrated below. Enclose the ellipsis in brackets only if there is an ellipsis in the original.

All the following examples quote from this passage about environmentalism:

Original quotation

"McLuhan, of course, coined the phrase the 'global village,' and instructed a generation about the world's interconnectedness in the age of modern communications. For some, interconnectedness reinforces impressions and realities of difference; for others, it enhances a sense of a common humanity. For still others, it provides fleeting and barely relevant images captured by the roving cameras of the western world's television networks. Whatever the individual reaction, the 'global village' does symbolize that previous links among states took a quantum leap in the post-war age. In particular, the 'global village' offers no escape from the cultural trends conveyed daily from news-making, trendsetting centres of the world."

—JEFFREY SIMPSON, *Faultlines*

1. Omission of the middle of a sentence

"McLuhan ... instructed a generation about the world's interconnectedness in the age of modern communications."

2. Omission of the end of a sentence

"For some, interconnectedness reinforces impressions and realities of difference. ..." [The sentence period, closed up to the last word, precedes the ellipsis mark.]

"For some, interconnectedness reinforces impressions and realities of difference ..." (Simpson 35). [When the quotation is followed by a parenthetical source citation, as here, the sentence period follows the citation.]

3. Omission of parts of two sentences

"For some, interconnectedness reinforces impressions and realities of difference; for others, ... it provides fleeting and barely relevant images captured by the roving cameras of the western world's television networks."

4. Omission of one or more sentences

"McLuhan, of course, coined the phrase the 'global village,' and instructed a generation about the world's interconnectedness in the age of modern communications. ... In particular, the 'global village' offers no escape from the cultural trends conveyed daily from news-making, trendsetting centres of the world."

...
44c

Note these features of the examples:

- The ellipsis mark indicates that material is omitted from the source when the omission would not otherwise be clear. Thus, use an ellipsis mark when the words you quote form a complete sentence that is different in the original. Don't use an ellipsis mark at the beginning or end of a partial sentence: *Simpson argues that interconnectedness offers "no escape."*
- If you omit one or more lines of poetry or paragraphs of prose from a quotation, use a separate line of ellipsis marks across the full width of the quotation to show the omission.

In "Song: Love Armed" from 1676, Aphra Behn contrasts two lovers' experiences of a romance:

> Love in fantastic triumph sate,
>
> Whilst bleeding hearts around him flowed,
>
>
>
> But my poor heart alone is harmed,
>
> Whilst thine the victor is, and free. (lines 1-2, 15-16)

(See pp. 412–13 for the format of displayed quotations like this one.)

(44d) Use brackets to indicate changes in quotations.

Brackets have specialized uses in mathematical equations, but their main use for all kinds of writing is to indicate that you have altered a quotation to explain, clarify, or correct it.

> "That Petro-Canada station [just outside Toronto] is one of the busiest in the nation," said a company spokesperson.

In the style of the Modern Language Association, brackets also surround ellipsis marks that you add to indicate omissions from quotations only if there is an ellipsis in the original.

The word *sic* (Latin for "in this manner") in brackets indicates that an error in the quotation appeared in the original and was not made by you. Do not underline or italicize *sic* in brackets.

> According to the newspaper report, "The car slammed thru [sic] the railing and into oncoming traffic."

But don't use *sic* to make fun of a writer or to note errors in a passage that is clearly nonstandard.

[ ]

44d

(44e) Use the slash between options, between lines of poetry run into the text, and in electronic addresses.

Option

Some teachers oppose pass/fail courses.

Poetry

Many readers have sensed an ambiguous relation to life and death in Irving Layton's lines "And brought my hand down on the butter-fly / And felt the rock move beneath my hand."

When separating lines of poetry in this way, leave a space before and after the slash. (See pp. 412–13 for more on quoting poetry.)

Electronic addresses

http://www.unbf.ca/arts/Culture_Lang/programs_world.html

See page 325 for more on electronic addresses.

6 Spelling and Mechanics

6 Spelling and Mechanics

45 Spelling and the Hyphen

You can train yourself to spell better, and this chapter will tell you how. But you can improve instantly by acquiring three habits:

- Carefully proofread your writing.
- Cultivate a healthy suspicion of your spellings.
- Compulsively check a dictionary whenever you doubt a spelling.

Note A word processor's spelling checker can help you find and track spelling errors in your papers. But its usefulness is limited, mainly because it can't spot the confusion of words with similar spellings, such as *their/they're/there*. A grammar and style checker may flag such words, but only the ones listed in its dictionary. You still must proofread your papers yourself.

45a Anticipate typical spelling problems.

Certain situations, such as misleading pronunciation, commonly lead to misspelling.

1 Pronunciation

In English, pronunciation of words is an unreliable guide to how they are spelled. Pronunciation is especially misleading with HOMONYMS, words pronounced the same but spelled differently. Some homonyms and near-homonyms appear in the following box.

Words commonly confused

accept (to receive)
except (other than)

affect (to have an influence on)
effect (result)

all ready (prepared)
already (by this time)

allusion (indirect reference)
illusion (erroneous belief or
 perception)

ascent (a movement up)
assent (agreement)

---

bare (unclothed)
bear (to carry, or an animal)

board (a plane of wood)
bored (uninterested)

brake (stop)
break (smash)

buy (purchase)
by (next to)

cite (to quote an authority)
sight (the ability to see)
site (a place)

desert (to abandon)
dessert (after-dinner course)

discreet (reserved, respectful)
discrete (individual, distinct)

fair (average, or lovely)
fare (a fee for transportation)

forth (forward)
fourth (after *third*)

hear (to perceive by ear)
here (in this place)

heard (past tense of *hear*)
herd (a group of animals)

hole (an opening)
whole (complete)

its (possessive of *it*)
it's (contraction of *it is*)

know (to be certain)
no (the opposite of *yes*)

lead (to guide, or a
    heavy metal)
led (past tense
    of *lead*)

meat (flesh)
meet (encounter)

passed (past tense of *pass*)
past (after, or a time gone by)

patience (forbearance)
patients (persons under
    medical care)

peace (the absence of war)
piece (a portion of something)

plain (clear)
plane (a carpenter's tool, or an
    airborne vehicle)

presence (the state of being at
    hand)
presents (gifts)

principal (most important, or
    the head of a school)
principle (a basic truth or law)

rain (precipitation)
reign (to rule)
rein (a strap for an animal)

right (correct)
rite (a religious ceremony)
write (to make letters)

road (a surface for driving)
rode (past tense of *ride*)

scene (where an action occurs)
seen (past participle of *see*)

stationary (unmoving)
stationery (writing paper)

their (possessive of *they*)
there (opposite of *here*)
they're (contraction of
    they are)

to (toward)
too (also)
two (following *one*)

waist (the middle of the body)
waste (discarded material)

weak (not strong)
week (Sunday through
    Saturday)

weather (climate)
whether (*if*, or introducing a
    choice)

which (one of a group)
witch (a sorcerer)

who's (contraction of *who is*)
whose (possessive of *who*)

your (possessive of *you*)
you're (contraction of
    you are)

2   Different forms of the same word

Often, the noun form and the verb form of the same word are spelled differently: for example, *advice* (noun) and *advise* (verb). Sometimes the noun and the adjective forms of the same word differ: *height* and *high*. Similar changes occur in the parts of some irregular verbs (*know, knew, known*) and the plurals of irregular nouns (*man, men*).

3   British vs. American spellings ESL

If you learned English in Canada or outside North America, you may be more accustomed to British than to American spellings. Here are the chief differences:

American	British
color, humor	colour, humour
theater, center	theatre, centre
canceled, traveled	cancelled, travelled
judgment	judgement
realize, civilize	realise, civilise
connection	connexion

Your dictionary may list both spellings, but it will specially mark the British one with *chiefly Brit* or a similar label.

For a note on Canadian spelling, see page 467.

(45b)   Follow spelling rules.

1   *ie* vs. *ei*

To distinguish between *ie* and *ei,* use the familiar jingle:

I before *e,* except after *c,* or when pronounced "ay" as in *neighbour* and *weigh.*

i before *e*	believe	thief	hygiene
ei after *c*	ceiling	conceive	perceive
ei sounded as "ay"	sleigh	eight	beige

Exceptions For some exceptions, remember this sentence:

The weird foreigner neither seizes leisure nor forfeits height.

2   Final *e*

When adding an ending to a word with a final *e,* drop the *e* if the ending begins with a vowel:

advise + able = advisable   surprise + ing = surprising

Keep the *e* if the ending begins with a consonant:

care + ful = careful   like + ly = likely

Exceptions Retain the *e* after a soft *c* or *g*, to keep the sound of the consonant soft rather than hard: *courageous, changeable.* And drop the *e* before a consonant when the *e* is preceded by another vowel: *argue + ment = argument, true + ly = truly.*

3 Final *y*

When adding an ending to a word with a final *y*, change the *y* to *i* if it follows a consonant:

beauty, beauties   worry, worried   supply, supplies

But keep the *y* if it follows a vowel, if it ends a proper name, or if the ending is -*ing:*

day, days   Minsky, Minskys   cry, crying

4 Final consonants

When adding an ending to a one-syllable word ending in a consonant, double the final consonant when it follows a single vowel. Otherwise, don't double the consonant.

slap, slapping   park, parking   pair, paired

5 Prefixes

When adding a prefix, do not drop a letter from or add a letter to the original word:

unnecessary   disappoint   misspell

6 Plurals

Most nouns form plurals by adding *s* to the singular form. Add *es* for the plural of nouns ending in *s, sh, ch,* or *x.*

boy, boys   kiss, kisses   church, churches

Nouns ending in *o* preceded by a vowel usually form the plural with *s.* Those ending in *o* preceded by a consonant usually form the plural with *es.*

ratio, ratios   hero, heroes

Some very common nouns form irregular plurals.

child, children   woman, women   mouse, mice

Some English nouns that were originally Italian, Greek, Latin, or French form the plural according to their original language:

analysis, analyses	criterion, criteria	phenomenon, phenomena
basis, bases	datum, data	thesis, theses
crisis, crises	medium, media	

A few such nouns may form irregular or regular plurals: for instance, *index, indices, indexes; curriculum, curricula, curriculums.* The regular plural is more contemporary.

With compound nouns, add *s* to the main word of the compound. Sometimes this main word is not the last word.

| city-states | fathers-in-law | passersby |

ESL Noncount nouns do not form plurals, either regularly (with an added *s*) or irregularly. Examples of noncount nouns include *equipment, intelligence,* and *wealth.* See page 224.

(45c) Use the hyphen in some compound words.

1 Compound adjectives

When two or more words serve together as a single modifier before a noun, a hyphen forms the modifying words clearly into a unit.

She is a well-known actor.
Some Spanish-speaking students work as translators.

When such a compound adjective follows the noun, the hyphen is unnecessary.

The actor is well known.
Many students are Spanish speaking.

The hyphen is also unnecessary in a compound modifier containing an *-ly* adverb, even before the noun: *clearly defined* terms.

When part of a compound adjective appears only once in two or more parallel compound adjectives, hyphens indicate which words the reader should mentally join with the missing part.

School-age children should have eight- or nine-o'clock bedtimes.

2 Fractions and compound numbers

Hyphens join the numerator and denominator of fractions: *one-half, three-fourths.* Hyphens also join the parts of the whole numbers *twenty-one* to *ninety-nine.*

_KEY TERM_____

COMPOUND WORD A word expressing a combination of ideas, such as *cross-reference* or *crossroads.*

3   Prefixes and suffixes

Do not use hyphens with prefixes except as follows:

- With the prefixes *self-*, *all-*, and *ex-*: *self-control, all-inclusive, ex-student.*
- With a prefix before a capitalized word: *anti-Canadian.*
- With a capital letter before a word: *T-shirt.*
- To prevent misreading: *de-emphasize, re-create a story.*

The only suffix that regularly requires a hyphen is *-elect,* as in *president-elect.*

(45d) Use the hyphen to divide words at the ends of lines.

You can avoid occasional short lines in your documents by dividing some words between the end of one line and the beginning of the next. If you write on a word processor, you can set the program to divide words automatically at appropriate breaks (in the Tools menu, select Language and then Hyphenation). To divide words manually, follow these guidelines:

- Divide words only between syllables—for instance, *win-dows,* not *wi-ndows.* Check a dictionary for correct syllable breaks.
- Never divide a one-syllable word.
- Leave at least two letters on the first line and three on the second line. If a word cannot be divided to follow this rule (for instance, *a-bus-er*), don't divide it.

If you must break an electronic address—for instance, in a source citation—do so only after a slash. Do not hyphenate, because readers may perceive any added hyphen as part of the address.

Not   http://www.library.miami.edu/staff/lmc/soc-
       race.html
But   http://www.library.miami.edu/staff/lmc/
       socrace.html

46 Capital Letters

The following conventions and a desk dictionary can help you decide whether to capitalize a particular word in most writing. The social, natural, and applied sciences require specialized capitalization for terminology, such as *Conditions A and B* or *Escherichia coli.* Consult one of the style guides listed on page 346 for the requirements of the discipline you are writing in.

Note A computerized grammar and style checker will flag overused capital letters and missing capitals at the beginnings of sentences. It will also spot missing capitals at the beginnings of proper nouns and adjectives—*if* the nouns and adjectives are in the checker's dictionary. For example, a checker caught *christianity* and *europe* but not *china* (for the country) or *Stephen king.* You'll need to proofread for capital letters on your own as well.

ESL Conventions of capitalization vary from language to language. English, for instance, is the only language to capitalize the first-person singular pronoun (*I*), and its practice of capitalizing proper nouns but not most common nouns also distinguishes it from some other languages.

46a Capitalize the first word of every sentence.

Every writer should own a good dictionary.

When quoting other writers, you should reproduce the capital letters beginning their sentences or indicate that you have altered the source's capitalization. Whenever possible, integrate the quotation into your own sentence so that its capitalization coincides with yours:

"Psychotherapists often overlook the benefits of self-deception," the author argues.

The author argues that "the benefits of self-deception" are not always recognized by psychotherapists.

If you need to alter the capitalization in the source, the MLA suggests that you indicate the change with brackets:

"[T]he benefits of self-deception" are not always recognized by psychotherapists, the author argues.

The author argues that "[p]sychotherapists often overlook the benefits of self-deception."

cap
46b

Note Capitalization of questions in a series is optional. Both of the following examples are correct:

Is the population a hundred? Two hundred? More?

Is the population a hundred? two hundred? more?

Also optional is capitalization of the first word in a complete sentence after a colon.

46b Capitalize proper nouns, proper adjectives, and words used as essential parts of proper nouns.

1 Proper nouns and proper adjectives

PROPER NOUNS name specific persons, places, and things: *Shakespeare, Manitoba, World War I.* PROPER ADJECTIVES are formed from some proper nouns: *Shakespearean, Manitoban.* Capitalize all proper nouns and proper adjectives but not the articles (*a, an, the*) that precede them:

Proper nouns and adjectives to be capitalized

Specific persons and things

Peter Mansbridge	Air Canada Centre
Napoleon Bonaparte	the West Edmonton Mall

Specific places and geographical regions

New York City	the Mediterranean Sea
China	the Maritimes, the North

But: northeast of the city, maritime climate

Days of the week, months, holidays

Monday	Yom Kippur
May	Christmas

Historical events, documents, periods, movements

the Riel Rebellion	the Renaissance
the Constitution	the Romantic Movement

Government offices or departments and institutions

House of Commons   City of Lethbridge
Ministry of Labour   Churchill High School

Political, social, athletic, and other organizations and associations and their members

Liberal Party, Liberals   Royal Society of Canada
Greenpeace   Montreal Canadiens
B'nai B'rith   Royal Winnipeg Ballet

Races, nationalities, and their languages

Native peoples   Germans
African Canadian   Swahili
Caucasian   Italian

But: blacks, whites

Religions, their followers, and terms for the sacred

Christianity, Christians God
Catholicism, Catholics   Allah
Judaism, Orthodox Jew   the Bible [but biblical]
Islam, Moslems or Muslims the Koran or Qur'an

2 Common nouns used as essential parts of proper nouns

Capitalize the common nouns *street, avenue, park, river, ocean, lake, company, college, county,* and *memorial* when they are part of proper nouns naming specific places or institutions:

Portage Avenue   Lake Superior
Avalon Peninsula   Ford Motor Company
Mackenzie River   Conestoga College
Pacific Ocean   Lions Gate Bridge

46c Capitalize most words in titles and subtitles of works.

Within your text, capitalize all the words in a title *except* the following: articles (*a, an, the*); *to* in infinitives; and connecting words (prepositions and conjunctions) of fewer than five letters.

Capitalize even these short words when they are the first or last word in a title or when they fall after a colon or semicolon.

"Disembarking at Quebec"   *Management: A New Theory*
A Diamond Is Forever   "From Colony to Nation"
"Knowing Whom to Ask"   *An End to Live For*
What's Bred in the Bone   *File Under Architecture*

Note The style guides of the academic disciplines have their own rules for capitals in titles. For instance, MLA style for English and some other humanities styles capitalize all subordinating conjunctions but no prepositions. In addition, APA style for the social sciences and CSE style for the sciences capitalize only the first word and proper names in book and article titles within source citations. (See pp. 448–56 on Chicago, 456–63 on CSE, and 423 on APA). See also IEEE style (p. 464).

46d   **Capitalize titles preceding persons' names.**

Before a person's name, capitalize his or her title. After or apart from the name, do not capitalize the title.

Professor Otto Osborne   Otto Osborne, a professor
Doctor Jane Covington   Jane Covington, a doctor
Premier Jean Charest   Jean Charest, the premier

Note Many writers capitalize a title denoting very high rank even when it follows a name or is used alone: *Bill Clinton, former President of the United States.*

46e   **Use capitals according to convention in online communication.**

Although common in electronic mail and other online communication, passages or whole messages written in all-capital letters or with no capital letters are difficult to read. Further, messages in all-capital letters may be taken as overly insistent, even rude. Use capital letters according to rules 46a–46d in all your online communication.

47 Italics or Underlining

Italic type and <u>underlining</u> indicate the same thing: the word or words are being distinguished or emphasized. If you underline two or more words in a row, underline the space between the words, too: <u>Criminal Statistics: Misuses of Numbers</u>.

Note Computerized grammar and style checkers cannot recognize problems with italics or underlining. Check your work yourself to ensure that you have used highlighting appropriately.

47a Use italics or underlining consistently and appropriately for your writing situation.

Word processors have made italic type possible in papers and other documents, and it is now used almost universally in business and most academic disciplines. (The *MLA Handbook for Writers of Research Papers* recommends italics over underlining although underlining is not incorrect. See p. 388.) Ask your instructor for his or her own preferences.

Depending on your instructor's preferences, use either italics or underlining consistently throughout a document. For instance, if you are writing an English paper and following MLA style for italicization in source citations, use italicization in the body of your paper as well.

47b Italicize or underline the titles of works that appear independently.

Within your text italicize or underline the titles of works, such as books and periodicals, that are published, released, or produced separately from other works. (See the box on the next page.) Use quotation marks for all other titles, such as songs, essays, short stories, articles in periodicals, and episodes of television series. (See pp. 272–73.)

Exceptions Legal documents, the Bible, the Koran, and their parts are generally not underlined or italicized:

NOT We studied the *Book of Revelation* in the *Bible*.
BUT We studied the Book of Revelation in the Bible.

Titles to be italicized or underlined

Other titles should be placed in quotation marks. (See pp. 272–73.)

Books	Long poems
Two Solitudes	*Beowulf*
War and Peace	*Paradise Lost*
The Stone Diaries	*Brébeuf and His Brethren*

Plays	Periodicals
Hamlet	*Maclean's*
The Phantom of the Opera	*Calgary Herald*

Pamphlets	Published speeches
The Truth About Alcoholism	Lincoln's *Gettysburg Address*

Long musical works	Movies and videotapes
Tchaikovsky's *Swan Lake*	*Schindler's List*
The Beatles' *Revolver*	*Jesus of Montreal*
But: Symphony in C	*How to Relax*

Television and radio programs	Works of visual art
The Royal Canadian Air Farce	Michelangelo's *David*
Canadian Idol	the *Mona Lisa*
Hockey Night in Canada	*Guernica*

(47c) Italicize or underline the names of ships, aircraft, spacecraft, and trains.

Challenger	*Orient Express*	*Queen Elizabeth 2*
Apollo XI	*Montrealer*	*Spirit of St. Louis*

(47d) Italicize or underline foreign words that are not part of the English language.

A foreign expression should be italicized or underlined when it has not been absorbed into our language. A dictionary will say whether a word is still considered foreign to English.

> The scientific name for the brown trout is *Salmo trutta*. [The Latin scientific names for plants and animals are always italicized or underlined.]

> The Latin *De gustibus non est disputandum* translates roughly as "There's no accounting for taste."

(47e) Italicize or underline words or characters named as words.

Use italics or underlining to indicate that you are citing a character or word as a word rather than using it for its meaning. Words you are defining fall under this convention.

> The word *syzygy* refers to a straight line formed by three celestial bodies, as in the alignment of the earth, sun, and moon.
>
> Some people say *th*, as in *thought*, with a faint *s* or *f* sound.

(47f) Occasionally, italics or underlining may be used for emphasis.

Italics or underlining can stress an important word or phrase, especially in reporting how someone said something. But use such emphasis very rarely, or your writing may sound immature or hysterical.

(47g) In online communication, use alternatives for italics or underlining.

Electronic mail and other forms of online communication often do not allow conventional highlighting such as italics or underlining for the purposes described in this chapter. The program may not be able to produce the highlighting or may reserve it for a special function. (On World Wide Web sites, for instance, underlining indicates a link to another site.)

To distinguish book titles and other elements that usually require italics or underlining, type an underscore before and after the element: *Measurements coincide with those in _Joule's Handbook_* . You can also emphasize words with asterisks before and after: *I *will not* be able to attend.*

Don't use all-capital letters for emphasis; they yell too loudly. (See also p. 290.)

48 Abbreviations

The following guidelines on abbreviations pertain to the text of a nontechnical document. All academic disciplines use abbreviations in source citations, and much technical writing, such as in the sciences and engineering, uses many abbreviations in the document text. Consult one of the style guides listed on page 346 for the in-text requirements of the discipline you are writing in.

Usage varies, but writers increasingly omit periods from abbreviations of two or more words written in all-capital letters: *US, BA, CUPE.* See pages 247–78 on punctuating abbreviations.

Note A computerized grammar and style checker may flag some abbreviations, such as *in.* (for *inch*) and *St.* (for *Street*). A spelling checker will flag abbreviations it does not recognize. But neither checker can tell you whether an abbreviation is appropriate for your writing situation or will be clear to your readers.

48a Use standard abbreviations for titles immediately before and after proper names.

Before the name	After the name
Dr. James Hsu	James Hsu, MD
Mr., Mrs., Ms., Hon.,	DDS, DVM, Ph.D.,
St., Rev., Msgr., Gen.	Ed.D., OSB, MP, SJ, Sr., Jr.

Do not use abbreviations such as *Rev., Hon., Prof., Rep., Sen., Dr.,* and *St.* (for *Saint*) unless they appear before a proper name.

48b Familiar abbreviations and acronyms are acceptable in most writing.

An ACRONYM is an abbreviation that spells a pronounceable word, such as WHO, NATO, and AIDS. These and other abbreviations using initials are acceptable in most writing as long as they are familiar to readers.

INSTITUTIONS	UWO, UBC, UPEI
ORGANIZATIONS	CIA, NDP, YMCA, PMO

Corporations	IBM, CTV, HBC
People	JFK, LBJ, PET
Countries	U.K. (or UK)

Note If a name or term (such as *operating room*) appears often in a piece of writing, then its abbreviation (*OR*) can cut down on extra words. Spell out the full term at its first appearance, indicate its abbreviation in parentheses, and then use the abbreviation.

(48c) Use *BC, AD, AM, PM, no.,* and *$* only with specific dates and numbers.

44 BC	11:26 AM (or a.m.)	no. 36 (or No. 36)
AD 1492	8:05 PM (or p.m.)	$7.41

The abbreviation BC ("before Christ") always follows a date, whereas AD (*anno Domini,* Latin for "in the year of the Lord") precedes a date.

Note BCE ("before the common era") and CE ("common era") are increasingly replacing BC and AD, respectively. Both follow the date: *44 BCE, 1492 CE.*

(48d) Generally reserve Latin abbreviations for source citations and comments in parentheses.

i.e.	*id est:* that is
cf.	*confer:* compare
e.g.	*exempli gratia:* for example
et al.	*et alii:* and others
etc.	*et cetera:* and so forth
NB	*nota bene:* note well

He said he would be gone a fortnight (i.e., two weeks).
Bloom et al., editors, *Anthology of Light Verse*
Trees, too, are susceptible to disease (e.g., Dutch elm disease).

(Note that these abbreviations are generally not italicized or underlined.)

Some writers avoid these abbreviations in formal writing, even within parentheses.

ab
48f

(48e) Use *Inc., Bros., Co.,* or *&* (for *and*) only in official names of business firms.

FAULTY   The Tremblay <u>bros.</u> operate a large trucking firm in Vancouver <u>&</u> the Lower Mainland.
REVISED   The Tremblay <u>brothers</u> operate a large trucking firm in Vancouver <u>and</u> the Lower Mainland.
REVISED   Tremblay <u>Bros.</u> is a large trucking firm that operates in Vancouver <u>and</u> the Lower Mainland.

(48f) Generally spell out units of measurement and names of places, calendar designations, people, and courses.

In most academic, general, and business writing, the types of words listed below should always be spelled out. (In source citations and technical writing, however, these words are more often abbreviated.)

Units of measurement
The dog is eighty <u>centimetres</u> [not <u>cm.</u>] high.

Geographical names
The publisher is in <u>Ontario</u> [not <u>Ont.</u> or <u>ON</u>].

Names of days, months, and holidays
The truce was signed on <u>Tuesday</u> [not <u>Tues.</u>], <u>April</u> [not <u>Apr.</u>] 16.

Names of people
<u>Robert</u> [not <u>Robt.</u>] Kroetsch writes Prairie poetry.

Courses of instruction
I'm majoring in <u>Canadian Literature</u> [not <u>Can. Lit.</u>].

49 Numbers

This chapter addresses the use of numbers (numerals versus words) in the text of a document. All disciplines use many more numerals in source citations.

Note Computerized grammar and style checkers will flag numerals beginning sentences and can be customized to ignore or to look for numerals. But they can't tell you whether numerals or spelled-out numbers are appropriate for your writing situation.

(49a) Use numerals according to standard practice in the field you are writing in.

Always use numerals for numbers that require more than two words to spell out:

The leap year has <u>366</u> days.
The population of Red Deer, Alberta, is about <u>54,400</u>.

In nontechnical academic writing, spell out numbers of one or two words:

<u>Twelve</u> nations signed the treaty.
The ball game drew <u>forty-two thousand</u> people. [A hyphenated number may be considered one word.]

In much business writing, use numerals for all numbers over ten: *five reasons, 11 participants*. In technical academic and business writing, such as in science and engineering, use numerals for all numbers over ten, and use numerals for zero through nine when they refer to exact measurements: *2 litres, 1 hour*. (Consult one of the style guides listed on p. 346 for more details.)

Note Use a combination of numerals and words for round numbers over a million: *26 million, 2.45 billion*. And use either all numerals or all words when several numbers appear together in a passage, even if convention would require a mixture.

ESL In English a comma separates the numerals in long numbers (*26,000*), and a period functions as a decimal point (*2.06*).

num
49c

(49b) Use numerals according to convention for dates, addresses, and other information.

Days and years
June 18, 1985   AD 12   456 BC   1999

Pages, chapters, volumes, acts, scenes, lines
Chapter 9, page 123
Hamlet, act 5, scene 3

Decimals, percentages, and fractions
22.5   3$^{1}/_{2}$
48% (or 48 percent)

Addresses
432 Marine Drive
Halifax, NS B3R 1A3

Scores and statistics
21 to 7   a ratio of 8 to 1
a mean of 26

Exact amounts of money
$3.5 million $4.50

The time of day
9:00 AM   3:45 PM

Exceptions Round dollar or cent amounts of only a few words may be expressed in words: *seventeen dollars; sixty cents.* When the word *o'clock* is used for the time of day, also express the number in words: *two o'clock* (not *2 o'clock*).

(49c) Spell out numbers that begin sentences.

For clarity, spell out any number that begins a sentence. If the number requires more than two words, reword the sentence so that the number falls later and can be expressed as a numeral.

NOT   3.5 billion people live in Asia.
BUT   The population of Asia is 3.5 billion.

Research and Documentation

7 Research and Documentation

Research writing gives you a chance to work like a detective solving a case. The mystery is the answer to a question you care about. The search for the answer leads you to consider what others think about your subject, but you do more than simply report their views. You build on them to develop and support your own opinion, and ultimately you become an expert in your own right.

Your investigation will be more productive and enjoyable if you take some steps described in this chapter: plan your work (below), keep a research journal (next page), find an appropriate topic and research question (p. 301), set goals for your research (p. 302), and keep a working bibliography (p. 305).

50a

(50a) Planning your work

Research writing is a *writing* process:

- You work within a particular situation of subject, purpose, audience, and other factors (see Chapter 1).
- You gather ideas and information about your subject (Chapter 2).
- You focus and arrange your ideas (Chapter 3).
- You draft to explore your meaning (Chapter 4).
- You revise and edit to develop, shape, and polish (Chapter 5).

Although the process seems neatly sequential in this list, you know from experience that the stages overlap—that, for instance, you may begin drafting before you've gathered all the information you expect to find, and then while drafting you may discover a source that causes you to rethink your approach. Anticipating the process of research writing can free you to be flexible in your search and open to discoveries.

A thoughtful plan and systematic procedures can help you follow through on the diverse activities of research writing. One step is to make a schedule like the one below that apportions the available time to the necessary work.

Complete
by:

_____ 1. Setting a schedule and beginning a research
journal (here and p. 300)
_____ 2. Finding a researchable topic and question (facing
page)
_____ 3. Setting research goals (p. 302)
_____ 4. Finding sources, both print and electronic (p. 302),
and making a working bibliography (p. 305)

_____ 5. Evaluating and synthesizing sources (pp. 323, 330)
_____ 6. Taking notes using summary, paraphrase, and
direct quotation (p. 331)

50b

_____ 7. Developing a thesis statement and creating a
structure (p. 348)
_____ 8. Drafting the paper (p. 349), integrating
summaries, paraphrases, and direct quotations
into your ideas (p. 331)

_____ 9. Revising and editing the paper (p. 349)
_____ 10. Citing sources in your text (p. 344)
_____ 11. Preparing the list of works cited or references
(p. 347)
_____ 12. Preparing the final manuscript (p. 350)
Final paper due

You can estimate that each segment marked off by a horizontal line
will occupy *roughly* one-quarter of the total time—for example, a
week in a four-week assignment or two weeks in an eight-week
assignment. The most unpredictable segments are the first two, so
it's wise to get started early enough to accommodate the unexpected.

(50b) Keeping a research journal

While working on a research project, carry index cards or a
notebook with you at all times to use as a RESEARCH JOURNAL, a place
to record your activities and ideas. (See p. 7 on journal keeping.) In
the journal's dated entries, you can write about the sources you
consult, the leads you want to pursue, any difficulties you
encounter, and, most important, your thoughts about sources,
leads, difficulties, new directions, relationships, and anything else
that strikes you. The very act of writing in the journal can expand
and clarify your thinking.

The research journal is the place for tracking and developing
your own ideas. Notes on what your sources actually say should be
taken and organized separately, as discussed on pages 331–35.

(50c) Finding a researchable topic and question

Before reading this section, you may want to review the suggestions given in Chapter 1 for finding and narrowing a writing subject (pp. 3–4). Generally, the same procedure applies to writing any kind of research paper. However, selecting and limiting a topic for a research paper can present special opportunities and problems. And before you proceed with your topic, you'll want to transform it into a question that can guide your search for sources.

1 Appropriate topic

Seek a research subject that interests you and that you care about. (It may be a subject you've already written about without benefit of research.) Starting with your own views will motivate you, and you will be a participant in a dialogue when you begin examining sources.

When you settle on a topic, ask the following questions about it. For each requirement, there are corresponding pitfalls.

- Are ample sources of information available on the topic?

  Avoid very recent topics, such as a newly announced medical discovery or a breaking story in today's newspaper.

- Does the topic encourage research in the kinds and number of sources required by the assignment?

  Avoid (*a*) topics that depend entirely on personal opinion and experience, such as the virtues of your hobby, and (*b*) topics that require research in only one source, such as a straight factual biography.

- Will the topic lead you to an objective assessment of sources and to defensible conclusions?

  Avoid topics that rest entirely on belief or prejudice, such as when human life begins or why women (or men) are superior. Your readers are unlikely to be swayed from their own beliefs.

- Does the topic suit the length of paper assigned and the time given for research and writing?

  Avoid broad topics that have too many sources to survey adequately, such as a major event in history.

2 Research question

Asking a question about your topic can give direction to your research by focusing your thinking on a particular approach. To discover your question, consider what about your subject intrigues or perplexes you, what you'd like to know more about. (See the next page for suggestions on using your own knowledge.)

Try to narrow your research question so that you can answer it in the time and space you have available. The question *How will the Internet affect business?* is very broad, encompassing issues as diverse as electronic commerce, information management, and employee training. In contrast, the question *How will Internet commerce benefit consumers?* or *How, if at all, should Internet commerce be taxed?* is much narrower. Each question also requires more than a simple *yes* or *no* answer, so that answering, even tentatively, demands thought about pros and cons, causes and effects.

As you read and write, your question will probably evolve to reflect your increasing knowledge of the subject, and eventually its answer will become your main idea, or thesis statement. (See p. 348.)

50d

(50d) Setting goals for the search

Before you start looking for sources, consider what you already know about your subject and where you are likely to find information on it.

1   Your own knowledge

Discovering what you already know about your topic will guide you in discovering what you don't know. Take some time to spell out facts you have learned, opinions you have heard or read elsewhere, and of course your own opinions. Use one of the discovery techniques discussed in Chapter 2 to explore and develop your ideas: keeping a journal (p. 7 and also p. 300), observing your surroundings (p. 8), freewriting (p. 8), brainstorming (p. 10), clustering (p. 11), asking questions (p. 12), and thinking critically (p. 13).

When you've explored your thoughts, make a list of questions for which you don't have answers, whether factual (*What laws govern taxes in Internet commerce?*) or more open-ended (*Who benefits from a tax-free Internet? Who doesn't benefit?*). These questions will give you clues about the sources you need to look for first.

2   Kinds of sources

For many research projects, you'll want to consult a mix of sources. (See pp. 303–04.) You may start by seeking the outlines of your topic—the range and depth of opinions about it—in reference works and articles in popular periodicals or through a search of the World Wide Web. Then, as you refine your views and your research question, you'll move on to more specialized sources, such as scholarly books and periodicals and your own interviews or surveys. (See pp. 312–22 for more on each kind of source.)

Library and Internet sources

The sources housed in your library—mainly reference works, periodicals, and books—have two big advantages over most of what you'll find on the Internet: they are catalogued and indexed for easy retrieval; and they are generally reliable, having been screened first by their publishers and then by the library's staff. In contrast, the Internet's retrieval systems are more difficult to use effectively, and online sources tend to be less reliable because most do not pass through any screening before being posted. (There are many exceptions, such as online scholarly journals and reference works and newspapers that are published both in print and online.)

Most instructors expect research writers to consult the print sources found in a library. But they'll accept online sources, too, if you have used them judiciously. Even with its disadvantages, the Internet can be a valuable resource for primary sources, scholarly contributions, current information, and a diversity of views. For guidelines on evaluating both print and online sources, see pages 323–30.

50d

Primary and secondary sources

As much as possible, you should rely on PRIMARY SOURCES, or firsthand accounts: historical documents (letters, speeches, and so on), eyewitness reports, works of literature, reports on experiments or surveys conducted by the writer, or your own interviews, experiments, observations, or correspondence.

In contrast, SECONDARY SOURCES report and analyze information drawn from other sources, often primary ones: a reporter's summary of a controversial issue, a historian's account of a battle, a critic's reading of a poem, a physicist's evaluation of several studies. Secondary sources may contain helpful summaries and interpretations that direct, support, and extend your own thinking. However, most research-writing assignments expect your own ideas to go beyond those in such sources.

Scholarly and popular sources

The scholarship of acknowledged experts is essential for depth, authority, and specificity. The general-interest views and information of popular sources can help you apply more scholarly approaches to daily life.

- *Check the publisher.* Is it a scholarly journal (such as *Education Forum*) or a publisher of scholarly books (such as University of Toronto Press), or is it a popular magazine (such as *Time* or *Maclean's*) or a publisher of popular books (such as Little, Brown)?

- *Check the author.* Have you seen the name elsewhere, which might suggest that the author is an expert?
- *Check the title.* Is it technical, or does it use a general vocabulary?
- *Check the electronic address.* Addresses for Internet sources often include an abbreviation that tells you something about the source: *edu* means the source comes from an educational institution, *gov* from an American and *gc.ca* from a Canadian government body, *org* from a nonprofit organization, *com* from a commercial organization such as a corporation. (See p. 325 for more on interpreting electronic addresses.)

50d

Older and newer sources

Check the publication date. For most subjects a combination of older, established sources (such as books) and current sources (such as newspaper articles, interviews, or Web sites) will provide both background and up-to-date information. Only historical subjects or very current subjects require an emphasis on one extreme or another.

Impartial and biased sources

Seek a range of viewpoints. Sources that attempt to be impartial can offer an overview of your subject and trustworthy facts. Sources with clear biases can offer a diversity of opinion. Of course, to discover bias, you may have to read the source carefully (see p. 323); but even a bibliographical listing can be informative.

- *Check the author.* You may have heard of the author as a respected researcher (thus more likely to be objective) or as a leading proponent of a certain view (less likely to be objective).
- *Check the title.* It may reveal something about point of view. (Consider these contrasting titles: "Keep the Internet Tax-Free" and "Taxation of Electronic Commerce: Issues and Questions.")

Note Online sources must be approached with particular care. See pages 324–28.

Sources with helpful features

Depending on your topic and how far along your research is, you may want to look for sources with features such as illustrations (which can clarify important concepts), bibliographies (which can direct you to other sources), and indexes (which can help you develop keywords for electronic searches; see p. 309).

(50e) Keeping a working bibliography

When you begin searching for sources, it may be tempting to pursue each possibility as you come across it. But that approach would prove inefficient and probably ineffective. Instead, you'll want to find out the full range of sources available and then decide on a good number to consult. For a paper of 1800 to 2500 words, try for ten to thirty promising titles as a start.

To keep track of where sources are and what they are, make a WORKING BIBLIOGRAPHY, a file of books, articles, Web sites, and other possibilities. By making a complete list, you'll have a record of all the information you'll need to find worthwhile sources and, eventually, to acknowledge them in your paper. When you have a substantial file, you can decide which sources seem most promising and look them up first or, if necessary, order them through interlibrary loan.

Note Some instructors require that the working bibliography be submitted on note cards (one source to a card), and this system has the advantage of allowing the sources to be shuffled easily. But many researchers have abandoned note cards because computers can print out source information, sort sources, and even transfer data to the user's own disk.

1   Source information

When you turn in your paper, you will be expected to attach a list of the sources you have used. So that readers can check or follow up on your sources, your list must include all the information needed to find the sources, in a format readers can understand. (See pp. 345–46.) The box on the next page shows the information you should record for each type of source so that you will not have to retrace your steps later.

2   Bibliographic information for online sources

Unlike that for printed materials, publication information for online sources can be difficult to find and make sense of. The screen shot on page 307 shows the first page of a Web site. Circled numbers refer to the following numbered explanations.

1. The source's address, or URL, usually appears in the Web browser's Address or Location field near the top of the screen. If the field does not appear, adjust the settings of the browser so that it displays the field.
2. Use as the source title the title of the page you are consulting. This information usually appears as a heading at the top of the page, but if not it may also appear in the bar along the top of the browser window.

Information for a working bibliography

For books

Library call number
Name(s) of author(s),
    editor(s), translator(s), or
    others listed
Title and subtitle
Publication data:
  Place of publication
  Publisher's name
  Date of publication
Other important data, such as
    edition or volume number

For periodical articles

Name(s) of author(s)
Title and subtitle of article
Title of periodical
Publication data:
  Volume number and issue
    number (if any) in which
    article appears
  Date of issue
  Page numbers on which
    article appears

For electronic sources

Name(s) of author(s)
Title and subtitle
Publication data if source is
    also published in print

Electronic publication data:
  Date of release, online post-
    ing, or latest revision
  Name and vendor (or pub-
    lisher) of a database or
    name of an online service or
    network (America Online,
    Lexis-Nexis, etc.)
  Medium (CD-ROM, online,
    etc.)
  Format of online source
    (e-mail, Web page, etc.)
Date you consulted the source
Search terms used to reach the
    source (for a database)
Complete electronic address

For other sources

Name(s) of author(s), govern-
    ment department, recording
    artist, or others listed
Title of the work
Format, such as unpublished
    letter or live performance
Publication or production
    data:
  Publisher's or producer's name
  Date of publication, release, or
    production
  Identifying numbers (if any)

3. Important information often appears at or near the bottom of
   each page. Look here for (*a*) the name of the author or the
   sponsoring organization, (*b*) an address for reaching the sponsor or author directly, and (*c*) the publication date or the date
   of the last revision.

If the page you are reading does not list publication information, look for it on the site's home page. There may be a link to the
home page, or you can find it by editing the address in the Address
or Location field: working backward, delete the end of the address
up to the preceding slash; then hit Enter. (For the address in the

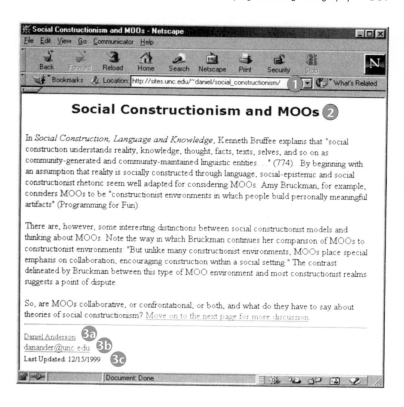

screen shot, you would delete *social_constructionism/*.) If that doesn't take you to the home page, delete the end of the remaining address up to the preceding slash and hit Enter. Editing the address in this way, you'll eventually reach the home page.

When scouting a discussion list, Web forum, or newsgroup, save messages that may serve as sources, and keep track of when and where they were posted. You may be able to discover information about the author of a message from the list's archive or from an archive site such as Deja (*http://groups.google.com*). See page 320 for more on discussion lists, forums, and newsgroups.

51 Finding Sources

This chapter discusses conducting electronic searches (below) and taking advantage of the range of sources, both print and electronic, that you have access to: reference works (p. 312), books (p. 312), periodicals (p. 313), the World Wide Web (p. 315), other online sources (p. 320), pamphlets and government publications (p. 321), and your own interviews, surveys, and other primary sources (p. 321).

51a Searching electronically

As you conduct research, the World Wide Web will be your gateway to ideas and information. You will use the Web to find many of your library's extensive resources, such as books, periodicals, and reference works. And you may use the Web to reach non-library resources, such as a discussion among experts in a field or the reports of a political or environmental group. Some of these resources are trustworthy; others are not. You need to be able to recognize both the type of source you're using and its likely validity.

Note Always begin your academic research on your library's Web site, not with a search engine such as *Google*. Although a direct Web search can be productive, you'll find a higher concentration of relevant and reliable sources through the library.

Two tips for researchers

- *A reference librarian can help.* If you are unsure of how to locate or use your library, either via the Web or at the library itself, consult a reference librarian. This person is very familiar with all the library's resources and with general and specialized research techniques. It is his or her job to help you and others with research. Even very experienced researchers often consult reference librarians.
- *You may be able to borrow from other libraries.* If sources you need are not available from your library, you may be able to obtain them from another library by mail, fax, or Internet. Ask your librarian for help, and plan ahead: interlibrary loans can take a week or longer.

1   Kinds of electronic sources

Your school's library and the Web offer several kinds of electronic resources that are suitable for academic research:

- *The library's catalogue of holdings* is a database that lists all the resources that the library owns or subscribes to: books, journals, magazines, newspapers, reference works, and more. The catalogue may include not only your library's holdings but also those of other schools nearby or in your province.
- *Online databases* include indexes, bibliographies, and other reference works. They are your main route to listings of specific journal articles and book chapters. Your library subscribes to the databases and makes them available through its Web site. Research engines like Research Navigator can also access these databases through a keyword search. (You may discover databases directly on the Web; however, a library or research engine search will be a more productive starting point.)
- *Databases on CD-ROM,* or compact disk, include the same information as online databases, but they must be read at a library computer terminal. Increasingly, libraries are providing CD-ROM databases through their Web sites or are moving away from CD-ROMs in favour of online databases.
- *Full-text resources* contain the entire contents of articles, book chapters, even whole books. Some of the library's online or CD-ROM databases provide access to the full text of listed sources. In addition, the Web sites of many periodicals and organizations, such as government agencies, offer the full text of articles, reports, and other publications.

51a

2   Keyword searches

Probably the most important element in an electronic search is appropriate KEYWORDS, or DESCRIPTORS, that name your subject for databases and Web search engines.

Databases vs. the Web

To develop keywords it helps to understand what they do when you use them for a search. Most databases index sources by authors, titles, and publication years and also by subject headings found in each database's directory or thesaurus. Electronic databases can usually search among their listings and subjects for uses of your keywords, but they work more efficiently when you use their subject headings for keywords. You can find a database's headings for your subject in two ways: consult its directory, or first use your own keywords to locate a promising source and then use the subject headings given with the source record to find more sources.

The Web has no overall directory of keywords. Some Web search engines do categorize sites into subject directories, but they include only a small portion of the Web's offerings. Other search engines, so-called crawlers, seek your keywords in the titles, summaries, and texts of sites. Their performance depends on how well your keywords describe your subject and anticipate the words used in sources. If you describe your subject too broadly or describe it specifically but don't match the vocabulary in relevant sources, your search will turn up few relevant sources and probably many that aren't relevant.

51a

Keyword refinement

Every database and search engine provides a system that you can use to refine your keywords for a productive search. The basic operations appear in the box on the next page, but resources do differ. For instance, some assume that *AND* should link two or more keywords, while others provide options specifying "Must contain all the words," "May contain any of the words," and other equivalents for the operations in the box.

Trial and error

You will probably have to use trial and error in developing your keywords, sometimes running dry (turning up few or no sources) and sometimes hitting uncontrollable gushers (turning up hundreds or thousands of mostly irrelevant sources). But the process is not busywork—far from it. Besides leading you eventually to worthwhile sources, it can also teach you a great deal about your subject: how you can or should narrow it, how it is and is not described by others, what others consider interesting or debatable about it, and what the major arguments are.

Ways to refine keywords

Most databases and search engines work with BOOLEAN OPERATORS, terms or symbols that allow you to expand or limit your keywords and thus your search.

- Use *AND* or + to narrow the search by including only sources that use all the given words. The keywords *Internet AND tax* request only the sources in the shaded area:

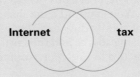

Internet   tax

- Use *NOT* or – *("minus")* to narrow the search by excluding irrelevant words. *Internet AND tax NOT access* excludes sources that use the word *access*.

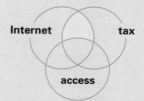

- Use *OR* to broaden the search by giving alternative keywords. *Internet OR (electronic commerce) AND tax* allows for sources that use *Internet* or *electronic commerce* (or both) along with *tax*.

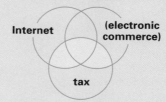

51a

- Use parentheses or quotation marks to form search phrases. For instance, *(electronic commerce)* requests the exact phrase, not the separate words.
- Use *NEAR* to narrow the search by requiring the keywords to be close to each other—for instance, *Internet NEAR tax*. Depending on the resource you're using, the words could be directly next to each other or many words apart. Some resources use *WITHIN* so that you can specify the exact number of words apart—for instance, *Internet WITHIN 10 tax*.
- Use wild cards to permit different versions of the same word. In *child**, for instance, the wild card * indicates that sources may include *child, children, childcare, childhood, childish, childlike,* and *childproof*. The example suggests that you have to consider all the variations allowed by a wild card and whether it opens up your search too much. If you seek only two or three from many variations, you may be better off using *OR: child OR children*. (Note that some systems use ?, :, or + for a wild card instead of *.)
- Be sure to spell your keywords correctly. Some search tools will look for close matches or approximations, but correct spelling gives you the best chance of finding relevant sources.

See pages 318–19 for a sample keyword search.

(51b) Finding reference works

REFERENCE WORKS, often available on CD-ROM or online, include encyclopedias, dictionaries, digests, bibliographies, indexes, atlases, almanacs, and handbooks. Your research *must* go beyond these sources, but they can help you decide whether your topic really interests you and whether it meets the requirements for a research paper (p. 301). Preliminary research in reference works can also help you develop keywords for computer searches (pp. 310–11) and can direct you to more detailed sources on your topic.

Often you can find reference works as well as other resources at Web sites devoted to fields or disciplines. The following list gives general Web references for all disciplines.

> National Library of Canada
> *http://www.nlc-bnc.ca*
> Internet Public Library
> *http://www.ipl.org*
> Library of Congress
> *http://www.loc.gov*
> The WWW Virtual Library
> *http://vlib.org/*

(51c) Finding books

Most academic libraries store their book catalogues on computer; however, older volumes—say, those acquired more than ten or fifteen years ago—may still be catalogued in bound volumes or on film.

You can search an electronic catalogue for authors' names, titles, or keywords describing your subject. As much as possible, the keywords should match words in *Library of Congress Subject Headings* (*LCSH*), a multivolume work that lists the headings under which the Library of Congress catalogues books. See pages 309–10 for more on keyword searches.

The following screen shot shows the features of a catalogue record for a book:

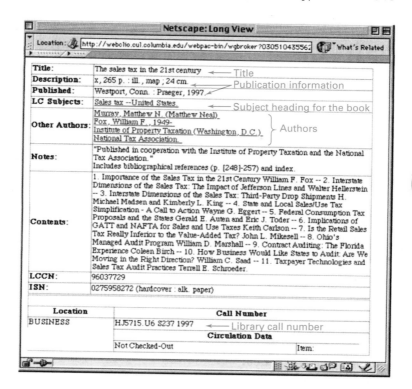

51d Finding periodicals

PERIODICALS—journals, magazines, and newspapers—are invaluable sources of both current and specialized information. The difference between journals and magazines lies primarily in their content, readership, and frequency of issue.

- Magazines—such as *Psychology Today, Maclean's,* and *Rolling Stone*—are nonspecialist publications intended for diverse readers. Most magazines appear weekly or monthly, and their pages are numbered anew with each issue.
- Journals are specialist publications written for other specialists, including students who, through their research, are developing specialist knowledge. The articles are written by academic experts in the area, and the articles are usually refereed for publication. Refereeing usually means that at least two other experts have read the article and recommended it for publication as an original contribution to knowledge in the area. Refereed articles and books will have the most credibility with other academic experts. Examples include *PMLA (Publication of the Modern Language Association), Canadian Journal of Political Science,* and

Journal of Chemical Education. Journals are usually published quarterly; some page each issue separately while others have continuous pagination from the beginning of the first issue to the end of the fourth (a difference reflected in the form of documentation; see p. 395).

1 Indexes to periodicals

51d

Various indexes to periodicals—most available on CD-ROM or online—provide information on the articles in journals, magazines, and newspapers. The following are a few of the most widely used indexes:

- *Research Navigator:* access to EBSCO ContentSelect, *The New York Times*, *Financial Times*, and Link Library.
- *Humanities Index:* journals in language and literature, history, philosophy, and other humanities.
- *MLA International Bibliography of Books and Articles on the Modern Languages and Literatures:* books and periodicals on literature, linguistics, and languages.
- *New York Times Index:* articles in the most comprehensive US newspaper.
- *Social Sciences Index:* journals in economics, psychology, political science, and other social sciences.
- *General Science Index:* journals in biology, chemistry, physics, and other sciences.
- *Readers' Guide to Periodical Literature:* over a hundred popular magazines.

Searching electronic periodical indexes is discussed under electronic searches on pages 308–311. The following record shows the results of an *InfoTrac* search:

[Subject: INTERNET Subdivision: DEMOGRAPHIC aspects] Subject heading and subheading

One Internet, two nations. (Internet usage by ethnic groups) (Column) Henry Louis Gates Jr. The New York Times Oct 31, 1999 s0 pWK15 (N) pWK15 (L) col 2 (20 col in)

What price will be paid by those not on the Net? (poor minorities denied use of the Internet) Pam Belluck. The New York Times Sept 22, 1999 pD12 (N) pG12 (L) col 1 (50 col in)

UNCF Examines Digital Divide On Campus. (United Negro College Fund) Ronald Roach. Black Issues in Higher Education August 5, 1999 v16 i11 p32

A Web That Looks Like the World. (Internet demographics (Abstract) Business Week March 22, 1999 i3621 pEB46 (1)

Who's on the Internet and why. Dan Johnson. The Futurist
August-Sep 1998 v32 n6 p11 (2)

Continental divide. (differences between Silicon Valley, CA, and
Washington DC) (Special Section: The Backbone of America)
Michael Kinsley. Time July 7, 1997 v150 n1 p97 (3)

| Periodical title | Date | Volume, issue, number, and page number |

2 Locations of periodicals

Every library lists its complete periodical holdings either in its
main catalogue or in a separate catalogue. Many periodicals are
available on CD-ROM or online. If a periodical is not available electronically, recent issues are probably held in the library's periodical
room. Back issues are usually stored elsewhere, either in bound volumes or on film that requires a special machine to read. A librarian
will show you how to operate the machine.

3 Abstracts

Many periodical indexes include ABSTRACTS, or summaries, of
articles along with bibliographic information. An abstract can tell
you in advance whether you want to pursue an article further. The
abstract is not the article, however, and should not be used or cited
as if it were. Whenever possible, consult the full article.

51e Finding sources on the World Wide Web

As an academic researcher, you enter the World Wide Web in
two ways: through your library's Web site, and through public search
engines such as *Yahoo!* and *Google*. The library entrance, covered in
the preceding sections, is your main path to the books and periodicals that, for most subjects, should make up most of your sources.
The public entrance, discussed here, can lead to a wealth of information and ideas, but it also has a number of disadvantages:

- *The Web is a wide-open network.* Anyone with the right hardware
  and software can place information on the Internet, and even a
  carefully conceived search can turn up sources with widely
  varying reliability: journal articles, government documents,
  scholarly data, term papers written by high school students,
  sales pitches masked as objective reports, wild theories. You
  must be especially diligent about evaluating Internet sources.
  (See p. 323.)
- *The Web changes constantly.* No search engine can keep up with
  the Web's daily additions and deletions, and a source you find

51e

Web search engines

The features of search engines change often, and new ones appear constantly. For the latest on search engines, see the links collected by *Search Engine Watch* at *http://www.searchenginewatch.com/links*.

Directories that review sites

BUBL Link
  http://bubl.ac.uk/
Internet Public Library
  http://www.ipl.org/div/subject
Internet Scout Project
  http://scout.wisc.edu/Archives/
Librarians' Internet Index
  http://lii.org

Most advanced and efficient engines

AlltheWeb
  http://www.alltheweb.com
  One of the fastest and most comprehensive engines, AlltheWeb updates its database frequently so that it returns more of the Web's most recent sites. It allows searches for news, pictures, and audio and video files.

Google Canada
  http://www.google.ca
  Also fast and comprehensive, Google ranks a site based not only on its content but also on the other sites that are linked to it, thus providing a measure of a site's usefulness. Google also allows searches for news, discussion groups, and images.

Other engines

AltaVista
  http://www.altavista.com
Ask.com
  http://www.ask.com
Dogpile
  http://www.dogpile.com
Excite
  http://search.excite.com
Lycos
  http://www.lycos.com
MetaCrawler
  http://www.metacrawler.com
Yahoo! Canada
  http://ca.yahoo.com

today may be different or gone tomorrow. Some sites are designed and labelled as archives: they do not change except with additions. But generally you should not put off consulting an online source that you think you may want to use.

- *The Web provides limited information on the past.* Sources dating from before the 1980s or even more recently probably will not appear on the Web.
- *The Web is not all-inclusive.* Most books and many periodicals are available only in the library, not via the Web.

Clearly, the Web warrants cautious use. It should not be the only resource you work with.

1 Search engines

51e

To find sources on the Web, you use a SEARCH ENGINE that catalogues Web sites in a series of directories and conducts keyword searches. Generally, use a directory when you haven't yet refined your topic or you want a general overview. Use keywords when you have refined your topic and you seek specific information.

Current search engines

The box on the opposite page lists the currently most popular search engines. To reach any one of them, enter its address in the Address or Location field of your Web browser.

Note For a good range of reliable sources, try out more than a single search engine, perhaps as many as four or five. No search engine can catalogue the entire Web—indeed, even the most powerful engine may not include half the sites available at any given time, and most engines include only a fifth or less. In addition, most search engines accept paid placements, giving higher billing to sites that pay a fee. These so-called sponsored links are usually marked as such, but they can compromise a search engine's method for arranging sites in response to your keywords.

A sample search engine

The screen shot on the next page, from the *Google* search engine, shows the features common to most engines. The circled numbers are keyed to the following comments:

1. To search by keywords, type them into the Search field. (See pp. 309–12 on developing keywords.)
2. Click on listings for specific kinds of sources and information— for instance, images or postings to discussion groups.
3. Click on pages from Canada if you wish to limit the search.

4. Click Advanced Search for limiting a search and for help using the search engine. Each engine has its own method of ranking HITS, or sites that match your search criteria, such as the number of times your keywords appear within a site or page, whether the terms appear in the title or the address, and (in *Google*'s case) which other sites have links to the site or page.

Search records

Your Web browser includes functions that allow you to keep track of Web sources and your search:

- Favorites *or* Bookmarks *save site addresses as links.* Click one of these terms near the top of the browser screen to add a site you want to return to. A favourite or bookmark remains on file until you delete it.
- *A browser's search history records the sites you visited over a certain period,* such as a single online session or a week's sessions. (After that period, the history is deleted.) If you forgot to bookmark a site, you can click History or Go to locate your search history and recover the site.

2   A sample search

The following sample Web search illustrates how the refinement of keywords can narrow a search to maximize the relevant hits and minimize the irrelevant ones. Kisha Alder, a student researching the feasibility of Internet taxes, first used the keywords *Internet taxes* on *Google*. But, as shown in the screen shot at the top of the next page, the search produced more than 3 million hits, an impractically large number and a sure sign that Alder's keywords needed revision.

1. First *Google* results

51e

After several tries, Alder arrived at two phrases, *sales tax* and *electronic commerce,* to describe her subject more precisely. Narrowed in this way, Alder's search produced a more manageable 915 hits—still a large number but including many potential sources on the first few screens. (See screen 2, below.)

2. Second *Google* results

(51f) Finding other online sources

Several online sources can put you directly in touch with experts and others whose ideas and information may inform your research. Because these sources, like Web sites, are unfiltered, you must always evaluate them carefully. (See pp. 324–28.)

1 Using electronic mail

As a research tool, e-mail allows you to communicate with others who are interested in your topic. You may, for instance, carry on an e-mail conversation with a teacher at your school or with other students. Or you may interview an expert in another province to follow up on a scholarly article he or she published. (See pp. 321–22 on conducting interviews.)

2 Using discussion lists

A DISCUSSION LIST (sometimes called a LISTSERV or just a LIST) uses e-mail to connect individuals who are interested in a common subject, often with a scholarly or technical focus. By sending a question to an appropriate list, you may be able to reach scores of people who know something about your topic. For an index of discussion lists, see *http://tile.net/lists* or *http://lists.topica.com*.

When conducting research on a discussion list, follow these guidelines for e-mail etiquette:

- *Lurk for a while*—read without posting messages. Make sure the discussion is relevant to your topic, and get a sense of how the group interacts.
- *Don't ask for information you can find elsewhere.* Most list members are glad to help with legitimate questions but resent messages that rehash familiar debates or that ask them to do someone else's work.
- *Evaluate messages carefully.* Many list subscribers are passionate experts with fair-minded approaches to their topics, but almost anyone with an Internet connection can post a message to a list. See pages 323–29 on evaluating online sources.

3 Using Web forums and newsgroups

Web forums and newsgroups are more open and less scholarly than discussion lists, so their messages require even more diligent evaluation. WEB FORUMS allow participants to join a conversation simply by selecting a link on a Web page. For a directory of forums, see *http://www.delphiforums.com*. NEWSGROUPS are organized under subject headings such as *soc* for social issues and *biz* for business. For a directory of newsgroups, see *http://groups.google.com*.

4   Using synchronous communication

With e-mail and discussion groups, there's a delay between a message you send and any response you receive. But with SYNCHRONOUS (or simultaneous) COMMUNICATION, you and others can converse in real time, the way you talk on the phone. Synchronous programs include instant-messaging applications, Web course-ware, Internet relay chat (IRC), and virtual environments called MOOs.

Synchronous communication can be used to conduct interviews or hold debates. Your instructor may ask you to use it for your course-work or research and will provide the software and instructions to get you started.

51h

(51g) Using pamphlets and government publications

Organizations such as social-service groups, professional societies, and all branches of government publish pamphlets, compilations of data, and other sources that usually cannot be retrieved through the library's book catalogue or periodicals listings.

Libraries store pamphlets and other loose materials in file drawers, called VERTICAL FILES. To find out what is available in pamphlet form, consult the *Vertical File Index: A Subject and Title Index to Selected Pamphlet Materials.*

Government publications provide a vast array of data, public records, and other historical and contemporary information. For Canadian government publications, search the Canadian government Web site (*http://canada.gc.ca*). For US government publications, consult the *Monthly Catalog of US Government Publications*, available on computer. Many federal, provincial, state, and local government agencies post important publications—legislation, reports, press releases—on their own Web sites.

(51h) Generating your own sources

Academic writing will often require you to conduct primary research for information of your own. For instance, you may need to analyze a poem, conduct an experiment, survey a group of people, or interview an expert.

An interview can be especially helpful for a research project because it allows you to ask questions precisely geared to your topic. You can conduct an interview in person, over the telephone, or online using electronic mail (see p. 320) or a form of synchronous communication (see above). A personal interview is preferable if you can arrange it, because you can see the person's expressions and gestures as well as hear his or her tone and words.

Here are a few guidelines for interviews:

- Call or write for an appointment. Tell the person exactly why you are calling, what you want to discuss, and how long you expect the interview to take. Be true to your word on all points.
- Prepare a list of open-ended questions to ask—perhaps ten or twelve for a one-hour interview. Plan on doing some research for these questions to discover background on the issues and your subject's published views on the issues.
- Give your subject time to consider your questions, and listen to your subject's answers so that you can ask appropriate follow-up questions.
- Take care in interpreting answers, especially if you are online and thus can't depend on facial expressions, gestures, and tone of voice to convey the subject's attitudes.
- For in-person and telephone interviews, keep careful notes or, if you have the equipment and your subject agrees, tape-record the interview. For online interviews, save the discussion in a file of its own.
- Before you quote your subject in your paper, check with him or her to ensure that the quotations are accurate.
- Send a thank-you note immediately after the interview. Promise your subject a copy of your finished paper, and send the paper promptly.

52 Working with Sources

Research writing is much more than finding sources and reporting their contents. The challenge and interest come from *interacting* with sources, reading them critically to discover their meanings, judge their quality, and create relationships among them. This chapter shows you how to use the sources you find to extend and support your own ideas, to make your topic your own. The chapter discusses evaluating and synthesizing sources (p. 323 and p. 330), taking notes (p. 331), and integrating sources into your text (p. 335).

ESL Making a topic your own requires thinking critically about sources and developing independent ideas. These goals may at first be uncomfortable for you if your native culture emphasizes understanding and respecting established authority over questioning and enlarging it. The information here will help you work with sources so that you can become an expert in your own right and convincingly convey your expertise to others.

(52a) Evaluating sources

Before you settle in to take notes, scan your sources to evaluate the kind and extent of ideas and information they offer.

52a

Note In evaluating sources, you need to consider how they come to you. The print and online sources you find through the library (including books and articles that are also released electronically) have been previewed for you by their publishers and by the library's staff. They still require your critical reading, but you can have some confidence in the information they contain. Online sources found on research engines like *Research Navigator* that access library and journal databases through links like *Ebsco* can be treated like sources found through your college or university library. With general online sources, however, you can't assume similar previewing, so your critical reading must be especially rigorous. Special tips for evaluating online sources appear on pages 324–28.

1   Relevance and reliability

Not all the sources you find will prove worthwhile: some may be irrelevant to your topic, and others may be unreliable. Gauging the relevance and reliability of sources is the essential task of evaluating them.

To determine whether sources are relevant, scan the introductions to books and articles and the tables of contents of books. You're looking for opinions and facts that pertain directly to your topic. You're also ensuring that your sources are appropriate in level: you can understand them (if with some effort), and they also expand your knowledge. If you don't see what you need or the source is too high-level or too simple, you can drop it from your list.

Reliability can be more difficult to judge than relevance. If you haven't already done so, study this book's Chapters 10 and 11 on critical thinking and argument. When scanning potential sources, look for claims, evidence, assumptions, tone, fairness, and other features discussed in Chapter 11. In addition, look for information about the author's background to satisfy yourself that the author has sufficient expertise in your subject. Then try to determine what his or her bias is. For instance, a book on parapsychology by someone identified as the president of the National Organization of Psychics may contain

Guidelines for evaluating sources

For online sources, supplement these guidelines with those opposite.

Determine *relevance:*

- Does the source devote some attention to your topic?
- Where in the source are you likely to find relevant information or ideas?
- Is the source appropriately specialized for your needs? Check the source's treatment of a topic you know something about, to ensure that it is neither too superficial nor too technical.
- How important is the source likely to be for your writing?

Judge *reliability:*

- How up to date is the source? If the publication date is not recent, be sure that other sources will give you more current views.
- Is the author an expert in the field? Look for an author biography, look up the author in a biographical reference, or try to trace the author over the Internet.
- What is the author's bias? Check biographical information or the author's own preface or introduction. Ask a librarian to direct you to book review indexes or citations indexes, which can help you find what others have written about the author or the source.
- Whatever his or her bias, does the author reason soundly, provide adequate evidence, and consider opposing views? (See pp. 88–90.)

52a

an authoritative explanation of psychic powers, but the author's view is likely to be biased. It should be balanced by research in other sources whose authors are more skeptical of psychic powers.

This balance or opposition is important. You probably will not find harmony among sources, for reasonable people often disagree in their opinions. Thus you must deal honestly with the gaps and conflicts in sources. Old sources, superficial ones, slanted ones—these should be offset in your research and your writing by sources that are more recent, more thorough, or more objective.

2   Evaluating a Web site

To a great extent, the same critical reading that helps you evaluate library sources will help you evaluate Web sites. But most Web sites have not undergone prior screening by editors and librarians. On your own, you must distinguish scholarship from corporate promotion, valid data from invented statistics, well-founded opinion from clever propaganda.

The following strategy can help you make such distinctions. We'll apply the strategy to the Web site shown on page 326, *Global Warming Information Center,* which turned up in a search for views and data on global warming.

Questions for evaluating Web sites

Supplement these questions with those on page 324.

- *What does the URL lead you to expect about the site?* Are those expectations fulfilled?
- *Who is the author or sponsor?* How credible is the person or group responsible for the site?
- *What is the purpose of the site?* What does the site's author or sponsor intend to achieve?
- *What does context tell you?* What do you already know about the site's subject that can inform your evaluation? What kinds of support or other information do the site's links provide?
- *What does presentation tell you?* Is the site's design well thought out and effective? Is the writing clear and error-free?
- *How worthwhile is the content?* Are the site's claims well supported by evidence? Is the evidence from reliable sources?

52a

Check the electronic address.

Every file on the Web has a unique address called a UNIFORM RESOURCE LOCATOR, or URL. In the screen shot here, the URL (seen in the Address field) is *http://www.nationalcenter.org/Kyoto.html.* For purposes of evaluation, the most important part of any URL is the domain name—here, *nationalcenter.org*—which generally contains the name of the organization that sponsors the site (*nationalcenter*) and an abbreviation that describes the type of organization (*org*). *Org* designates a nonprofit organization. The other major abbreviations are *gc* (government of Canada), *edu* (educational institution), *gov* (government body), *mil* (military), and *com* (commercial organization).

The domain abbreviation can inform your evaluation to some extent: a *com* site usually reflects the company's commercial purposes, an *edu* site usually supports and distributes scholarly pursuits, and an *org* site usually centres on the public interest. But the abbreviation should not unduly influence your evaluation. A *com* site may offer reliable data, an *edu* site may contain unfiltered student work, and an *org* site may promote a biased agenda.

Identify the author or sponsor.

A reputable site will list the author or group responsible for the site and will provide information or a link for contacting the author or group. If none of this information is provided, you should not use the source. If you have only the author or group name, you may be able to discover more in a biographical dictionary or through a keyword search. You should also look for mentions of the author or group in your other sources.

The Web site *Global Warming Information Center* names its sponsor right up front: the John P. McGovern M.D. Center for Environmental and Regulatory Affairs, which is part of the National Center for Public Policy Research in the United States (the *national-center* of the site's domain name). The McGovern Center sounds like an organization involved in research about the environment, but discovering more about it proves difficult. The site includes no links to the McGovern Center, so locating it involves following links to the National Center. When finally reached, the McGovern Center home page links to an informative explanation of the centre's mission and activities, as described on the next page.

Gauge purpose.

A Web site's purpose determines what ideas and information it offers. Inferring that purpose tells you how to interpret what you see on the site. If a site is intended to sell a product or an opinion, it will likely emphasize favourable ideas and information while ignoring or even distorting what is unfavourable. In contrast, if a site is intended to build knowledge—for instance, a scholarly project or journal—it will likely acknowledge diverse views and evidence.

Determining the purpose of a site often requires looking beneath the surface of words and images and beyond the first page. The elements of the *Global Warming* page—the title, the background, the photo of a child carrying a globe through a field of grass—suggest an environmentalist purpose of informing readers about the theory and consequences of rising earth temperatures caused by pollution. The site's purpose is actually different, though. Below the title box, a link to the "Bonn Global Warming Earth Summit Fact Kit" promises "A refutation of the most pervasive charges relating to the theory of man-made global warming." Explanations elsewhere on the site express an intention to inform readers about the evidence against global warming in the interest of reducing or overturning environmental regulations.

52a

Consider context.

Your evaluation of a Web site should be informed by considerations outside the site itself. Chief among these is your own knowledge: what do you already know about the site's subject and the prevailing views of it? In addition, you can follow some of the site's links to see how they support, or don't support, the site's credibility. For instance, links to scholarly sources lend authority to a site—but *only if* the scholarly sources actually relate to and back up the site's claims.

Examining the *Global Warming* site, you might register the antiregulatory bias but also recognize that this view is a significant one in the debates over global warming. That is, the bias does not necessarily disqualify the site as a source on global warming. The question then is the reliability of its information: does it come from trustworthy, less-biased sources? All the site's links lead to the McGovern Center's publications or the parent organization, the National Center for Public Policy Research. Because the links do not go outside the National Center, the question of reliability remains open, to be answered only by examining the *Global Warming* site further.

Look at presentation.

Considering both the look of a site and the way it's written can illuminate its intentions and reliability. Are the site's elements all functional and well integrated, or is the site cluttered with irrelevant material and graphics? Does the design reflect the apparent purpose of the site, or does it undercut or conceal that purpose in some way? Is the text clearly written, or is it difficult to understand? Is it error-free, or does it contain typos and grammatical errors?

At first glance, as noted earlier, the *Global Warming* site casts a pro-environmentalist image that turns out not to coincide with its purpose. Otherwise, the site is cleanly designed, with minimal elements, all of which are laid out clearly. The text on other pages is straightforward and readable. Together, design and readability indicate that the sponsor takes its purpose seriously and has thought out its presentation.

Analyze content.

With information about a site's author, purpose, and context, you're in a position to evaluate its content. Are the ideas and information slanted and, if so, in what direction? Are the views and data authoritative, or do you need to balance them—or even reject them? These questions require close reading of the text and its sources.

The *Global Warming* site links to a wealth of information on the issue it addresses, mostly reports and fact kits like the one listed on the home page. These documents offer statistics and quotations to support skepticism about global warming, with footnotes detailing sources. The footnotes are the crux of the site's reliability: the listed sources should be scholarly and should explain the methods of gathering and interpreting the cited data. Instead, however, they are newspaper and magazine articles and reports from the National Center and other conservative groups.

The public controversy on global warming reflects disagreement among scholars over whether the earth's temperatures are rising significantly, whether human-made pollution is an important cause, how serious the consequences may be, and how to solve the problem. Because the *Global Warming* site does not offer or refer to the scholarly research, its claims and evidence must be viewed suspiciously and probably rejected for use in a research paper. A usable source need not be less biased, but it must be more substantial.

3   Evaluating online discussions

The contributions to online discussions require the same critical scrutiny as Web sites do. On an e-mail discussion list, whose subscribers are likely to be professionals in the field, you will still find wrong or misleading data and skewed opinions. On more accessible Web forums and newsgroups, messages are even more suspect. A reliable discussion-group message may provide very current information or eyewitness testimony, but it will not have the authority of a scholarly publication.

Use the following strategy for evaluating messages in online discussions.

Identify the author.

As with a Web site, checking out the author of an online message can help you judge the reliability of the message. If the author uses a screen name, write directly to him or her requesting full name and credentials. Do not use the message as a source if the author fails to respond. Once you know an author's name, you may be able to obtain background information from a keyword search of the Web or a biographical dictionary.

52a

Questions for evaluating online discussions

Supplement these questions with those on page 325.

- *Who is the author?* How credible is the person writing?
- *What is the context of the message?* What do the other messages in the discussion thread tell you about the reliability of this message?
- *How worthwhile is the content?* Are the message's claims supported by evidence? Is the evidence from reliable sources? Is the tone moderate?
- *How does the message compare with other sources?* Do the author's claims seem accurate given what you've seen in sources you know to be reliable?

52a

Consider messages in context.

Messages are often more difficult to evaluate in isolation than in the context of the overall thread of conversation. By returning to the initial posting in the thread and reading forward, you can see how a message relates to other postings. Does the message respond fairly to others' views? Do others object to the message or confirm it?

Analyze content.

A reliable online message will offer evidence for claims and sources for evidence. If you don't see such supporting information, ask the author for it. (If the author does not respond, ignore the message.) Then verify the sources with your own research: are they reputable?

The tone of a message can also be a clue to its reliability. Online discussions are generally more rushed and heated than other kinds of dialogue, but look askance at a message that's contemptuous, dismissive, or shrill.

Compare with other sources.

Always consider discussion-group messages in the context of other sources so that you can distinguish singular, untested views from more mainstream views that have been subject to verification.

Be wary of postings that reproduce periodical articles, reports, or other publications. Try to locate the original version of the publication to be sure it has been reproduced fully and accurately, not quoted selectively or distorted. If you can't locate the original version, then don't use the publication as a source.

(52b) Synthesizing sources

When you begin to locate the differences and similarities among sources, you move into the most significant part of research writing: forging relationships for your own purpose. This SYNTHESIS is an essential step in reading sources critically and continues through the drafting and revision of a research paper. As you infer connections— say, between one writer's opinions and another's or between two works by the same author—you create new knowledge.

Your synthesis of sources will grow more detailed and sophisticated as you proceed through the research-writing process. Unless you are analyzing primary sources such as the works of a poet, at first read your sources quickly and selectively to obtain an overview of your topic and a sense of how the sources approach it. Don't get bogged down in taking detailed notes, but *do* record your ideas about sources in your research journal (p. 300).

1 Respond to sources

Write down what your sources make you think. Do you agree or disagree with the author? Do you find his or her views narrow, or do they open up new approaches for you? Is there anything in the source that you need to research further before you can understand it? Does the source prompt questions that you should keep in mind while reading other sources?

2 Connect sources

When you notice a link between sources, jot it down. Do two sources differ in their theories or their interpretations of facts? Does one source illuminate another—perhaps commenting or clarifying or supplying additional data? Do two or more sources report studies that support a theory you've read about or an idea of your own?

3 Heed your own insights

Apart from ideas prompted by your sources, you are sure to come up with independent thoughts: a conviction, a point of confusion that suddenly becomes clear, a question you haven't seen anyone else ask. These insights may occur at unexpected times, so it's good practice to keep a notebook handy to record them.

4 Use sources to support your own ideas

As your research proceeds, the responses, connections, and insights you form through synthesis will lead you to answer your starting research question with a statement of your thesis. (See p. 348.) They will also lead you to the main ideas supporting your thesis—conclusions you have drawn from your synthesis of sources, forming the main divisions of your paper. When drafting the paper, make sure each paragraph focuses on an idea of your own, with the support for the idea coming from your sources. In this way, your paper will synthesize others' work into something wholly your own.

(52c) Taking notes using summary, paraphrase, and direct quotation

You can accomplish a great deal of synthesis while taking notes from your sources. Note taking is not a mechanical process of copying from books. Rather, as you read and take notes you assess and organize the information in your sources.

Note A common trap in research writing is allowing your sources to control you, rather than vice versa. To avoid this trap, ask how each source illuminates the idea you are building. When you are taking notes, assign each note a heading from an outline (even a rough one) that you have devised to develop your idea.

1 Methods

You can take notes in any or all of four ways: handwriting on note cards, typing on a computer, photocopying, and downloading from online sources. Both handwritten notes and computer notes have disadvantages and advantages: handwriting notes can be tedious, but it is usually convenient; typing notes requires a handy computer, but the notes themselves are easy to incorporate into a draft. Both methods have the distinct advantage of requiring you to interact with sources as you decide what to write or type.

Photocopying and downloading sources can be the most convenient methods of note taking. Both can also reduce the risk that you will misrepresent or plagiarize a source: with photocopying, you need write out a quotation only once, into your draft; with downloading, you can move a quotation directly from your source into your draft.

However, photocopying and downloading function well as note taking only if you interact with the sources:

- Read the source as thoughtfully as you would any other. Highlight or annotate the relevant passages of a photocopy with underlining, circles, and marginal notes about their significance for your topic. You can accomplish the same work with a downloaded document by printing it out or by opening the downloaded file into your word-processing program and inserting highlights and comments at relevant passages.
- Do not import whole blocks of the source into your draft, especially with downloaded sources that you can excerpt electronically. The guidelines on pages 334–335 for judicious use of quotations apply to sources you photocopy or download as well as to those you take notes from.

52c

Whatever methods of note taking you use, make sure that each note has all the bibliographic information you'll need to cite the source in your paper if you decide to use the note. (See p. 306 for a list of information.) If you have a working bibliography, the note itself needs only a cross-reference to the full source information and then page numbers or other specifics about the note's location. Also give the note a topic heading that corresponds to a part of your subject, so you can see at a glance where the note fits. (See the samples below and on the following page.)

2   Summary

52c

When you SUMMARIZE, you condense an extended idea or argument into a sentence or more in your own words. Summary is most useful when you want to record the gist of an author's idea without the background or supporting evidence. The sample computer note below shows a summary of the following passage from a government agency report on the continuing and growing problem of child poverty in Canada:

Original quotation

- In an economy where young people struggle to establish themselves economically, it is perhaps not surprising that one out of five of Canada's young citizens—1.4 million—are growing up in poverty.
- Overall, over one-quarter of poor people in Canada were children in 1997.
- The rate of child poverty increased by 38 percent between 1989 and 1997, to 19.9 percent.

—Canadian Council on Social Development,
The Canadian Fact Book on Poverty 2000

Summary

> **Child poverty**
>
> Canadian Council on Social Development
>
> A large portion of children grow up poor in Canada, and they constitute, in turn, a large portion of the total number of poor people in Canada. The number of poor children increased in the 1990s by very significant amounts.

3   Paraphrase

When you PARAPHRASE, you follow much more closely the author's original presentation, but you still restate it in your own words. Paraphrase is most useful when you want to present or examine an author's line of reasoning but don't feel the original words merit direct quotation. Here is a paraphrase of the quotation from the Canadian Council on Social Development report on the previous page:

<u>Child poverty</u>

Canadian Council on Social Development

The chances of growing up poor in Canada:

The difficulty of entering into the Canadian economy means that almost 20 percent of young Canadians (one out of five or 1.4 million) grow up in poverty.

In 1997, children constituted 25 percent of all the poor people in Canada.

In the decade or so from 1989 to 1997, the number of poor children grew by 38 percent to 19.9 percent of all children.

52c

Paraphrasing a source

- Read the relevant material several times to be sure you understand it.
- Restate the source's ideas in your own words and sentence structures. You need not put down in new words the whole passage or all the details. Select what is relevant to your topic, and restate only that. If complete sentences seem too detailed or cumbersome, use phrases.
- Be careful not to distort meaning. Don't change the source's emphasis or omit connecting words, qualifiers, and other material whose absence will confuse you later or cause you to misrepresent the source.

Notice that the paraphrase follows the original but uses different words and different sentence structures. In contrast, an unsuccessful paraphrase—one that plagiarizes—copies the author's words or sentence structures or both *without quotation marks*. (See pp. 342–43 for examples.)

ESL If English is your second language, you may have difficulty paraphrasing the ideas in sources because synonyms don't occur to you or you don't see how to restructure sentences. Before attempting a paraphrase, read the original passage several times. Then, instead of "translating" line by line, try to state the gist of the passage without looking at it. Check your effort against the original to be sure you have captured the source author's meaning and emphasis without using his or her words and sentence structures. If you need a synonym for a word, look it up in a dictionary.

4 Direct quotation

When taking notes, you may be tempted to quote sources rather than bother to summarize or paraphrase them. But this approach has at least two disadvantages:

- Copying quotations does not encourage you to interact with sources, grappling with their meaning, analyzing them, testing them.
- Copying merely postpones the summarizing and paraphrasing until you are drafting your paper. The paper itself must be centred on *your* ideas, not stitched together from quotations.

In a paper analyzing primary sources such as literary works, you will use direct quotation extensively to illustrate and support your analysis. But you should quote from secondary sources only in the circumstances described in the box on the next page.

When taking a quotation from a source, copy the material *carefully*. Take down the author's exact wording, spelling, capitalization, and punctuation. Proofread every direct quotation *at least twice.*

If you want to make changes for clarity, use brackets. (See p. 279.) If you want to omit irrelevant words or sentences, use ellipsis marks, usually three spaced periods. (See pp. 277–79.)

Direct quotation

> Canadian Council on Social Development
>
> Large portion of poor children—"In an economy where young people struggle . . . , it is perhaps not surprising that one out of five of Canada's young citizens—1.4 million—are growing up in poverty."

Tests for direct quotations

- The author's original satisfies one of these requirements:

  The language is unusually vivid, bold, or inventive.

  The quotation cannot be paraphrased without distortion or loss of meaning.

  The words themselves are at issue in your interpretation.

52c

The quotation represents and emphasizes a body of opinion or the view of an important expert.
The quotation emphatically reinforces your own idea.
The quotation is a graph, diagram, or table.

- The quotation is as short as possible.
It includes only material relevant to your point.
It is edited to eliminate examples and other unneeded material.

(52d) Integrating sources into your text

52d

The evidence of others' information and opinions should back up, not dominate, your own ideas. To synthesize evidence, you need to smooth the transitions between your ideas and words and those of your sources, and you need to give the reader a context for interpreting the borrowed material.

Note The examples in this section use the MLA style of source documentation, discussed in Chapter 58. The source citations not only acknowledge that material is borrowed but also help to indicate where the borrowed material begins or ends. (See p. 380.)

1   Introduction of borrowed material

Readers will be distracted from your point if borrowed material does not fit into your sentence. In the passage below, the writer has not meshed the structures of her own and her source's sentences:

AWKWARD   One editor disagrees with this view and "a
                  good reporter does not fail to separate
                  opinions from facts" (Lyman 52).

In the following revision the writer adds words to integrate the quotation into her sentence:

REVISED   One editor disagrees with this view, <u>maintaining that</u> "a good reporter does not fail to separate opinions from facts" (Lyman 52).

To mesh your own and your source's words, you may sometimes need to make a substitution or addition to the quotation, signalling your change with brackets:

WORDS   "The tabloids [of England] are a journalistic
ADDED   case study in bad reporting," claims
                  Lyman (52).

52d

Conventions for handling quotations

- For guidelines on when to quote from sources, see pp. 334–35.
- For the punctuation of signal phrases such as *he insists*, see p. 259.
- For guidelines on when to run quotations into your text and when to display them separately from your text, see pp. 412–14 (MLA style) and 440 (APA style).
- For the use of brackets around your changes or additions in quotations, see p. 279.
- For the use of the ellipsis mark (. . .) to indicate omissions from quotations, see pp. 277–79.

VERB FORM CHANGED	A bad reporter, Lyman implies, is one who "[fails] to separate opinions from facts" (52). [The bracketed verb replaces *fail* in the original.]
CAPITALIZATION CHANGED	"[T]o separate opinions from facts" is the work of a good reporter (Lyman 52). [In the original, *to* is not capitalized.]
NOUN SUPPLIED FOR PRONOUN	The reliability of a news organization "depends on [reporters'] trustworthiness," says Lyman (52). [The bracketed noun replaces *their* in the original.]

2   Interpretation of borrowed material

Even when it does not conflict with your own sentence structure, borrowed material will be ineffective if you merely dump it in readers' laps without explaining how you intend it to be understood:

DUMPED	Many news editors and reporters maintain that it is impossible to keep personal opinions from influencing the selection and presentation of facts. "True, news reporters, like everyone else, form impressions of what they see and hear. However, a good reporter does not fail to separate opinions from facts" (Lyman 52).

Reading this passage, we must figure out for ourselves that the writer's sentence and the quotation state opposite points of view. In the following revision, the underlined additions tell us how to interpret the quotation:

REVISED

Many news editors and reporters maintain that it is impossible to keep personal opinions from influencing the selection and presentation of facts. <u>Yet not all authorities agree with this view. One editor grants that</u> "news reporters, like everyone else, form impressions of what they see and hear." <u>But, he insists</u>, "a good reporter does not fail to separate opinions from facts" (Lyman 52).

Signal phrases

The words *One editor grants* and *he insists* in the revised passage are SIGNAL PHRASES: they tell readers who the source is and what to expect in the quotations that follow. Signal phrases usually contain (1) the source author's name (or a substitute for it, such as *One editor* and *he*) and (2) a verb that indicates the source author's attitude or approach to what he or she says.

52d

Some verbs for signal phrases are in the list below. Use the present tense of verbs (as in the list) to discuss the writings of others, including literary works, opinions, and reports of conclusions from research. Use the past tense only to describe past events, such as historical occurrences and the procedures used in studies—for example, *In 1993 Holmes <u>stated</u> that he had lied a decade earlier* or *Riley <u>assessed</u> the participants' diets.*

Author is neutral	Author infers or suggests	Author argues	Author is uneasy or disparaging
comments	analyzes	claims	belittles
describes	asks	contends	bemoans
explains	assesses	defends	complains
illustrates	concludes	holds	condemns
notes	considers	insists	deplores
observes	finds	maintains	deprecates
points out	predicts		derides
records	proposes		disagrees
relates	reveals	Author agrees	laments
reports	shows		warns
says	speculates	admits	
sees	suggests	agrees	
thinks	supposes	concedes	
writes		grants	

Vary your signal phrases to suit your interpretation of borrowed material and also to keep readers' interest. A signal phrase may precede, interrupt, or follow the borrowed material:

PRECEDES

<u>Lyman insists</u> that "a good reporter does not fail to separate opinions from facts" (52).

INTERRUPTS	"However," <u>Lyman insists</u>, "a good reporter does not fail to separate opinions from facts" (52).
FOLLOWS	"[A] good reporter does not fail to separate opinions from facts," <u>Lyman insists</u> (52).

Background information

You can add information to a quotation to integrate it into your text and inform readers why you are using it. If your readers will recognize it, you can provide the author's name in the text:

AUTHOR NAMED	Harold Lyman grants that "news reporters, like everyone else, form impressions of what they see and hear." But, Lyman insists, "a good reporter does not fail to separate opinions from facts" (52).

If the source title contributes information about the author or the context of the quotation, you can provide it in the text:

TITLE GIVEN	Harold Lyman, <u>in his book *The Conscience of the Journalist*</u>, grants that "news reporters, like everyone else, form impressions of what they see and hear." But, Lyman insists, "a good reporter does not fail to separate opinions from facts" (52).

If the quoted author's background and experience reinforce or clarify the quotation, you can provide these credentials in the text:

CREDENTIALS GIVEN	Harold Lyman, <u>a newspaper editor for more than forty years</u>, grants that "news reporters, like everyone else, form impressions of what they see and hear." But, Lyman insists, "a good reporter does not fail to separate opinions from facts" (52).

You need not name the author, source, or credentials in your text when you are simply establishing facts or weaving together facts and opinions from varied sources. In the following passage, the information is more important than the source, so the name of the source is confined to a parenthetical acknowledgment:

To end the abuses of the British, many American colonists were urging three actions: forming a united front, seceding from Britain, and taking control of their own international relations (Wills 325–36).

53 Avoiding Plagiarism and Documenting Sources

PLAGIARISM (from a Latin word for "kidnapper") is the presentation of someone else's ideas or words as your own. Whether deliberate or accidental, plagiarism is a serious offence.

- *Deliberate* plagiarism:

    Copying or downloading a phrase, a sentence, or a longer passage from a source and passing it off as your own by omitting quotation marks and a source citation.

    Summarizing or paraphrasing someone else's ideas without acknowledging your debt in a source citation.

    Handing in as your own work a paper you have bought, copied off the Web, had a friend write, or accepted from another student.

Checklist for avoiding plagiarism

Type of source

Are you using
- your own independent material,
- common knowledge, or
- someone else's independent material?

You must acknowledge someone else's material.

Quotations

- Do all quotations exactly match their sources? Check them.
- Have you inserted quotation marks around quotations that are run into your text?
- Have you shown omissions with ellipsis marks and additions with brackets?
- Does every quotation have a source citation?

Paraphrases and summaries

- Have you used your own words and sentence structures for every paraphrase and summary? If not, use quotation marks around the original author's words.
- Does every paraphrase and summary have a source citation?

53a

The Web
- Have you obtained any necessary permission to use someone else's material on your Web site?

Source citations
- Have you acknowledged every use of someone else's material in the place where you use it?
- Does your list of works cited include all the sources you have used?

Working with a copy of this list, question every use you make of someone else's material.

- *Accidental* plagiarism:
  Forgetting to place quotation marks around another writer's words.
  Carelessly omitting a source citation for a paraphrase.
  Omitting a source citation for another's idea because you are unaware of the need to acknowledge the idea.

In most schools a code of academic honesty calls for severe consequences for deliberate or accidental plagiarism: a failing grade, suspension from school, or even expulsion.

The way to avoid plagiarism is to acknowledge your sources by documenting them. This chapter discusses plagiarism and the Internet, shows how to distinguish what doesn't require acknowledgment from what does, and provides an overview of source documentation.

ESL More than in many other cultures, teachers in Canada value students' original thinking and writing. In some other cultures, for instance, students may be encouraged to copy the words of scholars without acknowledgment, in order to demonstrate their mastery of or respect for the scholars' work. In Canada, however, the writing of an author is considered his or her property, and using that writing without a source citation is considered theft. When in doubt about the guidelines in this chapter, ask your instructor for advice.

(53a) Committing and detecting plagiarism on the Internet

The Internet has made it easier to plagiarize than ever before, but it has also made plagiarism easier to catch.

Even honest students risk accidental plagiarism by downloading sources and importing portions into their drafts. Dishonest students may take advantage of downloading to steal others' work. They may also use the term-paper businesses on the Web, which offer both ready-made research and complete papers, usually for a fee. *Paying for research or a paper does not make it the buyer's work.* Anyone who submits someone else's work as his or her own is a plagiarist.

Students who plagiarize from the Internet both deprive themselves of an education in honest research and expose themselves to detection. Teachers can use search engines to locate specific phrases or sentences anywhere on the Web, including among scholarly publications, all kinds of Web sites, and term-paper collections. They can search the term-paper sites as easily as students can, looking for similarities to papers they've received. Increasingly, teachers can use special detection programs that compare students' work with other work anywhere on the Internet, seeking matches as short as a few words.

Some instructors suggest that their students use plagiarism-detection programs to verify that their own work does not include accidental plagiarism from the Internet.

53b

(53b)   Knowing what you need not acknowledge

1   Your independent material

Your own observations, thoughts, compilations of facts, or experimental results—expressed in your words and format—do not require acknowledgment. You should describe the basis for your conclusions so that readers can evaluate your thinking, but you need not cite sources for them.

2   Common knowledge

Common knowledge consists of the standard information on a subject as well as folk literature and commonsense observations.

- *Standard information* includes the major facts of history, such as the dates during which Charlemagne ruled as emperor of Rome (800–14). It does *not* include interpretations of facts, such as a historian's opinion that Charlemagne was sometimes needlessly cruel in extending his power.
- *Folk literature,* such as the fairy tale "Snow White," is popularly known and cannot be traced to a particular writer. Literature traceable to a writer is *not* folk literature, even if it is very familiar.
- *A commonsense observation* is something most people know, such as that inflation is most troublesome for people with low and fixed incomes. However, an economist's argument about the effects of inflation on Chinese immigrants is *not* a commonsense observation.

If you do not know a subject well enough to determine whether a piece of information is common knowledge, make a record of the source as you would for any other quotation, paraphrase, or summary. As you read more about the subject, the information may come up repeatedly without acknowledgment, in which case it is probably common knowledge. But if you are still in doubt when you finish your research, always acknowledge the source.

53c Knowing what you *must* acknowledge

53c

You must always acknowledge other people's independent material—that is, any facts or ideas that are not common knowledge or your own. The source may be anything, including a book, an article, a movie, an interview, a microfilmed document, a Web page, a newsgroup posting, or an opinion expressed on the radio. You must acknowledge summaries or paraphrases of ideas or facts as well as quotations of the language and format in which ideas or facts appear: wording, sentence structures, arrangement, and special graphics (such as a diagram). You must acknowledge another's material no matter how you use it, how much of it you use, or how often you use it.

1 Using copied language: Quotation marks and a source citation

The following example baldly plagiarizes the original quotation from Jessica Mitford's *Kind and Usual Punishment*, page 9. Without quotation marks or a source citation, the example matches Mitford's wording (underlined) and closely parallels her sentence structure:

ORIGINAL   "The character and mentality of the keepers may be of more importance in understanding prisons than the character and mentality of the kept."

PLAGIARISM   But the character of prison officials (the keepers) is more important in understanding prisons than the character of prisoners (the kept).

To avoid plagiarism, the writer can paraphrase and cite the source (see the last two examples below) or use Mitford's actual words *in quotation marks* and *with a source citation* (here, in MLA style):

REVISION   According to one critic of the penal system,
(QUOTATION)   "The character and mentality of the keepers may be of more importance in understanding prisons than the character and mentality of the kept" (Mitford 9).

Even with a source citation and with a different sentence structure, the next example is still plagiarism because it uses some of Mitford's words (underlined) without quotation marks:

| PLAGIARISM | According to one critic of the penal system, the psychology of the kept may say less about prisons than the psychology of the keepers (Mitford 9). |
| REVISION (QUOTATION) | According to one critic of the penal system, the psychology of "the kept" may say less about prisons than the psychology of "the keepers" (Mitford 9). |

2   Using a paraphrase or summary: your own words and sentence structure and a source citation

The example below changes the sentence structure of the original Mitford quotation on the previous page, but it still uses Mitford's words (underlined) without quotation marks and without a source citation:

| PLAGIARISM | In understanding prisons, we should know more about the character and mentality of the keepers than of the kept. |

To avoid plagiarism, the writer can use quotation marks and cite the source (see above) or *use his or her own words* and still *cite the source* (because the idea is Mitford's, not the writer's):

| REVISION (PARAPHRASE) | Mitford holds that we may be able to learn more about prisons from the psychology of the prison officials than from that of the prisoners (9). |
| REVISION (PARAPHRASE) | We may understand prisons better if we focus on the personalities and attitudes of the prison workers rather than those of the inmates (Mitford 9). |

In the next example, the writer cites Mitford and does not use her words but still plagiarizes her sentence structure:

| PLAGIARISM | One critic of the penal system maintains that the psychology of prison officials may be more informative about prisons that the psychology of prisoners (Mitford 9). |
| REVISION (PARAPHRASE) | One critic of the penal system maintains that we may be able to learn less from the psychology of prisoners than from the psychology of prison officials (Mitford 9). |

(53d) Using and acknowledging online sources

Online sources are so accessible and so easy to download into your own documents that it may seem they are freely available, exempting you from the obligation to acknowledge them. They are not. Acknowledging online sources is somewhat trickier than acknowledging print sources, but no less essential. Further, if you are publishing your work online, you need to take account of sources' copyright restrictions as well.

1 Online sources in an unpublished project

When you use material from an online source in a print or online document to be distributed just to your class, your obligation to cite sources does not change: you must acknowledge someone else's independent material in whatever form you find it. With online sources, that obligation can present additional challenges:

- *Record complete publication information each time you consult an online source.* Online sources may change from one day to the next or even disappear entirely. See page 306 for the information to record, such as the electronic address and the publication date. Without the proper information, you *may not* use the source.
- *Acknowledge linked sites.* If you use not only a Web site but also one or more of its linked sites, you must acknowledge the linked sites as well. The fact that one person has used a second person's work does not release you from the responsibility to cite the second work.
- *Seek the author's permission before using an e-mail message or a contribution to a discussion group.* (See p. 325 for advice on tracing online authors.) Obtaining permission advises the author that his or her ideas are about to be distributed more widely and lets the author verify that you have not misrepresented the ideas.

2 Print and online sources in a Web composition

When you use material from print or online sources in a composition for the Web, you must not only acknowledge your sources but also take the additional precaution of observing copyright restrictions. A Web site is a form of publication just as a book or magazine is and so involves the same responsibility to obtain reprint permission from copyright holders.

The legal convention of fair use allows an author to quote a small portion of copyrighted material without obtaining the copyright holder's permission, as long as the author acknowledges the source. The online standards of fair use differ for print and online sources and are not fixed in either case. The guidelines below are conservative:

- *Print sources:* Quote without permission fewer than fifty words from an article or fewer than three hundred words from a book. You'll need the copyright holder's permission to use any longer quotation from an article or book; any quotation at all from a play, poem, or song; and any use of an entire work, such as a photograph, a chart, or another illustration.
- *Online sources:* Quote without permission text that represents just a small portion of the whole—say, forty words out of three hundred. Follow the print guidelines above for plays, poems, songs, and illustrations, adding multimedia elements (audio or video clips) to the list of works that require reprint permission for any use.
- *Links:* You may need to seek permission to link your site to another one—for instance, if you rely on the linked site to substantiate your claims or to provide a multimedia element.

Generally, you can find information about a site's copyright on the home page or at the bottoms of other pages: look for a notice using the symbol ©. Most worthwhile sites also provide information for contacting the author or sponsor. (See p. 307 for an illustration.) If you don't find a copyright notice, you *cannot* assume that the work is unprotected by copyright. Only if the site explicitly says it is not copyrighted or is available for free use can you exceed fair use without permission.

(53e) Documenting sources

Every time you borrow the words, facts, or ideas of others, you must DOCUMENT the source—that is, supply a reference (or document) telling readers that you borrowed the material and where you borrowed it from.

Editors and teachers in most academic disciplines require special documentation formats (or styles) in their scholarly journals and in students' papers. All the styles use a citation in the text that serves two purposes: it signals that material is borrowed, and it refers readers to detailed information about the source so that they can locate both the source and the place in the source where the borrowed material appears. The detailed source information appears either in footnotes or at the end of the paper.

Aside from these essential similarities, the disciplines' documentation styles differ markedly in citation form, arrangement of source information, and other particulars. Each discipline's style reflects the needs of its practitioners for certain kinds of information presented in certain ways. For instance, the currency of a source is important in

53e

the social sciences, where studies build on and correct each other; thus in-text citations in the social sciences include a source's date of publication. In the humanities, however, currency is less important, so in-text citations do not include date of publication.

The disciplines' documentation formats are described in style guides, including those in the following list. This book presents the styles of the guides marked *.

53e

Humanities

The Chicago Manual of Style. 15th ed. 2003. (See Chapter 60.)

*Gibaldi, Joseph. *MLA Handbook for Writers of Research Papers*. 7th ed. 2009. (See Chapter 58.)

*Turabian, Kate L. *A Manual for Writers of Term Papers, Theses, and Dissertations*. 7th ed. Rev. Wayne C. Booth, Gregory Colomb, and Joseph M. Williams. 2007. (See Chapter 60.)

Social sciences

American Anthropological Association. *AAA Style Guide*. 2003. *http://www.aaanet.org/publications/style_guide.htm*.

American Political Science Association. *Style Manual for Political Science*. 2006.

*American Psychological Association. *Publication Manual of the American Psychological Association*. 5th ed. 2001. (See Chapter 59.)

American Sociological Association. *ASA Style Guide*. 2nd ed. 1997.

The Bluebook: *A Uniform System of Citation* (law). 18th ed. 2005.

Sciences and mathematics

American Chemical Society. *ACS Style Guide: Effective Communication of Scientific Information*. 3rd ed. 2006.

American Institute of Physics. *Style Manual for Guidance in the Preparation of Papers*. 4th ed. 1990.

American Mathematical Society. *A Manual for Authors of Mathematical Papers*. Rev. ed. 1990.

American Medical Association. *Manual of Style*. 10th ed. 2007.

*Council of Science Editors. *Scientific Style and Format: The CSE Manual for Authors, Editors, and Publishers*. 7th ed. 2006. (See Chapter 61.)

Engineering

*Institute of Electrical and Electronics Engineers. *IEEE Editorial Style Manual*. 2008. *http://www.iee.org*. (See Chapter 62.)

Always ask your instructor which documentation style you should use. If your instructor does not require a particular style, use the one in this book that's most appropriate for the discipline in which you're writing. Do follow a single system for citing sources so that you provide all the necessary information in a consistent format.

Note Bibliography software, such as *Bibliocite* and *Endnote*, can help you format your source citations in the style of your choice. Always ask your instructors if you may use such software for your papers. The programs prompt you for needed information (author's name, book title, and so on) and then arrange, capitalize, underline, and punctuate the information as required by the style. But no program can anticipate all the varieties of source information, nor can it substitute for your own care and attention in giving your sources complete acknowledgment using the required form.

53e

Note To avoid plagiarism, you must correctly perform *three tasks* with your sources, whether print or online, as the checklist on pages 339–40 indicates:

- You must quote, paraphrase, or summarize the sources correctly and fairly, as discussed on pages 331–35. Words, phrases, sentences, or paragraphs of others must be acknowledged with quotation marks.
- You must *cite* the sources in your text, as discussed on pages 335–38, with the appropriate citation format or style, such as the style of the Modern Language Association (p. 380), the American Psychological Association (p. 423), the *Chicago Manual of Style* (p. 448), the Council of Science Editors (p. 456), or the Institute of Electrical and Electronics Engineers (p. 463). The citation acknowledges the source and directs your readers to the detailed information or documentation that will enable them to find the source for themselves.
- You must *document* the source fully at the end of the essay, as in MLA (p. 387) and APA (p. 427), or in a footnote or endnote, as in Chicago (CMS) (p. 448), CSE (p. 457), or IEEE (p. 463). As all the styles require, the documentation should be complete enough that readers can find the source.

All three stages are necessary to avoid plagiarism. Documentation of sources without correct quotation or paraphrase of the source's words, for example, is plagiarism. All writers must be especially careful with online sources that can be so easily downloaded and reprinted.

54 Writing the Paper

This chapter complements and extends the detailed discussion of the writing situation and the writing process in Chapters 1–5, which also include many tips for using a word processor and more links to helpful Web sites. If you haven't already done so, you may want to read Chapters 1–5 before this one.

54a

(54a) Focusing and organizing the paper

Before you begin using your source notes in a draft, give some thought to your main idea and your organization.

1 Thesis statement

You began research with a question about your subject (see p. 301). Though that question may have evolved during research, you should be able to answer it once you've consulted most of your sources. Try to state that answer in a THESIS STATEMENT, an assertion that narrows your subject to a single idea. Here, for example, are the research question and thesis statement of Stephen Butterworth, whose final paper appears on pages 441–45:

Research question
Has the problem of child poverty in Canada improved?

Thesis statement
Child poverty has only increased in the last ten years, and Canada must find solutions or be prepared to pay for the consequences.

A precise thesis statement will give you a focus as you organize and draft your paper. For more on thesis statements, see pages 14–16.

2 Organization

To structure your paper, you'll need to synthesize, or forge relationships among ideas (see pp. 330–31). Here is one approach:

- Arrange your notes in groups of related ideas and information according to the subject headings you wrote in your notes. Each group should correspond to a main section of your paper: a key idea of your own that supports the thesis.
- Review your research journal for connections between sources and other thoughts that can help you organize your paper.

- Look objectively at your groups of notes. If a group is skimpy, with few notes, consider whether you should drop the category or conduct more research to fill it out. If most of your notes fall into one or two groups, consider whether the categories are too broad and should be divided. (If any of this rethinking affects your thesis statement, revise it accordingly.)
- Within each group, distinguish between the main idea of the group (which should be your own) and the supporting ideas and evidence (which should come from your sources).

See pages 16–20 for more on organizing a paper, including samples of both informal and formal outlines.

54b

(54b)   Drafting, revising, and formatting the paper

1   First draft

In drafting your paper, you do not have to proceed methodically from introduction to conclusion. Instead, draft in sections, beginning with the one you feel most confident about. Each section should centre on a principal idea contributing to your thesis, a conclusion you have drawn from reading and responding to sources. Start the section by stating the idea; then support it with information, summaries, paraphrases, and quotations from your notes. Remember to insert source information from your notes as well.

If you have kept your notes on a computer, you can import them (and source information) directly into your draft and then rewrite and edit them so that they work for your ideas and fit into your sentences.

2   Revision and editing

For a complex project like a research paper, you'll certainly want to revise in at least two stages—first for thesis, structure, and other whole-paper issues, and then for clarity, grammar, and other sentence-level issues. Chapter 5 supports this two-stage approach with checklists for revision (pp. 25–26) and editing (pp. 29–30). The box below provides additional steps to take when revising a research paper:

Checklist for revising a research paper

These steps supplement the revision checklist on pages 25–26.

- Ensure that your thesis statement accurately describes your topic and your perspective as they emerged during drafting, so that the paper is unified and coherent.
- Be alert for structural problems (outlining your draft as suggested on pp. 18–20 can help you see your structure at a glance):

Illogical arrangements of ideas.

Inadequate emphasis of important points and overemphasis of minor points.

Irrelevant ideas and facts that crept in just because you had notes on them.

- Ensure that *your* ideas, not the ideas of others, drive the paper. Check for places where you neglected to draw conclusions from sources or allowed sources' views to overwhelm your own.
- Look for places where supporting evidence is weak.
- Examine your explanations to be sure your readers will understand them. Define terms and clarify concepts that readers may be unfamiliar with.
- Integrate source material smoothly and clearly into your sentences. (See pp. 335–38.)
- Double-check your source citations for the following:

A citation for every use of someone else's material, whether in summary, paraphrase, or quotation. (See p. 335.)

Quotation marks for quotations; your own words and sentence structures for summaries and paraphrases. (See p. 336.)

Accurate and complete source information.

Correct format for source information, following your instructor's preference for style. (See p. 346.)

3   Format

The final draft of your paper should conform to the document format recommended by your instructor or by the style guide of the discipline in which you are writing. (See p. 346.) This book details two common formats: Modern Language Association (pp. 380–421) and American Psychological Association (pp. 423–445).

In any discipline you can use a word processor to present your ideas effectively and attractively with readable type fonts, headings, illustrations, and other elements. See pages 52–63 for ideas.

8 Writing in the Disciplines

8 Writing in the Disciplines

55 Working with the Goals and Requirements of the Disciplines

Chapter 8 (p. 65) outlines the general concerns of subject, purpose, and audience that figure in most academic writing situations. The disciplines have more in common as well: methods of gathering evidence, kinds of assignments, scholarly tools, language conventions, and styles for source citations and document format. This chapter introduces these common goals and requirements. The next two chapters then distinguish the disciplines along the same lines, focusing on literature (Chapter 56), and on other humanities, the social sciences, and the natural and applied sciences (Chapter 57). The last five chapters outline the major documentation styles.

55a Using methods and evidence

The METHODOLOGY of a discipline is the way its practitioners study their subjects—that is, how they proceed when investigating the answers to questions. Methodology relates to the way practitioners analyze evidence and ideas. For instance, a literary critic and a social historian would probably approach Shakespeare's *Hamlet* quite differently: the literary critic might study the play for a theme among its poetic images; the historian might examine the play's relation to Shakespeare's context, England at the turn of the seventeenth century.

Whatever their approach, academic writers do not compose entirely out of their personal experience. Rather, they combine the evidence of their experience with that appropriate to the discipline, drawing well-supported conclusions about their subjects. The evidence of the discipline comes from research using primary or secondary sources.

- **Primary sources** are firsthand or original accounts, such as historical documents, works of art, and reports on experiments that the writer has conducted. When you use primary sources, you conduct original research, generating your own evidence. You might use your analysis of a painting as evidence for an interpretation of the painting. Or you might use data from your own survey of students to support your conclusions about students' attitudes.

Guidelines for academic writers

- Become familiar with the methodology and the kinds of evidence for the discipline in which you are writing.
- Analyze the special demands of each assignment. The questions you set out to answer, the assertions you wish to support, will govern how you choose your sources and evidence.
- Become familiar with the discipline's specialized tools and language.
- Use the discipline's style for source citations and document format.

- **Secondary sources** are books and articles written *about* primary sources. Much academic writing requires that you use such sources to spark, extend, or support your own ideas, as when you review the published opinions on your subject before contributing conclusions from your original research.

55b   Understanding writing assignments

For most academic writing, your primary purpose will be either to explain something to your readers or to persuade them to accept your conclusions. To achieve your purpose, you will adapt your writing process to the writing situation, particularly to your reader's likely expectations for evidence and how you use it. Most assignments will contain keywords that imply some of these expectations —words such as *compare, define, analyze,* and *illustrate* that express customary ways of thinking about and organizing a vast range of subjects. (See p. 12 for more on these so-called patterns of development.) You should be aware of them and alert to the wording in assignments that directs you to use them.

55c   Using tools and language

When you write in an academic discipline, you use the scholarly tools of that discipline, particularly its periodical indexes. In addition, you may use the aids developed by practitioners of the discipline for efficiently and effectively approaching research, conducting it, and recording the findings. Many of these aids, such as a system for recording evidence from sources, are discussed on pp. 299–347 and can be adapted to any discipline. Other aids are discussed in the next two chapters.

Pay close attention to the texts assigned in a course and any materials given out in class, for these items may introduce you to valuable references and other research aids, and they will use the specialized language of the discipline. This specialized language allows practitioners to write to each other both efficiently and precisely. It also furthers certain concerns of the discipline, such as accuracy and objectivity. Scientists, for example, try to interpret their data objectively, so they avoid *undoubtedly, obviously,* and other words that slant conclusions. Some of the language conventions like this one are discussed in the following chapters. As you gain experience in a particular discipline, keep alert for such conventions and train yourself to follow them.

(55d) Following styles for source citations and document format

Most disciplines publish journals that require authors to use a certain style for source citations and a certain format for documents. In turn, most instructors in a discipline require the same of students writing papers for their courses.

When you cite your sources, you tell readers which ideas and information you borrowed and where they can find your sources. Thus, source citations indicate how much knowledge you have and how broad and deep your research was. They also help you avoid PLAGIARISM, the serious offence of presenting the words, ideas, and data of others as if they were your own. (See pp. 339–47 on avoiding plagiarism.)

55d

Document format includes such features as margins and the placement of the title. But it also extends to special elements of the manuscript, such as tables or an abstract, that may be required by the discipline.

The style guides for various disciplines are listed on pages 369 (humanities), 373 (social sciences), 377–78 (natural and applied sciences), and 463 (engineering). If your instructor does not require a particular style, use that of the Modern Language Association, which is described and illustrated at length on pages 380–421.

56 Reading and Writing About Literature

By Sylvan Barnet

Writers of literature—stories, novels, poems, and plays—are concerned with presenting human experience concretely, with *showing* rather than *telling*, with giving a sense of the feel of life. Reading and writing about literature thus require extremely close attention to the feel of the words. For instance, the word *woods* in Robert Frost's "Stopping by Woods on a Snowy Evening" has a rural, folksy quality that *forest* doesn't have, and many such small distinctions contribute to the poem's effect.

When you read literature, you interpret distinctions like these, forming an idea of the work. When you write about literature, you state your idea as your thesis, and you support the thesis with evidence from the work. (See pp. 14–16 for more on thesis statements.)

Note Writing about literature is not merely summarizing literature. Your thesis is a claim about the meaning or effect of the literary work, not a statement of its plot. And your paper is a demonstration of your thesis, not a retelling of the work's changes or events.

(56a) Using the methods and evidence of literary analysis

1 Reading literature

Reading literature critically involves interacting with a text, not in order to make negative judgments but in order to understand the work and evaluate its significance or quality. Such interaction is not passive, like scanning a newspaper or watching television. Instead, it is a process of engagement, of diving into the words themselves.

You will become more engaged if you write while you read. If you own the book you're reading, don't hesitate to underline or highlight passages that especially interest you. Don't hesitate to annotate the margins, indicating your pleasures, displeasures, and uncertainties with remarks such as *Nice detail* or *Do we need this long description?* or *Not believable.* If you don't own the book, make these notes on separate sheets or on your computer.

An effective way to interact with a text is to keep a READING JOURNAL. A journal is not a diary in which you record your doings; instead, it is a place to develop and store your reflections on what you read, such as an answer to a question you may have posed in the margin of the text or a response to something said in class. You may, for instance, want to reflect on why your opinion is so different from that of another student. You may even make an entry in the form of a letter to the author or from one character to another. (See p. 7 for more on journal keeping.)

2   Meaning in literature

In analyzing literature, you face right off the question of *meaning.* Readers disagree all the time over the meanings of works of literature, partly because (as noted earlier) literature *shows* rather than *tells:* it gives concrete images of imagined human experiences, but it usually does not say how we ought to understand the images. Further, readers bring different experiences to their reading and thus understand images differently. In writing about literature, then, we can offer only our *interpretation* of the meaning rather than *the* meaning. Still, most people agree that there are limits to interpretation: it must be supported by evidence that a reasonable person finds at least plausible if not totally convincing.

56a

3   Questions for a literary analysis

One reason interpretations of meaning differ is that readers approach literary works differently, focusing on certain elements and interpreting those elements distinctively. For instance, some critics look at a literary work mainly as an artifact of the particular time and culture in which it was created, while other critics stress the work's effect on its readers.

This chapter emphasizes so-called formalist criticism, which sees a literary work primarily as something to be understood in itself. This critical framework engages the reader immediately in the work of literature, without requiring extensive historical or cultural background, and it introduces the conventional elements of literature that all critical approaches discuss, even though they view the elements differently. The list below poses questions for each element that can help you think constructively and imaginatively about what you read.

- *Plot:* **the relationships and patterns of events.** Even a poem has a plot—for instance, a change in mood from grief to resignation.

    What actions happen?
    What conflicts occur?
    How do the events connect to each other and to the whole?

- *Characters:* **the people the author creates,** including the narrator of a story or the speaker of a poem.

   Who are the principal people in the work?
   How do they interact?
   What do their actions, words, and thoughts reveal about their personalities and the personalities of others?
   Do the characters stay the same, or do they change? Why?

- *Point of view:* **the perspective or attitude of the speaker in a poem or the voice who tells a story.** The point of view may be FIRST PERSON (a participant, using *I*) or THIRD PERSON (an outsider, using *he, she, it, they*). A first-person narrator may be a major or a minor character in the narrative and may be RELIABLE or UNRELIABLE (unable to report events wholly or accurately). A third-person narrator may be OMNISCIENT (knows what goes on in all characters' minds), LIMITED (knows what goes on in the mind of only one or two characters), or OBJECTIVE (knows only what is external to the characters).

   Who is the narrator (or the speaker of a poem)?
   How does the narrator's point of view affect the narrative?

56a

- *Tone:* **the narrator's or speaker's attitude,** perceived through the words (for instance, joyful, bitter, or confident).

   What tone (or tones) do you hear? If there is a change, how do you account for it?
   Is there an ironic contrast between the narrator's tone (for instance, confidence) and what you take to be the author's attitude (for instance, pity for human overconfidence)?

- *Imagery:* **word pictures or details involving the senses of sight, sound, touch, smell, and taste.**

   What images does the writer use? What senses do they draw on?
   What patterns are evident in the images (for instance, religious or commercial images)?
   What is the significance of the imagery?

- *Symbolism:* **concrete things standing for larger and more abstract ideas.** For instance, the American flag may symbolize freedom, or a dead flower may symbolize mortality.

   What symbols does the author use? What do they seem to signify?
   How does the symbolism relate to the theme of the work?

- *Setting:* **the place where the action happens.**

   What does the locale contribute to the work?
   Are scene shifts significant?

- *Form:* **the shape or structure of the work.**

  What *is* the form? (For example, a story might divide sharply in the middle, moving from happiness to sorrow.)
  What parts of the work does the form emphasize, and why?

- *Theme:* **the central idea, a conception of human experience suggested by the work as a whole.** Theme is neither plot (what happens) nor subject (such as mourning or marriage). Rather it is what the author says with that plot about that subject.

  Can you state the theme in a sentence? For instance, you might state the following about Gerard Manley Hopkins' poem "Pied Beauty" (p. 364): *Beauty does not have to be and should not be pure.*
  Do certain words, passages of dialogue or description, or situations seem to represent the theme most clearly?
  How do the work's elements combine to develop the theme?

- *Appeal:* **the degree to which the work pleases you.**

  What do you especially like or dislike about the work? Why?
  Do you think your responses are unique, or would they be common to most readers? Why?

4   Using evidence in writing about literature

56a

The evidence for a literary analysis always comes from at least one primary source (the work or works being discussed) and may come from secondary sources (critical and historical works). For example, in the paper on pages 364–65 about Gerard Manley Hopkins' "Pied Beauty" the primary material is the poem itself, and the secondary material is the three critical studies of the poem. The bulk of the evidence is usually quotations from the work, although summaries and paraphrases can be useful as well.

KEY TERMS

PRIMARY SOURCE A firsthand account: for instance, a historical document, a work of literature, or your own observations. (See p. 351.)

SECONDARY SOURCE A report on or analysis of other sources, often primary ones: for instance, a historian's account of a battle or a critic's view of a poem. (See p. 352.)

QUOTATION An exact repetition of an author's words, placed in quotation marks. (See pp. 334–35.)

PARAPHRASE A restatement of an author's words, closely following the author's line of thought but using different words and sentence structures. (See pp. 332–33.)

SUMMARY A condensation of an extended passage into a sentence or more. (See p. 332.)

Your instructor will probably tell you if you are expected to consult secondary sources for an assignment. They can help you understand a writer's work, but your primary concern should always be the work itself, not what critics A, B, and C say about it. In general, then, quote or summarize secondary material sparingly. And always cite your sources.

56b   Understanding writing assignments in literature

A literature instructor may ask you to write one or more of the following types of papers. The first two are the most common.

- **A literary analysis paper:** your ideas about a work of literature—your interpretation of its meaning, context, or representations based on specific words, passages, characters, and events.
- **A literary research paper:** analysis of a literary work combined with research about the work and perhaps its author. A literary research paper draws on both primary and secondary sources.
- **A personal response or reaction paper:** your thoughts and feelings about a work of literature.
- **A book review:** a summary of a book and a judgment about the book's value.
- **A theatre review:** your reactions to and opinions about a theatrical performance.

56c   Using the tools and language of literary analysis

1   Writing tools

The fundamental tool for writing about literature is reading critically. Asking analytical questions such as those on pages 355–57 can help you focus your ideas. In addition, keeping a reading journal can help you develop your thoughts. Make careful, well-organized notes on any research materials. Finally, discuss the work with others who have read it. They may offer reactions and insights that will help you shape your own ideas.

2   Language considerations

Use the present tense of verbs to describe both the action in a literary work and the writing of an author: *The pied things live a double existence. Hopkins emphasizes how fresh each thing is. The critic Harry Shaw reads the lines as joyful.* Use the past tense to describe events that actually occurred in the past: *Hopkins was born in 1844.*

Some instructors discourage students from using the first-person *I* (as in *I felt sorry for the character*) in writing about literature. At least use *I* sparingly to avoid sounding egotistical. Rephrase sentences to avoid using *I* unnecessarily—for instance, *The character evokes the reader's sympathy.*

3   Research sources

In addition to the following resources on literature, you may also want to consult some on other humanities (pp. 368–69).

Specialized encyclopedias, dictionaries, and bibliographies

Bibliographical Guide to the Study of the Literature of the USA
Cambridge Bibliography of English Literature
Cambridge Encyclopedia of Language
Cambridge Guide to Literature in English
Dictionary of Literary Biography
Handbook to Literature
Literary Criticism Index
McGraw-Hill Encyclopedia of World Drama
MLA International Bibliography of Books and Articles on the Modern Languages and Literatures
New Princeton Encyclopedia of Poetry and Poetics
Oxford Companion to American Literature
Oxford Companion to Canadian Literature
Schomburg Center Guide to Black Literature from the Eighteenth Century to the Present

56c

Indexes

Abstracts of Folklore Studies
Dissertation Abstracts International (doctoral dissertations)
Humanities Index
Literary Criticism Index
MLA International Bibliography of Books and Articles on the Modern Languages and Literatures

Book reviews

Book Review Digest
Book Review Index
Index to Book Reviews in the Humanities

Web sources

Alex Catalog of Electronic Texts (http://infomotions.com/alex)
Canadian Encyclopedia (www.canadianencyclopedia.com/)
Internet Public Library: Online Literary Criticism (http://ipl.org/div/litcrit)
Key Sites on American Literature (http://usinfo.state.gov/products/pubs/oal/amlitweb.htm)
Literary Index (http://www.galenet.com/servlet/LitIndex)
Literary Resources on the Net (http://andromeda.rutgers.edu/~jlynch/Lit)

Online Books Page (http://onlinebooks.library.upenn.edu/)
Voice of the Shuttle: Drama, Theater, and Performance Art Studies (http://vos.ucsb.edu/browse.asp?id=782)
Voice of the Shuttle: Literature (in English) (http://vos.ucsb.edu/browse.asp?id=3)
Voice of the Shuttle: Literatures (Other than English) (http://vos.ucsb.edu/browse.asp?id=2719)

56d Documenting sources and formatting papers in literary analysis

Unless your instructor specifies otherwise, use the style of the Modern Language Association, detailed on pages 380–414 and in *MLA Handbook for Writers of Research Papers*, 7th edition, 2009. In MLA style, parenthetical citations in the text of the paper refer to a list of works cited at the end. Sample papers illustrating this style appear on pages 32–33 and on pages 415–21.

Use MLA format for headings, margins, long quotations, and other elements, as detailed on pages 410–14.

56e Examining two literary works and sample papers

The following pages reprint two works of literature (a short story and a poem), each followed by a student paper on the work. In each student paper the author develops a thesis about the work, supporting this main idea with quotations, paraphrases, and summaries from the work being discussed, a primary source. In the second paper (p. 364), the author also draws sparingly on secondary sources (other critics' views), which further support his own views.

Note the following features of the students' papers:

- The writers do not merely summarize the literary works they write about. Occasionally, they briefly summarize to make their meaning clear, but their essays consist mostly of their own analysis.
- Each writer uses many quotations from the literary work to provide evidence for his or her ideas and to let readers hear the voice of the work.
- Both writers integrate quotations smoothly into their own sentences. (See pp. 271–75.)
- The writers use the present tense of verbs (*Chopin shows*; *Mrs. Mallard dies*) to describe both the author's work and the action in the work.

1   A short story and an essay about it

Short story

Kate Chopin

The Story of an Hour

Knowing that Mrs. Mallard was afflicted with a heart trouble, great care was taken to break to her as gently as possible the news of her husband's death.

It was her sister Josephine who told her, in broken sentences, veiled hints that revealed in half concealing. Her husband's friend Richards was there, too, near her. It was he who had been in the newspaper office when intelligence of the railroad disaster was received, with Brently Mallard's name leading the list of "killed." He had only taken the time to assure himself of its truth by a second telegram, and had hastened to forestall any less careful, less tender friend in bearing the sad message.

She did not hear the story as many women have heard the same, with a paralyzed inability to accept its significance. She wept at once with sudden, wild abandonment, in her sister's arms. When the storm of grief had spent itself she went away to her room alone. She would have no one follow her.

There stood, facing the open window, a comfortable, roomy armchair. Into this she sank, pressed down by a physical exhaustion that haunted her body and seemed to reach into her soul.

She could see in the open square before her house the tops of trees that were all aquiver with the new spring life. The delicious breath of rain was in the air. In the street below a peddler was crying his wares. The notes of a distant song which some one was singing reached her faintly, and countless sparrows were twittering in the eaves.

There were patches of blue sky showing here and there through the clouds that had met and piled one above the other in the west facing her window.

She sat with her head thrown back upon the cushion of the chair quite motionless, except when a sob came up into her throat and shook her, as a child who has cried itself to sleep continues to sob in its dreams.

She was young, with a fair, calm face, whose lines bespoke repression and even a certain strength. But now there was a dull stare in her eyes, whose gaze was fixed away off yonder on one of those patches of blue sky. It was not a glance of reflection, but rather indicated a suspension of intelligent thought.

There was something coming to her and she was waiting for it, fearfully. What was it? She did not know; it was too subtle and elusive to name. But she felt it creeping out of the sky, reaching toward her through the sounds, the scents, the color that filled the air.

Now her bosom rose and fell tumultuously. She was beginning to recognize this thing that was approaching to possess her, and she was striving to beat it back with her will—as powerless as her two white slender hands would have been.

56e

When she abandoned herself a little whispered word escaped her slightly parted lips. She said it over and over under her breath: "Free, free, free!" The vacant stare and the look of terror that had followed it went from her eyes. They stayed keen and bright. Her pulses beat fast, and the coursing blood warmed and relaxed every inch of her body.

She did not stop to ask if it were not a monstrous joy that held her. A clear and exalted perception enabled her to dismiss the suggestion as trivial.

She knew that she would weep again when she saw the kind, tender hands folded in death; the face that had never looked save with love upon her, fixed and gray and dead. But she saw beyond that bitter moment a long procession of years to come that would belong to her absolutely. And she opened and spread her arms out to them in welcome.

There would be no one to live for her during those coming years; she would live for herself. There would be no powerful will bending her in the blind persistence with which men and women believe they have a right to impose a private will upon a fellow creature. A kind intention or a cruel intention made the act seem no less a crime as she looked upon it in that brief moment of illumination.

And yet she had loved him—sometimes. Often she had not. What did it matter! What could love, the unsolved mystery, count for in face of this possession of self-assertion which she suddenly recognized as the strongest impulse of her being.

"Free! Body and soul free!" she kept whispering.

Josephine was kneeling before the closed door with her lips to the keyhole, imploring for admission. "Louise, open the door! I beg; open the door—you will make yourself ill. What are you doing, Louise? For heaven's sake open the door."

"Go away. I am not making myself ill." No; she was drinking in the very elixir of life through that open window.

Her fancy was running riot along those days ahead of her. Spring days, and summer days, and all sorts of days that would be her own. She breathed a quick prayer that life might be long. It was only yesterday she had thought with a shudder that life might be long.

She arose at length and opened the door to her sister's importunities. There was a feverish triumph in her eyes, and she carried herself unwittingly like a goddess of Victory. She clasped her sister's waist and together they descended the stairs. Richards stood waiting for them at the bottom.

Some one was opening the front door with a latchkey. It was Brently Mallard who entered, a little travel-stained, composedly carrying his grip-sack and umbrella. He had been far from the scene of accident, and did not even know there had been one. He stood amazed at Josephine's piercing cry; at Richards' quick motion to screen him from the view of his wife.

But Richards was too late.

When the doctors came they said she had died of heart disease—of joy that kills.

Ironies of Life in Kate Chopin's
"The Story of an Hour"

Kate Chopin's "The Story of an Hour"—which takes only a few minutes to read—has an ironic ending: Mrs. Mallard dies just when she is beginning to live. On first reading, the ending seems almost too ironic for belief. On rereading the story, however, one sees that the ending is believable partly because it is consistent with other ironies in the story.

After we know how the story turns out, if we reread it we find irony at the very start. Because Mrs. Mallard's friends and her sister assume, mistakenly, that she was deeply in love with her husband, Brently Mallard, they take great care to tell her gently of his death. They mean well, and in fact they do well, bringing her an hour of life, an hour of joyous freedom, but it is ironic that they think their news is sad. True, Mrs. Mallard at first expresses grief when she hears the news, but soon (unknown to her friends) she finds joy in it. So Richards's "sad message" (12), though sad in Richards's eyes, is in fact a happy message.

Among the small but significant ironic details is the statement near the end of the story that when Mallard entered the house, Richards tried to conceal him from Mrs. Mallard, but "Richards was too late" (13). Almost at the start of the story, in the second paragraph, Richards "hastened" (12) to bring his sad news. But if Richards had arrived "too late" at the start, Brently Mallard would have arrived at home first, and Mrs. Mallard's life would not have ended an hour later but would simply have gone on as it had been. Yet another irony at the end of the story is the diagnosis of the doctors. They say she died of "heart disease—of joy that kills" (13). In one sense they are right: Mrs. Mallard has for the last hour experienced a great joy. But of course the doctors totally misunderstand the joy that kills her. It is not joy at seeing her husband alive, but her realization that the great joy she experienced during the last hour is over.

All of these ironic details add richness to the story, but the central irony resides not in the well-intentioned but ironic actions of Richards, or in the unconsciously ironic words of the doctors, but in Mrs. Mallard's own life. She "sometimes" (13) loved her husband, but in a way she has been dead, a body subjected to her husband's will. Now, his apparent death brings her new life. Appropriately, this new life comes to her at the season of the year when "the tops of trees [. . .] were all aquiver with the new spring life" (12). But, ironically, her new life will last only an hour. She is "Free, free, free" (12), but only until her husband walks through the doorway. She looks forward to "summer days" (13), but she will not see even the end of this spring day. If her years of marriage were ironic, bringing her a sort of living death instead of joy, her new life is ironic too, not only because it grows out of her moment of grief for her supposedly dead husband, but also because her vision of "a long procession of years" (12) is cut short within an hour on a spring day.

56e

[New page.]

Work Cited

Chopin, Kate. "The Story of an Hour." <u>Literature for Composition</u>.
    Ed. Sylvan Barnet et al. 5th ed. New York: Longman, 2000.
    12–13.

—JANET VONG (student)

2   A poem and an essay about it

Poem

Gerard Manley Hopkins
Pied Beauty
Glory be to God for dappled things—
For skies of couple-colour as a brinded cow;
For rose-moles in all stipple upon trout that swim;
Fresh-firecoal chestnut-falls; finches' wings;
Landscape plotted and pieced—fold, fallow, and plough;
And all trades, their gear and tackle and trim.

All things counter, original, spare, strange;
Whatever is fickle, freckled (who knows how?)
With swift, slow; sweet, sour; adazzle, dim;
He fathers-forth whose beauty is past change:
                    Praise him.

56e

An essay on poetry (with secondary sources)

Brent Reimer
Professor Robinson-Varahidis
English 102B
March 22, 2008

The Paradox of "Pied Beauty"

Gerard Manley Hopkins' "Pied Beauty" takes its theme from
the title. We usually think of beauty as pure, unmarked, or perfect.
"Pied" means just the opposite. Something pied has at least two
colours; however, the word also means mixed, spotted, marked in
some way. Something pied is anything but pure or perfect. The
title is a paradox, where two contradictory ideas or statements are
true. Pied things are beautiful, and through his words, images, and
the form of the poem the poet explores how that paradox can itself
be true.

Hopkins was especially interested in words. In his diaries, he
would write out long strings of words that sound the same or
rhyme or that mean the same thing or are synonyms. In the first
two lines, Hopkins uses words that have the same meaning as
"pied": "Glory be to God for dappled things— / For skies of couple-
colour like a brinded cow . . ." (30). "Dappled" and "brinded" are
synonyms for "pied." A brinded cat is streaked or spotted, what we
call a tabby. The list of things in the first stanza are all pied or
brinded, and they are everywhere in nature and life, in the air, in

water, fire, land, and the labour of people. Hopkins seems to be saying that everything is pied, including words.

Hopkins looked everywhere for pied things, which he identified with something he called "inscape." In one of his diary entries, he saw a sky that was brinded like the skies in "Pied Beauty," and he defined these as an "inscape":

> Another night from a gallery window I saw a brinded heaven, the moon just marked by a blue spot pushing its way through the darker cloud, underneath and on the skirts of the rack bold long flakes whitened and swaled like feathers, below the garden with the heads of the trees and shrubs furry grey: I read a broad careless inscape flowing throughout. (125)

"Inscape" seems to be something like an image, and Hopkins saw images everywhere that resembled one another or rhymed. The list of pied things in the first stanza all rhyme like this in their "inscape."

The first stanza of six lines has an actual rhyme scheme of abc/abc. The second stanza is strange in itself with four and a half lines and a rhyme scheme of dbcdc. Hopkins identified "Pied Beauty" as one of his "curtal sonnets" (228). A sonnet usually has fourteen lines. Hopkins didn't write a sonnet of ten and a half lines because he couldn't write fourteen. A "curtal" is something cut short or bobbed, like a horse's tail, as this sonnet is cut short. In other words, this sonnet is not perfect either. It's a pied thing. As Maria R. Lichtman argues, Hopkins deliberately created an asymmetrical structure in the poem (113). Hopkins deliberately makes the poem imperfect in form to render it pied.

56e

Why does he do this? The poem celebrates things that have a "couple-colour," that have a double nature, or have what Justus George Lawler calls "complementarity." In the second stanza, Hopkins describes these again and pairs together words that are opposite in meaning: "Whatever is fickle, freckled (who knows how?) / With swift, slow; sweet, sour; adazzle, dim. . . ." Those pairs of opposite words, "swift, slow; sweet, sour", are like paradoxes, opposite ideas that are both true. Two-word paradoxes like these are called oxymorons, and the title "Pied Beauty" is an oxymoron. The poem celebrates the double nature or paradox of all things. Only one thing in the sonnet is not paradoxical in this way: "He fathers-forth whose beauty is past change. . . ." Something past change is perfect, and the poem celebrates all created or imperfect things, as a way of celebrating the pied perfection of the world.

[New page.]

Works Cited

Hopkins, Gerard Manley. <u>Poems and Prose</u>. Ed. W. H. Gardner. Harmondsworth: Penguin, 1985.

Lawler, Justus George. <u>Hopkins Re-Constructed: Life, Poetry, and the Tradition</u>. New York: Continuum, 1998.

Lichtman, Maria R. <u>The Contemplative Poetry of Gerard Manley Hopkins</u>. Princeton: Princeton UP, 1989.

57 Writing in Other Disciplines

57a Writing in the humanities

The humanities include literature, the visual arts, music, film, dance, history, philosophy, and religion. The preceding chapter discusses the particular requirements of reading and writing about literature. This section concentrates on history. Although the arts, religion, and other humanities have their own concerns, they share many important goals and methods with literature and history.

1 Methods and evidence in the humanities

Writers in the humanities record and speculate about the growth, ideas, and emotions of human beings. Based on the evidence of written words, artworks, and other human traces and creations, humanities writers explain, interpret, analyze, and reconstruct the human experience.

The discipline of history focuses particularly on reconstructing the past. In Greek the word for history means "to inquire": historians inquire into the past to understand the events of the past. Then they report, explain, analyze, and evaluate those events in their context, asking such questions as what happened before or after the events or how the events were related to then existing political and social structures.

Historians' reconstructions of the past—their conclusions about what happened and why—are always supported with reference to the written record. The evidence of history is mainly primary sources, such as eyewitness accounts and contemporary documents, letters, commercial records, and the like. For history papers, you might also be asked to support your conclusions with those in secondary sources.

In reading historical sources, you need to weigh and evaluate their evidence. If, for example, you find conflicting accounts of the same event, you need to consider the possible biases of the authors. In general, the more a historian's conclusions are supported by public records such as deeds, marriage licences, and newspaper accounts, the more reliable the conclusions are likely to be.

2   Writing assignments in the humanities

Papers in the humanities generally perform one or more of the following operations:

- **Explanation:** for instance, showing how a painter developed a particular technique or clarifying a general's role in a historical battle.
- **Analysis:** examining the elements of a philosophical argument or breaking down the causes of a historical event.
- **Interpretation:** inferring the meaning of a film from its images or the significance of a historical event from contemporary accounts of it.
- **Synthesis:** finding a pattern in a historical period or in a composer's works.
- **Evaluation:** judging the quality of an architect's design or a historian's conclusions.

Most likely, you will use these operations in combination—say, interpreting and explaining the meaning of a painting and then evaluating it. (These operations are discussed in more detail on pp. 352–55.)

3   Tools and language in the humanities

The tools and language of the humanities vary according to the discipline. Major reference works in each field, such as those listed on the next pages, can clarify specific tools you need and language you should use.

57a

Writing tools

A useful tool for the arts is to ask a series of questions to analyze and evaluate a work. (A list of such questions for reading literature appears on pp. 355–58.) In any humanities discipline, a journal—a log of questions, reactions, and insights—can help you discover and record your thoughts.

In history the tools are those of any thorough and efficient researcher: a system for finding and tracking sources; a methodical examination of sources, including evaluating and synthesizing them; a system for gathering source information; and a separate system, such as a research journal, for tracking one's own evolving thoughts.

Language considerations

Historians strive for precision and logic. They do not guess about what happened or speculate about "what if." They avoid trying to influence readers' opinions with words having strongly negative or positive connotations, such as *stupid* or *brilliant*. Instead, historians show the evidence and draw conclusions from that.

Generally, they avoid using *I* because it tends to draw attention away from the evidence and toward the writer.

Writing about history demands some attention to the tenses of verbs to maintain consistency. Generally, historians use the past tense to refer to events that occurred in the past. They reserve the present tense only for statements about the present or statements of general truths. For example:

> Pierre Elliott Trudeau <u>died</u> in 2000. His political achievements <u>persist</u> in the current applications of his Canadian Charter of Rights and Freedoms.

Research sources on the Web

The following lists give resources in the humanities. (Resources for literature appear on pp. 359–60.)

General

BUBL Information Service (http://bubl.ac.uk/)
EDSITEment (http://edsitement.neh.gov)
Voice of the Shuttle (http://vos.ucsb.edu)

Art

Artnet (http://www.artnet.com)
World Wide Arts Resources (http://www.wwar.com/browse.html)

Dance

BUBL Link: Dance (http://bubl.ac.uk/link/d/dance.htm)
Google Directory: Dance Links (http://directory.google.com/Top/Arts/ Performing_Arts/Dance)

Film

Film Studies on the Internet (www.library.ualberta.ca/subject/film/ websites/index.cfm)
Internet Movie Database (http://www.imdb.com)

History

Best of History Web Sites (http://www.besthistorysites.net)
Librarians' Index to the Internet: History (http://search.lii.org/)

Music

American Music Resource (http://amrhome.net)
Web Resources for Research in Music (http://www.music.ucc.ie/wrrm)

Philosophy

EpistemeLinks (http://www.epistemelinks.com)
Intute: Philosophy (http://www.intute.ac.uk/artsandhumanities/ philosophy)

57a

Religion

Academic Info: Religion (http://www.academicinfo.net/religindex.html)
Virtual Religion Index (http://www.virtualreligion.net/vri)

Theatre

*McCoy's Brief Guide to Internet Resources in Theatre and Performance
    Studies (http://www2.stetson.edu/csata/thr_guid.html)*
Theater Connections (http://personal.uncc.edu/jvanoate/theater)

4   Documentation and format in the humanities

Writers in the humanities generally rely on one of the following
guides for source-citation style:

The Chicago Manual of Style. 15th ed. 2003.
Gibaldi, Joseph. *MLA Handbook for Writers of Research Papers.* 6th ed.
    2003
Turabian, Kate L. *A Manual for Writers of Term Papers, Theses, and
    Dissertations.* 7th ed. Rev. Wayne C. Booth, Gregory G. Colomb
    and Joseph M. Williams 2007.

See pages 380–414 for the recommendations of the *MLA
Handbook.* Unless your instructor specifies otherwise, use these recommendations for papers in English and foreign languages. In history, art history, and many other disciplines, however, writers rely
on *The Chicago Manual of Style* or the student reference adapted
from it, *A Manual for Writers.* Both books detail two documentation
styles. One, used mainly by scientists and social scientists, closely
resembles the style of the American Psychological Association. (See
pp. 423–437). The other style, used more in the humanities, calls for
footnotes or endnotes and an optional bibliography. This style is
described on pages 448–56.

57b

(57b)   Writing in the social sciences

The social sciences—including anthropology, economics, education, management, political science, psychology, and sociology—
focus on the study of human behaviour. As the name implies, the
social sciences examine the way human beings relate to themselves,
to their environment, and to one another.

1   Methods and evidence in the social sciences

Researchers in the social sciences systematically pose a question, formulate a **hypothesis** (a generalization that can be tested),
collect data, analyze those data, and draw conclusions to support,
refine, or disprove their hypothesis. This is the scientific method
developed in the natural sciences. (See p. 374.)

Social scientists gather data in several ways:

- **They make firsthand observations of human behaviour,** recording the observations in writing or on audio- or videotape.
- **They interview subjects about their attitudes and behaviour,** recording responses in writing or on tape. (See pp. 321–22 for guidelines on conducting an interview.)
- **They conduct broader surveys using questionnaires,** asking people about their attitudes and behaviour. (See the box below.)
- **They conduct controlled experiments,** structuring an environment in which to encourage and measure a specific behaviour.

In their writing, social scientists explain their own research or analyze and evaluate others' research.

The research methods of social science generate two kinds of data:

- *Quantitative data* **are numerical,** such as statistical evidence based on surveys, polls, tests, and experiments. When public-opinion pollsters announce that 47 percent of Canadian citizens polled approve of the prime minister's leadership, they are offering quantitative data gained from a survey. Social science

57b

Conducting a survey

- **Decide what you want to find out—what your hypothesis is.** The questions you ask should be dictated by your purpose.
- **Define your population.** Think about the kinds of people your hypothesis is about—for instance, college men, or five-year-old children. Plan to sample this population so that your findings will be representative.
- **Write your questions.** Surveys may contain closed questions that direct the respondent's answers (checklists and multiple-choice, true/false, or yes/no questions) or open-ended questions allowing brief, descriptive answers. Avoid loaded questions that reveal your own biases or make assumptions about subjects' answers, such as "Do you want Canada to support democracy in China?" or "How much more money does your father make than your mother?"
- **Test your questions.** Use a few respondents with whom you can discuss the answers. Eliminate or recast questions that respondents find unclear, discomforting, or unanswerable.
- **Tally the results.** Count the actual numbers of answers, including any nonanswers.
- **Seek patterns in the raw data.** Such patterns may confirm or contradict your hypothesis. Revise the hypothesis or conduct additional research if necessary.

writers present quantitative data in graphs, charts, and other illustrations that accompany their text.

- *Qualitative data* **are not numerical but more subjective:** they are based on interviews, firsthand observations, and inferences, taking into account the subjective nature of human experience. Examples of qualitative data include an anthropologist's description of the initiation ceremonies in a culture she is studying or a psychologist's interpretation of interviews he conducted with a group of adolescents.

2   Writing assignments in the social sciences

Depending on what social science courses you take, you may be asked to complete a variety of assignments:

- **A summary or review of research** reports on the available research literature on a subject, such as infants' perception of colour.
- **A case analysis** explains the components of a phenomenon, such as a factory closing.
- **A problem-solving analysis** explains the elements of a problem, such as unreported child abuse, and suggests ways to solve it.
- **A research paper** interprets and sometimes analyzes and evaluates the writings of other social scientists about a subject, such as the effect of national appeals in advertising.
- **A research report** explains the author's own original research or the author's attempt to replicate someone else's research. (See pp. 441–45 for an example of a research report.)

57b

Many social science disciplines have special requirements for the content and organization of each kind of paper. The requirements appear in the style guides of the disciplines, listed on pages 372–73. For instance, the American Psychological Association specifies the outline for research reports, which is illustrated on pages 437–40. Because of the differences among disciplines and even among different kinds of papers in the same discipline, you should always ask your instructor what he or she requires for an assignment.

3   Tools and language in the social sciences

The following guidelines for tools and language apply to most social sciences. However, the particular discipline you are writing in, or an instructor in a particular course, may have additional requirements.

Writing tools

Many social scientists rely on a **research journal** or **log,** in which they record their ideas throughout the research-writing process. Even if a research journal is not required in your courses, you may want to use one. As you begin formulating a hypothesis, you can record preliminary questions. Then when you are in the field conducting research, you can use the journal to react to the evidence you are collecting, to record changes in your perceptions and ideas, and to assess your progress.

To avoid confusing your reflections on the evidence with the evidence itself, keep records of actual data—notes from interviews, observations, surveys, and experiments—separately from the journal.

Language considerations

Each social science discipline has specialized terminology for concepts basic to the discipline. In sociology, for example, the words *mechanism, identity,* and *deviance* have specific meanings different from those of everyday usage. And *identity* means something different in sociology, where it applies to groups of people, than in psychology, where it applies to the individual. Social scientists also use precise terms to describe or interpret research. For instance, they say *The subject expressed a feeling of* rather than *The subject felt* because human feelings are not knowable for certain; or they say *These studies indicate* rather than *These studies prove* because conclusions are only tentative.

Just as social scientists strive for objectivity in their research, so they strive to demonstrate their objectivity through language in their writing. They avoid expressions such as *I think* in order to focus attention on what the evidence shows rather than on the researcher's opinions. (However, many social scientists prefer *I* to the artificial *the researcher* when they refer to their own actions, as in *I then interviewed the subjects.* Ask your instructor for his or her preferences.) Social scientists also avoid direct or indirect expression of their personal biases or emotions, either in discussions of other researchers' work or in descriptions of research subjects. Thus one social scientist does not call another's work *sloppy* or *immaculate* and does not refer to his or her own subjects as *drunks* or *innocent victims.* Instead, the writer uses neutral language and ties conclusions strictly to the data.

Research sources on the Web
General

Data on the Net (http://3stages.org/idata)
Social Science Information Gateway (http://intute.ac.uk/socialsciences)
WWW Virtual Library: Social and Behavorial Sciences (http://vlib.org/ SocialSciences)

Anthropology

Anthro.Net (http://home1.gte.net/ericjw1/index.html)
Anthropology Resources on the Internet (http://www.anthropologie.net)

Business and economics

Resources for Economics on the Internet (http://rfe.org)
Virtual International Business and Economic Sources (http://library. uncc.edu/vibes)

Education

Educator's Reference Desk (http://www.eduref.org)
Your provincial ministry of education

Ethnic and gender studies

Diversity and Ethnic Studies (http://www.public.iastate.edu/~savega/ divweb2.htm)
Voice of the Shuttle: Gender Studies (http://vos.ucsb.edu/browse.asp? id=2711)

Political science and law

Librarians' Index to the Internet: Law (http://lii.org/search/file/law)
Political Science Resources (http://www.psr.keele.ac.uk)

Psychology

PsychCentral (http://psychcentral.com)
Psych Web (http://psywww.com)

Sociology

SocioWeb (http://www.socioweb.com)
WWW Virtual Library: Sociology (http://socserv2.mcmaster.ca/ w3virtsoclib)

57b

4   Documentation and format in the social sciences

Some of the social sciences publish style guides that advise practitioners how to organize, document, and type papers. The following is a partial list:

American Anthropological Association. *AAA Style Guide.* 2003. *http://www.aaanet.org/publications/style_guide.pdf*
American Political Science Association. *Style Manual for Political Science.* 2006.
American Psychological Association. *Publication Manual of the American Psychological Association,* 5th ed., 2001
American Sociological Association. *ASA Style Guide,* 2nd ed. 1997.
Linguistic Society of America. "LSA Style Sheet." Published every December in *LSA Bulletin.*
The Bluebook: A Uniform System of Citation (law). 18th ed. 2005.

By far the most widely used style is that of the American Psychological Association, detailed on pages 427–37. Always ask your instructor in any discipline what style you should use.

57c   Writing in the natural and applied sciences

The natural and applied sciences include biology, chemistry, physics, mathematics, engineering, computer science, and their branches. Their purpose is to understand natural and technological phenomena. (A *phenomenon* is a fact or event that can be known by the senses.) Scientists conduct experiments and write to explain the step-by-step processes in their methods of inquiry and discovery.

1   Methods and evidence in the sciences

Scientists investigate phenomena by the SCIENTIFIC METHOD, a process of continual testing and refinement.

The scientific method

- **Observe carefully.** Accurately note all details of the phenomenon being researched.
- **Ask questions about the observations.**
- **Formulate a *hypothesis*,** or preliminary generalization, that explains the observed facts.
- **Test the hypothesis** with additional observations or controlled experiments.
- **If the hypothesis proves accurate, formulate a *theory*,** or unified model, that explains *why*.
- **If the hypothesis is disproved, revise it or start anew.**

Scientific evidence is almost always quantitative—that is, it consists of numerical data obtained from the measurement of phenomena. These data are called EMPIRICAL (from a Greek word for "experience"): they result from observation and experience, generally in a controlled laboratory setting but also (as sometimes in astronomy or biology) in the natural world. Often the empirical evidence for scientific writing comes from library research into other people's reports of their investigations. Surveys of known data or existing literature are common in scientific writing.

2   Writing assignments in the sciences

No matter what your assignment, you will be expected to document and explain your evidence carefully so that anyone reading can check your sources and replicate your research. It is important for your reader to know the context of your research—both the previous experimentation and research on your particular subject (acknowledged in the survey of the literature) and the physical conditions and other variables surrounding your own work.

Assignments in the natural and applied sciences include the following:

- **A summary** distills a research article to its essence in brief, concise form. (Summary is discussed in detail on pp. 74–76.)
- **A critique** summarizes and critically evaluates a scientific report.
- **A laboratory report** explains the procedure and results of an experiment conducted by the writer.
- **A research report** explains the experimental research of other scientists and the writer's own methods, findings, and conclusions.
- **A research proposal** reviews the relevant literature and explains a plan for further research.

A laboratory report has four or five major sections:

1. **"Abstract"**: a summary of the report.
2. **"Introduction"** or **"Objective"**: a review of why the study was undertaken, a summary of the background of the study, and a statement of the problem being studied.
3. **"Method"** or **"Procedure"**: a detailed explanation of how the study was conducted, including any statistical analysis.
4. **"Results"**: an explanation of the major findings (including unexpected results) and a summary of the data presented in graphs and tables.
5. **"Discussion"**: an interpretation of the results and an explanation of how they relate to the goals of the experiment. This section also describes new hypotheses that might be tested as a result of the experiment. If the discussion is brief, it may be combined with the results in a single section labelled "Conclusions."

In addition, laboratory or research reports may include a list of references (if other sources were consulted). They almost always include tables and figures (graphs and charts) containing the data from the research.

3   Tools and language in the sciences

Tools and language concerns vary from discipline to discipline in the sciences. Consult your instructor for specifics about the field in which you are writing.

Writing tools

In the sciences a LAB NOTEBOOK or SCIENTIFIC JOURNAL is almost indispensable for accurately recording the empirical data from observations and experiments. Use such a notebook or journal for these purposes:

- **Record observations** from reading, from class, or from the lab.
- **Ask questions and refine hypotheses.**

57c

- **Record procedures.**
- **Record results.**
- **Keep an ongoing record of ideas and findings** and how they change as data accumulate.
- **Sequence and organize your material** as you compile your findings and write your report.

Make sure that your records of data are clearly separate from your reflections on the data so that you don't mistakenly confuse the two in drawing your conclusions.

Language considerations

Science writers prefer to use objective language that removes the writer as a character in the situation and events being explained, except as the impersonal agent of change, the experimenter. Although usage is changing, scientists still rarely use *I* in their reports and evaluations, and they often resort to the passive voice of verbs, as in *The mixture <u>was</u> then <u>subjected</u> to centrifugal force.* This conscious objectivity focuses attention (including the writer's) on the empirical data and what they show. It discourages the writer from, say, ascribing motives and will to animals and plants. For instance, instead of asserting that the sea tortoise *evolved* its hard shell *to protect* its body, a scientist would write only what could be observed: that the hard shell *covers and thus protects* the tortoise's body.

Science writers typically change verb tenses to distinguish between established information and their own research. For established information, such as that found in journals and other reliable sources, use the present tense: *Baroreceptors <u>monitor</u> blood pressure.* For your own and others' research, use the past tense: *The bacteria <u>died</u> within three hours. Marti <u>reported</u> some success.*

Each discipline in the natural and applied sciences has a specialized vocabulary that permits precise, accurate, and efficient communication. Some of these terms, such as *pressure* in physics, have different meanings in the common language and must be handled carefully in science writing. Others, such as *enthalpy* in chemistry, have no meanings in the common language and must simply be learned and used correctly.

Research sources on the Web
General

Google Directory: Science Links (directory.google.com/Top/Science)
Librarians' Index to the Internet: Science (lii.org/search/file/scitech)
WWW Virtual Library: Natural Sciences and Mathematics (vlib.org/ Science.html)

57c

Biology

Biology Online (http://www.biology-online.org)
National Biological Information Infrastructure (http://www.nbii.gov)

Chemistry

American Chemical Society (http://www.acs.org)
*WWW Virtual Library: Links for Chemists (http://www.liv.ac.uk/
Chemistry/Links/links.html)*

Computer science

IEEE Computer Society (http://www.computer.org)
*University of Texas Virtual Computer Library (http://www.utexas.
edu/computer/vcl)*

Engineering

*BUBL: Technology
(http://bubl.ac.uk/link/linkbrowse.cfm?menuid=8178)*
*Internet Guide to Engineering, Mathematics, and Computing
(http://www.eevl.ac.uk)*

Environmental science

EE-link: Environmental Education on the Internet (http://eelink.net)
EnviroLink (http://www.envirolink.org)

57c

Geology

American Geological Institute (http://www.agiweb.org)
US Geological Survey Library (http://libraryusgs.gov)

Health sciences

Hardin MD (http://www.lib.uiowa.edu/hardin/md)
World Health Organization (http://www.who.int)

Mathematics

Math on the Web (http://www.ams.org/mathweb)
*BUBL: Natural Sciences and Mathematics (http://bubl.ac.uk/link/
linkbrowse.cfm?menuid=6402)*

Physics and astronomy

American Institute of Physics (http://aip.org)
PhysicsWorld (http://physicsworld.com)

4 Documentation and format in the sciences

Within the natural and applied sciences, practitioners use one of
two styles of documentation, varying slightly from discipline to discipline. Following are some of the style guides most often consulted:

American Chemical Society. *ACS Style Guide: Effective Communication of Scientific Information.* 3rd ed. 2006

American Institute of Physics. *Style Manual for Guidance in the Preparation of Papers*. 4th ed. 1990.

American Mathematical Society. *The AMS Author Handbook: General Instructions for Preparing Manuscripts*. Rev. ed. 1996.

American Medical Association Manual of Style, 9th ed., 1998.

Council of Science Editors. *Scientific Style and Format: The CSE Manual for Authors, Editors, and Publishers*. 7th ed. 2006.

The most thorough and widely used of these guides is the last one, *Scientific Style and Format*. See pages 456–63 for a description of CSE style.

57c

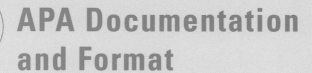

APA Documentation and Format

APA Documentation and Format

59 APA Documentation and Format

The style guide for psychology and some other social sciences is the *Publication Manual of the American Psychological Association* (5th ed., 2001). In the APA documentation style, you acknowledge each of your sources twice:

- In your text, a brief parenthetical citation adjacent to the borrowed material directs readers to a complete list of all the works you refer to.
- At the end of your paper, the list of references includes complete bibliographical information for every source.

Every entry in the list of references has at least one corresponding citation in the text, and every in-text citation has a corresponding entry in the list of references.

This chapter describes APA text citations (p. 424) and references (p. 427), details APA document format (p. 437), and concludes with a sample APA paper (p. 440).

APA
59

(59a) Writing APA parenthetical text citations

In the APA documentation style, parenthetical citations within the text refer the reader to a list of sources at the end of the text. See the tabbed divider for an index to the models for various kinds of sources.

Note Models 1 and 2 below show the direct relationship between what you include in your text and what you include in a parenthetical citation. The citation always includes a publication date and may include a page number. It also includes the author's name if you do *not* name the author in your text (model 1). It does not include the author's name if you *do* name the author in your text (model 2).

1. Author not named in your text

One critic of Milgram's experiments said that the subjects "should have been fully informed of the possible effects on them" (Baumrind, 2003, p. 34).

When you do not name the author in your text, place the author's name and the date of the source in parentheses. The APA requires page number(s) preceded by "p." or "pp." for direct quotations (as in the example) and recommends them for paraphrases. Separate the elements with commas. Position the reference so that it is clear what material is being documented *and* so that the reference fits as smoothly as possible into your sentence structure. (See pp. 385–87 for guidelines.) The following would also be correct:

In the view of one critic of Milgram's experiments (Baumrind, 2003), the subjects "should have been fully informed of the possible effects on them" (p. 34).

2. Author named in your text

Baumrind (2003) said that the subjects in Milgram's study "should have been fully informed of the possible effects on them" (p. 34).

When you use the author's name in the text, do not repeat it in the reference. Place the date after the author's name and any page reference after the borrowed material. If you cite the same source again in the paragraph, you need not repeat the reference as long as it is clear that you are using the same source.

3. A work with two authors

Pepinsky and DeStefano (2002) demonstrate that a teacher's language often reveals hidden biases.

One study (Pepinsky & DeStefano, 2002) demonstrates hidden biases in teachers' language.

When given in the text, two authors' names are connected by "and." In a parenthetical citation, they are connected by an ampersand, "&."

4. A work with three to five authors

Pepinsky, Dunn, Rentl, and Corson (1993) further demonstrate the biases evident in gestures.

In the first citation of a work with three to five authors, name all the authors, as in the example above. In the second and subsequent references to the work, generally give only the first author's name, followed by "et al." (Latin for "and others"):

In the work of Pepinsky et al. (1993), the loaded gestures include head shakes and eye contact.

However, two or more sources published in the same year could shorten to the same form—for instance, two references shortening to Pepinsky et al., 1993. In that case, cite the last names of as many authors as you need to distinguish the sources, and then give "et al.": for instance, Pepinsky, Dunn, et al., 1993 and Pepinsky, Bradley, et al., 1993.

5. A work with six or more authors

One study (Rutter et al., 2001) attempts to explain these geographical differences in adolescent experience.

For six or more authors, even in the first citation of the work, give only the first author's name, followed by "et al." If two or more sources published in the same year shorten to the same form, follow the instructions for model 4 above.

6. A work with a group author

An earlier prediction was even more sombre (Lorenz Research, 2007).

APA

59a

For a work that lists an institution, agency, corporation, or other group as author, treat the name of the group as if it were an individual's name.

7. An anonymous work

One article ("Future Offenders," 2001) noted that young offenders require individual attention.

For an anonymous or unsigned work, use the first two or three words of the title in place of an author's name, excluding an initial *The, A,* or *An.* Underline book and journal titles. Place quotation marks around article titles. (In the list of references, however, do not use quotation marks for article titles. See p. 428.) Capitalize the significant words in all titles cited in the text. (But in the reference list, treat only journal titles this way. See p. 428.)

8. One of two or more works by the same author(s)

At about age seven, most children begin to use appropriate gestures to reinforce their stories (Gardner, 1973a).

If your reference list includes two or more works published by the same author(s) *in the same year,* the works should be lettered in the reference list. (See p. 430.) Then your parenthetical citation should include the appropriate letter, as in "1973a" in the example.

9. Two or more works by different authors

Two studies (Herskowitz, 2000; Marconi & Hamblen, 2002) found that periodic safety instruction can dramatically reduce employees' accidents.

List the sources in alphabetical order by the first author's name. Insert a semicolon between sources.

10. An indirect source

Supporting data appear in a study by Wong (cited in Marconi & Hamblen, 2002).

The phrase "cited in" indicates that the reference to Wong's study was found in Marconi and Hamblen. Only Marconi and Hamblen then appears in the list of references.

11. An electronic source

APA

59a

Ferguson and Hawkins (2008) did not anticipate the "evident hostility" of participants.

Electronic sources can be cited like printed sources, usually with the author's last name and the publication date. If the source does not have page numbers, provide just the author's name and the date.

(59b) Preparing the APA reference list

In APA style, the in-text parenthetical citations refer to the list of sources at the end of the text. This list, titled "References," includes full publication information on every source cited in the paper. The list falls at the end of the paper, numbered in sequence with the preceding pages. The sample below shows the elements and their spacing.

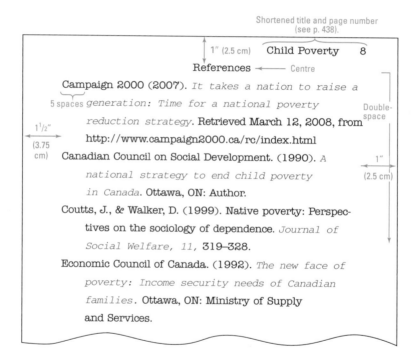

Shortened title and page number (see p. 438).

1″ (2.5 cm)   Child Poverty   8

References ◄── Centre

Campaign 2000 (2007). *It takes a nation to raise a*

5 spaces *generation: Time for a national poverty*

Double-space

1½″ *reduction strategy.* Retrieved March 12, 2008, from

(3.75 cm)   http://www.campaign2000.ca/rc/index.html

Canadian Council on Social Development. (1990). *A*

national strategy to end child poverty   1″

in Canada. Ottawa, ON: Author.   (2.5 cm)

Coutts, J., & Walker, D. (1999). Native poverty: Perspec-

tives on the sociology of dependence. *Journal of*

Social Welfare, 11, 319–328.

Economic Council of Canada. (1992). *The new face of*

poverty: Income security needs of Canadian

families. Ottawa, ON: Ministry of Supply

and Services.

Arrangement

Arrange sources alphabetically by the author's last name or, if there is no author, by the first main word of the title. Do *not* group sources by type (books, journals, and so on).

Spacing

Double-space all entries.

Indention

The APA recommends hanging indentions, in which the first line is not indented and the others are:

> Speck, D. C. (1998). *The pleasure of the crown: Anthropol-*
>
> > *ogy, law, and First Nations.* Burnaby, BC:
> >
> > Talonbooks.

The hanging indention is used in the sample on the previous page and in the following models for references, with a 1/2-inch (1.25 cm) indention for the second and subsequent lines of each entry.

Punctuation

Separate the parts of the reference (author, date, title, and publication information) with a period and one space. Do not use a final period in references to electronic sources that conclude with an electronic address or Digital Object Identifier (DOI). (See pp. 433–35.)

Authors

List all authors with last name first, separating names and parts of names with commas. Use initials for first and middle names. Use an ampersand (&) before the last author's name.

Publication date

Place the publication date in parentheses after the author's or authors' names, followed by a period. Generally, this date is the year only, though for some sources (such as magazine and newspaper articles) it includes the month and sometimes the day as well.

Titles

In titles of books and articles, capitalize only the first word of the title, the first word of the subtitle, and proper nouns; all other words begin with small letters. In titles of journals, capitalize all significant words. (See pp. 289–90.) Unless your instructor specifies underlining, italicize the titles of books and journals, along with any comma or period following. Do not italicize or use quotation marks around the titles of articles.

City of publication

For print sources that are not periodicals (such as books or government publications), give the city of publication. The following U.S. cities do not require state names: Baltimore, Boston, Chicago, Los Angeles, New York, Philadelphia, and San Francisco. Follow their names with a colon. For all other U.S. cities, add a comma

APA

59b

after the city name and give the two-letter postal abbreviation of the province or state, unless the province or state appears in the publisher's name (e.g., University of Missouri Press), and follow with a colon. Canadian cities require provincial postal abbreviations.

Publisher's name

For nonperiodical print sources, give the publisher's name after the place of publication and a colon. Use shortened names for many publishers (such as "Morrow" for William Morrow), and omit "Co.," "Inc.," and "Publishers." However, give full names for associations, corporations, and university presses (such as "University of Toronto Press"), and do not omit "Books" or "Press" from a publisher's name.

Page numbers

Use the abbreviation "p." or "pp." before page numbers in books and in newspapers, but *not* in other periodicals. For inclusive page numbers, include all figures: "667–668."

Note An index to the following models appears at the tabbed divider. If you don't see a model listed for the kind of source you used, try to find one that comes close, and provide ample information so that readers can trace the source. Often, you will have to combine models to provide the necessary information on a source—for instance, combining "A book with two or more authors" (2) and "An article in a journal" (11) for a journal article with two or more authors.

1   Books

1. A book with one author

Speck, D. C. (1998). *The pleasure of the Crown: Anthropology, law, and First Nations.* Burnaby, BC: Talonbooks.

The initials "D. C." appear instead of the author's first name, even though the author's full first name appears on the source. In the title, only the first words of title and subtitle and the proper name are capitalized.

2. A book with two or more authors

Kline, S., Dyer-Witheford, N., & de Peuter, G. (2003). *Digital play: The interaction of technology, culture, and marketing.* Montreal, QC: McGill-Queen's University Press.

An ampersand (&) separates the last author's names.

APA
59b

3. A book with an editor

Treat, J. W. (Ed.). (1996). *Contemporary Japan and popular culture*. Honolulu: University of Hawaii Press.

List the editors' names as if they were authors, but follow the last name with "(Eds.)."—or "(Ed.)." with only one editor. Note the periods inside and outside the final parenthesis and the omission of the state name when it is part of the publisher's name.

4. A book with a translator

Bourdieu, P. (1990). *In other words: Essays towards a reflexive sociology*. (M. Adamson, Trans.). Stanford, CA: Stanford University Press.

The name of the translator appears in parentheses after the title, followed by a comma, "Trans.", a closing parenthesis, and a final period.

5. A book with a group author

Lorenz Research. (2007). *Research in social studies teaching*. Baltimore: Arrow Books.

For a work with a group author—such as a research group, government agency, institution, or corporation—begin the entry with the group name. In the references list, alphabetize the work as if the first main word (excluding *The, A,* and *An*) were an author's last name.

6. An anonymous book

Gage Canadian dictionary (2nd ed.). (1997). Toronto, ON: Gage Educational.

When no author is named, list the work under its title, and alphabetize it by the first main word (excluding *The, A, An*).

7. Two or more works by the same author(s)

Frye, N. (1963a). *T. S. Eliot*. Edinburgh: Oliver and Boyd.

Frye, N. (1963b). *The well-tempered critic*. Toronto, ON: University of Toronto Press.

When citing two or more works by exactly the same author(s), published in the same year, arrange them alphabetically by the first main word of the title and distinguish the sources by adding a letter (a, b, c . . .) to the date. Both the date *and* the letter are used in citing the source in the text. (See p. 426.)

When citing two or more works by exactly the same author(s) but *not* published in the same year, arrange the sources in order of their publication dates, earliest first.

8. A later edition

Ihde, D. (2007). *Listening and voice: Phenomenologies of sound*. (2nd ed). Albany: State University of New York Press.

The edition number in parentheses follows the title and is followed by a period.

9. A work in more than one volume

Montgomery, L. M. (1985). *Selected journals of L. M. Montgomery* (M. Rubio & E. Waterston, Eds.). (Vol. 3). Toronto, ON: Oxford University Press.

Montgomery, L. M. (1985). *Selected journals of L. M. Montgomery* (M. Rubio & E. Waterston, Eds.). (Vols. 1–4). Toronto, ON: Oxford University Press.

The first entry cites a single volume (3) in the four-volume set. The second cites all four volumes. In the absence of an editor's name, the description of volumes would follow the title directly: *Selected journals of L. M. Montgomery* (Vol. 3).

10. An article or chapter in an edited book

Keating, N. C. (1992). Older rural Canadians. In D. A. Hay & G. S. Basran (Eds.), *Rural sociology in Canada* (pp. 134–154). Toronto, ON: Oxford University Press.

Give the publication date of the collection (1992 above) as the publication date of the article or chapter. After the word "In," provide the editors' names (in normal order), "(Eds.)" and a comma, the title of the collection, and the page numbers of the article in parentheses.

APA
59b

2   Periodicals: Journals, magazines, newspapers

11. An article in a journal with continuous pagination throughout the annual volume

Emery, R. E. (2005). Marital turmoil: Interpersonal conflict

and the children of discord and divorce. *Psychological*

Bulletin, 92, 310–330.

See page 395 for an explanation of journal pagination. Note that you do not place the article title in quotation marks and that you capitalize only the first words of the title and subtitle. In contrast, you italicize the journal title and capitalize all significant words. Separate the volume number from the title with a comma, and italicize the number. Do not add "pp." before the page numbers.

12. An article in a journal that pages issues separately

Dacey, J. (1998). Management participation in

corporate buy-outs. *Management Perspectives,*

7(4), 20–31.

Again, consult page 395 for an explanation of journal pagination. In this case, place the issue number in parentheses after the volume number without intervening space. Do *not* italicize the issue number.

13. An abstract of a journal article

Emery, R. E. (2005). Marital turmoil: Interpersonal

conflict and the children of discord and divorce.

Psychological Bulletin, 92, 310–330.

Abstract obtained from *Psychological Abstracts,*

69, Item 1320.

When you cite the abstract of an article, rather than the article itself, give full publication information for the article, followed, in parentheses, by the information for the collection of abstracts, including title, volume number, and either page number or other reference number ("Item 1320" above). If it is not otherwise clear that you are citing an abstract (because the word *abstract* does not appear in the title of the periodical or of the abstracts collection), add "[Abstract]" between the article title and the following period. See model 19, page 434, for an example.

14. An article in a magazine

Barker, P. (2007, November 10). Revolution at the London
    Library. *The Spectator*, 24.

If a magazine has volume and issue numbers, give them as in models 11 and 12. Also give the full date of the issue: year, followed by a comma, month, and day (if any). Give all page numbers even when the article appears on discontinuous pages, without "pp."

15. An article in a newspaper

Rupert, J. (2006, February 5). Ontario to Ottawa: Soaring taxes
    your problem. *Ottawa Citizen*, p. A1.

Give month *and* date along with year of publication. Use *The* in the newspaper name if the paper itself does. For a newspaper (unlike a journal or magazine), precede the page number(s) with "p." or "pp."

16. An unsigned article

Winter fed birds yield healthier chicks. (2008, February 6).
    Vancouver Sun, p. A6.

List and alphabetize the article under its title, as you would an anonymous book (model 6, p. 430).

17. A review

Drainie, B. (2003, April). Slouching towards paradise. [Review of
    the book *Oryx and Crake*]. *Quill & Quire*, 38.

If the review is not titled, use the bracketed information as the title, keeping the brackets.

3 Electronic sources

The *APA Style Guide to Electronic References* (2007) includes models for documenting electronic sources. Most of the models for

APA
59b

electronic sources can be accessed through the APA Web site (*http://www.apastyle.org/elecref.html*).

In general, the APA's electronic-source references begin as those for print references do: author(s), date, and title. Then you usually add the information on where you retrieved the source, and provide a date of retrieval if the material is likely to be changed or updated. For example, the entry for an online source that may be changed or updated might end Retrieved August 19, 2004, from http://www.liasu.edu/finance-dl/46732 (in APA style, no period follows an electronic address at the end of the reference). Some scholarly journals use a Digital Object Identifier (DOI), a unique string of numbers and letters, which provides a more stable link to the document than a URL. Try to locate all the information required in the following models. However, if you search for and still cannot find some information, then give what you can find. Remember that the purpose of documentation is to allow your reader to find and review the sources you use.

18. An abstract on a database

Willard, B. L. (1992). *Changes in occupational safety standards, 1970–1990* (Dissertation Abstract UMI No. 7770763) [Abstract]. Retrieved November 12, 2001, from UMI-ProQuest database.

19. An online journal article

To cite a journal article you access online, use the same basic journal reference. (See models 11 and 12.) Then add information about how you retrieved the source by giving the URL or Digital Object Identifier (DOI), an identifier that provides a stable link to the article. A retrieval date is not necessary because the content is in its final form.

If you retrieve an article through a database, you are not required to include the name of the database in the entry. But if you do, do not include the URL.

Journal article with a DOI:

Chappell, N. L., & Dujela, C. (2008). Caregiving: Predicting at-risk status. *Canadian Journal on Aging, 27*, 169–179. doi: 10.3138/cha.27.2.169

APA
59b

Journal article without a DOI:

If anybody can access the journal article, give the exact URL. But if you can access the content only by subscription, then give the URL of the home page of the journal.

Grady, G. F. (2003). The here and now of hepatitis
    B immunization. *Today's Medicine*, *13*, 145–151.
    Retrieved from http://www.fmrt.org/todaysmedicine/
    Grady050203.html

20. An online newspaper article

Keenan, G. (2008, February 14). Emission changes could limit
    car choices. *Globe and Mail* Retrieved from
    http://www.globeandmail.com

21. An online posting

Tourville, M. (1999, January 6). European currency reform.
    Message posted to *news://sci.international.finance*,
    archived at http://www. liasu.edu/finance-dl/46732

Use this format for messages posted to newsgroups, forums, or discussion groups. If only a screen name is available, list that in place of the author's name. Include the date of the posting, the title of the thread, the URL of the thread, and the URL of where the posting is archived. If the message has an identifier, such as a number, put it in brackets after the title.

22. A personal e-mail message

At least one member of the research team has expressed
reservations about the design of the study (L. Kogod,
personal communication, February 6, 2007).

Personal electronic mail should be cited only in your text, as in the example above.

23. Weblog entry

Yong, E. (2009, May 20). Darwinius changes everything.
    Message posted to http://scienceblogs.com/
    notrocketscience/2009/05/everything_changes.php

24. Software

Project Scheduler 8000 [Computer software]. (1999). Orlando,
    FL: Scitor.

If you downloaded the software from the Web, instead of the location add the words "Available from:" and end with the URL.

APA
59b

4   Other sources

25. A report

Gerald, K. (1958). *Medico-moral problems in obstetric care* (Report No. NP–71). St. Louis, MO: Catholic Hospital Association.

Treat the report like a book, but provide any report number in parentheses immediately after the title, with no punctuation between them.

For a report from the Educational Resources Information Center (ERIC), provide the ERIC document number in parentheses at the end of the entry:

Jolson, M. K. (1981). *Music education for preschoolers* (Report No. TC–622). New York: Teachers College, Columbia University. (ERIC Document Reproduction Service No. ED 264 488).

26. A government publication

House of Commons Task Force on Employment. (1981). *Work for tomorrow*. Ottawa, ON, Canada: Author.

U.S. House Committee on Ways and Means. (1991). *Medicare payment for outpatient physical and occupational therapy services*. 102d Cong., 2d Sess. Washington, DC: U.S. Government Printing Office.

Hawaii. Department of Education. (1998). *Kauai district schools, profile 1998-99*. Honolulu, HI: Author.

If no individual is given as the author, list the publication under the name of the sponsoring agency. When the agency is both the author and the publisher, use "Author" in place of the publisher's name.

27. An abstract of an unpublished dissertation

Steciw, S. K. (1986). Alterations to the Pessac project of Le Corbusier (Doctoral dissertation, University of Cambridge, England, 1986). *Dissertation Abstracts International, 46,* 565C.

For an abstract of an unpublished doctoral dissertation, give the university and the year of the dissertation in parentheses after the title. Then give the source of the abstract, the volume number, and the page number.

28. An interview

Brisick, W. C. (1988, July 1). [Interview with Ishmael Reed]. *Publishers Weekly,* 41–42.

List a published interview under the interviewer's name. Provide the publication information appropriate for the kind of source the interview appears in (here, a magazine). Immediately after the date, in brackets, specify that the piece is an interview and, if necessary, provide other identifying information. If the interview has its own title, insert it after the date, as with a review (model 17, p. 433).

Note that interviews you conduct yourself are not included in the list of references. Instead, use an in-text parenthetical citation, as shown in model 23 (p. 435) for a nonretrievable online posting.

29. A motion picture, recording, or other audiovisual source

Siberry, J. (1995). Caravan. *Maria* [CD]. Burbank, CA: Reprise.

Spielberg, S. (Director). (1993). *Schindler's list* [Motion picture]. Los Angeles: Viacom.

For audiovisual sources such as films, videotapes, television or radio programs, or recordings, begin with the name of the person whose work you are citing, followed by his or her function, if appropriate, in parentheses. Immediately after the title, add the notation [Motion picture]. Then give the location and name of the distributor.

(59c) Formatting a paper in APA style

The APA *Publication Manual* distinguishes between documents intended for publication (which will be set in type) and those submitted by students (which are the final copy). The guidelines below apply to most undergraduate papers. Check with your instructor for any modifications to this format.

APA
59c

Note See pages 427–37 for the APA format of a reference list. And see pages 52–63 for guidelines on type spacing, type fonts, lists, and other elements of document design.

Structure and format

- The title page includes the full title, your name, the course title, the instructor's name, and the date. Include a shortened form of the title along with the page number at the top of this and all other pages. Number the title page 1. The APA allows either the centred layout below or the layout shown on page 441, in which all title-page information appears on the top half of the page.

Title page

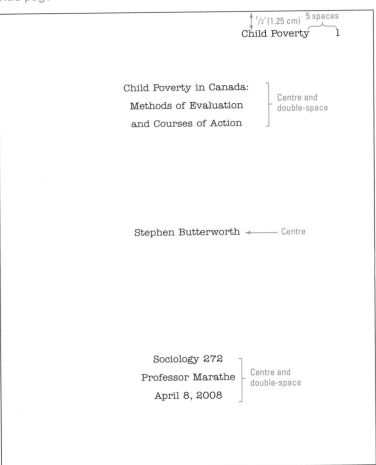

APA
59c

- The first section, labelled "Abstract," summarizes (in about 100 words—and not more than 120) your subject, research method, findings, and conclusions. Put the abstract on a page by itself.

Abstract

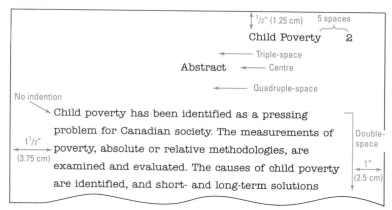

- The body of the paper begins with a restatement of the paper's title and then an introduction (not labelled). The introduction concisely presents the problem you researched, your research method, the relevant background (such as related studies), and the purpose of your research.

First page of body

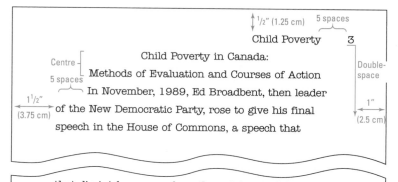

APA
59c

Spacing, page numbers, and illustrations

- Use a 1½-inch (3.75-cm) margin on the left and 1-inch (2.5-cm) margins on the other sides. (The wider left margin allows for a binder.)
- Number pages consecutively, starting with the title page. Identify each page (including the title page) with a shortened version of the title as well as a page number, as illustrated in the samples on the previous page and opposite.
- Run into your text all quotations of less than 40 words, and enclose them in quotation marks. For quotations of 40 or more words, set them off from your text by indenting all lines five spaces, double-spacing above and below. For student papers, the APA allows single-spacing of displayed quotations:

Echoing the opinions of other Europeans at the time, Freud had a poor view of Americans:

> The Americans are really too bad. . . . Competition is much more pungent with them, not succeeding means civil death to every one, and they have no private resources apart from their profession, no hobby, games, love or other interests of a cultured person. And success means money. (1961, p. 86)

Do not use quotation marks around a quotation displayed in this way.

- Present data in tables and figures (graphs or charts), as appropriate. (See the samples on pp. 61–62 for a clear format to follow.) Begin each illustration on a separate page. Number each kind of illustration consecutively and separately from the others (Table 1, Table 2, etc., and Figure 1, Figure 2, etc.). Refer to all illustrations in your text—for instance, "See Figure 3." Generally, place illustrations immediately after the text references to them. (See pp. 59–63 for more discussion of illustrations, along with samples.)

(59d)   A sample paper in APA style

The following excerpts from a sociology paper illustrate elements of a research paper using the APA style of documentation and format.

APA

59d

Alternative title page layout **(see p. 438)**.

Shortened title and page number.

Child Poverty in Canada:

Methods of Evaluation and Courses of Action

Stephen Butterworth

Sociology 272

Professor Marathe

April 8, 2008

Double-space all information: title, name, course title, instructor, date.

New page.

Abstract: summary of research, research method, conclusion.

Abstract

Child poverty has been identified as a pressing problem for Canadian society. The measurements of poverty, absolute or relative methodologies, are examined and evaluated. The causes of child poverty are identified, and short- and long-term solutions proposed.

New page.

Child Poverty in Canada:

Methods of Evaluation and Courses of Action

In November, 1989, Ed Broadbent, then leader of the New Democratic Party, rose to give his final speech in the House of Commons, a speech that prompted the following resolution: "That this house express concern for the more than one million Canadian children currently living in poverty and seek to achieve the goal of eliminating poverty among Canadian children by the year 2000" (cited in Canadian Council on Social Development, 1990, p. 1). Since then, there have been many public and private studies of child poverty in Canada, including some that diminish or even deny the existence of the problem. Child poverty has only increased in the last nineteen years, and Canada must find solutions or be prepared to pay for the consequences.

Introduction: presentation of the problem researched by the writer.

APA

59d

Child Poverty   4

Everyone admits that an objective definition of poverty is hard to find. Indeed, the authors of *The Canadian Fact Book on Poverty 2000* (Ross, Scott, & Smith, 2000) list eight commonly used measures of poverty. All these methods divide into either absolute or relative methods (pp. 4–5). Basically, an absolute method takes into account only the actual cost of necessities, whereas a relative method tries to consider the entire context.

The economist Christopher A. Sarlo (1996, p. 2) uses an absolute or what he calls a "basic needs" method. He argues that relative approaches measure "inequality," not poverty, which he defines as the inability to supply life's basic necessities (pp. 3–13). Using this method, he has come up with a poverty rate that is only a quarter of that resulting from the most commonly used relative method. This number leads him to argue that poverty "is simply not a major problem in Canada" (p. 2).

The most commonly used relative measure, the one used by the federal government and the basis for Ed Broadbent's motion, is the LICO or Low Income Cut Off set by Statistics Canada:

> There is a LICO for each family size, and LICOs also vary according to the size of the community in which the family lives. In simple terms, each LICO, which is a measure of family income, on average, spends at least 60 percent of their income on the basic necessities of food, clothing and shelter. (Economic Council of Canada, 1992, pp. 1–2).

Using LICO criteria, the Standing Senate Committee on Social Affairs, Sciences, and Technology (1991, p. 4) determined that in 1988 there were 913,000 children under the age of 16 living in poverty and that with the addition of children aged 16 and 17 Aboriginal children living on reserves, "the

Citation form: source with three to five authors, named in the text.

Citation form: author named in the text.

Quotation of 40 or more words set off without quotation marks, indented one-half inch (1.25 cm) and single-spaced.

APA
59d

figure would exceed one million, hovering at 1.1 million." By 1997, however, Ross et al. report that this number had increased to 1.4 million, so that one in five children in Canada live below the poverty line (2000).

Roughly 20% of Canadian children, then, are poor. This number may compare favourably with the 20% figure in the United States, but looks less impressive beside Sweden's 5.2% (Standing Senate Committee, 1991, p. 5). This number also does not include the "near poor," those whose family income is only slightly above the LICO (p. 9). The other statistics are bad enough. Over 40% of all users of food banks are children (p. 8). Ross et al. report that the child mortality rate among poor children is twice the national average (2000). The situation of Aboriginal children is especially perilous. More than 50% of Aboriginal children live in poverty; their life expectancy is eight years less than the national average; 60% of their homes have no plumbing (Coutts & Walker, 1999, p. 322; Standing Senate Committee, 1991, pp. 9–11).

These last figures demonstrate that disagreements over absolute vs. relative measures are really unimportant for the children themselves, though they may be important for policy makers, advocacy groups, and others. However you measure the number, however small or large you make it, there are many children suffering hunger, disease, and death. In order to make the situation better, Canadians have to identify both the causes of child poverty and the short- and long-term solutions.

Discussion section: moves from analysis of problem to causes.

The obvious immediate cause of child poverty is parent poverty. Poor parents raise poor children, and these parents are not who we think they are. The Canadian Council on Social Development (CCSD) (1990, p. 2) notes that of the 913,000 poor children

APA
59d

Child Poverty   6

(1988 figure cited above) 51% lived in two-parent homes, and only 39.1% lived with lone-parent mothers. All these parents need short-term assistance through tax credits, minimum wage adjustments, subsidized housing, retraining and education, and child care. A national child-care policy is especially needed. The CCSD study reports that even though 1.9 million Canadian children needed day care in 1988, only 243,500 spaces were available (p. 6).

These short-term adjustments will work toward the long-term solution, which as the Standing Senate Committee puts it (1991, p. 13), must be "more preventative than curative." The key to ending the cycle of poverty is education. The dropout rate for poor children is 2.5 times the national average (Ross et al., 2000, pp. 1–2). Those who do stay in school are hampered by hunger, exhaustion, and anxiety. Without education and training, poor children become poor adults.

All Canadians pay when this happens. The 187,000 children projected to drop out of high school in the twenty years after 1991 will cost $610 million in unemployment insurance and $710 million in other assistance (Standing Senate Committee, 1991, pp. 5–6). Of all street and residential crime, between 40% and 60% is committed by juveniles (p. 20). Why should poor children respect us or our laws if we let them grow up hungry?

In the years since the House of Commons resolution to eliminate child poverty by the year 2000, little has been accomplished. Campaign 2000 (2007), a nonprofit national organization that advocates on behalf of poor children, issues an annual report card on child poverty. Their latest, the 2007 report, "It takes a nation to raise a generation: Time for a national poverty reduction strategy," argues that even though the Canadian economy has grown by

APA
59d

Child Poverty   7

50% since 1989, no real progress has been made
against child poverty (2007, p. 3). Indeed, the figures
are still shocking: 49% of children of recent immigrants,
for example, live in poverty. The organization calls for
a three-pronged approach of a comprehensive child
benefit, the building of affordable housing, and a
national strategy for early childhood education. In an
era of surplus, we can do no less.

New page.   Child Poverty   8

References

Campaign 2000 (2007). *It takes a nation to raise*   A retrievable online
a generation: Time for a national poverty   posting.
reduction strategy. Retrieved March 12, 2008,
from http://www.campaign2000.ca/rc/index.
html

Canadian Council on Social Development. (1990). *A*   An article in a print
national strategy to end child poverty   journal.
in Canada. Ottawa, ON, Canada: Author.

Coutts, J., & Walker, D. (1999). Native poverty:
Perspectives on the sociology of dependence.
Journal of Social Welfare, 11, 319–328.

Economic Council of Canada. (1992). *The new face*
of poverty: Income security needs of
Canadian families. Ottawa, ON, Canada:
Ministry of Supply and Services.

Ross, D. P., Scott, K., & Smith, P. J. (2000). *The*
Canadian fact book on poverty 2000. Ottawa,
ON, Canada: Canadian Council on Social
Development.

Sarlo, C. A. (1996). *Poverty in Canada* (2nd ed.).   A book.
Vancouver, BC, Canada: Fraser Institute.

Standing Senate Committee on Social Affairs, Sciences,
and Technology. (1991). *Children in poverty:*
Toward a better future. Ottawa, ON, Canada:
Ministry of Supply and Services Canada.

APA
59d

Chicago, CSE, and IEEE Documentation

Chicago, CSE, and IEEE Documentation

60 Chicago Documentation

History, art history, philosophy, and some other humanities use endnotes or footnotes to document sources, following one style recommended by *The Chicago Manual of Style* (15th ed., 2003) and the student guide adapted from it, Kate L. Turabian's *A Manual for Writers of Term Papers, Theses, and Dissertations* (7th ed., 2007). The Chicago note style is described below.

60a Distinguishing Chicago notes and works-cited entries

In the Chicago note style, raised numerals in the text refer to footnotes (bottoms of pages) or endnotes (end of paper) that contain complete source information. A separate list of works cited is optional: ask your instructor for his or her preference.

Single-space both footnotes and endnotes. Separate footnotes from the text with a short line:

> In 1901, Madras, Bengal, and Punjab were a few of the huge Indian provinces governed by the British viceroy.[6]
>
> 1″ (2.5 cm) → British rule, observes Stuart Cary Welch, "seemed as permanent as Mount Everest."[7]   1″ (2.5 cm)
>
> ——————— Line
> 5 spaces
> 6. Martin Gilbert, *Atlas of British History* (New York: Dorset Press, 1968), 96.   ] Single-space
>
> ——— Double-space
>
> 7. Stuart Cary Welch, *India: Art and Culture* (New York: Metropolitan Museum of Art, 1985), 421.   ] Single-space
>
> ↕ 1″ (2.5 cm)

With endnotes, use the format on the following page for a list of works cited, substituting the heading "NOTES" and numbered entries as for footnotes.

For the list of sources at the end of the paper, use the format on the next page. Arrange the sources alphabetically by the authors' last names.

The following examples illustrate the essentials of a note and a works-cited entry:

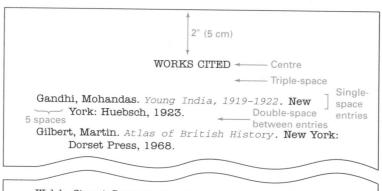

6. Martin Gilbert, *Atlas of British History* (New York: Dorset Press, 1968), 96.

Gilbert, Martin. *Atlas of British History*. New York: Dorset Press, 1968.

Notes and works-cited entries share certain features:

- Italicize or underline the titles of books and periodicals (ask your instructor for his or her preference).
- Enclose in quotation marks the titles of parts of books or articles in periodicals.
- Do not abbreviate publishers' names, but omit "The," as well as "Inc.," "Co.," and similar abbreviations.
- Do not use "p." or "pp." before page numbers.

Notes and works-cited entries also differ in important ways:

Note	Works-cited entry
Start with a number (typed on the line and followed by a period) that corresponds to the note number in the text.	Do not begin with a number.
Indent the first line five spaces.	Indent the second and subsequent lines five spaces.
Give the author's name in normal order.	Begin with the author's last name.

Chic

60b

Use commas between elements.	Use periods between elements.
Enclose publication information in parentheses, with no preceding punctuation.	Precede the publication information with a period, and don't use parentheses.
Include the specific page number(s) you borrowed from, omitting "p." or "pp."	Omit page numbers except for parts of books or articles in periodicals.

Many computerized word processors will automatically position footnotes at the bottoms of appropriate pages. Some will automatically number notes and even renumber them if you add or delete one or more.

(60b) Models of Chicago notes and works-cited entries

In the following models for common sources, notes and works-cited entries appear together for easy reference. (An index to the models appears at the tabbed divider.) Be sure to use the numbered note form for notes and the unnumbered works-cited form for works-cited entries. Works cited are to be listed alphabetically using the author's last name.

1   Books

1. A book with one, two, or three authors

1. Suzanne Norton, *At Odds: Gambling and Canadians, 1919–1969* (Toronto: University of Toronto Press, 2003), 101.

Norton, Suzanne. *At Odds: Gambling and Canadians, 1919–1969*. Toronto: University of Toronto Press, 2003.

1. Deidre F. Baker, and Ken Setterington, *A Guide to Canadian Children's Books*. (Toronto: McClelland and Stewart, 2003), 102–203.

Baker, Deidre F., and Ken Setterington. *A Guide to Canadian Children's Books*. Toronto: McClelland and Stewart, 2003.

2. A book with more than three authors

2. Celia Haig-Brown et al., *Making the Spirit Dance Within: Joe Duquette High School and an Aboriginal Community* (Toronto: James Lorimer, 1997), 121–27.

Haig-Brown, Celia, Kathy L. Hodgson-Smith, Robert Regnier, and Jo-Ann Archibald. *Making the Spirit Dance Within: Joe Duquette High School and an Aboriginal Community*. Toronto: James Lorimer, 1997.

3. A book with an editor

3. Kathleen Kufeldt and Brad McKenzie, eds., *Child Welfare: Connecting Research, Policy, and Practice* (Waterloo, ON: Wilfrid Laurier University Press, 2003).

Kufeldt, Kathleen, and Brad McKenzie, eds. *Child Welfare: Connecting Research, Policy, and Practice*. Waterloo, ON: Wilfrid Laurier University Press, 2003.

4. A book with an author and an editor

4. Lewis Mumford, *The City in History*, ed. Donald L. Miller (New York: Pantheon, 1986), 216–17.

Mumford, Lewis. *The City in History*. Edited by Donald L. Miller. New York: Pantheon, 1986.

5. A translation

5. Dante Alighieri, *The Inferno*, trans. John Ciardi (New York: New American Library, 1971), 51.

Alighieri, Dante. *The Inferno*. Translated by John Ciardi. New York: New American Library, 1971.

6. An anonymous work

6. *Gage Canadian Dictionary*, 2nd ed. (Toronto: Gage Educational, 1997).

Gage Canadian Dictionary. 2nd ed. Toronto: Gage Educational, 1997.

7. A later edition

7. Don Ihde, *Listening and Voice: Phenomenologies of Sound*, 2nd ed. (Albany: State University of New York Press, 2007), 20.

Ihde, Don. *Listening and Voice: Phenomenologies of Sound*. 2nd ed. Albany: State University of New York Press, 2007.

8. A work in more than one volume

Citation of one volume without a title:

8. L. M. Montgomery, *Selected Journals of L. M. Montgomery*, ed. Mary Rubio and Elizabeth Waterston (Toronto: Oxford University Press, 1985), 3:16–21.

Montgomery, L. M. *Selected Journals of L. M. Montgomery*. Edited by Mary Rubio and Elizabeth Waterston. Vol. 3. Toronto: Oxford University Press, 1985.

Citation of one volume with a title:

8. Linda B. Welkin, *The Age of Balanchine*, vol. 3 of *The History of Ballet* (New York: Columbia University Press, 1969), 56.

Welkin, Linda B. *The Age of Balanchine*. Vol. 3 of *The History of Ballet*. New York: Columbia University Press, 1969.

9. A selection from an anthology

9. Assefaw Bariagher, "Ethnicity and Constitutionalism in Ethiopia," in *Emancipating Cultural Pluralism*, ed. Chris C. Toffols (Albany: State University of New York Press, 2003), 230.

Bariagher, Assefaw. "Ethnicity and Constitutionalism in Ethiopia." In *Emancipating Cultural Pluralism*, edited by Chris C. Toffols, 231–38. Albany: State University of New York Press, 2003.

10. A work in a series

10. Ingmar Bergman, *The Seventh Seal*, Modern Film Scripts Series, no. 12 (New York: Simon and Schuster, 1968), 27.

Bergman, Ingmar. *The Seventh Seal*. Modern Film Scripts Series, no. 12. New York: Simon and Schuster, 1968.

11. An article in a reference work

The abbreviation "s.v." in the first example stands for the Latin *sub verbo*, "under the word." Note that well-known reference works such as dictionaries and encyclopedias are usually cited in the notes but not in a works-cited list.

11. *Merriam-Webster's Collegiate Dictionary*, 10th ed., s.v. "reckon."

11. Mark F. Herman, "Polymers," in *The New Encyclopaedia Britannica: Macropaedia*, 16th ed.

2   Periodicals: Journals, magazines, newspapers

12. An article in a journal with continuous pagination throughout the annual volume

12. Donald J. Savoie, "The Rise of Court Government in Canada," *Canadian Journal of Political Science* 32 (1999): 637.

Savoie, Donald J. "The Rise of Court Government in Canada." *Canadian Journal of Political Science* 32 (1999): 635–64.

13. An article in a journal that pages issues separately

13. Jane E. Kennard, "False Analogies: Teaching Gay and Lesbian Texts," *Modern Language Studies* 28, no. 3 (1998): 180.

Kennard, Jane E. "False Analogies: Teaching Gay and Lesbian Texts." *Modern Language Studies* 28, no. 3 (1998): 173–86.

14. An article in a popular magazine

14. Paul Barker, "Revolution at the London Library," *Spectator*, November 10, 2007, 24.

Barker, Paul. "Revolution at the London Library." *Spectator*, November 10, 2007, 24.

15. An article in a newspaper

15. Jake Rupert, "Ontario to Ottawa: Soaring Taxes Your Problem," *Ottawa Citizen*, February 5, 2008, A1+.

Rupert, Jake. "Ontario to Ottawa: Soaring Taxes Your Problem." *Ottawa Citizen*, February 5, 2008.

16. A review

16. John Gregory Dunne, "The Secret of Danny Santiago," review of *Famous All over Town*, by Danny Santiago, *New York Review of Books*, August 16, 1984, 25.

Dunne, John Gregory. "The Secret of Danny Santiago." Review of *Famous All over Town*, by Danny Santiago. *New York Review of Books*, August 16, 1984, 17–27.

3   Electronic sources

Models for documenting electronic sources are listed in the 15th edition of the *Chicago Manual* according to their types: that is, whether they are online books, journals, magazines, and so forth.

Note For line breaks in electronic addresses follow Chicago style: break only after slashes and before a tilde (~), period, comma, hyphen, underline, question mark, number sign, or percent symbol. Do not hyphenate for line breaks, and do not break a URL at an already existing hyphen.

17. A source on a periodical CD-ROM

A source also published in print:

17. Peter H. Lewis, "Many Updates Cause Profitable Confusion," *New York Times*, January 21, 1999, national ed. *New York Times Ondisc*, CD-ROM (UMI-ProQuest, March 1999).

Lewis, Peter H. "Many Updates Cause Profitable Confusion." *New York Times*, January 21, 1999, national ed. *New York Times Ondisc*. CD-ROM. UMI-ProQuest, March 1999.

A source not published in print:

17. "Vanguard Forecasts," *Business Outlook*, CD-ROM (Information Access, March 1998).

"Vanguard Forecasts." *Business Outlook*. CD-ROM. Information Access, March 1998.

18. A source on a nonperiodical CD-ROM

18. Mary Wollstonecraft Shelley, *Frankenstein*, in *Classic Library*, CD-ROM (Alameda, CA: Andromeda, 1993).

Shelley, Mary Wollstonecraft. *Frankenstein*. In *Classic Library*. Alameda, CA: Andromeda, 1993. CD-ROM.

19. An online book

19. Jane Austen, *Emma*, ed. Ronald Blythe (Harmondsworth, UK: Penguin, 1972; Oxford Text Archive), ftp://ota.ox.ac.uk/public/english/Austen/emma.1519.

Austen, Jane. *Emma*. Edited by Ronald Blythe. Harmondsworth, UK: Penguin, 1972. Oxford Text Archive. ftp://ota.ox.ac.uk/public/english/Austen/emma.1519.

20. An article in an online periodical

Access dates are not used now (unless the source is no longer available or is likely to be altered), but they can be required for scientific material.

20. Andrew Palfrey, "Choice of Mates in Identical Twins," *Modern Psychology* 4, no. 1 (1996), par. 10, http://www.liasu.edu/modpsy/palfrey4(1).htm (accessed February 25, 2000).

Palfrey, Andrew. "Choice of Mates in Identical Twins." *Modern Psychology* 4, no. 1 (1996). http://www.liasu.edu/modpsy/palfrey4(1).htm (accessed February 25, 2000).

21. An online database

21. *Scots Teaching and Research Network*, ed. John Corbett (Glasgow: University of Glasgow), http://www.arts.gla.ac.uk/www/comet/starn.htm (accessed March 5, 1999).

Scots Teaching and Research Network. Edited by John Corbett. Glasgow: University of Glasgow. http://www.arts.gla.ac.uk/www/comet/starn.htm (accessed March 5, 1999).

4   Other sources

22. A government publication

22. Parliamentary Committee on Equality Rights, *Equality for All*, 1st sess., 33rd Parliament (Ottawa: Queen's Printer for Canada, 1984–85).

Parliamentary Committee on Equality Rights. *Equality for All*. 1st sess., 33rd Parliament. Ottawa: Queen's Printer for Canada, 1984–85.

23. A letter

A letter from a published collection can be cited in a note, but the full collection should be cited in a works-cited list. (See the first example.) Unpublished personal communications are cited in notes but not in a works-cited list. (See the second example.)

A published letter:

> 23. Robertson Davies to Margaret Atwood, June 30, 1982, in *For Your Eyes Only: Letters 1976–1995*, ed. Judith Skelton Grant (Toronto: McClelland & Stewart, 1999), 104.

> Davies, Robertson. *For Your Eyes Only: Letters 1976–1995*. Edited by Judith Skelton Grant. Toronto: McClelland & Stewart, 1999.

A personal letter:

> 23. Ann E. Packer, letter to author, June 15, 2008.

24. An interview

> 24. John Ralston Saul, interview by Darryl Konynenbelt, *Politics and People*, CBC, June 21, 2004.

> Saul, John Ralston. Interview by Darryl Konynenbelt. *Politics and People*. CBC, June 21, 2004.

25. A work of art

> 25. John Singer Sargent, *In Switzerland*, watercolour, 1908, Metropolitan Museum of Art, New York.

> Sargent, John Singer. *In Switzerland*. Watercolour, 1908. Metropolitan Museum of Art, New York.

26. A film or video recording

> 26. George Balanchine, *Serenade*, VHS, San Francisco Ballet (PBS Video, 1985).

> Balanchine, George. *Serenade*. VHS. San Francisco Ballet. PBS Video, 1985.

27. A sound recording

> 27. Johannes Brahms, *Concerto no. 2 in B-flat*, Artur Rubinstein, Philadelphia Orchestra, Cond. Eugene Ormandy, RCA BRC4–6731, ℗1992.

> Brahms, Johannes. *Concerto no. 2 in B-flat*. Artur Rubinstein. Philadelphia Orchestra. Eugene Ormandy. RCA BRC4–6731. ℗1992.

5   Two or more citations of the same source

To minimize clutter and give a quick sense of how often you cite a source, the Chicago style allows a shortened form for subsequent citations of a source you have already cited fully. Your instructor may also allow the shortened form for a first citation of a source if full information appears in a list of works cited.

You may use the Latin abbreviation "ibid." (meaning "in the same place") to refer to the same source cited in the preceding note:

> 8. Donald J. Savoie, "The Rise of Court Government in Canada," *Canadian Journal of Political Science* 32 (1999): 637.
>
> 9. Ibid., 653.

For any source already cited in your notes, not just immediately before, you may use the author's name and (if the author is responsible for more than one cited source) a shortened form of the title.

> 1. Carol Gilligan, *In a Different Voice: Psychological Theory and Women's Development* (Cambridge, MA: Harvard University Press, 1993), 27.
>
> 2. Carol Gilligan, "Moral Development in the College Years," *The Modern American College*, ed. A. Chickering (San Francisco: Jossey-Bass, 1981), 286.
>
> 3. Gilligan, *In a Different Voice*, 47.

Omit the title if you are using only one source by the cited author.

The Chicago style recommends in-text parenthetical citations when you cite one or more works repeatedly. This practice allows you to avoid many notes saying "ibid." or giving the same author's name. In the example following, the note number refers to the complete source information in an endnote; the numbers in parentheses are page numbers in the same source.

> British rule, observes Stuart Cary Welch, "seemed as permanent as Mount Everest."[7] Most Indians submitted, willingly or not, to British influence in every facet of life (423–24).

61 CSE Documentation

Writers in the life sciences, physical sciences, and mathematics rely for documentation style on *Scientific Style and Format: The CSE Style Manual for Authors, Editors, and Publishers* (7th ed., 2006). This book details two styles of in-text citation: one using author and date and one using numbers. Both types of text citation refer to a list

61b

of references at the end of the paper (p. 458). Ask your instructor which style you should use.

61a Writing CSE name-year text citations

In the CSE name-year style, parenthetical text citations provide the last name of the author being cited and the source's year of publication. At the end of the paper, a list of references, arranged alphabetically by authors' last names, provides complete information on each source. (See p. 458.)

The CSE name-year style closely resembles the APA name-year style detailed on pages 424–27. You can follow the APA examples for in-text citations, making several notable changes for CSE:

- Do not use a comma to separate the author's name and the date: (Baumrind 1968, p. 34).

- For sources with two authors, separate their names with "and" (not "&"): (Pepinsky and DeStefano 1987).

- For sources with three or more authors, use "and others" (not "et al.") after the first author's name: (Rutter and others 1996).

- For anonymous sources, give the author as "Anonymous" both in the text citation—(Anonymous 1976)—and in the list of references (model 6, p. 461).

61b Writing CSE numbered text citations

In the CSE number style, raised numbers in the text refer to a numbered list of references at the end of the paper.

Two standard references[1,2] use this term.

These forms of immunity have been extensively researched.[3]

According to one report,[4] research into some forms of viral immunity is almost nonexistent.

Hepburn and Tatin[2] do not discuss this project.

Assignment of numbers

The number for each source is based on the order in which you cite the source in the text: the first cited source is 1, the second is 2, and so on.

CSE
61c

Reuse of numbers

When you cite a source you have already cited and numbered, use the original number again. (See the last example above, which reuses the number 2 from the first example.)

This reuse is the key difference between the CSE numbered citations and numbered references to footnotes or endnotes (pp. 457–63). In the CSE style, each source has only one number, determined by the order in which the source is cited. With notes, in contrast, the numbering proceeds in sequence, so that sources have as many numbers as they have citations in the text.

Citation of two or more sources

When you cite two or more sources together, arrange their numbers in sequence and separate them with a comma and no space, as in the first example on the previous page.

(61c) Preparing the CSE reference list

For both the name-year and the number styles of in-text citation, provide a list, titled "References," of all sources you have cited. Format the page as shown for APA references on page 427 (but you may omit the shortened title before the page number).

Follow these guidelines for references, noting the important differences in name-year and number styles:

Spacing

Single-space each entry, and double-space between entries.

Arrangement

The two styles differ in their arrangement of entries:

Name-year style
Arrange entries alphabetically by authors' last names.

Number style
Arrange entries in numerical order—that is, in order of their citation in the text.

Format

In both styles, begin the first line of each entry at the left margin and indent subsequent lines:

Name-year style

Hepburn PX, Tatin JM. 1995. Human physiology. New York:
    Columbia Univ Pr. 1026 p.

Number style
> 2. Hepburn PX, Tatin JM. Human physiology. New York: Columbia
>   Univ Pr; 1995. 1026 p.

Authors

List each author's name with the last name first, followed by initials for first and middle names. (See the examples above and on the previous page.) Do not use a comma between an author's last name and initials, and do not use periods or space with the initials. Do use a comma to separate authors' names.

Placement of dates

The two styles differ, as shown in the examples on the facing page.

Name-year style
The date follows the author's or authors' names.

Number style
The date follows the publication information (for a book) or the periodical title (for a journal, magazine, or newspaper).

Journal titles

Do not underline or italicize journal titles. For titles of two or more words, abbreviate words of six or more letters (without periods) and omit most prepositions, articles, and conjunctions. Capitalize each word. For example, *Annals of Medicine* becomes Ann Med, and *Journal of Chemical and Biochemical Studies* becomes J Chem Biochem Stud. See the Rowell examples below and on the next page.

Book and article titles

Do not underline, italicize, or use quotation marks around a book or an article title. Capitalize only the first word and any proper nouns. See the Rowell examples below and model 2 on the next page.

Publication information for journal articles

Both the name-year and the number styles give the journal's volume number, a colon, and the inclusive page numbers of the article: 28:329–33 in the Rowell examples following. (If the journal has an issue number, it follows the volume number in parentheses: 62(2):26–40.) However, the styles differ in the punctuation as well as the placement of the date:

Name-year style
The date, after the author's name and a period, is followed by a period:

> Rowell LB. 1996. Blood pressure regulation during exercise. Ann
>   Med 28:329–33.

Number style
The date, after the journal title and a space, is followed by a semi-colon:

> 3. Rowell LB. Blood pressure regulation during exercise. Ann Med 1996;28:329–33.

The following examples show both a name-year reference and a number reference for each type of source. An index to the models appears after the tabbed divider.

1   Books

1. A book with one author

Gould SJ. 1987. Time's arrow, time's cycle. Cambridge: Harvard Univ Pr. 222 p.

1. Gould SJ. Time's arrow, time's cycle. Cambridge: Harvard Univ Pr; 1987. 222 p.

2. A book with two to ten authors

Hepburn PX, Tatin JM. 1995. Human physiology. New York: Columbia Univ Pr. 1026 p.

2. Hepburn PX, Tatin JM. Human physiology. New York: Columbia Univ Pr; 1995. 1026 p.

3. A book with more than ten authors

Evans RW, Bowditch L, Dana KL, Drummond A, Wildovitch WP, Young SL, Mills P, Mills RR, Livak SR, Lisi OL, and others. 1998. Organ transplants: ethical issues. Ann Arbor: Univ of Michigan Pr. 498 p.

3. Evans RW, Bowditch L, Dana KL, Drummond A, Wildovitch WP, Young SL, Mills P, Mills RR, Livak SR, Lisi OL, and others. Organ transplants: ethical issues. Ann Arbor: Univ of Michigan Pr; 1998. 498 p.

4. A book with an editor

Jonson P, editor. 1997. Anatomy yearbook. Los Angeles: Anatco. 628 p.

4. Jonson P, editor. Anatomy yearbook. Los Angeles: Anatco; 1997. 628 p.

5. A selection from a book

Krigel R, Laubenstein L, Muggia F. 1997. Kaposi's sarcoma. In: Ebbeson P, Biggar RS, Melbye M, editors. AIDS: a basic guide for clinicians. 2nd ed. Philadelphia: WB Saunders. p 100–26.

5. Krigel R, Laubenstein L, Muggia F. Kaposi's sarcoma. In: Ebbeson P, Biggar RS, Melbye M, editors. AIDS: a basic guide

for clinicians. 2nd ed. Philadelphia: WB Saunders; 1997.
p 100–26.

6. An anonymous work

[Anonymous]. 1992. Health care for multiple sclerosis. New York:
US Health Care. 86 p.

6. [Anonymous]. Health care for multiple sclerosis. New York: US
Health Care; 1992. 86 p.

7. Two or more cited works by the same author published in the same year

Gardner H. 1973a. The arts and human development. New York:
J Wiley. 406 p.

Gardner H. 1973b. The quest for mind: Piaget, Lévi-Strauss,
and the structuralist movement. New York: AA Knopf.
492 p.

(The number style does not require such forms.)

2   Periodicals: Journals, magazines, newspapers

8. An article in a journal with continuous pagination throughout the annual volume

Ancino R, Carter KV, Elwin DJ. 1983. Factors contributing to
viral immunity: a review of the research. Dev Biol.
30:156–9.

8. Ancino R, Carter KV, Elwin DJ. Factors contributing to
viral immunity: a review of the research. Dev Biol.
1983;30:156–9.

9. An article in a journal that pages issues separately

Kim P. 1986 Feb. Medical decision making for the dying.
Milbank Quar. 64(2):26–40.

9. Kim P. Medical decision making for the dying. Milbank Quar.
1`986 Feb;64(2):26–40.

10. An article in a newspaper

Immen W. 1996 July 2. ASA helps heart but hurts brain. Globe
and Mail;Sect. A:3 (col2).

10. Immen W. ASA helps heart but hurts brain. Globe and Mail.
1996 July 2;Sect. A:3 (col2).

11. An article in a magazine

Van Gelder L. 1996 Dec. Countdown to motherhood: when should
you have a baby? Ms. 37–9.

11. Van Gelder L. Countdown to motherhood: when should you
have a baby? Ms. 1996 Dec:37–9.

3 Electronic sources

The CSE's *Scientific Style and Format* includes just a few models for electronic sources, and they form the basis of the following examples.

Note Break electronic addresses only after slashes, and do not hyphenate. A period may be used after an URL only if the last character is a slash.

12. A source on CD-ROM or DVD-ROM

Reich WT, editor. 2005. Encyclopedia of bioethics [DVD]. New York: Co-Health.

12. Reich WT, editor. Encyclopedia of bioethics [DVD]. New York: Co-Health; 2005.

13. An online journal article

Grady GF. 1993 May 2. The here and now of hepatitis B immunization. Today's Med [Internet]. [cited 1999 Dec 27]. Available from: http://www.fmrt.org/todaysmedicine/Grady050293.html.

13. Grady GF. The here and now of hepatitis B immunization. Today's Med [Internet] 1993 May 2. [cited 1999 Dec 27]. Available from: http://www.fmrt.org/todaysmedicine/Grady050293.html.

14. An online book

Ruch BJ, Ruch DB. 1999. Homeopathy and medicine: resolving the conflict [Internet]. New York: Albert Einstein Coll of Medicine. [cited 2000 Jan 28]. Available from: http://www.einstein.edu/medicine/books/ruch.html.

14. Ruch BJ, Ruch DB. Homeopathy and medicine: resolving the conflict [Internet]. New York: Albert Einstein Coll of Medicine; 1999. [cited 2000 Jan 28]. Available from: http://www.einstein.edu/medicine/books/ruch.html.

15. Computer software

Project scheduler 8000 [computer program]. 1999. Version 4.1. Orlando (FL): Scitor. 1 computer disk: 3 1/2 in. Accompanied by: 1 manual. System requirements: IBM PC or fully compatible computer; Windows 95 or higher; 8 MB RAM; hard disk with a minimum of 2 MB of free space.

15. Project scheduler 8000 [computer program]. Version 4.1. Orlando (FL): Scitor; 1999. 1 computer disk: 3 1/2 in. Accompanied by: 1 manual. System requirements: IBM PC or fully compatible computer; Windows 95 or higher; 8 MB RAM; hard disk with a minimum of 2 MB of free space.

4   Other sources

16. A government publication

Parliamentary Committee on Equality Rights. 1984. Equality for all. 33rd Parl., 1st Sess. Queen's Printer Canada.

16. Parliamentary Committee on Equality Rights. Equality for all. 33rd Parl, 1st Sess. Queen's Printer Canada; 1984.

17. A nongovernment report

Warnock M. 1992. Report of the Committee on Fertilization and Embryology. Baylor University, Department of Embryology. Waco (TX): Baylor Univ. Report nr BU/DE.4261.

17. Warnock M. Report of the Committee on Fertilization and Embryology. Baylor University, Department of Embryology. Waco (TX): Baylor Univ; 1992. Report nr BU/DE.4261.

18. A sound recording, video recording, or film

Teaching Media. 1993. Cell mitosis [videocassette]. White Plains (NY): Teaching Media. 1 videocassette: 40 min, sound, black and white, 1/2 in.

18. Cell mitosis [videocassette]. White Plains (NY): Teaching Media; 1993. 1 videocassette: 40 min, sound, black and white, 1/2 in.

62 IEEE Documentation

Writers in engineering rely for documentation style on the Institute of Electrical and Electronics Engineers's "IEEE Editorial Style Manual" (available at *http://www.ieee.org*).

The Manual prescribes a footnote and numbered reference system. Footnotes are numbered consecutively throughout the text, and the notes appear at the bottom of the text column in which they were cited. References do not have to be cited in the text. When they are cited in text, they appear on the line in square brackets, inside the punctuation, and in reference to their numbered position in the list of references.

Mathematical equations within the text are numbered consecutively from the beginning to the end of the text.

Citations of tables and figures within the text are also in numerical order, and citation to figures always carry the abbreviation "Fig." followed by the figure number.

(62a) Preparing the IEEE reference list

Numbering

Reference numbers should be set flush left in a column spaced beyond the body of the reference. All reference numbers are in square brackets and are on the line.

Author name

The author's given names are abbreviated to the initial only and appear before the last name. Give all the names listed as authors. Use *et al.* only if author names are not given.

Titles

For titles of book chapters, periodical articles, and other shorter texts, capitalize the first word, first word after a colon, and all proper nouns only. Book chapters and journal articles appear in quotation marks. Magazine articles appear without quotation marks.

For titles of books, capitalize all words except articles (*a, an, the*), coordinating conjunctions (*and, but, yet, or, for, nor, so*), and prepositions of less than four letters (*in, on, etc.*), unless they are the first or last word of the title or appear after a colon. All book titles should appear in italics.

For periodicals, the title of the periodical should be abbreviated and appear in italics.

Publication information

For books, all publication information should be given in this sequence: full title of book, edition number or series where applicable, abbreviation of publisher, city, abbreviation of state (unless the state is indicated, e.g. New York) or country if other than the United States, year, followed by chapter, section, pages, and URL where applicable.

For periodicals, all publication information should be given in this sequence: abbreviation of periodical title, series where applicable, volume, number, pages, abbreviation of month, year, and URL where applicable. When the article has been accessed on an electronic source, the date and abbreviation of the month of access should appear in parentheses after the author's name and the type of medium in square brackets after the title, which does not appear in quotation marks. When the article has been accessed online on www, the day of the month should also be given.

(62b) Models for IEEE references

1   Books

1. A book with one author or editor

1. G. V. Tsoulos, Ed., *Adaptive Antennas for Wireless Communication*. New York: Wiley, 2001.

2. A book with two authors or editors

2. J. L. Volakis, A. Chatterjee, and L. C. Kempel, *Finite Elements for Electronics: Antennas, Microwave Circuits, and Scattering Applications*. New York: Oxford University Press, 1998.

3. A chapter in a book

3. C. Bolchinim, A. Lapiana, and G. Mulas, "Adaptive network," in *Mobile Information Systems: Infrastructure Design for Adaptivity and Flexibility*, B. Pernici, Ed. Berlin, Germany: Springer, 2006, pp. 117–154.

4. A book in a series

4. *Microwave Antenna for Avionics* (AGARD Lecture Series 151). Neuilly-sur-Seine, France: AGARD, 1987.

5. A handbook

5. *Westinghouse Instruction Literature Design Manual*, Westinghouse Electric Corporation, East Pittsburg, PA, 1963.

2   Periodicals

6. A journal article with one author

6. J. Capon, "High resolution frequency-wavenumber spectral analysis," *Proc. of the IEEE*, vol. 57, no. 8, pp. 1408–1418, Aug. 1969.

7. A journal article with two or more authors

7. D. B. Ward, R. A. Kennedy, and R. C. Williamson, "Theory and design of broadband sensor arrays with frequency invariant for field beam patterns," *Jour. of Acoustic Society of Am.*, vol. 97, no. 2, pp. 1023–1034, Feb. 1995.

3   Electronic sources

8. An online book

8. S. Khutaina. (2007, Aug. 19). *EMBASE handbook* (3rd ed.) [Online]. 3(21). Available: Knowledge Index File: EMBASE Handbook (EMHB)

62b

9. An article in an online journal

9. M. Malesich, Advances in DoD's ATS framework, *IEEE Aerospace and Electronic System Magazine*. [Online]. 23(2). Available: http://ieeexplore.ieee.org

10. An article in an online magazine

10. B. Snyder. (2008, Mar. 8). Cloud computing: Tales from the front. *CIO Magazine*. [Online]. Available: http://www.cio.com/article/192701/Cloud_Computing_Tales_from_the_Front

11. An e-mail message

11. S. H. Gold. (2006, Apr. 11). *Inter-Network Talk* [Online]. Available e-mail: COMSERVE@RPIECS Message: Get NETWORK TALK

4   Other sources

12. A dissertation

12. G. Tsoulos, "Smart antennas for third generation wireless personal communications," Ph.D. dissertation, Dept. Elect. Eng., Bristol Univ., England, 1997.

13. A patent

13. P. W. Howells, "Intermediate frequency sidelobe canceller," U.S. Patent 3 202 990, May 1, 1959.

14. A paper presented at a conference

14. Y. Lu, X. Cair, and Z. Gao, "Optimal design of special corner reflector antennas by the real-coded genetic algorithm," presented at the 2000 Asia-Pacific Microwave Conf., Vancouver, BC.

Glossary of Usage and Index

Glossary of Usage
and Index

Glossary of Usage

This glossary provides notes on words or phrases that often cause problems for writers. The recommendations for standard written English are based on current dictionaries and usage guides. Items labelled NONSTANDARD should be avoided in speech and especially in writing. Those labelled COLLOQUIAL and SLANG occur in speech and in some informal writing but are best avoided in the more formal writing usually expected in college and business. (Words and phrases labelled *colloquial* include those labelled by many dictionaries with the equivalent term *informal*.)

Spelling presents a special problem in Canadian English because of the difference between spellings in the United Kingdom and those in the United States. Because of Canada's historical relation to Britain and proximity to the United States, Canadian spelling has tended to waver between the two. The principal forms of the variants are the following (British first): *civilise/civilize; colour/color; centre/center; fulfil/fulfill; defence/defense; travelled/traveled; anaemia/anemia*. A widely recognized authority on Canadian spelling is the *Gage Canadian Dictionary* (1983, revised 1997). In this text, we have followed Gage for the most part, preferring the British spellings for centre, fulfil, defence, and travelled, while preferring the U.S. spellings for civilize and anemia. We have preserved American spellings as used in quoted material.

a, an Use *a* before words beginning with consonant sounds, including those spelled with an initial pronounced *h* and those spelled with vowels that are sounded as consonants: *a historian, a one-o'clock class, a university*. Use *an* before words that begin with vowel sounds, including those spelled with an initial silent *h: an orgy, an L, an honour*.

The article before an abbreviation depends on how the abbreviation is to be read: *She was once an AEC undersecretary* (*AEC* is to be read as three separate letters). *Many Americans opposed a SALT treaty* (*SALT* is to be read as one word, *salt*).

See also pages 224–25 on the uses of *a/an* versus *the*.

accept, except *Accept* is a verb meaning "receive." *Except* is usually a preposition or conjunction meaning "but for" or "other than"; when it is used as a verb, it means "leave out." *I can accept all your suggestions except the last one. I'm sorry you excepted my last suggestion from your list.*

advice, advise *Advice* is a noun, and *advise* is a verb: *Take my advice; do as I advise you.*

affect, effect Usually *affect* is a verb, meaning "to influence," and *effect* is a noun, meaning "result": *The drug did not affect his driving; in fact, it seemed to have no effect at all*. But *effect* occasionally is used as a verb meaning "to bring about": *Her efforts effected a change*. And *affect* is used in psychology as a noun meaning "feeling or emotion": *One can infer much about affect from behaviour.*

agree to, agree with *Agree to* means "consent to," and *agree with* means "be in accord with": *How can they agree to a treaty when they don't agree with each other about the terms?*

467

all ready, already *All ready* means "completely prepared," and *already* means "by now" or "before now": *We were all ready to go to the movie, but it had already started.*

all right *All right* is always two words. *Alright* is a common misspelling.

all together, altogether *All together* means "in unison" or "gathered in one place." *Altogether* means "entirely." *It's not altogether true that our family never spends vacations all together.*

allusion, illusion An *allusion* is an indirect reference, and an *illusion* is a deceptive appearance: *Paul's constant allusions to Shakespeare created the illusion that he was an intellectual.*

almost, most *Almost* means "nearly"; *most* means "the greater number (or part) of." In formal writing, *most* should not be used as a substitute for *almost*: *We see each other almost [not most] every day.*

a lot *A lot* is always two words, used informally to mean "many." *Alot* is a common misspelling.

among, between In general, use *among* for relationships involving more than two people or for comparing one thing to a group to which it belongs. *The four of them agreed among themselves that the choice was between Toronto and Vancouver.*

amount, number Use *amount* with a singular noun that names something not countable (a noncount noun): *The amount of food varies.* Use *number* with a plural noun that names more than one of something countable (a plural count noun): *The number of calories must stay the same.*

and/or *And/or* indicates three options: one or the other or both: *The decision is made by the mayor and/or the council.* If you mean all three options, *and/or* is appropriate. Otherwise, use *and* if you mean "both," *or* if you mean "either."

ante-, anti- The prefix *ante-* means "before" (*antedate, antebellum*); *anti-* means "against" (*antiwar, antinuclear*). Before a capital letter or *i*, *anti-* takes a hyphen: *anti-Freudian, anti-isolationist.*

anxious, eager *Anxious* means "nervous" or "worried" and is usually followed by *about*. *Eager* means "looking forward" and is usually followed by *to*. *I've been anxious about getting blisters. I'm eager [not anxious] to get new running shoes.*

anybody, any body; anyone, any one *Anybody* and *anyone* are indefinite pronouns; *any body* is a noun (*body*) modified by *any*; *any one* is a pronoun or adjective (*one*) modified by *any*. *How can anybody communicate with any body of government? Can anyone help Amy? She has more work than any one person can handle.*

any more, anymore *Any more* means "no more"; *anymore* means "now." Both are used in negative constructions. *He doesn't want any more. She doesn't live here anymore.*

apt, liable, likely *Apt* and *likely* are interchangeable. Strictly speaking, though, *apt* means "having a tendency to": *Horace is apt to forget his* *lunch in the morning. Likely* means "probably going to": *Horace is leaving so early today that he's likely to catch the first bus.*

    Liable normally means "in danger of" and should be confined to situations with undesirable consequences: *Horace is liable to trip over that hose.* Strictly, *liable* means "responsible" or "exposed to": *The owner will be liable for Horace's injuries.*

are, is Use *are* with a plural subject (*books are*), *is* with a singular subject (*book is*).

as Substituting for *because, since,* or *while, as* may be vague or ambiguous: *As we were stopping to rest, we decided to eat lunch.* (Does *as* mean "while" or "because"?) *As* should never be used as a substitute for *whether* or *who. I'm not sure whether* [not *as*] *we can make it. That's the man who* [not *as*] *gave me directions.*

as, like In formal speech and writing, *like* should not introduce a full clause (with a subject and a verb) because it is a preposition. The preferred choice is *as* or *as if: The plan succeeded as* [not *like*] *we hoped. It seemed as if* [not *like*] *it might fail. Other plans like it have failed.*

as, than In comparisons, *as* and *than* precede a subjective-case pronoun when the pronoun is a subject: *I love you more than he* [*loves you*]. *As* and *than* precede an objective-case pronoun when the pronoun is an object: *I love you as much as* [*I love*] *him.* See also page 210.

assure, ensure, insure *Assure* means "to promise": *He assured us that we would miss the traffic. Ensure* and *insure* often are used interchangeably to mean "make certain," but some reserve *insure* for matters of legal and financial protection and use *ensure* for more general meanings: *We left early to ensure that we would miss the traffic. It's expensive to insure yourself against floods.*

at The use of *at* after *where* is wordy and should be avoided: *Where are you meeting him?* is preferable to *Where are you meeting him at?*

awful, awfully Strictly speaking, *awful* means "awe-inspiring." As intensifiers meaning "very" or "extremely" (*He tried awfully hard*), *awful* and *awfully* should be avoided in formal speech or writing.

awhile, a while *Awhile* is an adverb; *a while* is an article and a noun. *I will be gone awhile* [not *a while*]. *I will be gone for a while* [not *awhile*].

bad, badly In formal speech and writing, *bad* should be used only as an adjective; the adverb is *badly. He felt bad because his tooth ached badly.* In *He felt bad,* the verb *felt* is a linking verb and the adjective *bad* describes the subject. See also page 220.

being as, being that Colloquial for *because,* the preferable word in formal speech or writing: *Because* [not *Being as*] *the world is round, Columbus never did fall off the edge.*

beside, besides *Beside* is a preposition meaning "next to." *Besides* is a preposition meaning "except" or "in addition to" as well as an adverb meaning "in addition." *Besides, several other people besides you want to sit beside Dr. Christensen.*

Usage

better, had better *Had better* (meaning "ought to") is a verb modified by an adverb. The verb is necessary and should not be omitted: *You had better* [not *better*] *go.*

between, among See *among, between.*

bring, take Use *bring* only for movement from a farther place to a nearer one and *take* for any other movement. *First take these books to the library for renewal; then take them to Mr. Daniels. Bring them back to me when he's finished.*

but, hardly, scarcely These words are negative in their own right; using *not* with any of them produces a double negative. See page 223. *We have but* [not *haven't got but*] *an hour before our plane leaves. I could hardly* [not *couldn't hardly*] *make out her face.*

but, however, yet Each of these words is adequate to express contrast. Don't combine them. *He said he had finished, yet* [not *but yet*] *he continued.*

can, may Strictly, *can* indicates capacity or ability, and *may* indicates permission: *If I may talk with you a moment, I believe I can solve your problem.*

censor, censure To *censor* is to edit or remove from public view on moral or some other grounds; to *censure* is to give a formal scolding. *The lieutenant was censured by Major Taylor for censoring the letters her soldiers wrote home from boot camp.*

centre around *Centre on* is more logical than, and preferable to, *centre around.*

cite, sight, site *Cite* is a verb usually meaning "quote," "commend," or "acknowledge": *You must cite your sources. Sight* is both a noun meaning "the ability to see" or "a view" and a verb meaning "perceive" or "observe": *What a sight you see when you sight Venus through a strong telescope. Site* is a noun meaning "place" or "location" or a verb meaning "situate": *The builder sited the house on an unlikely site.*

climatic, climactic *Climatic* comes from *climate* and refers to the weather: *Last winter's temperatures may indicate a climatic change. Climactic* comes from *climax* and refers to a dramatic high point: *During the climactic duel between Hamlet and Laertes, Gertrude drinks poisoned wine.*

complement, compliment To *complement* something is to add to, complete, or reinforce it: *Her yellow blouse complemented her black hair.* To *compliment* something is to make a flattering remark about it: *He complimented her on her hair. Complimentary* can also mean "free": *complimentary tickets.*

conscience, conscious *Conscience* is a noun meaning "a sense of right and wrong"; *conscious* is an adjective meaning "aware" or "awake." *Though I was barely conscious, my conscience nagged me.*

contact Often used imprecisely as a verb instead of a more exact word such as *consult, talk with, telephone,* or *write to.*

Usage

continual, continuous *Continual* means "constantly recurring": *Most movies on television are continually interrupted by commercials. Continuous* means "unceasing": *Some cable channels present movies continuously without commercials.*

could of See *have, of.*

credible, creditable, credulous *Credible* means "believable": *It's a strange story, but it seems credible to me. Creditable* means "deserving of credit" or "worthy": *Steve gave a creditable performance. Credulous* means "gullible": *The credulous Claire believed Tim's lies.* See also *incredible, incredulous.*

criteria The plural of *criterion* (meaning "standard for judgment"): *Our criteria are strict. The most important criterion is a sense of humour.*

Usage

data The plural of *datum* (meaning "fact"). Though *data* is often used as a singular noun, most careful writers still treat it as plural: *The data fail* [not *fails*] *to support the hypothesis.*

device, devise *Device* is the noun, and *devise* is the verb: *Can you devise some device for getting his attention?*

different from, different than *Different from* is preferred: *His purpose is different from mine.* But *different than* is widely accepted when a construction using *from* would be wordy: *I'm a different person now than I used to be* is preferable to *I'm a different person now from the person I used to be.*

differ from, differ with To *differ from* is to be unlike: *The twins differ from each other only in their hairstyles.* To *differ with* is to disagree with: *I have to differ with you on that point.*

discreet, discrete *Discreet* (noun form *discretion*) means "tactful": *What's a discreet way of telling Maud to be quiet? Discrete* (noun form *discreteness*) means "separate and distinct": *Within a computer's memory are millions of discrete bits of information.*

disinterested, uninterested *Disinterested* means "impartial": *We chose Pete, as a disinterested third party, to decide who was right. Uninterested* means "bored" or "lacking interest": *Unfortunately, Pete was completely uninterested in the question.*

don't *Don't* is the contraction for *do not,* not for *does not: I don't care, you don't care,* and *he doesn't* [not *don't*] *care.*

due to the fact that Wordy for *because.*

eager, anxious See *anxious, eager.*

effect See *affect, effect.*

elicit, illicit *Elicit* is a verb meaning "bring out" or "call forth." *Illicit* is an adjective meaning "unlawful." *The crime elicited an outcry against illicit drugs.*

emigrate, immigrate *Emigrate* means "to leave one place and move to another": *The Chus emigrated from Korea. Immigrate* means "to move into a place where one was not born": *They immigrated to Canada.*

ensure See *assure, ensure, insure.*

enthused Used colloquially as an adjective meaning "showing enthusiasm." The preferred adjective is *enthusiastic: The coach was enthusiastic* [not *enthused*] *about the team's victory.*

et al., etc. Use *et al.,* the Latin abbreviation for "and other people," only in source citations: *Jones et al.* Avoid *etc.,* the Latin abbreviation for "and other things," in formal writing, and do not use it to refer to people or to substitute for precision, as in *The government provides health care, etc.*

everybody, every body; everyone, every one *Everybody* and *everyone* are indefinite pronouns: *Everybody* [*everyone*] *knows Tom steals. Every one* is a pronoun (*one*) modified by *every,* and *every body* a noun (*body*) modified by *every.* Both refer to each thing or person of a specific group and are typically followed by *of: The game commissioner has stocked every body of fresh water in the province with fish, and now every one of our rivers is a potential trout stream.*

everyday, every day *Everyday* is an adjective meaning "used daily" or "common"; *every day* is a noun (*day*) modified by *every: Everyday problems tend to arise every day.*

everywheres Nonstandard for *everywhere.*

except See *accept, except.*

except for the fact that Wordy for *except that.*

explicit, implicit *Explicit* means "stated outright": *I left explicit instructions. Implicit* means "implied, unstated": *We had an implicit understanding.*

farther, further *Farther* refers to additional distance (*How much farther is it to the beach?*), and *further* refers to additional time, amount, or other abstract matters (*I don't want to discuss this any further*).

fewer, less *Fewer* refers to individual countable items (a plural count noun), *less* to general amounts (a noncount noun, always singular). *Skim milk has fewer calories than whole milk. We have less milk left than I thought.*

flaunt, flout *Flaunt* means "show off"; *If you have style, flaunt it. Flout* means "scorn" or "defy": *Hester Prynne flouted convention and paid the price.*

flunk A colloquial substitute for *fail.*

fun As an adjective, *fun* is colloquial and should be avoided in most writing: *It was a pleasurable* [not *fun*] *evening.*

further See *farther, further.*

get This common verb is used in many slang and colloquial expressions: *get lost, that really gets me, getting on. Get* is easy to overuse: watch out for it in expressions such as *it's getting better* (substitute *improving*) and *we got done* (substitute *finished*).

good and Colloquial for "very": *I was very* [not *good and*] *tired.*

good, well *Good* is an adjective, and *well* is nearly always an adverb: *Larry's a good dancer. He and Linda dance well together. Well* is properly used as an adjective only to refer to health: *You look well.* (*You look good,* in contrast, means "Your appearance is pleasing.")

had better See *better, had better.*

had ought The *had* is unnecessary and should be omitted: *He ought* [not *had ought*] *to listen to his mother.*

hanged, hung Though both are past-tense forms of *hang, hanged* is used to refer to executions and *hung* is used for all other meanings: *Tom Dooley was hanged* [not *hung*] *from a white oak tree. I hung* [not *hanged*] *the picture you gave me.*

hardly See *but, hardly, scarcely.*

have, of Use *have,* not *of,* after helping verbs such as *could, should, would, may,* and *might: You should have* [not *should of*] *told me.*

he, she; he/she Convention has allowed the use of *he* to mean "he or she": *After the infant learns to creep, he progresses to crawling.* However, many writers today consider this usage inaccurate and unfair because it seems to exclude females. The construction *he/she,* one substitute for *he,* is awkward and objectionable to most readers. The better choice is to make the pronoun plural, to rephrase, or, sparingly, to use *he or she.* For instance: *After infants learn to creep, they progress to crawling. After learning to creep, the infant progresses to crawling. After the infant learns to creep, he or she progresses to crawling.* See also pages 143–44 and 213–14.

herself, himself See *myself, herself, himself, yourself.*

hisself Nonstandard for *himself.*

hopefully *Hopefully* means "with hope": *Freddy waited hopefully for a glimpse of Eliza.* The use of *hopefully* to mean "it is to be hoped," "I hope," or "let's hope" is now very common; but since many readers continue to object strongly to the usage, try to avoid it. *I hope* [not *Hopefully*] *the law will pass.*

idea, ideal An *idea* is a thought or conception. An *ideal* (noun) is a model of perfection or a goal. *Ideal* should not be used in place of *idea: The idea* [not *ideal*] *of the play is that our ideals often sustain us.*

if, whether For clarity, use *whether* rather than *if* when you are expressing an alternative: *If I laugh hard, people can't tell whether I'm crying.*

illicit See *elicit, illicit.*

illusion See *allusion, illusion.*

immigrate, emigrate See *emigrate, immigrate.*

implicit See *explicit, implicit.*

imply, infer Writers or speakers *imply,* meaning "suggest": *Jim's letter implies he's having a good time.* Readers or listeners *infer,* meaning "conclude": *From Jim's letter I infer he's having a good time.*

incredible, incredulous *Incredible* means "unbelievable"; *incredulous* means "unbelieving": *When Nancy heard Dennis's incredible story, she was frankly incredulous.* See also *credible, creditable, credulous.*

individual, person, party *Individual* should refer to a single human being in contrast to a group or should stress uniqueness: *The U.S. Constitution places strong emphasis on the rights of the individual.* For other meanings *person* is preferable: *What person* [not *individual*] *wouldn't want the security promised in that advertisement? Party* means "group" (*Can you seat a party of four for dinner?*) and should not be used to refer to an individual except in legal documents. See also *people, persons.*

infer See *imply, infer.*

in regards to Nonstandard for *in regard to, as regards,* or *regarding.*

inside of, outside of The *of* is unnecessary when *inside* and *outside* are used as prepositions: *Stay inside* [not *inside of*] *the house. The decision is outside* [not *outside of*] *my authority. Inside of* may refer colloquially to time, though in formal English *within* is preferred: *The law was passed within* [not *inside of*] *a year.*

insure See *assure, ensure, insure.*

irregardless Nonstandard for *regardless.*

is, are See *are, is.*

is because See *reason is because.*

is when, is where These are faulty constructions in sentences that define: *Adolescence is a stage* [not *is when a person is*] *between childhood and adulthood. Socialism is a system in which* [not *is where*] *government owns the means of production.* See also page 243.

its, it's *Its* is the pronoun *it* in the possessive case: *That plant is losing its leaves. It's* is a contraction for *it is: It's likely to die if you don't water it.* Many people confuse *it's* and *its* because possessives are most often formed with *-'s;* but the possessive *its,* like *his* and *hers,* never takes an apostrophe.

-ize, -wise The suffix *-ize* changes a noun or adjective into a verb: *revolutionize, immunize.* The suffix *-wise* changes a noun or adjective into an adverb: *clockwise, otherwise, likewise.* Avoid the two suffixes except in established words: *I'm highly sensitive* [not *sensitized*] *to that kind of criticism. Financially* [not *Moneywise*], *it's a good time to buy real estate.*

kind of, sort of, type of In formal speech and writing, avoid using *kind of* or *sort of* to mean "somewhat": *He was rather* [not *kind of*] *tall.*

Kind, sort, and *type* are singular and take singular modifiers and verbs: *This kind of dog is easily trained.* Agreement errors often occur when these singular nouns are combined with the plural adjectives *these* and *those: These kinds* [not *kind*] *of dogs are easily trained. Kind, sort,* and *type* should be followed by *of* but not by *a: I don't know what type of* [not *type* or *type of a*] *dog that is.*

Use *kind of, sort of,* or *type of* only when the word *kind, sort,* or *type* is important: *That was a strange* [not *strange sort of*] *statement.*

lay, lie *Lay* means "put" or "place" and takes a direct object: *We could lay the tablecloth in the sun.* Its main forms are *lay, laid, laid. Lie* means "recline" or "be situated" and does not take an object: *I lie awake at night. The town lies east of the river.* Its main forms are *lie, lay, lain.* See also pages *178–79.*

leave, let *Leave* and *let* are interchangeable only when followed by *alone*; *leave me alone* is the same as *let me alone.* Otherwise, *leave* means "depart" and *let* means "allow": *Jill would not let Sue leave.*

less See *fewer, less.*

liable See *apt, liable, likely.*

lie, lay See *lay, lie.*

like, as See *as, like.*

like, such as Strictly, *such as* precedes an example that represents a larger subject, whereas *like* indicates that two subjects are comparable. *Steve has recordings of many great saxophonists such as Ben Webster and Lee Konitz. Steve wants to be a great jazz saxophonist like Ben Webster and Lee Konitz.*

likely See *apt, liable, likely.*

literally This word means "actually" or "just as the words say," and it should not be used to qualify or intensify expressions whose words are not to be taken at face value. The sentence *He was literally climbing the walls* describes a person behaving like an insect, not a person who is restless or anxious. For the latter meaning, *literally* should be omitted.

lose, loose *Lose* means "mislay": *Did you lose a brown glove? Loose* means "unrestrained" or "not tight": *Ann's canary got loose. Loose* also can function as a verb meaning "let loose": *They loose the dogs as soon as they spot the bear.*

lots, lots of Colloquial substitutes for *very many, a great many,* or *much.* Avoid *lots* and *lots of* in college or business writing.

may, can See *can, may.*

may be, maybe *May be* is a verb, and *maybe* is an adverb meaning "perhaps": *Tuesday may be a legal holiday. Maybe we won't have classes.*

may of See *have, of.*

media *Media* is the plural of *medium* and takes a plural verb: *All the news media are increasingly visual.* The singular verb is common, even in the media, but most careful writers still use the plural verb.

might of See *have, of.*

moral, morale As a noun, *moral* means "ethical conclusion" or "lesson": *The moral of the story escapes me. Morale* means "spirit" or "state of mind": *Victory improved the team's morale.*

Usage

most, almost See *almost, most.*

must of See *have, of.*

myself, herself, himself, yourself The *-self* pronouns refer to or intensify another word or words: *Paul helped himself; Jill herself said so.* The *-self* pronouns are often used colloquially in place of personal pronouns, but that use should be avoided in formal speech and writing: *No one except me* [not *myself*] *saw the accident. Our delegates will be Susan and you* [not *yourself*].

nowheres Nonstandard for *nowhere.*

number See *amount, number.*

of, have See *have, of.*

off of *Of* is unnecessary. Use *off* or *from* rather than *off of*: *He jumped off* [or *from*, not *off of*] *the roof.*

OK, O.K., okay All three spellings are acceptable, but avoid this colloquial term in formal speech and writing.

on account of Wordy for *because of.*

on the other hand This transitional expression of contrast should be preceded by its mate, *on the one hand*: *On the one hand, we hoped for snow. On the other hand, we feared that it would harm the animals.* However, the two combined can be unwieldy, and a simple *but, however, yet,* or *in contrast* often suffices: *We hoped for snow. Yet we feared that it would harm the animals.*

outside of See *inside of, outside of.*

owing to the fact that Wordy for *because.*

party See *individual, person, party.*

people, persons In formal usage, *people* refers to a general group: *We the people of the United States . . . Persons* refers to a collection of individuals: *Will the person or persons who saw the accident please notify . . .* Except when emphasizing individuals, prefer *people* to *persons.* See also *individual, person, party.*

per Except in technical writing, an English equivalent is usually preferable to the Latin *per*: *$10 an* [not *per*] *hour; sent by* [not *per*] *parcel post; requested in* [not *per* or *as per*] *your letter.*

percent (per cent), percentage Both these terms refer to fractions of one hundred. *Percent* always follows a numeral (*40 percent of the voters*), and the word should be used instead of the symbol (%) in general writing. *Percentage* stands alone (*the percentage of voters*) or follows an adjective (*a high percentage*).

person See *individual, person, party.*

persons See *people, persons.*

phenomena The plural of *phenomenon* (meaning "perceivable fact" or "unusual occurrence"): *Many phenomena are not recorded. One phenomenon is attracting attention.*

plenty A colloquial substitute for *very*: *The reaction occurred very* [not *plenty*] *fast.*

plus *Plus* is standard as a preposition meaning "in addition to": *His income plus mine is sufficient.* But *plus* is colloquial as a conjunctive adverb: *Our organization is larger than theirs; moreover* [not *plus*], *we have more money.*

practice, practise In Canadian usage, *practice* is a noun and *practise* is a verb: *Practice* makes perfect, so *practise* every day.

precede, proceed The verb *precede* means "come before": *My name precedes yours in the alphabet.* The verb *proceed* means "move on": *We were told to proceed to the waiting room.*

Usage

prejudice, prejudiced *Prejudice* is a noun; *prejudiced* is an adjective. Do not drop the *-d* from *prejudiced*: *I was fortunate that my parents were not prejudiced* [not *prejudice*].

pretty Overworked as an adverb meaning "rather" or "somewhat": *He was somewhat* [not *pretty*] *irked at the suggestion.*

previous to, prior to Wordy for *before.*

principal, principle *Principal* is an adjective meaning "foremost" or "major," a noun meaning "chief official," or, in finance, a noun meaning "capital sum." *Principle* is a noun only, meaning "rule" or "axiom." *Her principal reasons for confessing were her principles of right and wrong.*

proceed, precede See *precede, proceed.*

question of whether, question as to whether Wordy substitutes for *whether.*

raise, rise *Raise* means "lift" or "bring up" and takes a direct object: *The Kirks raise cattle.* Its main forms are *raise, raised, raised.* *Rise* means "get up" and does not take an object: *They must rise at dawn.* Its main forms are *rise, rose, risen.* See also page 179.

real, really In formal speech and writing, *real* should not be used as an adverb; *really* is the adverb and *real* an adjective. *Popular reaction to the announcement was really* [not *real*] *enthusiastic.*

reason is because Although colloquially common, this expression should be avoided in formal speech and writing. Use a *that* clause after *reason is*: *The reason he is absent is that* [not *is because*] *he is sick.* Or: *He is absent because he is sick.* See also page 243.

respectful, respective *Respectful* means "full of (or showing) respect": *Be respectful of other people.* *Respective* means "separate": *The French and the Germans occupied their respective trenches.*

rise, raise See *raise, rise.*

scarcely See *but, hardly, scarcely.*

sensual, sensuous *Sensual* suggests sexuality; *sensuous* means "pleasing to the senses." *Stirred by the sensuous scent of meadow grass and flowers, Cheryl and Paul found their thoughts growing increasingly sensual.*

set, sit *Set* means "put" or "place" and takes a direct object: *He <u>sets</u> the pitcher down.* Its main forms are *set, set, set.* *Sit* means "be seated" and does not take an object: *She <u>sits</u> on the sofa.* Its main forms are *sit, sat, sat.* See also pages *178–79.*

shall, will *Will* is the future-tense helping verb for all persons: *I <u>will</u> go, you <u>will</u> go, they <u>will</u> go.* The main use of *shall* is for first-person questions requesting an opinion or consent: *<u>Shall</u> I order a pizza? <u>Shall</u> we dance? Shall* can also be used for the first person when a formal effect is desired (I *<u>shall</u> expect you around three*), and it is occasionally used with the second or third person to express the speaker's determination (*You <u>shall</u> do as I say*).

should of See *have, of.*

sight, site, cite See *cite, sight, site.*

since *Since* mainly relates to time: *I've been waiting <u>since</u> noon.* But *since* is also often used to mean "because": *<u>Since</u> you ask, I'll tell you.* Revise sentences in which the word could have either meaning, such as *<u>Since</u> you left, my life is empty.*

sit, set See *set, sit.*

site, cite, sight See *cite, sight, site.*

so Avoid using *so* alone or as a vague intensifier: *He was <u>so</u> late. So* needs to be followed by *that* and a clause that states a result: *He was <u>so</u> late <u>that</u> I left without him.*

somebody, some body; someone, some one *Somebody* and *someone* are indefinite pronouns; *some body* is a noun (*body*) modified by *some*; and *some one* is a pronoun or an adjective (*one*) modified by *some*. *Somebody ought to invent a shampoo that will give hair <u>some body</u>. <u>Someone</u> told Janine she should choose <u>some one</u> plan and stick with it.*

sometime, sometimes, some time *Sometime* means "at an indefinite time in the future": *Why don't you come up and see me <u>sometime</u>? Sometimes* means "now and then": *I still see my old friend Joe <u>sometimes</u>. Some time* means "a span of time": *I need <u>some time</u> to make the payments.*

somewheres Nonstandard for *somewhere.*

sort of, sort of a See *kind of, sort of, type of.*

such Avoid using *such* as a vague intensifier: *It was <u>such</u> a cold winter. Such* should be followed by *that* and a clause that states a result: *It was <u>such</u> a cold winter <u>that</u> Napoleon's troops had to turn back.*

such as See *like, such as.*

supposed to, used to In both these expressions, the *-d* is essential: *I <u>used to</u>* [not *use to*] *think so. He's <u>supposed to</u>* [not *suppose to*] *meet us.*

sure Colloquial when used as an adverb meaning *surely: Pierre Trudeau <u>sure</u> was right about the need for the Charter.* If you merely want to be emphatic, use *certainly: Trudeau <u>certainly</u> was right.* If your goal is to convince a possibly reluctant reader, use *surely: Trudeau <u>surely</u> was right.*

sure and, sure to; try and, try to *Sure to* and *try to* are the correct forms: *Be sure to* [not *sure and*] *buy milk. Try to* [not *Try and*] *find some decent tomatoes.*

take, bring See *bring, take.*

than, as See *as, than.*

than, then *Than* is a conjunction used in comparisons, *then* an adverb indicating time: *Holmes knew then that Moriarty was wilier than he had thought.*

that, which *That* introduces an essential clause: *We should use the lettuce that Susan bought* (*that Susan bought* limits the lettuce to a particular lettuce). *Which* can introduce both essential and nonessential clauses, but many writers reserve *which* only for nonessential clauses: *The leftover lettuce, which is in the refrigerator, would make a good salad* (*which is in the refrigerator* simply provides more information about the lettuce we already know of). Essential clauses (with *that* or *which*) are not set off by commas; nonessential clauses (with *which*) are. See also pages 252–56.

that, which, who Use *that* for animals, things, and sometimes collective or anonymous people: *The rocket that failed cost millions. Infants that walk need constant tending.* Use *which* only for animals and things: *The river, which flows south, divides two countries.* Use *who* only for people and for animals with names: *Dorothy is the girl who visits Oz. Her dog, Toto, who accompanies her, gives her courage.*

their, there, they're *Their* is the possessive form of *they*: *Give them their money. There* indicates place (*I saw her standing there*) or functions as an expletive (*There is a hole behind you*). *They're* is a contraction for *they are*: *They're going fast.*

theirselves Nonstandard for *themselves.*

then, than See *than, then.*

these kind, these sort, these type, those kind See *kind of, sort of, type of.*

this, these *This* is singular: *this car* or *This is the reason I left. These* is plural: *these cars* or *These are not valid reasons.*

thru A colloquial spelling of *through* that should be avoided in all academic and business writing.

to, too, two *To* is a preposition; *too* is an adverb meaning "also" or "excessively"; and *two* is a number. *I too have been to Europe two times.*

too Avoid using *too* as an intensifier meaning "very": *Monkeys are too mean.* If you do use *too*, explain the consequences of the excessive quality: *Monkeys are too mean to make good pets.*

toward, towards Both are acceptable, though *toward* is preferred. Use one or the other consistently.

try and, try to See *sure and, sure to; try and, try to.*

type of See *kind of, sort of, type of.* Don't use *type* without *of*: *It was a family type of* [not *type*] *restaurant.* Or better: *It was a family restaurant.*

uninterested See *disinterested, uninterested.*

unique *Unique* means "the only one of its kind" and so cannot sensibly be modified with words such as *very* or *most*: *That was a unique* [not *a very unique* or *the most unique*] *movie.*

usage, use *Usage* refers to conventions, most often those of a language: *Is "hadn't ought" proper usage? Usage* is often misused in place of the noun *use: Wise use* [not *usage*] *of insulation can save fuel.*

use, utilize *Utilize* can be used to mean "make good use of": *Many teachers utilize computers for instruction.* But for all other senses of "place in service" or "employ," prefer *use.*

used to See *supposed to, used to.*

wait for, wait on In formal speech and writing, *wait for* means "await" (*I'm waiting for Paul*) and *wait on* means "serve" (*The owner of the store herself waited on us*).

ways Colloquial as a substitute for *way: We have only a little way* [not *ways*] *to go.*

well See *good, well.*

whether, if See *if, whether.*

which, that See *that, which.*

which, who, that See *that, which, who.*

who's, whose *Who's* is the contraction of *who is: Who's at the door? Whose* is the possessive form of *who: Whose book is that?*

will, shall See *shall, will.*

-wise See *-ize, -wise.*

would have Avoid this construction in place of *had* in clauses that begin *if* and state a condition contrary to fact: *If the tree had* [not *would have*] *withstood the fire, it would have been the oldest in town.* See also pages 196–97.

would of See *have, of.*

you In all but very formal writing, *you* is generally appropriate as long as it means "you, the reader." In all writing, avoid indefinite uses of *you*, such as *In one ancient tribe your first loyalty was to your parents.* See also page 218.

your, you're *Your* is the possessive form of *you: Your dinner is ready. You're* is the contraction of *you are: You're bound to be late.*

yourself See *myself, herself, himself, yourself.*

Credits

ABC, photographs. Walt Disney Internet Group, ABC, *Extreme Makeover*, 2005. ABC Photo Archives.

American Society for Aesthetic Plastic Surgery, graph: "Cosmetic Surgery Trends" from *Statistics: 2004*. Reprinted by permission.

Columbia University. Catalogue record from the Columbia University online catalogue.

Chopin, Kate. "The Story of an Hour" by Kate Chopin. *Literature for Composition*. Ed. Sylvan Barnet et al. 5th ed. New York: Longman, 2000.

Drucker, Peter F. From "How Best to Protect the Environment," *Harper's* Magazine, January 1972. Copyright © 1971 by Minneapolis Star and Tribune Co.

Dyson, Freeman J. Excerpt from *Disturbing the Universe* by Freeman J. Dyson. Copyright © 1979 by Freeman J. Dyson. Reprinted by permission of HarperCollins Publishers, Inc.

Google. Screen images used by permission from Google.

Goreau, Angeline. Excerpt from "Worthy Women Revisited" by Angeline Goreau, *The New York Times*, December 11, 1986. Copyright © 1986 by The New York Times Co. Reprinted by permission.

Ik, Kim Yong. Excerpt from "A Book-Writing Venture" by Kim Yong Ik. Originally published in *The Writer*, October 1965. Copyright © Kim Yong Ik. Reprinted by permission of Faith M. Leigh.

Mahler, Gregory, and MacInnes, Donald J., *Comparative Politics: An Institutional and Cross-National Approach*, Canadian Edition. Copyright © 2002 Pearson Education Canada Inc., Toronto, Ontario.

Mayer, Lawrence A. Excerpt from "The Confounding Enemy of Sleep" by Lawrence A. Mayer. *Fortune*, June 1974. Copyright © 1975 Time Inc. All rights reserved. Reprinted by permission.

Microsoft Corporation. Screen shots reprinted by permission from Microsoft Corporation.

Milk Processor Education Program, photo. Courtesy U.S. National Fluid Milk Processor Promotion Board.

Netscape Communicator browser window © 1999 Netscape Communications Corporation. Used with permission. Netscape Communications has not authorized, sponsored, endorsed, or approved this publication and is not responsible for its content. Reprinted with permission.

Ouchi, William G. Excerpt from *Theory Z: How American Business Can Meet the Japanese Challenge* by William G. Ouchi. Addison Wesley Publishing Company, Inc., 1981.

Rosen, Ruth. "Search for Yesterday" by Ruth Rosen from *Watching Television*, Todd Gitlin, editor. New York: Pantheon Books, 1986.

Sowell, Thomas, "Student Loans" from *Is Reality Optional?* by Thomas Sowell. Copyright © 1993 by Thomas Sowell. Reprinted by permission of the author.

Standard & Poor's, graph: "Five-Year Cumulative Return for Equities in Standard & Poor's 500 Index, 1996–2000." Reprinted by permission.

Statistics Canada, *Juristat*, Cat. 85–002, Vol. 19, No. 9.

Thomas, Dylan. Excerpt from "Fern Hill" from *Collected Poems of Dylan Thomas, 1934–1952* by Dylan Thomas. Copyright © 1971 by W. W. Norton and Company.

Tuchman, Barbara. Excerpt from "The Decline of Quality" by Barbara Tuchman. Reprinted by permission of Russell and Volkening, as agents for the author. Copyright © 1980 by Barbara Tuchman.

United Way Toronto. "Way Out" advertising campaign 2008. Advertising Agency of Record: Publicis Toronto.

University of Michigan Press, figure: "Lifetime prevalence of use of alcohol, compared with other drugs, among twelfth graders in 2000. Data from *Monitoring the Future: National Survey Results on Drug Use, 1975–2000. Vol. 1: Secondary School Students.* Bethesda, MD: National Institute on Drug Abuse, 2001. Reprinted by permission.

Woolf, Virginia. Excerpt from *The Waves* by Virginia Woolf. Copyright © 1988 by Harcourt Brace.

Index

Index

Index

Index

Index

Index

Index

Index

Editing Symbols

Italic numbers and letters refer to chapters and sections of the handbook.

ab	Faulty abbreviation, *48*		⌄	Comma, *39*
ad	Misused adjectives or adverbs, *33*		;	Semicolon, *40*
agr	Error in agreement, *29, 31*		:	Colon, *41*
ap	Apostrophe needed or misused, *42*		⌄	Apostrophe, *42*
appr	Inappropriate word, *18a*		""	Quotation marks, *43*
arg	Faulty argument, *11b–d*		— () . . . [] /	Dash, parentheses, ellipsis mark, brackets, slash, *44*
awk	Awkward construction		par, ¶	Start new paragraph, *6*
cap	Use capital letter, *46*		¶ coh	Paragraph not coherent, *6b*
case	Error in case form, *30*		¶ dev	Paragraph not developed, *6c*
cit	Missing source citation or error in form of citation, *52d*		¶ un	Paragraph not unified, *6a*
coh	Coherence lacking, *3b–3, 6b*		pass	Ineffective passive voice, *28a*
con	Be more concise, *20*		pn agr	Error in pronoun-antecedent agreement, *31*
coord	Coordination needed, *15c*		ref	Error in pronoun reference, *32*
crit	Think or read more critically, *10a*		rep	Unnecessary repetition, *20c*
cs	Comma splice, *36*		rev	Revise or proofread, *5*
d	Ineffective diction (word choice), *18*		run-on	Run-on (fused) sentence, *36*
des	Ineffective or incorrect document design, *7*		shift	Inconsistency, *26d, 27b, 28b, 32d*
det	Error in use of determiner, *33f*		sp	Misspelled word, *45*
dm	Dangling modifier, *34b*		spec	Be more specific, *6c, 18b–3*
emph	Emphasis lacking or faulty, *15*		sub	Subordination needed or faulty, *15d*
exact	Inexact word, *18b*		t	Error in verb tense, *26*
frag	Sentence fragment, *35*		t seq	Error in tense sequence, *26e*
fs	Fused sentence, *36*		trans	Transition needed, *6b–6*
gr	Error in grammar, *21–24*		und	Underline or italicize, *47*
hyph	Error in use of hyphen, *45*		usage	See Glossary of Usage, p. 467
inc	Incomplete construction, *19*		var	Vary sentence structure, *13b*
ital	Italicize or underline, *47*		vb	Error in verb form, *25*
k	Awkward construction		vb agr	Error in subject-verb agreement, *29*
lc	Use lower case letter, *46*		w	Wordy, *20*
mixed	Mixed construction, *37*		ww	Wrong word, *18b–2*
mm	Misplaced modifier, *34a*		//	Faulty parallelism, *16*
mng	Meaning unclear		#	Separate with space
no cap	Unnecessary capital letter, *46*		⌒	Close up the space
no ⌄	Comma not needed, *39h*		⟋	Delete
no ¶	No new paragraph needed, *6*		t/e\h|	Transpose letters or words
num	Error in use of numbers, *49*		x	Obvious error
p	Error in punctuation, *38–44*		^	Something missing, *19*
. ? !	Period, question mark, exclamation point, *38*		??	Document illegible or meaning unclear